Reasoned Programming

Prentice Hall International Series in Computer Science

C.A.R. Hoare, Series Editor

BACKHOUSE, R.C., *Program Construction and Verification*
BACKHOUSE, R.C., *Syntax of Programming Languages*
DE BAKKER, J.W., *Mathematical Theory of Program Correctness*
BARR, M. and WELLS, C., *Category Theory for Computing Science*
BEN-ARI, M., *Principles of Concurrent and Distributed Programming*
BEN-ARI, M., *Mathematical Logic for Computer Science*
BIRD, R. and WADLER, P., *Introduction to Functional Programming*
BORNAT, R., *Programming from First Principles*
BOVET, D.P. and CRESCENZI, P., *Introduction to the Theory of Complexity*
DE BROCK, B., *Foundations of Semantic Databases*
BUSTARD, D., ELDER, J. and WELSH, J., *Concurrent Program Structures*
CLARK, K. and McCABE, F.G., *Micro-Prolog: Programming in Logic*
DAHL, O.-J., *Verifiable Programming*
DROMEY, R.G., *How to Solve It by Computer*
DUNCAN, E., *Microprocessor Programming and Software Development*
ELDER, J., *Construction of Data Processing Software*
ELDER, J., *Compiler Construction*
ELLIOTT, R.J. and HOARE, C.A.R. (eds), *Scientific Applications of Multiprocessors*
FREEMAN, T.L. and PHILLIPS, R.C., *Parallel Numerical Algorithms*
GOLDSCHLAGER, L. and LISTER, A., *Computer Science: A modern introduction (2nd edn)*
GORDON, M.J.C., *Programming Language Theory and Its Implementation*
GRAY, P.M.D., KULKARNI, K.G. and PATON, N.W., *Object-oriented Databases*
HAYES, I. (ed.), *Specification Case Studies (2nd edn)*
HEHNER, E.C.R., *The Logic of Programming*
HENDERSON, P., *Functional Programming: Application and implementation*
HOARE, C.A.R., *Communicating Sequential Processes*
HOARE, C.A.R. and GORDON, M.J.C. (eds), *Mechanized Reasoning and Hardware Design*
HOARE, C.A.R. and JONES, C.B. (eds), *Essays in Computing Science*
HOARE, C.A.R. and SHEPHERDSON, J.C. (eds), *Mechanical Logic and Programming Languages*
HUGHES, J.G., *Database Technology: A software engineering approach*
HUGHES, J.G., *Object-oriented Databases*
INMOS LTD, *Occam 2 Reference Manual*
JACKSON, M.A., *System Development*
JOHNSTON, H., *Learning to Program*
JONES, C.B., *Systematic Software Development Using VDM (2nd edn)*
JONES, C.B. and SHAW, R.C.F. (eds), *Case Studies in Systematic Software Development*
JONES, G., *Programming in Occam*
JONES, G. and GOLDSMITH, M., *Programming in Occam 2*
JONES, N.D., GOMARD, C.K. and SESTOFT, P., *Partial Evaluation and Automatic Program Generation*
JOSEPH, M., PRASAD, V.R. and NATARAJAN, N., *A Multiprocessor Operating System*
KALDEWAIJ, A., *Programming: The derivation of algorithms*
KING, P.J.B., *Computer and Communications Systems Performance Modelling*
LALEMENT, R., *Computation as Logic*
LEW, A., *Computer Science: A mathematical introduction*
McCABE, F.G., *Logic and Objects*
McCABE, F.G., *High-level Programmer's Guide to the 68000*
MEYER, B., *Introduction to the Theory of Programming Languages*
MEYER, B., *Object-oriented Software Construction*
MILNER, R., *Communication and Concurrency*
MITCHELL, R., *Abstract Data Types and Modula 2*
MORGAN, C., *Programming from Specifications*
PEYTON JONES, S.L., *The Implementation of Functional Programming Languages*
PEYTON JONES, S. and LESTER, D., *Implementing Functional Languages*

Series listing continued at back of book

Reasoned Programming

K. Broda, S. Eisenbach, H. Khoshnevisan and S. Vickers
Imperial College of Science, Technology and Medicine

Prentice Hall
New York   London   Toronto   Sydney   Tokyo   Singapore

First published 1994 by
Prentice Hall International (UK) Limited
Campus 400, Maylands Avenue
Hemel Hempstead
Hertfordshire, HP2 7EZ
A division of
Simon & Schuster International Group

© Prentice Hall International (UK) Limited 1994

All rights reserved. No part of this publication may be reproduced,
stored in a retrieval system, or transmitted, in any form, or by any
means, electronic, mechanical, photocopying, recording or otherwise,
without prior permission, in writing, from the publisher.
For permission within the United States of America
contact Prentice Hall Inc., Englewood Cliffs, NJ 07632

Printed and bound in Great Britain at
The University Press, Cambridge

Library of Congress Cataloging-in-Publication Data

Available from the publisher

British Library Cataloguing in Publication Data

A catalogue record for this book is available from
the British Library

ISBN 0-13-098831-6

1 2 3 4 5   98 97 96 95 94

Contents

Foreword	xi
Preface	xiii
1 Introduction	**1**
1.1 How do you know a program does what you want it to?	1
1.2 Why bother?	1
1.3 What *did* you want your program to do?	2
1.4 Local versus global behaviour	3
1.5 Reasoned programs	4
1.6 Reasoned program*ming*	5
1.7 Modules	6
1.8 Programming in the large	7
1.9 Logical notation	8
1.10 The need for formality	10
1.11 Can programs be proved correct?	11
1.12 Summary	12
I Programming	**13**
2 Functions and expressions	**15**
2.1 Functions	15
2.2 Describing functions	16
2.3 Some properties of functions	21
2.4 Using a functional language evaluator	22
2.5 Evaluation of expressions	22
2.6 Notations for functions	24

	2.7	Meaning of expressions	25
	2.8	Summary	26
	2.9	Exercises	26
3	**Specifications**	**27**
	3.1	Specification as contract	27
	3.2	Formalizing specifications	28
	3.3	Defensive specifications — what happens if the input is bad?	29
	3.4	How to use specifications: `fourthroot`	30
	3.5	Proof that `fourthroot` satisfies its specification	31
	3.6	A little unpleasantness: error tolerances	34
	3.7	Other changes to the contract	35
	3.8	A careless slip: positive square roots	36
	3.9	Another example, `min`	37
	3.10	Summary	38
	3.11	Exercises	38
4	**Functional programming in Miranda**	**40**
	4.1	Data types — `bool`, `num` and `char`	40
	4.2	Built-in functions over basic types	41
	4.3	User-defined functions	44
	4.4	More constructions	47
	4.5	Summary	51
	4.6	Exercises	52
5	**Recursion and induction**	**53**
	5.1	Recursion	53
	5.2	Evaluation strategy of Miranda	54
	5.3	Euclid's algorithm	55
	5.4	Recursion variants	57
	5.5	Mathematical induction	60
	5.6	Double induction — Euclid's algorithm without division	63
	5.7	Summary	65
	5.8	Exercises	65
6	**Lists**	**68**
	6.1	Introduction	68
	6.2	The list aggregate type	68
	6.3	Recursive functions over lists	72
	6.4	Trapping errors	75
	6.5	An example — insertion sort	76
	6.6	Another example — sorted merge	81
	6.7	List induction	82
	6.8	Summary	86

6.9	Exercises	87

7 Types   91
7.1 Tuples   91
7.2 More on pattern matching   93
7.3 Currying   94
7.4 Types   96
7.5 Enumerated types   100
7.6 User-defined constructors   100
7.7 Recursively defined types   102
7.8 Structural induction   106
7.9 Summary   111
7.10 Exercises   112

8 Higher-order functions   117
8.1 Higher-order programming   117
8.2 The higher-order function `map`   117
8.3 The higher-order function `fold`   120
8.4 Applications   121
8.5 Implementing `fold` — `foldr`   122
8.6 Summary   123
8.7 Exercises   124

9 Specification for Modula-2 programs   129
9.1 Writing specifications for Modula-2 procedures   129
9.2 Mid-conditions   131
9.3 Calling procedures   133
9.4 Recursion   135
9.5 Examples   136
9.6 Calling procedures in general   138
9.7 Keeping the reasoning simple   139
9.8 Summary   139
9.9 Exercises   140

10 Loops   141
10.1 The coffee tin game   141
10.2 Mid-conditions in loops   144
10.3 Termination   145
10.4 An example   145
10.5 Loop invariants as a programming technique   148
10.6 `FOR` loops   149
10.7 Summary   151
10.8 Exercises   151

11 Binary chop — 154
- 11.1 A telephone directory — 154
- 11.2 Specification — 155
- 11.3 The algorithm — 156
- 11.4 The program — 158
- 11.5 Some detailed checks — 159
- 11.6 Checking for the presence of an element — 160
- 11.7 Summary — 161
- 11.8 Exercises — 162

12 Quick sort — 164
- 12.1 Quick sort — 164
- 12.2 Quick sort — functional version — 164
- 12.3 Arrays as lists — 166
- 12.4 Quick sort in Modula-2 — 167
- 12.5 Dutch national flag — 169
- 12.6 Partitions by the Dutch national flag algorithm — 172
- 12.7 Summary — 174
- 12.8 Exercises — 174

13 Warshall's algorithm — 176
- 13.1 Transitive closure — 176
- 13.2 First algorithm — 178
- 13.3 Warshall's algorithm — 181
- 13.4 Summary — 184
- 13.5 Exercises — 184

14 Tail recursion — 186
- 14.1 Tail recursion — 186
- 14.2 Example: `gcd` — 188
- 14.3 General scheme — 189
- 14.4 Example: `factorial` — 190
- 14.5 Summary — 192
- 14.6 Exercises — 193

II Logic — 195

15 An introduction to logic — 197
- 15.1 Logic — 197
- 15.2 The propositional language — 198
- 15.3 Meanings of the connectives — 200
- 15.4 The quantifier language — 203
- 15.5 Translation from English — 205

	15.6 Introducing equivalence	208
	15.7 Some useful predicate equivalences	209
	15.8 Summary	210
	15.9 Exercises	211

16 Natural deduction — 214
    16.1 Arguments — 214
    16.2 The natural deduction rules — 215
    16.3 Examples — 230
    16.4 Summary — 235
    16.5 Exercises — 235

17 Natural deduction for predicate logic — 237
    17.1 $\forall$-elimination ($\forall\mathcal{E}$) and $\exists$-introduction ($\exists\mathcal{I}$) rules — 237
    17.2 $\forall$-introduction ($\forall\mathcal{I}$) and $\exists$-elimination ($\exists\mathcal{E}$) rules — 242
    17.3 Equality — 247
    17.4 Substitution of equality — 249
    17.5 Summary — 255
    17.6 Exercises — 256

18 Models — 260
    18.1 Validity of arguments — 260
    18.2 Disproving arguments — 264
    18.3 Intended structures — 267
    18.4 Equivalences — 268
    18.5 Soundness and completeness of natural deduction — 271
    18.6 Proof of the soundness of natural deduction — 273
    18.7 Proof of the completeness of natural deduction — 275
    18.8 Summary — 279
    18.9 Exercises — 280

A Well-founded induction — 282
    A.1 Exercises — 287

B Summary of equivalences — 288

C Summary of natural deduction rules — 289

Further reading — 293

Index — 294

Foreword

How do you describe what a computer program does without getting bogged down in how it does it? If the program hasn't been written yet, we can ask the same question using a different tense and slightly different wording: How do you *specify* what a program should do without determining exactly how it should do it? Then we can add the question: When the program is written, how do you judge that it satisfies its specification?

In civil engineering, one can ask a very similar pair of questions: How can you specify what a bridge should do without determining its design? And, when it has been designed, how can you judge whether it does indeed do what it should?

This book is about these questions for software engineering, and its answers can usefully be compared with what happens in civil engineering. First, a specification is a different *kind* of thing from a design; the specification of a bridge may talk about load-bearing capacity, deflection under high winds and resistance of piers to water erosion, while the design talks about quite different things such as structural components and their assembly. For software, too, specifications talk about external matters and programs talk about internal matters.

The second of the two questions is about judging that one thing satisfies another. The main message of the book, and a vitally important one, is that *judgement relies upon understanding*. This is obviously true in the case of the bridge; the judgement that the bridge can bear the specified load rests on structural properties of components, enshrined in engineering principles, which in turn rest upon the science of materials. Thus the judgement rests upon a tower of understanding.

This tower is well-established for the older engineering disciplines; for software engineering, it is still being built. (We may call it 'software science'.) The authors have undertaken to tell students in their first or second year about the tower as it now stands, rather than dictate principles to them. This is refreshing; in software engineering there has been a tendency to substitute formality for understanding. Since a program is written in a very formal language, and the specification is also often written in formal logical terms, it is natural to emphasize formality in making the judgement that one satisfies the other. But in teaching it is stultifying to formalize before understanding, and software science is no exception — even if the industrial significance of a formal verification is increasingly being recognized.

This book is therefore very approachable. It makes the interplay between specification and programming into a human and flexible one, albeit guided by rigour. After a gentle introduction, it treats three or four good-sized examples, big enough to give confidence that the approach will scale up to industrial software; at the same time, there is a spirit of scientific enquiry. The authors have made the book self-contained by including an introduction to logic written in the same spirit. They have tempered their care for accuracy with a light style of writing and an enthusiasm which I believe will endear the book to students.

Robin Milner
University of Edinburgh
January 1994

Preface

Can we ever be sure that our computer programs will work reliably? One approach to this problem is to attempt a mathematical proof of reliability, and this has led to the idea of Formal Methods: if you have a formal, logical *specification* of the properties meant by 'working reliably', then perhaps you can give a formal mathematical proof that the program (presented as a formal text) satisfies them.

Of course, this is by no means trivial. Before we can even get started on a formal proof we must turn the informal ideas intended by 'working reliably' into a formal specification, and we also need a formal account of what it means to say that a program satisfies a specification (this amounts to a *semantics* of the programming language, an account of the meaning of programs). None the less, Formal Methods are now routinely practised by a number of software producers.

However, a tremendous overhead derives from the stress on *formality*, that is to say, working by the manipulation of symbolic forms. A *formal* mathematical proof is a very different beast from the kind of proof that you will see in mathematical text books. It includes the minutest possible detail, both in proof steps and in background assumptions, and is not for human consumption — sophisticated software support tools are needed to handle it. For this reason, Formal Methods are often considered justifiable only in 'safety critical' systems, for which reliability is an overriding priority.

The aim of this book is to present *informal* formal methods, showing the benefits of the approach even without strict formality: although we use logic as a notation for the specifications, we rely on informal semantics — a programmer's ordinary intuitions about what small, linear stretches of code actually do — and we use proofs to the level of rigour of ordinary mathematics.

This can, of course, serve as a first introduction to strict Formal Methods, but it should really be seen much more broadly. The benefits of Formal

Methods do not accrue just from the formality. The very effort of writing a specification prior to the coding focuses attention on what the user wants to get out of the program, as opposed to what the computer has to do, and the satisfaction proof, even if informal, expresses our idea of how the algorithm works. This does not require support tools, and the method — which amounts really to methodical commenting — is practicable in *all* programming tasks.

Moreover, the logic plays a key role in modularization, because it bundles the code up into small, self-contained chunks, each with its specific task defined by the logic.

Although most of the techniques presented are not new (and can be found, for instance, in the classic texts of Gries and Reynolds), we believe that many aspects of our approach are of some novelty. In particular:

Functional programming: Functional programming is presented as a programming language in its own right (and we include a description of the main features of Miranda); but we also use it as a reasoning tool in imperative programming. This is useful because the language of functional programming is very often much clearer and more concise than that of imperative programming (the reason being that functional programs contain less detail about *how* to solve a problem than do imperative programs).

Procedures: It is difficult to give a semantics that covers procedures, and many treatments (though not Reynolds') ignore them. This is reinforced by the standard list of ingredients of structured programming (sequence, decision and iteration), which are indeed all that is structurally necessary; but in fact procedures are the single most effective structure in making large programs tractable to human minds and this is because they are the basic unit of interface between specification and code — both inwards, between the specification and implementing code, and outwards, between the specification and calling code. The role of the logical specification in promoting modularity is crucial, and we have paid unusual attention to showing not only how specifications may be satisfied but also to how they may be used.

Loop invariants: We have tried hard to show loop invariants as an expression of initial intuitions about the computation, rather than as either a *post hoc* justification or as something that appears by magic by playing with the post-condition. Often they arise naturally out of diagrams; nearly always they can function as statements of intent for what sections of the code are to do. We have never shirked the duty of providing them. Experience even with machine code shows that the destinations of jumps are critical places at which comments are vital, and this covers the case of loop invariants.

Real programming languages: We have done our best to address real programming problems by facing up to the complexities of real imperative languages, saying what can be said rather than restricting ourselves to artificial simplicities. Thus, while pointing out that reasoning is simpler if features such as side-effects are avoided, we have tried to show how the more complicated features might be attacked, at least informally.

The book is divided into two complementary parts, the first on Programming and the second on Logic. Though they are both about logical reasoning, the first half concerns the ideas about programs that the reasoning is intended to capture, while the second half is more about the formal machinery. The distinction is somewhat analogous to that often seen in books about programming languages: a first part is an introduction to programming using the language, and a second part is a formal report on it.

To read our book from scratch, one would most likely read the two parts in parallel, and this is in fact how we teach the material for our main computer science course at Imperial. However, the division into two reasonably disjoint parts means that people who already have some background in logic can see the programming story told without interruption.

The approach to the logic section has been strongly influenced by our experience in teaching the subject as part of a computer science course. We put great stress right from the start on the use of the full predicate logic as a means of expression, and our formal treatment of logical proof is based on natural deduction because it *is* natural — its formal structure does reflect the way informal mathematical reasoning is carried out (in the first part, for instance). We have taken the opportunity to use the two parts to enrich each other, so, for instance, some of the proofs about programs in the first part are presented as illustrations of the box proof techniques of the second part, and many of the logic examples in the second part are programs.

Part I *Programming*
1 Introduction
2 Functions and expressions
3 Specifications
4 Functional programming in Miranda
5 Recursion and induction
6 Lists
7 Types
8 Higher-order functions
9 Specification for Modula-2 programs
10 Loops
11 Binary chop
12 Quick sort
13 Warshall's algorithm
14 Tail recursion

Part II *Logic*
15 An introduction to logic

16 Natural deduction

17 Natural deduction for predicate logic
18 Models

The preceding contents list shows the order in which we cover the material in the first year of our undergraduate computer science course. The gap in Part I, between Chapters 8 and 9, is where we teach Modula-2 as a language. Students who have already been taught an imperative programming language would be able to carry straight on from Chapter 8 to Chapter 9.

There are other courses that could be based on this book. Either part makes a course without the other, and indeed in a different class we successfully teach the Part II material separately with Part I following. For the more mathematically minded who find imperative program reasoning inelegant, Chapters 9 through 14 could be omitted and this would then enable the material to be taught in a single semester course.

Acknowledgements

We would like our first acknowledgement to be to David Turner and Research Associates for the elegant Miranda language and the robust Miranda system. Much of the written material has been handed out as course notes over the years and we thank those students and academic staff who attempted the exercises and read, puzzled over and commented on one section or another.

We would also like to thank Paul Taylor for his box proof macros; Lee McLoughlin for helping with the diagrams; Kevin Twidle for keeping our production system healthy; Mark Ryan for helping to turn Word files into LaTeX; Peter Cutler, Iain Stewart and Ian Moor for designing and testing many of the programs; special thanks must go to Roger Bailey whose Hope course turned into our Miranda lectures.

Lastly, we would like to credit those who have inspired us. Courses evolve rather than emerge complete. *Reasoned Programming* could not have existed in its current form without the ideas of Samson Abramsky and Dov Gabbay, for which we are most grateful.

Krysia Broda,
Susan Eisenbach
Hessam Khoshnevisan,
Steve Vickers
Imperial College,
January 1994

Chapter 1

Introduction

1.1 How do you know a program does what you want it to?

You write a computer program in order to get the computer to do something for you, so it is not difficult to understand that when you have written a program you want to be reasonably confident that it does what you intended. A common approach is simply to run it and see. If it does something unexpected, then you can try to correct the errors. (It is common to call these 'bugs', as though the program had blamelessly caught some disabling infection. Let us instead be ruthlessly frank and call them 'errors', or 'mistakes'.) Unfortunately, as the computer scientist Edgser Dijkstra has pointed out, testing can only establish the *presence* of errors, not the absence, and it is common to regard programs as hopelessly error-prone. It would be easy to say that the answer is simple: Don't write any errors! Get the program right first time! Novice programmers quickly see the fatuity of this, but then fall into the opposite trap of not taking care to keep errors out.

In practical programming there are various techniques designed to combat errors. Some help you to write error-free programs in the first place, while others aim to catch errors early when they are easier to correct. This book explains one particular and fundamental idea: *the better you understand what it is that the program is supposed to do, the easier it is to write it correctly.*

1.2 Why bother?

Here is the warranty on a well-known and perfectly reputable operating system:

> The Supplier makes no warranty or representation, either express or implied, with respect to this software, its quality, performance, merchantability, or fitness for a particular purpose. As a result, this software is sold 'as is'

and you the purchaser are assuming the entire risk as to its quality and performance.

Fortunately, the programmers engaged to write the software did not treat this legal disclaimer as the definitive statement of what the program was supposed to do. They worked hard and conscientiously to produce a well-thought-out and useful product of which they could be proud. None the less, the potential is for even the tiniest of software errors to produce catastrophic failures. This worries the legal department, and, for the sake at least of legal consequences, they do their best to dissociate the company from uses to which the software is put in the real world.

There are other contexts where litigation is not even a theoretical factor. For instance, if you work in a software house, your colleagues may need to use your software, and they will want to be confident that it works. If something goes wrong, blanket disclaimers are quite beside the point. The management will want to know what went wrong and what you are doing about it.

More subtly, you are often *your own customer* when you write different parts of the program at different times or reuse parts of other programs. This is because, by the time you come to reuse the code, it is easy to forget what it did.

All in all, therefore, we see that the quality you are trying to achieve in your software, and the responsibility for avoiding errors, goes beyond what can be defined by legal or contractual obligations.

1.3 What *did* you want your program to do?

Your finished software will contain lots of *code* — instructions for the computer written in some programming language or other. It is important to recognize that the activity that this describes is essentially meaningless from the point of view of the users because they do not need to know what is happening inside the computer. This remains true even for users who are able to read and understand the code. Users are interested in such questions as:

- What is the program's overall effect?
- Is it easy to understand what it does?
- Is it easy to use?
- Does it help you detect and correct your mistakes, or does it cover them up and punish you for them?
- How fast is it?
- How much memory does it use?
- Does it contain any errors?

None of these is expressed directly by the code. Generally speaking, the collection of computer instructions in itself tells you nothing about what the program achieves when run in the real world.

It follows that in progressing from your first vague intention to the completed software you have done two distinct things: first, you have turned the vague ideas into something precise enough for the computer to execute; and second, you have converted the users' needs and requirements into something quite different — instructions for the computer.

The sole purpose of this book is to show how to divide this progression into two parts: first, to turn the vagueness into a precise account *of the users' needs and wants*; and then to turn that into computer instructions.

This 'precise account of the users' needs and wants' is called a *specification*, and the crucial point to understand is that it is expressing something quite different from the code, that is, the users' interests instead of the computer's. If the specification and code end up saying the same thing in different ways — and this can easily happen if you think too much from the computer's point of view when you specify — then doing both of them is largely a waste of time.

1.4 Local versus global behaviour

One distinction between the code and the specification is that whereas the code describes individual execution steps — *local* behaviour — the specification is often about the overall, *global* behaviour. The following is an example (though it does not use an orthodox programming language).

WALKIES: Walking According to Local Kommands In Easy Steps. The following is an example WALKIES program:

```
GO 3 METRES; TURN LEFT 90 DEGREES;
GO 3 METRES; TURN LEFT 90 DEGREES;
GO 3 METRES; TURN LEFT 90 DEGREES;
GO 3 METRES; TURN LEFT 90 DEGREES
```

The *local* behaviour of this is that it does four walks with right angles in between; a *global* property is that it ends up at the starting position. The program does not explicitly describe this global property; we need some geometry to deduce it. This is not trivial because, with the wrong geometry, the global property can fail! Therefore, the geometric reasoning must be deep enough to resolve this.

Consider this program:

```
GO 10000 km; TURN LEFT 90 DEGREES;
GO 10000 km; TURN LEFT 90 DEGREES;
GO 10000 km; TURN LEFT 90 DEGREES;
GO 10000 km; TURN LEFT 90 DEGREES
```

4 Introduction

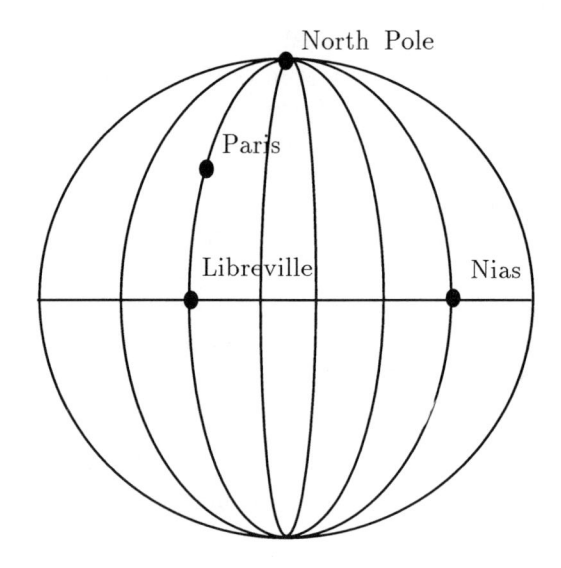

Figure 1.1

You would not end up where you started, if you started at the North Pole and walked round the Earth (Figure 1.1).

The metre was originally defined as one ten millionth part of the Earth's circumference from the North Pole to the Equator via Paris, so the WALKIES trip here goes from the North Pole to Libreville (via Paris), then near to a little island called Nias, then back to the North Pole, and then *on to Libreville again*. You don't get back to where you started. Thus the global properties of a program can depend very much on hidden geometrical assumptions: is our world flat or round? They are not explicit in the program.

WALKIES is not a typical programming language, and properties of programs do not typically depend on geometry, although like WALKIES, their behaviour may depend on environmental factors. But it is nevertheless true that program code usually describes just the individual execution steps and how they are strung together, not their overall effect.

1.5 Reasoned programs

Once we have made both the code and the specification precise, then it is a valid and useful exercise to try and compare them as precisely as possible. In later chapters we shall see specific mathematical techniques for making this comparison. What they amount to is that we try to give mathematical precision not only to the vague overall intention (obtaining a specification), but also to all the comments in the program. They can be written logically, and whether they fit the code can be analyzed precisely.

When code is supported by this kind of careful specification and reasoning, it is a much more stable product. When you have written it, you have greater confidence that it works. When you reuse it, you know exactly what it is supposed to do. When you modify it, you have a clearer idea of how your changes fit into its structure.

Here, then, is our overall goal:

$$\boxed{\text{specification} + \text{reasoning} + \text{code} \longrightarrow \text{a } Reasoned\ Program}$$

1.6 Reasoned program*ming*

We have presented the Reasoned Program as the desired software end product, but there is also something important to say about the process of developing it, in other words about *Reasoned Programming*.

It is possible to see the purpose of the specification as being to say what the code does; but that is the wrong way round. Really, the purpose of the code is to achieve what the specification sets out. This means that it is much better to specify first and then to code. In everyday terms, you can perform a task more effectively if you can understand first what it is that you are trying to achieve.

In the words of Hamming,

$$\boxed{\text{'Typing is no substitute for thinking.'}}$$

This means make your ideas precise before you type them in — work out what you want before you tell the computer how to do it. In the thirty years since Hamming formulated his ideas, our ideas of how to set about this have advanced greatly, and this book is written to teach you, in practical terms, how the modern ideas work.

It is always tempting to start straight off on the code. You gain your initial experience in very short programs and find that this method works. It gets something into the computer, and you get feedback that is gratifyingly quick, even if it often shows that mistakes are present. Many programmers continue to work in this way for the whole of their careers. They find that even if they accept the idea of aiming for Reasoned Programs, it all seems an impossible dream 'Yes, all right in theory, but ...'. They write the code, and *then* — perhaps just before a deadline — try to clarify the reasons.

This is a mistake. There are two essential aspects to the final product that distinguish it from the initial vague intentions, namely precision and local execution steps, and if you go for the code first, you are trying to obtain both aspects at once. On the other hand, if you first think about the specification, then you are just looking for precision. After all, it is the specification that

6 *Introduction*

lies closer to the original vague intentions, not the code. So the first step should always be to think carefully about your intentions and try to refine them to a more precise specification.

After that, the next step is to convert globality (specification) into locality (code), and this is much easier after the initial thought. In fact, there are specific mathematical techniques, which we shall discuss later, that make much of this process automatic. At the same time, they tie the specification and code carefully together so you know *as part of the coding process* that the link between them is made. Figure 1.2 illustrates the progression from vague intention to precise code via precise specification.

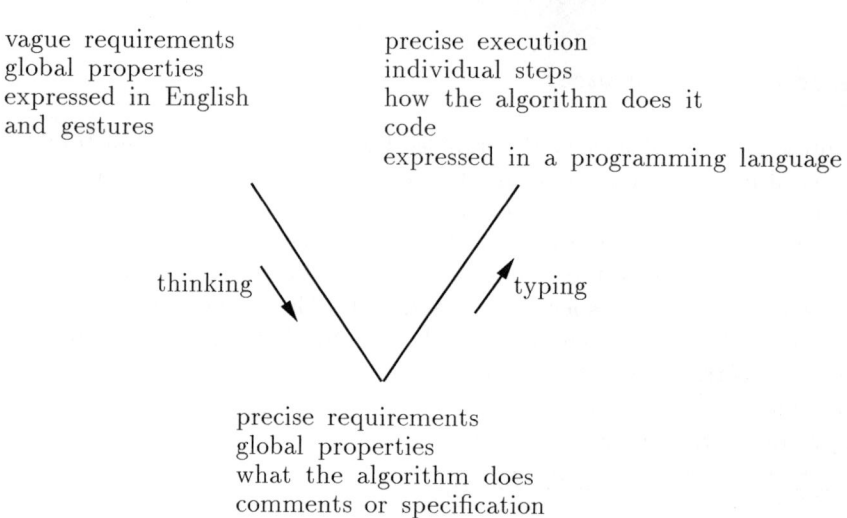

```
vague requirements            precise execution
global properties             individual steps
expressed in English          how the algorithm does it
and gestures                  code
                              expressed in a programming language


         thinking  ↘        ↗ typing


                precise requirements
                global properties
                what the algorithm does
                comments or specification
                expressed in logic
```

Figure 1.2

1.7 Modules

This distinction that we have made between specification and code, corresponding to users and computer, also makes sense inside a program. It is common to find that part of the program, with a well-defined task, can be made fairly self-contained and it is then called — in various contexts — a *subprogram*, or *subroutine*, or *procedure* or *function*, or, for larger, more structured pieces of program, a *module*. The idea is that the overall program is a composite thing, made up *using* components: so it takes on the role of *user*.

A module can be specified, and this describes how its environment, the rest of the program, can call on it and what that achieves. The specification describes all that the rest of the program needs to know about the module. The implementation of the module, the code that it contains, its inner workings, is hidden and can be ignored by the rest of the program.

Modularization is crucial when you want to write a large program because it divides the overall coding problem into independent subproblems. Once you have specified a module, you can code up the inside while forgetting the outside, and vice versa. The specifications of the modules also act as *bulkheads*, like the partitions in the hold of a ship that stop water from a hole spreading everywhere and sinking the ship. The specifications compartmentalize the program so that if an error is discovered in one module you can easily check whether or not correcting it has any consequences for the others. This helps to avoid the 'Hydra' problem, in which correcting one error introduces ten new ones.

1.8 Programming in the large

This book makes a significant simplifying assumption, namely that *specifications can be got right first time*. This is usually (though not always) realistic for small programs, and so the techniques that we shall present are called those of programming *in the small*. The underlying idea, of understanding the users' point of view through a specification, is still important in large-scale programs, but the techniques cannot be applied in such a pure form (specify first, then code). To understand why, you must understand what could possibly be wrong with a specification.

The ultimate test — in fact the definition — of *quality* of software is that it is fit for its purpose. To be sure, the specification is supposed to capture formally this idea of fitness, and if that has been done well then a *correct* program, one for which the code satisfies the specification, will indeed be a quality one. But, conversely, *specifications can have mistakes in them,* and this will manifest itself in unexpected and unwanted features in a formally correct program. Hence *correctness* is only an approximation to *quality*.

Now there are many advantages to forgetting quality and working for correctness. For instance, we have precise objectives (write the code to satisfy the specification) that are susceptible to mathematical analysis, and we can modularize the program and work for correctness of small, easy parts, forgetting the wider issues. The widget manufacturer who takes an order for 2000 blue, size 15 widgets will find life easier if he does not ask himself whether they are really the right colour, let alone whether or not their end use is to help train dolphins to run suicide missions smuggling cocaine.

However, the true proof of the program is, despite all we have said, its behaviour in real life, and ultimately no programmer should forget that. The specification and reasoning are merely a means to an end. Never forget the

8 *Introduction*

possibility that the specification is faulty. This will be obvious if correct code plainly gives undesirable behaviour, but earlier warning signs are when the coding is unexpectedly complicated or perhaps even impossible.

If the specification is faulty, then it can be revised, which will involve checking existing code against the revised specifications. Alternatively, the specification can be left as it is for the time being, with the intention of revising it for future versions or in the light of future experience. This is often quite reasonable, and provides some stability to the project, but it should be chosen after consideration and not out of inertia. The universal experience is that the later corrections are left, the more expensive it is to make them (A Stitch in Time Saves Nine), and large software projects have been destroyed by the accumulation of uncorrected errors.

For programming in the large, many of the practical techniques that people use can be seen as being there to help to correct specificational faults as early as possible, while they are still cheap to fix. For instance, *requirements elicitation* is about how to communicate as effectively as possible with the users, to find out what they really do need and want; then a number of design methodologies help to obtain a good specification before coding starts; and prototyping produces some quick, cheap code in order to find those faults (such as difficulty of use in practice) that are best exposed by a working version. All of these are important issues but they are ignored in the rest of this book.

1.9 Logical notation

English is not always precise and unambiguous — that is why computer programming languages were invented. In general, the fewer things that a language needs to talk about, the more precise it can be.

In our specifications, we are going to make use of *logic* to make precise one particular aspect of what we want to say, namely how different properties connect together. In English there are connecting words such as 'and', 'or', 'but', 'not', 'all', 'some', and so on, and in logic these are systematized and given individual symbols. The reason for the importance of these *connectives* is that it is the logical connections between the given properties that allow us to deduce new ones.

For instance, suppose an instruction manual tells you:

> 'If anyone envelops the distal pinch-screw parascopically, then the pangolin will unbundle.'

Suppose you also know that the anterior proctor has just enveloped the distal pinch-screw parascopically. You do not need to be an expert on pangolins to realize that it is likely to unbundle. The reason is that you have spotted the underlying *logical* structure of these facts, and it does not depend on the nature of pinch-screws, pangolins or proctors.

This logical structure shows up best if we introduce some abbreviations:

$E(x)$ (where x stands for any person or thing) stands for 'x envelops the distal pinch-screw parascopically'.
A stands for 'the anterior proctor'.
P stands for 'the pangolin unbundles'.

As a special case of this notation, if we substitute A for x then:

$E(A)$ stands for 'the anterior proctor envelops the distal pinch-screw parascopically'.

These abbreviations are not in themselves logical notation; that comes in when we connect these statements together. Logic writes —

$\wedge$ for 'and'
$\forall$ for 'for all' (reflecting 'anyone')
$\rightarrow$ for 'implies' (reflecting 'if ... then ...')

Now our known facts appear as
$$\forall x. \ [E(x) \rightarrow P] \wedge E(A)$$
and just from this logical structure we can deduce P.

Much of logic is about making such deductions based on the logical structure of statements. The general pattern is that we start from some statements A called the *premisses*, and then deduce a *conclusion* B. The argument from A to B is *valid* if in any situation where A is true, it follows inevitably that B is true, too. Logic gives *formal* rules — that is to say, rules that depend just on the *form* of the statements and not on their content or meaning — for making valid deductions, and if these rules give us an argument from A to B then we write $A \vdash B$ (A entails B).

For example,

If I have loads of money, then I buy lots of goods.
I have loads of money.
$\vdash$ I buy lots of goods.

is a valid argument There are situations where the premisses are false (for instance, if, as it happens, I am a miser then the first premiss is false), but that does not affect the validity of the argument. *So long as* the premisses are true, the conclusion ('I buy lots of goods') will be, too. However,

If I have loads of money, then I buy lots of goods.
I go on a spending spree.

⊢ I have loads of money.

is not a valid argument. Even if the premisses are true, the conclusion *need not* be since I might be making imprudent use of my credit card.

In this book we shall use logic to help us with, broadly speaking, two kinds of deduction related to a given specification of a program: first, deducing new facts about how the program will behave when we come to use it; and, second, deducing that the program code, or implementation, really does meet the specification. Part II of this book is entirely devoted to logic itself.

1.10 The need for formality

English, and natural language in general, is tremendously rich and can express not only straightforward assertions and commands but also aspects of emotion, time, possibility and probability, meaning of life, and so on. But there is a cost. Much of it relies on common understanding and experience, and on the context. Look at the following three examples, and see how they contain progressively more that is unspoken:

1. 'She sang like her sister.'
2. 'She sang like a nightingale.'
3. 'He sang like a canary.'

(1) is fairly literal, but (2) is not — the comparison is not of the songs themselves but of their beauty, and the compliment works only because everyone knows (even if only by repute) that nightingales sing beautifully. As for (3), in a gangster film "He" might well be a criminal who, on arrest, told the police all about his accomplices. But it is extremely inexplicit, and would be hard to understand out of context.

Different people lead different lives, so these unspoken background assumptions of experience and understanding are imprecise, and this leads to an imprecision in English. To say anything precisely and unambiguously you must drastically restrict the range of what can be said, to the point where any background assumptions can also be made explicit. Then there is a direct correspondence between the language and its meaning, and you can treat the language 'formally', that is, as symbols to be manipulated (which, after all, is what a computer has to do), and be confident that such manipulations are reflected validly in the meaning.

An important example of a formal language that you must already know is algebra, the formal language of numbers. Problems can often be solved *symbolically* by algebraic manipulations without thinking about the numbers behind the symbols, and you still obtain correct answers. An extension of this is calculus. Again the symbolic manipulations — the various rules for differentiating and integrating — can be carried through without you having to remember what the derivatives and integrals really mean.

In fact, this is only a particular application of the word 'calculus', which is Latin for 'little stone'. In ancient times, one method of *calcula*ting was by using little stones roughly like an abacus, and the idea is that you can obtain correct answers about unmanipulable things through surrogate manipulations of the little stones. We now use formal symbols instead of little stones, but the word 'calculus' is still often used for such a formal language — for instance, one part of logic is often called the 'predicate calculus'.

The other formal languages that you will see in this book are as follows:

logic This is the language of logical connections between statements. This is a very narrow aspect of the statements and so the logical notation will usually need to be combined with other notations, but once we have the logical symbols expressing the logical structure, we can describe what are logically correct arguments. Another point is that the logical symbols are more precisely defined than English words. For instance, there is a logical connective '$\vee$' that, by and large, means 'or': 'A or B' has the logical structure '$A \vee B$'. But sometimes the English 'or' carries an implicit restriction 'but not both' (the so-called *exclusive or*), and then the logic must take care to express this, as $(A \vee B) \wedge \neg(A \wedge B)$.

programming languages These are the languages of computer actions (roughly — this is more true for the imperative language Modula-2 than for the functional language Miranda). Once they are made formal then one can work with them by symbolic manipulation and this is exactly what computers do when they compile and interpret programs.

1.11 Can programs be proved correct?

We have already distinguished between quality and correctness, and explained how 'correctness', conformance to the specification, is only relative: if the specification is wrong (that is, not what the user wanted) then so, too, will be the code, however 'correct' it is. But at least the specification and code are both formal, so there is the possibility of giving formal proofs of this relative correctness — one might say that this is the objective of *formal methods* in computer software.

It is worth pointing out that what you will see in this book are really only 'informal formal methods'. There are two main reasons for this.

The first is that to give a formal correctness proof you need a formal *semantics* of your programming language, a mathematical account of what the programs actually mean in relation to the specifications. We shall not attempt to do this at all, but instead will rely on your informal understanding of what the programming constructs mean.

The second is that true formal reasoning has to include every last detail. This might be fine if it is a computer (via a software tool) that is checking the reasoning, but for humans such reasoning is tedious to the point of impracticability, and hides the overall shape of the argument — you cannot see the wood for the trees. Even in pure mathematics, proofs are 'rigorous' — to a high standard that resolves doubts — but not formal. Our aim is to introduce you to rigorous reasoning.

Now even rigorous reasoning runs the risk of containing errors, so if in this book we cannot claim unshakable mathematical correctness you might wonder what the point is. We do not seem to be working to a Reasoned Program as an error-free structure. Nevertheless, the structure of the Reasoned Program, with its specification and reasoning included, is much more stable than an Unreasoned Program, that is, code on its own. We have a clearer understanding of its working, and this helps us both to avoid errors in the first place and, when errors do slip through, to understand why we made them and how to correct them.

1.12 Summary

- The *code* is directed towards the computer, giving it its instructions.
- The *specification* is directed towards the users, describing what they will get out of the program. It is concerned with *quality* (fitness for purpose).
- By reasoning that the code satisfies the specification, you link them together into a *reasoned program*.
- By putting the specification first, as objectives to be achieved by the code, you engage in *reasoned programming*. Coding is then concerned with *correctness* (conformance with specification).
- This separation also underlies *modularization*. The specification of a module or subroutine is its interface with the rest of the program, the coding is its (hidden) internal workings.
- This book is about *programming in the small*. It makes the simplifying assumption that specifications can be got right first time.
- In practice, specifications can be faulty — so that correctness does not necessarily produce quality. Be on your guard against this.
- The earlier faults are corrected, the better and cheaper.
- There are numerous practices aimed at obtaining good specifications early rather than late, for instance talking to the customer, thinking hard about the design and prototyping, but this book is not concerned with these.
- To match the formality of the programming language, we use formal logical notation for specifications. It is also possible to use formal semantics to link the two, but we will not do this here.

Part I

Programming

Chapter 2

Functions and expressions

2.1 Functions

From the specification point of view a function is a *black box* which converts input to output. 'Black box' means you cannot see — or are not interested in — its internal workings, the implementing code. Mathematically speaking, the input and output represent the *argument* to the function and the computed *result* (Figure 2.1).

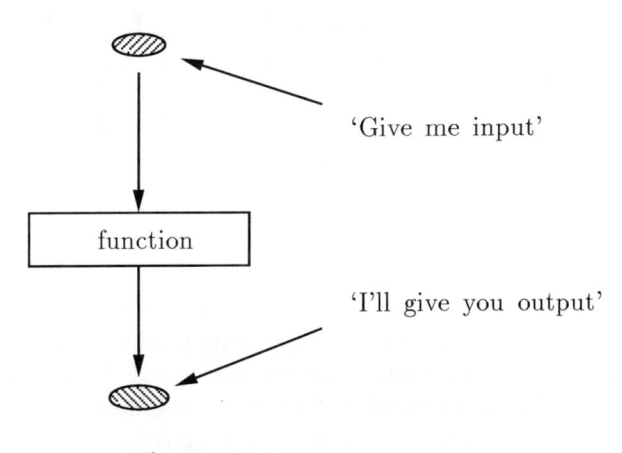

Figure 2.1

In Figure 2.2 the function `add1` simply produces a result which is one more than its given argument. The number 16 is called an argument or an *actual parameter* and the process of supplying a function with a parameter is called *function application*. We say that the function `add1` is *applied* to 16. Similarly, the function `capital` takes arguments which are countries and returns the capital city corresponding to the given country.

16 *Functions and expressions*

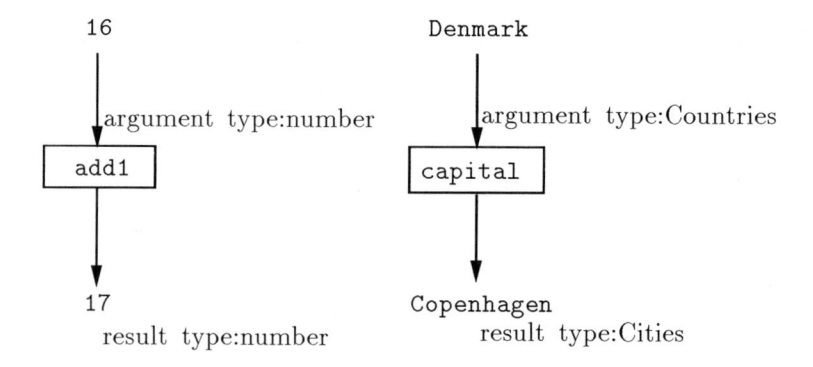

```
       16                            Denmark
        │                               │
        │ argument type:number          │ argument type:Countries
     ┌──▼──┐                         ┌──▼────┐
     │ add1│                         │capital│
     └──┬──┘                         └──┬────┘
        │                               │
        ▼                               ▼
       17                           Copenhagen
  result type:number              result type:Cities
```

Figure 2.2

From mathematics we are all familiar with functions which take more than one argument. For example, functions + and * require two numbers as arguments. Figure 2.3 gives some examples of applications of multi-argument functions.

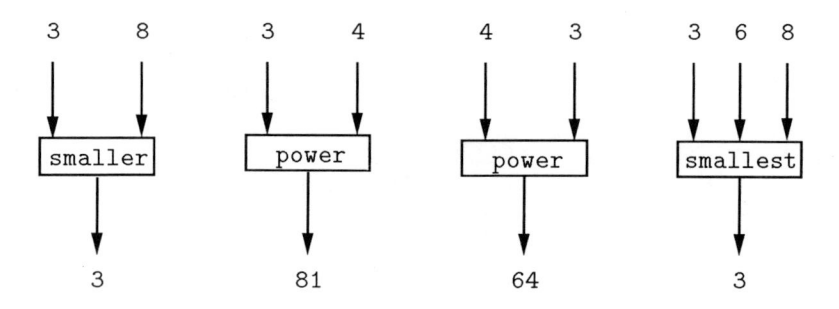

```
  3   8          3   4          4   3          3   6   8
  │   │          │   │          │   │          │   │   │
  ▼   ▼          ▼   ▼          ▼   ▼          ▼   ▼   ▼
┌───────┐      ┌───────┐      ┌───────┐      ┌─────────┐
│smaller│      │ power │      │ power │      │smallest │
└───┬───┘      └───┬───┘      └───┬───┘      └────┬────┘
    ▼              ▼              ▼               ▼
    3             81              64              3
```

Figure 2.3

When we first define a function we need to pay attention both to the way it works as a rule for calculation (the code) and also to its overall global, external behaviour (the specification). But, when a function comes to be used, only its external behaviour is significant and the local rule used in calculations and evaluations becomes invisible (a black box). For example, whenever `double` is used the same external behaviour will result whether `double n` is defined as `2*n` or as `n+n`.

2.2 Describing functions

We can describe functions in a number of ways. We can specify the function value explicitly by giving one equation for each individual input element; or

Describing functions 17

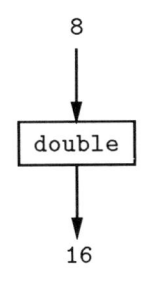

```
        8
        │
        ▼
    ┌────────┐
    │ double │
    └────────┘
        │
        ▼
       16
```

Figure 2.4

we can draw a diagram — a *mapping diagram* showing for each input element its corresponding result (Figure 2.5). However, often there will be many, even infinitely many, individual elements to consider and such methods will clearly be inconvenient.

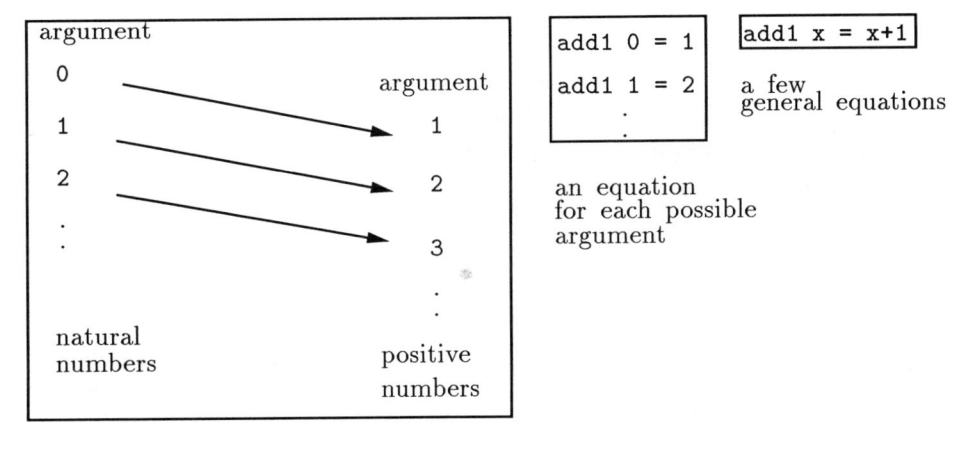

```
argument          argument
  0 ─────────────────╲
  1 ─────────────────╲╲ 1
                      ╲╲
  2 ─────────────────── 2
                        ╲
                         3
  ·                      ·
  ·                      ·
natural              positive
numbers              numbers
```

```
add1 0 = 1
add1 1 = 2
    ·
```

an equation
for each possible
argument

```
add1 x = x+1
```

a few
general equations

showing individual mappings

Figure 2.5

An alternative method is to describe the function using a few general equations (Figure 2.5). Here we can make use of *formal parameters*, which are names that we give to represent any argument to which the function will be applied. For example, the formal parameter x in the definition of add1 stands for any number. The *right hand side* of the *rule* (or *equation*) describes the result computed in terms of the formal parameter. In the functional language Miranda, add1 is described in a notation which is very close to the mathematical notation used above:

```
add1 :: num -> num
add1 x = x+1
```

18 *Functions and expressions*

The first line *declares* the function by indicating the function's argument and result types. The argument type, which precedes the arrow, states the expected type of the argument to which the function will be applied. The result type, which follows the arrow, states the type of the value returned by the function. A function is said to *map* a value from an argument type to another value of a result type. The second line is an equation which *defines* the function.

Now let us look at some more programs: for example, consider the problems of finding the area and circumference of a circle given its radius. We need the constant value π, which is built-in to the Miranda evaluator under the name `pi`, but note that even if `pi` were not built-in we could define our own constant as shown for `mypi`:

```
mypi :: num
mypi = 3.14159
circumference, areaofcircle :: num -> num
areaofcircle  radius =  pi * radius * radius
circumference  r = 2 * pi * r
```

(This also illustrates how a formal parameter is not restricted to a single letter such as n.) Similarly, we can define a function to convert a temperature given in degrees Fahrenheit to degrees Celsius by:

```
fahr_to_celsius :: num -> num
fahr_to_celsius temp = (temp - 32) / 1.8
```

Multi-argument functions can be defined similarly. For example, see the function below, which, given the base area and the height of a uniform object, computes the volume of the object:

```
volume :: num -> num -> num
volume  hgt area = hgt * area
```

The declaration is read as follows: `volume` is a function which takes two numbers as arguments and returns a number as its result. The reason for using `->` to separate the two number arguments will become clear later when we discuss typing in more detail. Each `->` marks the type preceding it as an argument type.

Joining functions together

More complex functions can be defined by *functional composition*, making the result of one function application an argument of another function application. This can be viewed pictorially as joining the output wire of one black box onto an input wire of another black box (Figure 2.6). In this way several functions can be combined, for example `double (4 * 6)` combines the functions `double` and `*`. This combination can be pictured by connecting up the wires:

Describing functions 19

```
    4   6
    ↓   ↓
    ┌─┐
    │*│
    └─┘
     ↓
   ┌──────┐
   │double│
   └──────┘
      ↓
     48
```

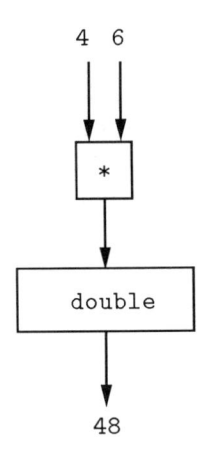

Figure 2.6

There is no restriction on the number of times this principle may be employed as long as the result and argument types of the various pairs of functions match.

If we use functional composition without explicit (that is, actual) arguments then the combination can be regarded as a new function (a *composition* of double and *), which we will call doubleprod (Figure 2.7). This new function

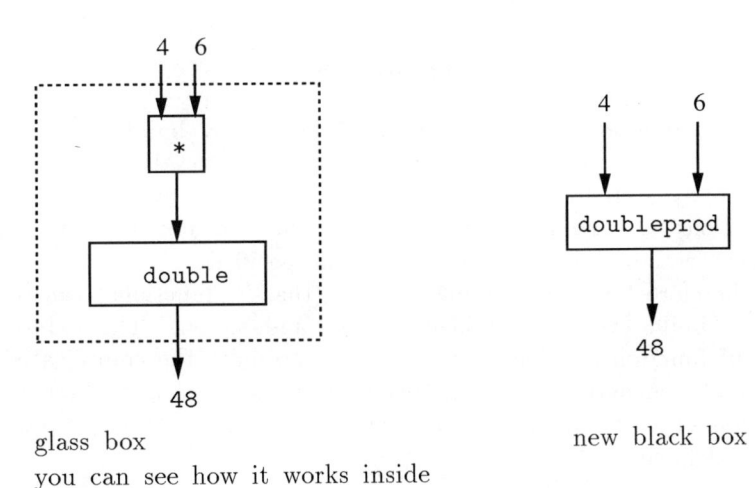

```
glass box                           new black box
you can see how it works inside
```

Figure 2.7

has the property that, for all numbers x and y,

```
doubleprod :: num -> num -> num
doubleprod x y = double(x*y)
```

20 *Functions and expressions*

As another example consider the following function, which computes the volume of a cylinder of height h and radius r (Figure 2.8). A cylinder is a particular kind of 'uniform object' whose volume we calculate by multiplying its height, which is h, by its base area, which we calculate using `areaofcircle`. Hence, assuming that `volume` and `areaofcircle` compute correctly (conform to their specifications), our function for the volume of a cylinder can be computed by

```
cylinderV :: num -> num -> num
cylinderV h r = volume h(areaofcircle r)
```

This is an example of *top-down* design. Ultimately, we want to implement

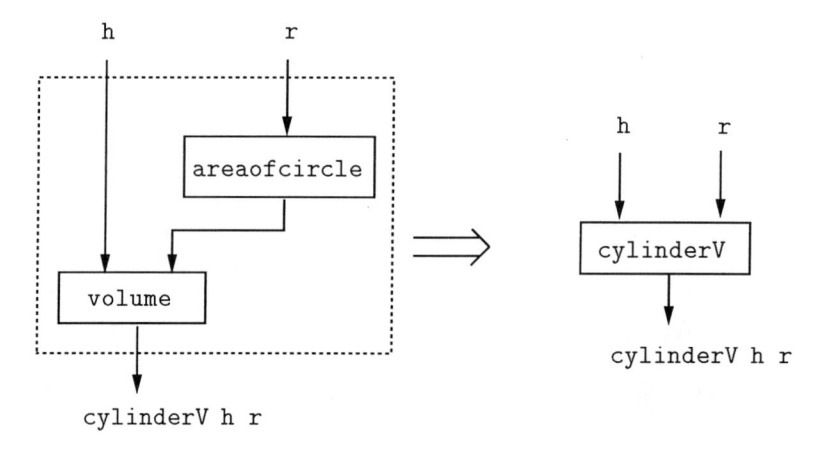

Figure 2.8

the high-level functions, the ones we really want, by building them up from the low-level, *primitive* functions, that are built-in to Miranda. But we can do this step by step from the top down, for instance by defining `cylinderV` using functions `volume` and `areaofcircle` that do not need to have been implemented yet, but do need to have been specified.

It can therefore be seen that black boxes (that is, functions) can be plugged together to build even bigger black boxes, and so on. The external, black box view of functions, which allows us to encapsulate the complicated internal plugging and concentrate on the specification, has an important impact on the cohesion of large programs. To see an example of this, suppose we had mistakenly defined

```
areaofcircle radius = pi*pi*radius
```

Of course, `cylinderV` will then give wrong answers. But we are none the less convinced that *the definition of* `cylinderV` *is correct*, and that is because our use of `areaofcircle` in it is based on the *specification* of `areaofcircle`, not on the erroneous definition. (`volume` asks for the base area, and `areaofcircle` is supposed to compute this.)

There may be lots of parts of a large program, all using `areaofcircle` correctly, and all giving wrong answers. As soon as `areaofcircle` has been corrected, all these problems will vanish.

On the other hand, someone might have been tempted to correct for the error by defining

```
cylinderV h r = volume h ((areaofcircle r)*r/pi)
```

This is a perfect recipe for writing code that is difficult to understand and debug: as soon as `areaofcircle` is corrected, `cylinderV` goes wrong. The rule is:

> When you use a function, rely on its *specification*, not its *definition*.

2.3 Some properties of functions

Functions map each combination of elements of the argument types to *at most one* element of the result type: when there is a result at all, then it is a well-defined, unique result. There *may* be argument combinations for which the result is not defined, and then we call the function *partial*. An example is `bitNegate`, which is undefined for all numbers other than 0 and 1 (Figure 2.9):

```
bitNegate ::  num -> num
bitNegate x = 1,   if x=0
            = 0,   if x=1
```

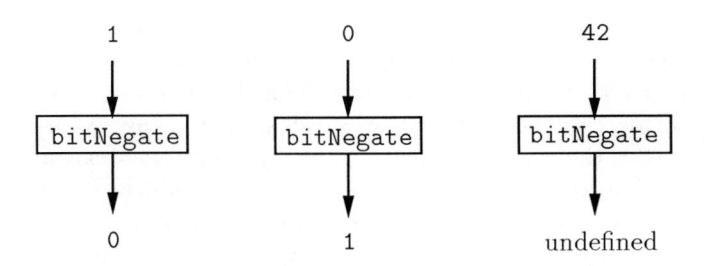

<pre>
       1   0   42
       ↓   ↓   ↓
  ┌─────────┐   ┌─────────┐   ┌─────────┐
  │bitNegate│   │bitNegate│   │bitNegate│
  └─────────┘   └─────────┘   └─────────┘
       ↓   ↓   ↓
       0   1   undefined
</pre>

Figure 2.9

Similarly, division is a partial function and is said to be undefined for cases where its second argument is zero. A function that is not partial, one for which the result is always defined (at least for arguments of the right type), is called *total*.

22 *Functions and expressions*

Just as an illustration of some different possible behaviours of functions, here are two more kinds:

1. A function is *onto* if every value of the result type is a possible result of the function.
2. A function is *one-to-one* if two different combinations of arguments must lead to two different results.

For instance, `double` is one-to-one (if $x \neq y$ then `double` $x \neq$ `double` y) but not onto (for example, 3 is not a possible result because the results are all even). On the other hand, `volume` is onto (for example, any number z is a possible result because $z =$ `volume` z 1) but not one-to-one (for example, `volume` 2 3 = 6 = `volume` 3 2 — different argument combinations (2,3) and (3,2) lead to the same result).

2.4 Using a functional language evaluator

In order to construct a program in a functional language to solve a given problem one must define a function which solves the problem. If this definition involves other functions, then those must also be defined. Thus a functional program is just a collection of function definitions supplied by the programmer. To run a program one simply presents the functional language evaluator with an expression and it will do the rest. This expression can contain references to functions defined in the program as well as to built-in functions and constant values.

The functional language evaluator will have a number of *built-in* (or *primitive*) functions, together with their definitions: for example, the basic arithmetic functions `+`, `-`, `*`, `/` etc. The computer will evaluate your expression using your function definitions and those of its primitive functions and then print the result. Therefore, the computer just acts as a giant calculator.

Expressions that do not involve user-defined functions can be evaluated without using any program (just like a calculator). The evaluator, however, is more powerful than an ordinary calculator since you can introduce new function definitions in addition to those already built-in. Expressions can involve the name of these functions and are evaluated by using their definitions. This view of a functional language evaluator is illustrated in Figure 2.10.

2.5 Evaluation of expressions

When you present a functional evaluator with an expression, you can imagine it reducing the expression through a sequence of equivalent expressions to its 'simplest equivalent form' (or *normal* form), with no functions left to be

Evaluation of expressions 23

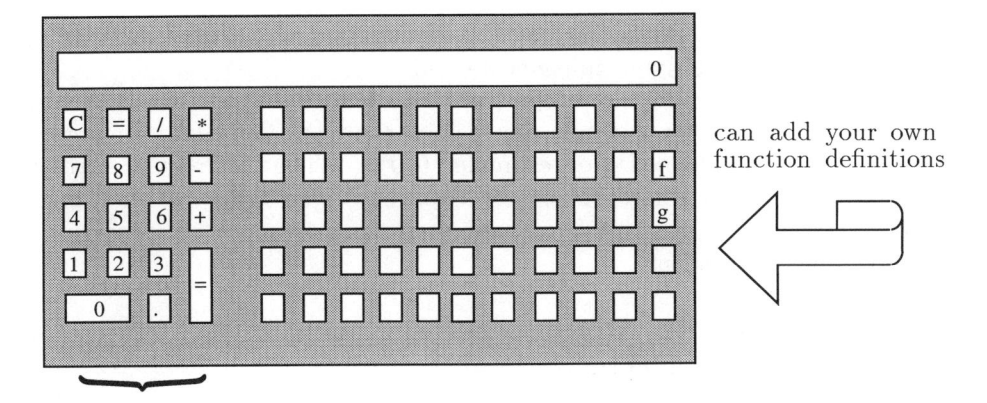

primitive functions and values

Figure 2.10 One view of a functional language evaluator

applied. This is the answer, which is then displayed. You can mimic this by 'hand evaluation', as in

```
double(3 + 4)
=   double 7            by built-in rules for +
=   7 + 7               by the rule for double
=   14                  by built-in rules for +
```

14 will be printed by the evaluator. (At each stage we have underlined the part that gets reduced next.) Other reduction sequences are possible, though of course they lead to the same answer in the end. Here is another one:

```
double (3 + 4)
=   (3 + 4) +(3 + 4)    by the rule for double
=   7 +(3 + 4)          by built-in rules for +
=   7 + 7               by built-in rules for +
=   14                  by built-in rules for +
```

Thus evaluation is a simple process of *substitution* and *simplification*, using both primitive rules and rules (that is, definitions) supplied by the programmer. In order to simplify a function application, a *new copy* of the right-hand side of the function definition is created with each occurrence of the formal parameter replaced by a copy of the actual parameter. Function applications of the resulting expression are then simplified in the same manner until a normal form is reached.

It should be noted that in the above discussion there has been no mention of *how* the evaluation mechanism is implemented. Indeed, functional languages

24 Functions and expressions

offer the considerable advantage that programmers need not pay much (if any) attention to the underlying implementation.

Some expressions do not represent well-defined values in the normal mathematical sense, for example any partial function applied to an argument for which it is undefined (for example, 6/0). When confronted with such expressions (that is, whose values are undefined), the computer may give an error message, or it may go into an infinitely long sequence of reductions and remain perpetually silent.

2.6 Notations for functions

So far we have seen functions in prefix and infix notations. In *prefix* notation the function symbol precedes its argument, as in `double 3` or `smaller x y`. *Infix* notation should also be familiar from school mathematics, where the function (also called operator) symbol appears between its arguments (also called operands), as in `2+6` or `x*y`.

In mathematics, $f(x,y)$ is written for the result of applying f to x and y. In Miranda, we can omit the parentheses and comma, and in fact it would be wrong to include them. Instead, we write `f x y` (with spaces) (Figure 2.11).

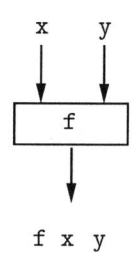

Figure 2.11

However, we cannot do without parentheses altogether, for we need them to package `f x y` as a single unit (`f x y`) when it is used within a larger expression. You can see this in

```
cylinderV h r = volume h(areaofcircle r)
```

Precedence

In expressions such as (2+3*4), where there are several infix operators, it is ambiguous whether the expression is meant to represent ((2+3)*4) or (2+(3*4)). Such ambiguities are resolved by a set of simple *precedence* (priority) rules. For example, the above expression really means (2+(3*4)) because, by long-standing convention, multiplication has a higher precedence relative to addition.

The purpose of precedence rules is to resolve possible ambiguity and to allow us to use fewer parentheses in expressions. Such rules of precedence will also be built-in to the evaluator to enable it to recognize the intended ordering. A hand evaluation example illustrating this is shown in Figure 2.12. Where necessary, the programmer can use extra parentheses to force a different order of grouping. For instance, 2*(3+4)*5 = 2*7*5 = 70.

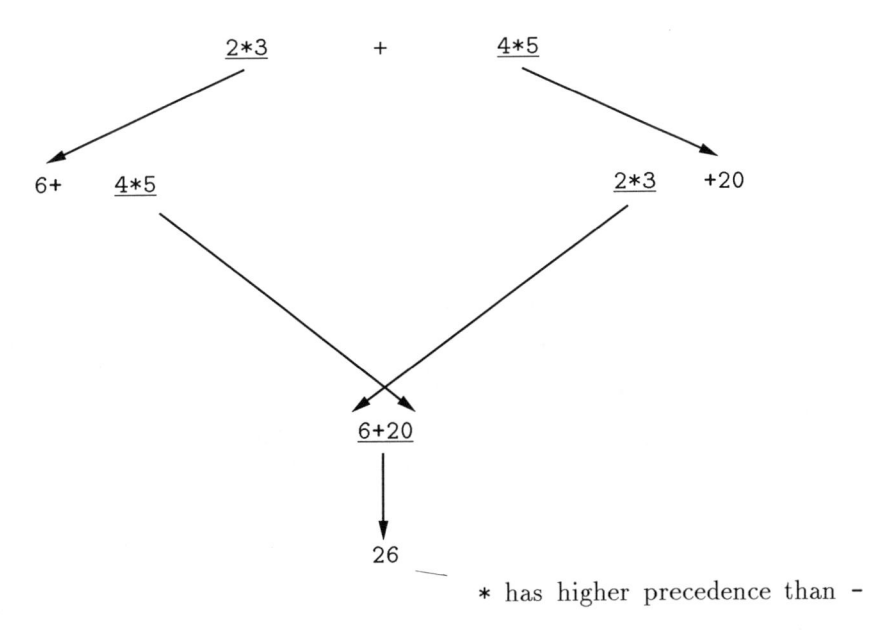

```
       2*3         +           4*5

6+    4*5                   2*3     +20


                  6+20

                   26
                          * has higher precedence than -
```

Figure 2.12 $2*3 + 4*5 = 6 + 20 = 26$

2.7 Meaning of expressions

The meaning of an expression *is* the value which it *represents*. This value cannot be changed by any part of the computation. Evaluating an expression only alters its form, never its value. For example, in the following evaluation sequence all expressions have the same value — the abstract integer value 30:

doubleprod 5 3 = double (5*3) = double 15 = 30

Note that an expression (in whatever form, even in its normal form) is not a value but, rather, a representation of it. There are many representations for one and the same value. For example, the above expressions are just four of infinitely many possible representations for the abstract integer value 30.

Expressions in a functional language may contain names which stand for unknown quantities, but, as in mathematics, different occurrences of the same name refer to the same unknown quantity, for example x in double(x) + $\frac{x}{2}$. Such names are usually called *variables*.

2.8 Summary

- A functional program consists of a collection of function definitions. To run a program one presents the evaluator with an expression and it will evaluate it. This expression can contain references to functions defined in the program, as well as to built-in functions and constant values.
- Functions are defined in a notation which is very close to mathematical notation.
- *Functional composition* (that is, passing the output of one function as an argument to another function) is used to define more complex functions in terms of simpler ones.
- Evaluation of an expression is by *reduction*, meaning simplification. The expression is repeatedly simplified until it has no more functions left to be applied.
- The meaning of an expression is the value which it *represents*. This value cannot be changed by any part of the computation. Evaluating an expression only alters its form, never its value.

2.9 Exercises

1. Define a function hypotenuse which, given the lengths of the two shorter sides of a right-angled triangle, returns the length of the third side. (There is a built-in function sqrt that calculates square roots.)
2. Write a function addDigit of two arguments which will concatenate a single-digit integer onto the right-hand end of an arbitrary-sized integer. For instance, addDigit 123 4 should give 1234. Ignore the possibility of the number becoming too large (called integer overflow).
3. Define a function celsius_to_fahr that converts celsius temperatures to Fahrenheit. Show for any value of temp that the following hold:

   celsius_to_fahr(fahr_to_celsius temp) = temp
   fahr_to_celsius(celsius_to_fahr temp) = temp

Chapter 3

Specifications

A conscientious programmer wants the customer to be entirely satisfied with the program, so their aims are the same overall: they both want to see a satisfactory and useful product at the end. None the less, there are certain tensions between the programmer's wish for an easy task, and the customer's desire for a powerful and comprehensive ('All singing, all dancing') program. This may boil down to money. A more powerful program will cost more to produce, the customer must balance his needs against his budget and the programmer must be able to make plain the difference between the more and the less powerful specifications.

In this vague sense, the specification represents part of a contract between programmer and customer. The full contract says 'Programmer will implement software to this specification, and customer will pay such-and-such amount of money.' However, there is also a sense in which *the specification itself* represents a contract.

3.1 Specification as contract

PUNTER (the customer) and HACKER (the programmer) have done business together before, and usually find they understand each other.

> Act 1
> PUNTER: Can you write me a program to calculate the square root of a real number?
> HACKER: Can I assume it is non-negative?
> PUNTER: Yes.
> HACKER: OK, I can do that.
> [Shake hands and exeunt]

They now have a gentlemen's agreement that HACKER will write a square root program: this is an oral contract between PUNTER as software purchaser, and HACKER as software producer. But there is also a more subtle contract involved, between PUNTER as software user, and HACKER 'as software'. This says that if PUNTER uses the program, then, *provided that* the input is a non-negative number, the output will be a square root of it. This is a contract because it embodies some interlocking rights and obligations governing the way in which the program is to be used.

First, the input must be non-negative. This is an obligation on PUNTER, but a right for HACKER, who is entitled to expect, for the sake of his implementation, that the input is non-negative. But, then, he is obliged to calculate a square root, and PUNTER has the right to expect that this is what the output will be.

A specification such as this can be divided into the following two parts:

- The *pre-condition* is the condition on the input that the user guarantees: for example, the input is a non-negative real number.
- The *post-condition* is the condition on the output that the programmer guarantees: for example, the output is the square root of the input.

There is a certain asymmetry here (which is due to the fact that the input comes first). The pre-condition can only refer to the input, whereas the post-condition will probably refer to both the input and the output.

Note also the underlying tension: the customer would like weak pre-conditions (so the program works for very general input) and strong post-conditions (so it computes many, or very precise, answers). The programmer, on the other hand, would like the reverse.

Therefore, there must be some kind of dialogue in order to agree on the terms of the contract. Figure 3.1 shows these tensions with springs. The programmer would have the pre- and post-conditions the same, then he doesn't have to do anything at all. The customer's spring pulls the conditions apart.

The strength of the springs depends on various factors. For instance, if the customer is prepared to pay a lot of money for some software, or if the software is a procedure that is called very often, then it is worth putting a lot of work into programming it — 'the customer's spring is powerful'.

3.2 Formalizing specifications

Let us introduce a very specific format for writing such specifications as part of a Miranda program. It has three parts, namely typing information and the pre- and post-conditions.

The *typing information* gives the types of the input (argument) and output (result), and also the name of the program (function), and there is a standard Miranda notation for this. In many programming languages this is an essential part of the program definition, required by the compiler. In Miranda, it is

Defensive specifications — what happens if the input is bad?

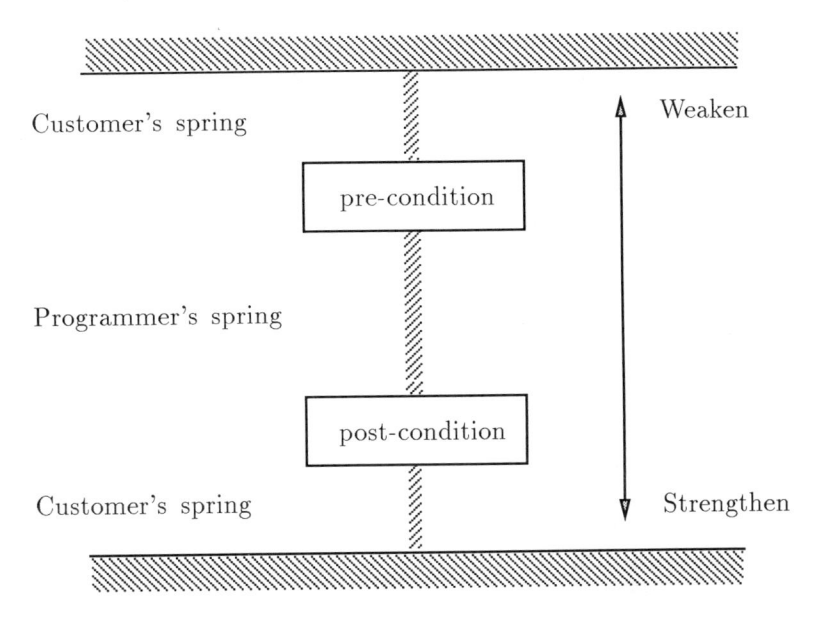

Figure 3.1

optional because the compiler can deduce the types from the rest of the definition. However, they may not be the intended types so type declarations should always be included in all programs.

The *pre- and post-conditions* are written using English and logical notation, and made into comments (that is, they follow the symbols '||'). Note that in Miranda any part of your program which starts with ||, together with all the text to its right (on the same line), is regarded as being a comment and hence is ignored by the evaluator.

The square root function could be specified by

```
sqrt :: num -> num
||pre:  x >= 0
||post: (sqrt x)^2 = x
sqrt x= HACKER must fill this in
```

3.3 Defensive specifications — what happens if the input is bad?

This is a relatively convenient specification for HACKER because he doesn't have to worry about the possibility of negative input. That worry has been passed over to PUNTER, who must therefore be careful. If, by mistake, he gives a negative input, then the contract is off and there is no knowing what

30 *Specifications*

might happen. He might obtain a sensible answer, or a nonsense answer, or an apparently sensible but actually erroneous answer, or an error message, or an infinite loop, or a system crash, or World War III, or anything. ('Garbage in, garbage out'; the contract itself is 'Non-garbage in, non-garbage out'.)

This balance of worry is usually sensible if the only way in which PUNTER uses HACKER's square root program is by calling it from a program of his own. He needs to look at every place where it is called, and convince himself that he would never use a negative input. Thus in exchange for some care at the programming stage, the `sqrt` function can run efficiently without checking inputs all the time.

On the other hand, PUNTER may intend to use the program at an exposed place (for instance, in a calculator) where any input at all may conceivably be provided. In that case, PUNTER would prefer a 'defensive specification' for a function that defends itself against bad arguments. When HACKER asks if he can assume that the input is non-negative, PUNTER replies: 'No. If it is negative, stop and print an error message.'

```
defensivesqrt :: num -> num
||pre:  none
||post: (x < 0 & error reported) \/
||      (x >= 0 & (defensivesqrt x)^2 = x)
```

(We would like to use the logical notation ∧ and ∨ for 'and' and 'or' but for a program comment, where it is impossible to type logical symbols we use the notation & and \/ instead. This matches Miranda's own notation.) The point is that different ideas about how to handle erroneous input must be reflected in different specifications.

3.4 How to use specifications: `fourthroot`

Suppose PUNTER wants to write a Miranda function to calculate fourth roots:

```
fourthroot :: num -> num
||pre:  x >= 0
||post: (fourthroot x)^4 = x
```

Essentially, he wants to apply HACKER's `sqrt` twice, but he also notices a nuisance — the specification of `sqrt` doesn't specify the *positive* square root. So he splits the function definition into two cases:

```
fourthroot x = sqrt y,      if y>=0
             = sqrt(-y),    otherwise
               where y = sqrt x
||Would help if sqrt gave positive square roots.
```

PUNTER now wishes to show that this definition of fourthroot satisfies its specification. It is important to understand that he does not need to know anything at all about how HACKER calculates square roots. He just assumes that sqrt satisfies *its* specification. The specification is all that PUNTER knows, or is entitled to assume, about the sqrt function.

Note there is something important for PUNTER to do. He uses sqrt in three places, and at each one he must check that the pre-condition holds: that the argument of sqrt is non-negative.

3.5 Proof that fourthroot satisfies its specification

We want to *prove* (or explain why) fourthroot works correctly, that is,
$$\forall x : num.\ (x \geq 0 \rightarrow (\texttt{fourthroot } x)^4 = x)$$
We do this on the *assumption* that sqrt works correctly, that is,
$$\forall x : num.\ (x \geq 0 \rightarrow (\texttt{sqrt } x)^2 = x)$$
(Of course, it is possible that it doesn't, but fourthroot should not have to worry about that. It is the responsibility of sqrt to get its answer right.)

We shall put the reasoning in a framework where the assumptions go at the top, the conclusion (what is to be proved) goes at the bottom and the proof goes in the middle, as in Figure 3.2. What we want to end up with is a

$\forall x : num.\ (x \geq 0 \rightarrow (\texttt{sqrt } x)^2 = x)$ assumption

⋮

proof

⋮

$\forall x : num.\ (x \geq 0 \rightarrow (\texttt{fourthroot } x)^4 = x)$ conclusion

Figure 3.2

proof that, as you read down through it, steadily accumulates more and more true consequences of the assumptions until it reaches the desired conclusion. That is how the proof can be read, but we can see already that writing it does not go straight down from top to bottom — we are going to have an interplay between working forwards from the assumptions and backwards from the desired conclusions.

The method is fully investigated in Chapter 16. In this example we give a rather informal introduction to it.

Here is a typical backward step. To prove the conclusion, we must show that if someone gives us a number — and we don't care what number it is

— as long as it is non-negative, `fourthroot` will calculate a fourth root of it. Once we have the number it is fixed, so let us give it a different name c to indicate this. So we are now working in a hypothetical context where

1. we have been given our c
2. c is a number
3. $c \geq 0$

and given all these assumptions we must prove $(\texttt{fourthroot}\ c)^4 = c$. Figure 3.3 shows a box drawn around the part of the proof where these temporary assumptions are in force. For the final conclusion we have left c behind, so we

$\forall x : num.\ (x \geq 0 \to (\texttt{sqrt}\ x)^2 = x)$ assumption

$c : num \quad c \geq 0$ temporary assumptions

$\vdots$

proof

$\vdots$

$(\texttt{fourthroot}\ c)^4 = c$ to prove

$\forall x : num.\ (x \geq 0 \to (\texttt{fourthroot}\ x)^4 = x)$ conclusion

Figure 3.3

can come out of the box. What this purely logical, and automatic, analysis has given us is a context (the box) where we can begin to come to grips with the programming issues. Since $c \geq 0$, we can use our original assumption (that `sqrt` works) to deduce that `sqrt` c gives an answer y (with $y^2 = c$), and either $y \geq 0$ or $y < 0$.

We thus — again by automatic logic, but working forwards this time — have two cases to work with, which again we put in boxes because each case has a temporary assumption ($y \geq 0$ for one, $y < 0$ for the other). In each case, we must prove $(\texttt{fourthroot}\ c)^4 = c$, so this equation ends up by being written down three times. This can be seen in Figure 3.4. The two cases may then be argued by chains of equations as in the final box proof, Figure 3.5. Notice the following features of box proofs:

1. Each box marks the scope, or region of validity, of some names or assumptions. For instance, within the left-hand innermost box we are working in a context where

    - we have a number c
    - $c \geq 0$
    - $y = \texttt{sqrt}\ c \geq 0$

Proof that fourthroot satisfies its specification

$\forall x : num. \ (x \geq 0 \to (\text{sqrt } x)^2 = x)$ assumption

---
$c : num$ $c \geq 0$ assumption

$(\text{sqrt } c)^2 = c$ spec of sqrt

$y^2 = c$ write y for sqrt c

$y \geq 0 \lor y < 0$

$y \geq 0$		$y < 0$	
$\vdots$	case 1	$\vdots$	case 2
$(\text{fourthroot } c)^4 = c$	to prove	$(\text{fourthroot } c)^4 = c$	to prove

$(\text{fourthroot } c)^4 = c$

$\forall x : num. \ (x \geq 0 \to (\text{fourthroot } x)^4 = x)$ conclusion

Figure 3.4 Working forwards

$F = \text{fourthroot } c$

$\forall x : num. \ (x \geq 0 \to (\text{sqrt } x)^2 = x)$ assumption

---
$c : num$ $c \geq 0$ assumption

$(\text{sqrt } c)^2 = c$ spec of sqrt

$y^2 = c$ y for sqrt c

$y \geq 0 \lor y < 0$

$y \geq 0$		$y < 0$	
$(F)^4 = ((F)^2)^2$	arithmetic	$(F)^4 = ((F)^2)^2$	arithmetic
$= ((\text{sqrt } y)^2)^2$	def F	$= ((\text{sqrt } (-y))^2)^2$	def F
$= y^2$	spec sqrt	$= (-y)^2$	spec sqrt
$= c$	as required	$= y^2$	arithmetic
		$= c$	as required

$(\text{fourthroot } c)^4 = c$

$\forall x : num. \ (x \geq 0 \to (\text{fourthroot } x)^4 = x)$ conclusion

Figure 3.5 The final box proof for fourthroot

These are not permanent; for instance outside the boxes nothing is known of c, and the right-hand innermost box does not know that $y \geq 0$.

2. When you read a box proof, you can read it straight down from the top: each new line is either a temporary hypothesis or is derived from lines higher up. But when you *construct* a box proof you work both forwards, from assumptions, and backwards, from your goal. Hence there is a definite difference between *proof* and *proving*. (It is very similar to that between the Reasoned Program and Reasoned Programming.)

Box proofs can be translated into English as follows:

Let $c : num$ with $c \geq 0$, and let $y = \mathtt{sqrt}\ c$. Since $c \geq 0$ (pre-condition of $\mathtt{sqrt}$), we know $y^2 = c$.

There are two cases.

If $y \geq 0$, then
$(\mathtt{fourthroot}\ c)^4 = (\mathtt{sqrt}\ y)^4 = ((\mathtt{sqrt}\ y)^2)^2$
$= y^2$ (because $y \geq 0$ and so satisfies the pre-condition of $\mathtt{sqrt}$)
$= c$

If $y < 0$, then
$(\mathtt{fourthroot}\ c)^4 = ((\mathtt{sqrt}\ (-y))^2)^2$
$= (-y)^2$ (because $-y \geq 0$)
$= y^2 = c$

Either way, we obtain the required result. □

However, the virtue of box proofs for beginners is that certain steps are automatic, and the box proofs give you a framework for making these steps. They take you to a context where you have disentangled the logic and have something to prove about concrete programs.

3.6 A little unpleasantness: error tolerances

Act 2

HACKER: I can't calculate exact square roots. There has to be an error tolerance.

PUNTER: But the programs I've just had ROMmed assume the roots *are* exact. It'll cost me £5m to have them changed.

HACKER: I'm sorry, you'll just have to.

PUNTER: You shall hear from my solicitors.

[*Exeunt scowling*]

The story has a happy ending. HACKER's legal department had prudently included the following general disclaimer clause in his software:

This software might do anything at all, but there again it might not. Anything HACKER says about it is inoperative.

PUNTER stopped thinking in legal terms, and negotiated the following revised specification with HACKER:

```
sqrt :: num -> num
||pre:  x >= 0
||post: |(sqrt x)^2-x| < tolerance
```

where `tolerance` was a number still to be negotiated.

This is a perfectly common occurrence, that specifications must be revised in the light of attempts to implement them. It is a nuisance, but it happens, and you must understand how to deal with it.

In this case, the post-condition has been weakened for HACKER's benefit, and this makes extra work for PUNTER. He must look at every place where he has called `sqrt` and check whether his reasoning still works with the revised specification. If it does still work, PUNTER is happy. If not, PUNTER may yet be able to modify his program and his reasoning to cope. But in this case, PUNTER realizes that he cannot compute exact fourth roots after all, so he must go back apologetically to *his* customer and negotiate a revised specification for `fourthroot`.

The reasoning is the same if HACKER and PUNTER are collaborators, or even the same person (a programmer calling his own procedures).

3.7 Other changes to the contract

The error tolerance was a *weakened post-condition*. Other possibilities are as follows:

- *Strengthened pre-condition:* HACKER might decide he needs to assume more for his routine to work. Again, PUNTER must check every call to ensure that the new pre-conditions are still set up properly.
- *Weakened pre-condition or strengthened post-condition:* Now the specification is better for PUNTER, so he has no checking to do. This time it is HACKER who must check his routine to ensure that it still satisfies the new conditions. He might find that it does, or that he can modify it so that it does, or that he has to go to the people who wrote the functions he calls and negotiate a revised specification for them.

Either way, we see that when a specification is changed, programs have to be checked to make sure that they still fit the revised specification. This checking is boring, but routine: because of the way the specifications have given *logical* structure to the program, you know exactly which parts of the program you need to examine, and exactly what you are checking for. If you don't bother, you are likely to run into the *Hydra* problem: for every mistake you correct, you make ten new ones.

There are also mixed changes to specification, for instance if you strengthen both pre- and post-conditions. This might happen if the customer wants a strengthened post-condition but the programmer needs a strengthened

36   *Specifications*

pre-condition before he can deliver it. The customer may be happy with that. Perhaps by chance his existing applications already set up the strong pre-condition. On the other hand, he may find that the new pre-condition requires too much work to be worth while. Thus the new specification may or may not be a good idea. The customer and programmer must negotiate the best compromise.

Simultaneously weakened conditions are similar.

3.8   A careless slip: positive square roots

The story so far: PUNTER and HACKER have agreed a specification for `sqrt` with error tolerances.

> Act 3, Scene 1
> PUNTER: The result of `sqrt` always seems to be non-negative. Is that right?
> HACKER: [*looks at code*] Yes.
> PUNTER: Good. That's useful to know.
> [*exeunt*]

This is how, validly, coding may feed back into the specification. If they agree on a new, strengthened post-condition:

$$\mid (\text{sqrt } x)^2 - x \mid \leq \text{\textit{tolerance}} \ \land \ (\text{sqrt } x) \geq 0$$

then this is better for PUNTER, so he is happy, and HACKER is no worse off because his code does it anyway. PUNTER thinks they have agreed, but unfortunately HACKER never wrote it into the comments for the `sqrt` function.

> Act 3, Scene 2
> [*It is very late at night.* HACKER *sits in front of a computer terminal.*]
> HACKER: Eureka! I can make `sqrt` go 0.2% faster by making its result negative.
> [*Erases old version of* `sqrt`]

> Act 3, Scene 3
> PUNTER: My programs have suddenly stopped working.
> HACKER: [*looks at code*] It's not my fault. `sqrt` satisfies its specification.
> [*exeunt*]

This kind of misunderstanding is just as common *when you are your own customer* (that is, when you write your own procedure). It is easy to assume that you can understand a simple program just by looking at the code; but this is dangerous. The code can only tell you what the computer does, not what the result was meant to be. Avoid the problem with a strong specification discipline: only assume what is specified. Equivalently, everything that is assumed must be in the specification.

3.9 Another example, min

The minimum function is easily enough defined as

```
min :: num -> num -> num
min x y = x,   if x <= y
        = y,   otherwise
```

However, there is an unnatural asymmetry in the way the cases are divided between x≤y and x>y, when they could equally well have been x<y and x≥y. This case division is not part of what you need to know to be able to use min. Perhaps a more natural specification would be

```
min :: num -> num -> num
||pre:  none
||post: ((min x y) = x \/ (min x y) =y) &
||      ((min x y) <= x & (min x y) <=y)
```

Proposition 3.1 The definition of min satisfies the specification.
Proof Suppose x and y are real numbers. There are two cases — either $x \leq y$, or $x > y$.

case 1: $x \leq y$, then $(\min\ x\ y) = x$. This immediately proves $((\min\ x\ y) = x \vee (\min\ x\ y) = y)$ and $(\min\ x\ y) \leq x$; and $(\min\ x\ y) \leq y$ because $x \leq y$.
case 2: $x > y$, then $(\min\ x\ y) = y$. Immediately, $((\min\ x\ y) = x \vee (\min\ x\ y) = y)$ and $(\min\ x\ y) \leq y$; and $(\min\ x\ y) \leq x$ because $y < x$. □

We can now prove properties of min solely from the specification.
Proposition 3.2 $(\min\ x\ y)$ is uniquely determined by the specification.
Proof Let $m1$ and $m2$ be two possible values of $(\min\ x\ y)$ according to the specification (not the definition). We wish to show that $m1 = m2$. We know that

$(m1 = x \vee m1 = y) \wedge (m1 \leq x) \wedge (m1 \leq y) \wedge$
$(m2 = x \vee m2 = y) \wedge (m2 \leq x) \wedge (m2 \leq y)$

We first show that $m1 \leq m2$. From $(m2 = x \vee m2 = y)$, there are two cases, two possible values for $m2$, and, either way, $m1 \leq m2$. By symmetry, $m2 \leq m1$, so $m1 = m2$. □

38   *Specifications*

Specifications do not have to specify uniquely; there may be several different possible answers, equally satisfactory. But uniqueness of specification is a useful property, as is illustrated by the next result.

Proposition 3.3 (*Commutativity*) (min x y) = (min y x).

Proof The specification of (min x y) is symmetrical in x and y, so it is also satisfied by (min y x). Hence, by uniqueness (the previous proposition), (min y x) = (min x y). □

3.10 Summary

- A specification of a procedure can be expressed as typing information, pre-condition and post-condition.
- You can write these down as part of a Miranda program using logical notation.
- To show that a function definition satisfies the specification you assume that you are given arguments satisfying the pre-condition, and show that the result satisfies the post-condition.
- When you use a function, you rely on its *specification*, not its *definition*.
- Any change to a specification requires a methodical examination of the function definition, and all calls of the function. This may entail no changes, or changes to the program only, or to other specifications, or to both.

3.11 Exercises

1. Write pre- and post-conditions for the functions (both in the text and the exercises) in Chapter 2. Try to get to the heart of what each function is meant to achieve.

2. Use pre- and post-conditions to write a specification for calculating square roots. Try to think of as many ideas as possible for what the customer might want. Choosing one interpretation rather than another may be a *design decision*, or it may call for clarification from the customer.

3. Suppose you want a procedure to solve the quadratic equation $ax^2 + bx + c = 0$:

   ```
   solve :: num -> num -> num -> (num, num)
   ||pre:   ?
   ||post: x1 and x2 are the solutions of a*x^2+b*x+c = 0,
           where (x1,x2) = (solve a b c)
   ```

Assume that you intend to use the formula

$$x = \frac{-b \pm \sqrt{(b^2 - 4ac)}}{2a}$$

What are suitable pre- and post-conditions? Try to write them in logic. (NOTE: the result type (num, num) is the type of *pairs* of numbers, such as (19, 2.6).)

4. Using the uniqueness property of min prove the associative property, that is,

   (*Associativity*)   (min x (min y z)) = (min(min x y) z)

5. Directly from the *definition* of min prove associativity.

6. Use pre- and post-conditions to write specifications for the standard Miranda functions abs and entier. (Of course, these are already coded unalterably. Your 'specification' expresses your understanding of what the standard functions do.)
   abs takes a number and makes it non-negative by removing its sign: for instance, abs -1.3 = abs 1.3 = 1.3.
   entier takes a number x and returns an integer, the biggest that is no bigger than x. For instance,

   entier 3 = 3   entier 2.9 = 2   entier -3 = -3   entier -2.9 = -3

7. (a) Specify a function round :: num -> num that rounds its argument to the nearest integer. Try to capture the idea that, of all the integers, round x is as close as you can get to x.

   (b) Show that the definition round1 satisfies the specification of round:

   ```
   round1 x = e,   if abs (e-x)< abs (e+1-x)
                   || i.e. if e is closer to x than e+1
             = e+1, otherwise
                   where e = entier x
   ```

   (c) Show that this definition round2 computes the same function as round1.

   ```
   round2 x = entier (x+0.5)
   ```

   (HINT: express the condition $abs(e - x) < abs(e + 1 - x)$ without using abs.)

Chapter 4

Functional programming in Miranda

In the preceding chapters, where we were illustrating rather general issues of programming, we did not probe too deeply into the details of Miranda but relied on its closeness to mathematical notation to make the meaning clear. We now turn to a more careful description of Miranda itself.

4.1 Data types — `bool`, `num` and `char`

Every value in Miranda has a type; the simplest are `num` (which you have already seen), `bool` and `char`.

The data type `num` includes both whole numbers (or *integers*) and fractional numbers (or *reals*, or floating-point numbers). A whole number is a number whose fractional part is zero. Here are some data values of type `num`:

```
56  -78  0  -87.631  0.29e-7  4.68e13  -0.62e-4  12.891
```

Although there are infinitely many numbers, computers have finite capacity and can only store a limited range. Similarly, within a finite range, there are infinitely many fractional numbers, so not all of them can be stored exactly. Although such practical limitations can be important when you are doing numerical calculations, especially when you are trying to obtain a fractional answer that is as accurate as possible, we shall largely ignore them here. The theory of *numerical analysis* deals with these questions.

Booleans are the truth-values `True` and `False` and their Miranda type is called `bool`. Truth-values are produced as a result of the application of the *comparison* operators (for example, `>`, `>=`, `=`, `<`). They can also be returned by user-defined functions, for example the function `even`. Expressions of type `bool` are really, rather, like logical formulas, and on this analogy functions that return a `bool` as their result are often called *predicates*.

If the evaluator is presented with an expression which is already in its normal form, then it will simply echo back the same expression since it cannot reduce the expression any further. For example,

```
Miranda False
False
```

char is the type of *characters*, the elements of the ASCII character set. They include printable symbols such as letters ('a', 'A', ...), digits ('0' to '9'), punctuation marks (',', ...) and so on, as well as various layout characters such as newline '\n'. Obviously, characters are most useful when strung together into lists such as "Reasoned Programming" (note the double quotes for strings, single quotes for individual characters), so we shall defer more detailed consideration until the chapter on lists (Chapter 6).

4.2 Built-in functions over basic types

Values of the basic built-in types can be manipulated by a host of built-in functions and operators. Most such built-in functions and operators are binary (that is, operate on two arguments) and can be used in infix form.

Arithmetic

These operations are on numbers. Each is used as a *binary infix* operator. The minus sign can also be used as a *unary prefix* operator.

+	addition
-	subtraction
*	multiplication
/	division
^	exponentiation
div	integer division
mod	integer remainder

All except / return exact integer results when arguments are integers, provided that the integers are in the permitted range. Representation for floating-point numbers may not be exact, so operations on fractional numbers may not produce the same results as ordinary arithmetic. For example, (x*y)/y and x may not be equal. div and mod can be specified in tandem by

```
div  :: num -> num -> num
mod  :: num -> num -> num
||pre:   int(x) & int(y) & y ~= 0
||       (where int(x) means x is a whole number and ~ means not)
||post: x = (x div y) * y + (x mod y)
||       & y>0 -> (0 <= (x mod y) < y)
||       & y<0 -> (y < (x mod y) <= 0)
```

Arithmetic expressions can be entered directly into the evaluator, for example after the computer has displayed the `Miranda` prompt:

```
Miranda 14 div 5
2
Miranda 14 mod 5
4
Miranda 2^4
16
```

The relative precedence of these operators is as follows:

```
+ -
* / div mod    ⇓ increasing precedence
^
```

Function application always binds more tightly than any other operator! Parentheses are used when one is not sure of binding powers or when one wishes to force a different order of grouping, for example,

```
Miranda double 5 + 8 mod 3 = 10+2
12
Miranda double (5 + 8) mod 3 = double 13 mod 3 = 26 mod 3
2
```

Comparisons

=	equals
~=	not equals
<	less than
>	greater than
<=	less than or equal
>=	greater than or equal

All have the same level of precedence.

Their precedence is lower than that of the arithmetic operators.

Comparison operators are made up of *relational* operators (>, >=, <, <=) and *equality* operators (=, ~=) and their result is of type `bool`. The following are some examples:

```
Miranda  5 = 9
False
Miranda  6 >= 2+3
True
```
As the second example suggests, the precedence of comparison operators is lower than that of the arithmetic operators. Note that comparison operators cannot be combined so readily; for example, the expression (2<3<4) would give a type error since it would be interpreted as

((<u>2<3</u>)<4) = True<4.

When operating on numbers '=' may not return the correct result unless the numbers are integers in the permitted range. This is because fractional numbers should be compared up to a specific tolerance. For example,

```
Miranda  sqrt(2)^2 = 2
False
```
We can define a function `within` as follows:

```
within eps x y = abs(x-y) < eps
```

`within` can then be used instead of '=' when comparing fractional numbers to a certain tolerance. For example, (`within 0.001 a b`) can be used to see if `a` and `b` are closer than 0.001 apart.

Logical operators

Boolean values may be combined using the following logical operators:

&	conjunction (logical ∧ 'and')
\/	disjunction (logical ∨ 'or')
~	negation (logical ¬ 'not')

in order of ⇓ increasing precedence

Their precedence is lower than that of comparisons. They can be defined in Miranda itself (not that you will need to do this) as in Figure 4.1. Defining these primitives in Miranda not only gives their meaning but also illustrates the use of pattern matching with Booleans. EXERCISE: we have used one equation to define **and** and two for **or**. Try writing **and** with two equations and **or** with one.

It is always a good idea to use parentheses whenever — as is often the case with logical connectives — there is the slightest doubt about the intended meaning:

```
Miranda  4>6 & (3<2 \/ 9=0)
False
```

```
and ::        bool -> bool -> bool
||pre:        none
||post:       and x y = x & y
or ::         bool -> bool -> bool
||pre:        none
||post:       or x y = x \/ y
not ::        bool -> bool
||pre:        none
||post:       not x = ~x

and x y    = y,        if x
           = False,    otherwise

or True x   = True
or False x  = x

not True   = False
not False  = True
```

Figure 4.1

4.3 User-defined functions

Identifiers

Before introducing a new function the programmer must decide on an appropriate name for it. Names, also called *identifiers*, are subject to some restrictions in all programming languages.

Throughout a program, identifiers are used for variables, function names and type names. In Miranda, identifiers must start with a *lower case* letter. The remaining characters in the identifier can be letters, digits, _, or ' (single quote). However, not all such identifiers are valid as there are a number of special words (*reserved words*) which have a particular meaning to the evaluator, for example **where**, **if**, **otherwise**. Clearly, the programmer cannot use a reserved word for an identifier as this would lead to ambiguities. Furthermore, there are also a number of predefined names (for example, those of built-in functions such as `div`, `mod`) which must be avoided.

Meaningful identifiers for functions and variables will make a program easier to read. Longer names are usually better than shorter names, although the real criterion is *clarity*. For example, the identifier `record` is probably a better choice than `r`. But deciding whether it is better than, say, `rec` is not as straightforward. In fact, in most cases modest abbreviations need not reduce the clarity of the program.

A good rule is that identifiers should have long explanatory names if they are used in many different parts of the program. This is because it may be difficult to refer to the definition if it is a long way from the use. On the other hand, identifiers with purely local significance can safely have short names — such as x for a function argument. If the variable in question is a general purpose one then nothing is gained by having a long name such as theBiggestNumberNeeded; an identifier such as n may be just as clear. Finally, it is worth mentioning that it is best to avoid acronyms for identifiers. For example, tBNN is even worse than theBiggestNumberNeeded.

Defining values

It is often useful to give a name to a value because the name can then be used in other expressions. For example, we have already seen the definition of mypi:

```
mypi :: num
mypi = 3.14159
```

As usual, the choice of meaningful names will make the program easier to read. The following is a simple example of an expression which involves names that have been previously defined using '=':

```
hours_in_day = 24
days = 365
hours_in_year = days * hours_in_day
```

If you are already familiar with imperative languages such as Pascal or BASIC, then it is important to understand that a definition like this is *not* like an assignment to a variable, but, rather, like declaring a constant. The identifier days has the value 365 and this cannot be changed except by rewriting the program. What is more, if you have conflicting definitions within a program, then only the first will ever have any effect. At this point it may also appear natural to be able to give names not only to values such as numbers or truth-values but also to functions, for example

```
    dd :: num -> num
    dd = double
```

dd behaves identically to double in every respect. This indicates that functions are not only 'black boxes' that map values to other values, but are *values* in themselves. Thus in functional languages functions are also first-class citizens (just like numbers, Booleans, etc.) which can be passed to other functions as parameters or returned as results of other functions. This is discussed in much more detail in Chapter 8.

Thus entering a function's name without any parameters is the equivalent of entering a value. However, the major difference between a function value and other values is that two functions may not be tested for equality. This is the case even if they both have precisely the same code or precisely the same mappings for all possible input values. Thus the expression (`dd = double`) will result in an error.

Defining functions

In Miranda, new functions are introduced in three steps:

1. Declare the function name and its type (its argument and result types):
   ```
   square :: num -> num
   ```
2. Provide the appropriate pre- and post-conditions:
   ```
   ||pre:  none
   ||post: square n = n^2
   ```
3. Describe the function using one or more equations:
   ```
   square n = n*n
   ```

Although type declarations are not mandatory for functions, it is good programming practice to include them with definitions in all programs. Type declarations act as a design aid since the programmer is forced to consider the nature of the input and output of functions before defining them. They also document the program and make it more readable since any programmer can immediately see what types of objects are mapped by the function. Of course, the second step is also optional in that the evaluator won't even notice if you miss it out. But we hope by now you are beginning to understand why it is essential.

Consider quadratic equations of the form $ax^2 + bx + c = 0$, where x is a variable and a, b and c are constants. Now the solutions for such a quadratic equation are given by
$$\frac{-b \pm \sqrt{b^2 - 4ac}}{2a}$$
We can define a function `hasSolutions` which given a, b and c returns `True` or `False` indicating whether there will be any solution for x:

```
hasSolutions:: num -> num -> num -> bool
||pre: none
||post: hasSolutions a b c iff a*x*x + b*x +c = 0 for some real x
hasSolutions a b c = ((a~=0) & (b*b>=4*a*c)) \/
                     ((a=0) & ((b~=0)\/(c=0)))
```

More constructions 47

This uses the fact that the roots of the quadratic equation are given by the formula above.
NOTE:

- The specification is quite different from the definition, and it takes some mathematical reasoning to relate the two.
- `(a~=0 & b*b>=4*a*c) \/ ((a=0) & ((b~=0) \/ (c=0)))`, the right-hand side of the definition, has type `bool` and its value is exactly the Boolean result you want for the function application.

In the above definition a b c are called the *formal parameters*. We talk about the left-hand or the right-hand side of an *equation* or *rule*. The right-hand side describes how the result is constructed using the parameters.

Layout — the offside rule

Miranda assumes that the *entire* right-hand side of an equation lies *directly below or to the right* of the *first* symbol of the right-hand side. This enables the evaluator to spot automatically when the right-hand side of a rule has finished. An advantage of this is that no special character or symbol such as a semi-colon is required to indicate the end of definition — less typing for the programmer! This is possible because as soon as the evaluator comes across a symbol that violates the offside rule it will take the violation to mean that the right-hand side of the definition has been completed. On the negative side, however, care must be taken by the programmer to use safe layout. For long definitions leave a blank line before starting the right-hand side and indent a small standard amount. For example,

```
functionWithALongName =
    xxxx
```

or

```
functionWithALongName
    = xxxx
```

Remember that the boundary is set by the first symbol of the right-hand side and *not* by the preceding =.

4.4 More constructions

Case analysis

Often, we want to define a function by case analysis. For example,

```
pdifference ::   num -> num -> num
||pre:    none
||post:   pdifference x y = abs (x-y)
pdifference x y = x-y,    if x>=y
                = y-x,    if y>x
```

This definition is a *single* equation consisting of two expressions, each of which is distinguished by a Boolean-valued expressions called a *guard*. The first alternative says that the value of (`pdifference x y`) is `x-y` provided that the expression `x>=y` evaluates to `True`; `pdifference` is defined for all numbers since the two guards *exhaust* all possibilities. In the above the order in which the alternatives are written is *not* significant because the two cases are *disjoint* (that is, the guards are *mutually exclusive*), they can't both succeed. However, if cases are *not* disjoint then the order in which the alternatives are written *is* significant.

Thus guards allow us to choose between two or more alternative values of the same type and only one alternative will be selected and evaluated. If there is a possibility of more than one guard evaluating to `True`, then the alternative selected will be the *first* whose guard evaluates to `True`. Actually, it is good programming practice to write order-independent code, so it is better if guards are mutually exclusive. Also, writing order-independent code aids in the portability of your program: then your program is more like a set of equations. For example, if your guards are mutually exclusive then porting your Miranda program to a parallel machine in which guards may be evaluated simultaneously will not require any alterations to your code.

An equivalent definition for `pdifference` is

```
pdifference x y = x-y,    if x >= y
                = y-x,    otherwise
```

The reserved word `otherwise` can be regarded as a convenient abbreviation for the condition which returns `True` when all previous guards return `False`.

Pattern matching on basic types

Pattern matching is one of the more powerful features of functional languages. As we shall see in Chapter 6, it is most powerful when used with composite structures such as lists because it lets you delve into the structure. With the basic types it can still be used, though it tends to appear much like case analysis. The idea is that the formal parameters are not just variables, but 'patterns' to be matched against the actual parameter. For example,

```
bitNegate :: num -> num
||pre:   x = 0 \/ x = 1
||post:  (x = 0 & b = 1) \/ (x = 1 & b = 0)
||       where b= bitNegate x
bitNegate 0 = 1
bitNegate 1 = 0
```

Thus pattern matching can be used to select amongst alternative defining equations of a function based on the format of the actual parameter. This facility has a number of advantages, including enhancing program readability and providing an alternative to the use of guards, which are inflexible at times. Furthermore, pattern matching often helps the programmer when considering all possible inputs to a function. For example, it is clear from the above equations that `bitNegate` is currently only defined for the values 0 and 1.

The notions of disjointedness and exhaustiveness apply to patterns just as for guards; similarly, for non-disjoint patterns, it is the *first* match that is used. The `otherwise` guard corresponds to a final pattern that is simply a variable (and so matches everything). Note that pattern matching and guards can be used together:

```
sign ::  num -> num
||pre:   none
||post:  (n=0 & sign n=0) \/
||       (n>0 & sign n=1) \/ (n<0 & sign n = -1)
sign 0   = 0
sign n   = 1,    if n>0
         = -1,   if n<0
```

Special facilities for pattern matching on natural numbers

Patterns can be used to define functions which operate on natural numbers (that is, non-negative integers). The operator + is special as it can be used in patterns of the form `p+k` where `p` is a pattern and `k` is a positive integer constant. A number `x` will match the pattern only if `x` is an integer and $x \geq k$. For example, `y+1` matches any positive integer, and `y` gets bound to that integer-minus-one. So,

```
pred :: num -> num
||pre:   nat(x)
||post:  (pred x = 0 & x = 0) \/ (x > 0 & pred x = x-1)
pred 0 = 0
pred (n + 1) = n
```

(`nat(x)` means that n is a natural number: $int(x) \wedge x \geq 0$.) Notice that patterns can contain variables. This definition describes a version of the predecessor function. The pattern `n+1` can only be 'matched' by a value if n matches a natural number forcing `pred` to be defined for natural numbers only. Here the patterns are exhaustive and hence cover all natural numbers. Furthermore, we know that the order of equations will not be important in this example since the patterns are disjoint as no natural number can match more than one pattern.

Prefix and infix functions

In Miranda, enclosing an infix operator in parentheses converts it to an ordinary prefix function, which can be applied to its arguments like any other function. This can be useful in the context of Chapter 8, where functions are used as arguments of other functions:

```
Miranda  (+) 8 9
17

Miranda  (>) 8 9
False
```

Conversely, user-defined binary functions can also be applied in an infix form by prefixing their name with the special character `$`:

```
Miranda  9 $smaller 8
8
```

One simple way of determining whether it is a good idea to have an operator as an infix one is to see if it is associative — `(x $f y) $f z = x $f(y $f z)` This is because `x $f y $f z` is then unambiguous.

Local definitions

In mathematical descriptions one often finds expressions that are qualified by a phrase of the form 'where ...'. The same device can also be used in function definitions. For example, `balance*i where i = interestRate/100`. In fact, we have already used `where` in the definition of `fourthroot` in Chapter 3. The special reserved word `where` can be used to introduce local definitions whose context (or scope) is the expression on the entire right-hand side of the definition which contains it. For example,

```
f x y = x + a,    if x > 10
      = x - a,    otherwise
        where a = square (y+1)
```

In any one equation the `where` clause is written after the last alternative.

Its local definitions govern the whole of the right-hand side of that equation, including the guards, but do not apply to any other equation.

Furthermore, following a `where` there can be any number of definitions. These definitions are just like ordinary definitions and may therefore contain nested `where`s or be recursive definitions.

Note that the whole of the `where` clause must be indented, to show that it is part of the right-hand side of the equation. The evaluator determines the scopes of nested `where`s by looking at their indentation levels. In the next example it is clear that the definition of `g` is not local to the right-hand side of the definition of `f`, but those of `y` and `z` are

```
f x     = g y z
          where y = (x+1) * 4
                z = (x-1) * x
g x z = (x + 1) * (z-1)
```

Let us consider some uses of local definitions. Firstly, as in `fourthroot`, they can be used to avoid repeated evaluation. In an expression a subexpression may appear several times, for example

`z+(smaller x y)*(smaller x y)`

Here the subexpression `(smaller x y)` appears twice, and will be evaluated twice, which is rather wasteful. By using a local definition we can give a name to an expression and then use the name in the same way that we use a formal parameter:

`z+w*w where w = smaller x y`

If you like, you can view this use of local definitions as a mechanism for extending the existing set of formal parameters.

Local definitions can also be used to decompose compound structures or user-defined data types by providing names for components (as will be seen later, in Chapter 7).

It is good programming practice to avoid unnecessary nesting of definitions. In particular, use local definitions only if logically necessary. Furthermore, a third level of definition should be used only very occasionally. Failure to follow these simple programming guidelines will result in definitions that are difficult to read, understand and reason about.

4.5 Summary

- Miranda has three primitive data types: numbers, truth-values and characters (`num`, `bool` and `char` respectively).

- Miranda also provides many built-in operators and functions.
- A new function is defined in three stages. The function's type is declared, the function is specified in a comment and then it is defined using one or more equations.
- Although type declarations and specifications are not mandatory for functions, it is good programming practice to include them with all definitions.
- Miranda is layout-sensitive in that it assumes that the *entire* right-hand side of an equation lies *directly below or to the right* of the *first* symbol of the right-hand side (excluding the initial =). This is the *offside rule*.
- To aid in the portability of programs try, wherever possible, to write order-independent code. This means writing mutually exclusive guards or patterns.
- Functions (or other values) can also be defined *locally* to a definition. Such local definitions can be used to avoid repeated evaluation or to decompose compound structures, as will be seen in Chapter 7.

4.6 Exercises

1. Write definitions for the functions specified in the exercises at the end of Chapter 3.
2. Define istriple, which returns whether the sum of the squares of two numbers is equal to the square of a third number. A *Pythagorean triple* is a triple of whole numbers x, y and z that satisfy $x^2 + y^2 = z^2$. The Miranda function istriple should be declared as follows:

```
istriple :: num -> num -> num -> bool
||pre:   none
||post:  (istriple a b c) <-> a,b,c are the lengths of the
||                            sides of a right angle triangle
```

The function takes as arguments three numbers and returns true if they form such a triple. Evaluate the function on the triples

```
3 4 5
5 12 13
12 14 15
```

and check that the first two are Pythagorean triples and the third is not. Do this exercise twice: first assume that c is the hypotenuse and then rewrite it so that any of the parameters could be the hypotenuse.

Chapter 5

Recursion and induction

5.1 Recursion

Suppose we want to write a function sum n which gives us the sum of the natural numbers up to n, that is, $\sum_{i=0}^{n} i$:

sum $n = 0 + 1 + 2 + 3 + \ldots + (n-1) + n$

Inspecting the above expression we see that if we remove '$+n$' we obtain an expression which is equivalent to sum$(n-1)$, at least if $n \geq 1$.

This suggests that

$$\text{sum } n = \text{sum } (n-1) + n \qquad (5.1)$$

We say that the equation exhibits a *recurrence relationship*. To complete the definition we must define a *base case* which specifies where the *recursion* process should end. For sum this is when the argument is 0. Thus the required definition is

```
sum ::   num -> num
||pre:   nat(n)
||post:  sum n = sum(i=0 to n) i
sum n    = 0,                if n = 0
         = sum (n-1) + n,    if n > 0
```

'sum(i=0 to n) i' is intended to be a typewriter version of '$\sum_{i=0}^{n} i$'. If we just used the recurrence relation (5.1), forgetting the base case, then we would obtain non-terminating computations as illustrated in Figure 5.1. Function definitions, like that of sum, that call themselves are said to be *recursive*. Obviously, the computation of sum involves repetition of an action.

Often when describing a function — such as sum — there are infinitely many cases to consider. In conventional imperative programming languages this is solved by using a *loop*, but in functional languages there are no explicit looping constructs. Instead, solutions to such problems are expressed

54   *Recursion and induction*

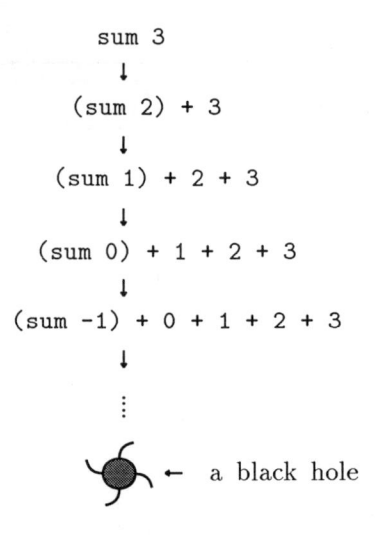

$$
\begin{array}{c}
\text{sum } 3 \\
\downarrow \\
(\text{sum } 2) + 3 \\
\downarrow \\
(\text{sum } 1) + 2 + 3 \\
\downarrow \\
(\text{sum } 0) + 1 + 2 + 3 \\
\downarrow \\
(\text{sum } -1) + 0 + 1 + 2 + 3 \\
\downarrow \\
\vdots
\end{array}
$$

⟵ a black hole

Figure 5.1

by defining a *recursive* function. Clearly, the recursive call must be in terms of a simpler problem — otherwise the recursion will proceed forever.

The example given above illustrated the technique of writing recursive functions, which can be summarised as follows:

1. Define the base case(s).
2. Define the recursive case(s):

    (a) reduce the problem to simpler cases of the same problem,

    (b) write the code to solve the simpler cases,

    (c) combine the results to give required answer.

5.2   Evaluation strategy of Miranda

We have seen that evaluation is a simple process of *substitution* and *simplification*, using primitive and user-defined function definitions. More precisely, a function application is rewritten (reduced) in two steps. First the actual parameters are substituted for the formal parameters in the defining equation of the function: this is called *instantiation*. Then the application is replaced by the instantiated right-hand side expression (see Figure 5.2).

During evaluation an expression may contain more than one *redex* — place where reduction is possible. But in functional languages if an expression has a well-defined value then the final result is independent of the reduction route (this is known as the *Church-Rosser property*). However, an evaluator selects

Euclid's algorithm 55

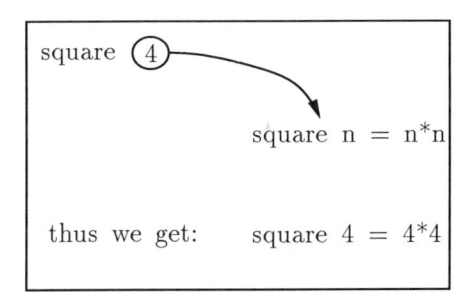

```
square  ④─────┐
              │
              ▼
         square n = n*n


thus we get:  square 4 = 4*4
```

Figure 5.2

the next reduction (from the set of possible ones) in a consistent way. This is called the evaluator's *reduction strategy*. We will not discuss reduction strategies here except to mention that Miranda's reduction strategy is called *lazy evaluation*. Lazy evaluation works as follows:

| Reduce a particular part *only* if its result is needed. |

Therefore, because of lazy evaluation you can write function definitions such as

```
f n = 1,     if n = 0
    = n * y, otherwise
    where y = f(n-1)
```

Although the scope of the local definition of y is the entire right-hand side of the equation for f, we know that by lazy evaluation *y* will only be evaluated if it is needed (that is, if and only if the first guard fails).

5.3 Euclid's algorithm

Consider the problem of finding the greatest common divisor, gcd, of two natural numbers:

```
gcd :: num -> num -> num
||pre:  nat(x) & nat(y)
||post: nat(z) & z|x & z|y (ie z is a common divisor)
||      &(A)n:nat(n|x & n|y -> n|z)
||          (ie any other common divisor divides it)
||      where z = (gcd x y)
```

We have introduced some notation in the pre- and post-conditions:

- (A) just means ∀, that is, 'for all', written in standard keyboard characters. ∃ would be (E). Chapter 15 contains more detailed

descriptions of logical symbols.
- '|' means 'divides', or 'is a factor of'. (Note that it is not the same symbol as the division sign '/'.)

$$z|x \Leftrightarrow \exists y : nat. \ (x = z \times y)$$

- When we write '$y : nat$', we are using the predicate nat as though it were a Miranda type, though it is not. You can think of '$nat(y)$' and '$y : nat$' as meaning exactly the same, namely that y is a natural number. But the type-style notation is particularly useful with quantifiers:

$\exists y : nat. \ P$ means $\exists y. \ (nat(y) \wedge P)$
('there is a natural number y for which P holds')
$\forall y : nat. \ P$ means $\forall y. \ (nat(y) \rightarrow P)$
('for all natural numbers y, P holds')

Be sure to understand these, and in particular why it is that $\exists$ goes naturally with $\wedge$, and $\forall$ with $\rightarrow$. They are patterns that arise very frequently when you are translating from English into logic (see Chapter 15).

There is a small unexpected feature. You might expect the post-condition to say that any other common divisor is *less* than z, rather than dividing it: in other words that z is indeed the *greatest* common divisor. There is just a single case where this makes a difference, namely when x and y are both 0. All numbers divide 0, so amongst the common divisors of x and y there is no greatest one. The specification as given has the effect of specifying

    gcd 0 0 = 0

Proposition 5.1 For any two natural numbers x and y, there is at most one z satisfying the specification for (gcd x y).

Proof Let $z1$ and $z2$ be two values satisfying the specification for (gcd x y); we must show that they are equal. All common divisors of x and y divide $z2$, so, in particular, $z1$ does. Similarly, $z2$ divides $z1$. Hence for some positive natural numbers p and q, we have $z1 = z2 \times p$, $z2 = z1 \times q$, so $z1 = z1 \times p \times q$. It follows that either $z1 = 0$, in which case also $z2 = 0$, or $p \times q = 1$, in which case $p = q = 1$. In either case, $z1 = z2$. $\square$

Note that we have not actually proved that there is *any* value z satisfying the specification; only that there cannot be more than one. But we shall soon have an implementation showing how to find a suitable z, so then we shall know that there is exactly one possible result.

Euclid's algorithm relies on the following fact.

Proposition 5.2 Let x and y be natural numbers, $y \neq 0$. Then the common divisors of x and y are the same as those of y and (x mod y).

Proof For natural numbers x and y there are two fundamental properties of integer division, which in fact are enough to specify it uniquely: if $y \neq 0$ (pre-condition), then (post-condition)

$$x = y \times (x \text{ div } y) + (x \text{ mod } y)$$
$$0 \leq (x \text{ mod } y) < y$$

Suppose n is a common divisor of y and $(x \text{ mod } y)$. That is, there is a p such that $y = n \times p$ and a q such that $(x \text{ mod } y) = n \times q$. Then

$$x = y \times (x \text{ div } y) + (x \text{ mod } y) = n \times (p \times (x \text{ div } y) + q)$$

so n also divides x. Hence every common divisor of y and $(x \text{ mod } y)$ is also a common divisor of x and y. The converse is also true, by a similar proof. □

It follows that, provided $y \neq 0$, (gcd x y) must equal (gcd y (x mod y)). (EXERCISE: show this.) On the other hand, (gcd x 0) must be x. This is because $x \mid x$ and $x \mid 0$, and any common divisor of x and 0 obviously divides x, so x satisfies the specification for (gcd x 0). We can therefore write the following function definition:

```
gcd x y = x,              if y=0
        = gcd y (x mod y), otherwise
```

QUESTION: does this definition satisfy the specification?

Let us follow through the techniques that we discussed in Chapter 3. Let x and y be natural numbers, and let $z = (\text{gcd } x \, y)$. We must show that z has the properties given by the post-condition, and there are two cases corresponding to the two clauses in the definition:

$y = 0 : z = x$ We have already noted that this satisfies the specification.

$y \neq 0 : z = (\text{gcd } y \, (x \text{ mod } y))$ What we have seen shows that *provided that* z satisfies the specification for (gcd y (x mod y)), then it also satisfies the specification for (gcd x y), as required.

□

But how do we know that the recursive call gives the right answer? How do we know that it gives any answer at all? (Conceivably, the recursion might never bottom out.) Apparently, we are having to *assume* that gcd satisfies its specification in order to *prove* that it satisfies its specification.

5.4 Recursion variants

The answer is that we *are* allowed to assume it! But there is a catch. This apparently miraculous circular reasoning must be justified, and the key is to notice that the recursive call uses simpler arguments: the pair of arguments y with $x \text{ mod } y$ is 'simpler' than the pair x with y, in the sense that the second argument is smaller: $x \text{ mod } y < y$.

As we go down the recursion, the second argument, always a natural number, becomes smaller and smaller, but never negative. This cannot go on for ever, so the recursion must eventually terminate. This at least proves termination, but it also justifies the *circular reasoning*. For suppose that gcd does not always work correctly. What might be the smallest bad y for which gcd x y may go wrong (for some x)? Not 0 — gcd x 0 always works correctly. Suppose Y is the smallest bad y, and gcd X Y goes wrong. Then $Y > 0$, so

gcd X Y = gcd Y (X mod Y)

But X mod Y is good (since X mod $Y < Y$), so the recursive call works correctly, so (we have already reasoned) gcd X Y does also — a contradiction.

We call the value y in gcd x y a *recursion variant* for our definition of gcd. It is a rough measure of the depth of recursion needed, and always decreases in the recursive calls.

Let us now state this as a reasoning principle:

> In proving that a recursive function satisfies its specification, you are *allowed to assume* that the recursive calls work correctly — *provided that* you can define a recursion variant for the function.

A recursion variant for a function must obey the following rules:

- It is calculated from the arguments of the function.
- It is a natural number (at least when the pre-conditions of the function hold). For instance, in gcd the recursion variant is y.
- It is calculated (trivially) from the function's arguments (x and y).
- It always decreases in the recursive calls. For the recursive call gcd y (x mod y), the recursion variant x mod y is less than y, the variant for gcd x y.

Though these rules may look complicated when stated in the abstract like this, the underlying intuitions are very basic. Although we did not mention this explicitly when deriving gcd, the driving force behind recursive definitions is usually to reduce the computation to simpler cases. If you can quantify this notion of simplicity, find an approximate numerical measure for it, then that is probably the basic idea for your recursion invariant.

Another example — multiplication without multiplying

Some processor chips can add and subtract, but do not have hardware instructions to multiply or divide. These operations have to be programmed. Here, in Miranda, is one method for doing this. It uses multiplication and integer division by 2, but these are easy in binary arithmetic.

A similar method can be used for exponentiation — computing x^n by using $x^{n \ div \ 2}$ (Exercise 5):

```
mult   ::     num -> num -> num
||pre:        nat(n)
||post:       mult x n = x*n
||recursion variant = n
mult x n = 0,         if n=0
         = y,         if n>0 & n mod 2=0
         = y+x,       otherwise
              where y=2*(mult x(n div 2))
```

The recursion variant is n. The recursive call, used to calculate y, has variant n div 2. It is used when y is used, that is, the second and third alternatives, and in both of these we have $n > 0$ and so n div $2 < n$ — the variant has decreased.

Proposition 5.3 mult satisfies its specification

Proof There are three cases, corresponding to the three alternatives in the definition:

$n = 0$: mult $x \ n = 0 = x \times n$.
$n > 0, n$ **even:** mult $x \ n = 2 \times ($mult $x(n/2))$
$\phantom{n > 0, n \text{ even: } \text{mult } x \ n} = 2 \times x \times (n/2)$
$\phantom{n > 0, n \text{ even: } \text{mult } x \ n} = x \times n$
$n > 0, n$ **odd:** mult $x \ n = 2 \times ($mult $x((n-1)/2)) + x$
$\phantom{n > 0, n \text{ odd: } \text{mult } x \ n} = 2 \times x \times ((n-1)/2) + x$
$\phantom{n > 0, n \text{ odd: } \text{mult } x \ n} = x \times (n-1) + x = x \times n$

$\square$

More general properties of functions

The reasoning principle stated above concerned a particular property of a function, namely whether it satisfied its specification. But actually, the argument applied to any property of the function that you are interested in proving: as long as you have a recursion variant, then you can reason circularly by assuming that the property holds for recursive calls.

For example, consider the sum function of Section 5.1. The recursion variant in sum n is easy — it is just n itself. Having found a recursion variant, we can now prove the properties of sum, such as the following well-known equation:

Proposition 5.4 $\forall n. \ ($sum $n = \frac{1}{2}n(n+1))$

60 Recursion and induction

Proof In the non-recursive case, $n = 0$, this is obvious: both sides of the equation evaluate to 0. In the recursive case we have

$$\begin{aligned} \mathtt{sum}\ n &= \mathtt{sum}(n-1) + n \\ &= \tfrac{1}{2}(n-1)((n-1)+1) + n \quad &&\text{because we assume the equation holds} \\ & &&\text{for the recursive call} \\ &= \tfrac{1}{2}n(n+1) &&\text{by a little algebra.} \end{aligned}$$

□

5.5 Mathematical induction

The reasoning principle given in the preceding section was really a packaged form of *mathematical induction*. There are two basic forms of induction and they are equivalent to each other (see Exercise 7): *simple induction* and *course of values* induction. Both should be familiar from school mathematics, but let us review them here. Both are used for proving properties of the *natural numbers*, that is, non-negative whole numbers, and both have the same underlying idea. You give a general method that shows how you can prove a property for the natural numbers one by one, starting at 0 and working up.

Simple induction

The ingredients of a simple induction proof are as follows:

- a predicate P or property on the natural numbers for which you wish to prove $\forall n : nat.\ P(n)$ (P holds for all natural numbers n);
- the **base case**: a proof of $P(0)$;
- the **induction step**: a proof of $\forall n : nat.\ (P(n) \to P(n+1))$, in other words a general method that shows for all natural numbers n how, if you had a proof of $P(n)$ (the *induction hypothesis*), you could prove $P(n+1)$.

Given these, you can indeed deduce $\forall n : nat.\ P(n)$. This is the *Principle of Mathematical Induction*. The separate parts can be put in the box proof format, as can be seen in Figure 5.3. If you were using ordinary 'forall-arrow-introduction', as in Chapter 17, you would produce a box proof such as that given in Figure 5.4. You could then consider two cases, $M = 0$ and $M = N + 1$ for some N, and so you end up more or less as in induction, proving $P(0)$ and $P(N+1)$. However, in induction, you have a free gift, the induction hypothesis $P(N)$, as an extra assumption. Without it, the proof would be difficult or even impossible.

Mathematical induction

```
┌─────────────────────────────┐  ┌─────────────────────────────────────┐
│        ⋮                    │  │ N : nat    P(N)                     │
│      P(0)       base case   │  │        ⋮              induction step│
│                             │  │      P(N + 1)                       │
└─────────────────────────────┘  └─────────────────────────────────────┘
         ∀n : nat. P(n)                                    simple induction
```

Figure 5.3 Box proof for simple induction

```
┌──────────────────────────────────────────────────────────────┐
│ M : nat                                                      │
│    ⋮                                                         │
│   P(M)                                                       │
└──────────────────────────────────────────────────────────────┘
      ∀n : nat. P(n)                                       ∀ℐ
```

Figure 5.4

To show how this works, suppose, for instance, you want to prove $P(39976)$. The ingredients of the induction show that you can first prove $P(0)$; from this you can obtain a proof of $P(1)$; from this a proof of $P(2)$; and so on up to $P(39976)$. Of course, you never need to go through all these steps. It is sufficient to know that it can be done, and then you know that P does hold for 39976.

Another way of justifying the induction principle is by contradiction: if $\forall n : nat. P(n)$ is false, then there is a *smallest* n for which $P(n)$ is false. What is n? Certainly not 0, for you have proved the base case. So taking $N = n - 1$, which is still a natural number, we have $P(N)$ because n was the smallest counter-example. But now the induction step shows how to prove $P(N + 1)$, that is, $P(n)$, a contradiction. The following is a simple example.

Proposition 5.5 For all n,
$$\sum_{i=0}^{n} i^2 = \frac{n}{6}(n+1)(2n+1)$$

Proof Let $P(n)$ be the above equation, considered as a property of n. We prove $\forall n : nat. P(n)$ by simple induction.

base case: $n = 0$ and both sides of the equation are 0.

induction step: Suppose that P holds for N; then in the equation for $N+1$,

$$\begin{aligned}
\text{LHS} &= \sum_{i=0}^{N+1} i^2 \\
&= \sum_{i=0}^{N} i^2 + (N+1)^2 \\
&= \tfrac{N}{6}(N+1)(2N+1) + (N+1)^2 \quad \text{by the induct. hyp.} \\
&= \tfrac{N+1}{6}(N+2)(2N+3) \\
&= \text{RHS}
\end{aligned}$$

□

Course of values induction

Think of how $P(39976)$ was to be proved under simple induction: you work up to $P(39975)$, and then use the induction step. But in working up to $P(39975)$, you actually proved P for *all* natural numbers less than 39976, and it might be helpful in the induction step to use this additional information. This idea leads to a revised, *course of values* induction step (with n playing the role of what before was $n+1$):

> a general proof that shows how, if you already know that P holds for all $m < n$, you can show that P also holds for n. In logical notation,

$$\forall n : nat.\ (\forall m : nat.\ (m < n \to P(m)) \to P(n))$$

Curiously enough, this also replaces the base case. When you put $n = 0$, the induction step says *if* you know $P(m)$ for all $m < 0$, then you can deduce $P(0)$; but there are no $m < 0$ (remember that we are dealing with natural numbers), so of course you know $P(m)$ for all $m < 0$. When proving the induction step, the effect is that for $n = 0$ there is no special assumption that can be used and $P(0)$ has to be proved just as before.

The *Principle of Course of Values Induction* says that if you prove the course of values induction step, then you can deduce $\forall n : nat.\ P(n)$. In box proof form, a course of values induction proof has the form seen in Figure 5.5. The following is an example.

Proposition 5.6 Every positive natural number is a product of primes. (Recall that n is prime iff it cannot be written as $p \times q$ unless either $p = 1, q = n$, or the other way round.)

Proof Let $P(n)$ be the property 'n is a product of primes' for positive natural numbers n.

Let n be a positive natural number, and suppose (course of values induction hypothesis) that every $m < n$ is a product of primes. We show that n is, too.

```
┌─────────────────────────────────────────────────────────────┐
│ N : nat                                                     │
│                                                             │
│       ∀m : nat. (m < N → P(m))        induction hypothesis  │
│       ⋮                                                     │
│                                                             │
│       P(N)                                                  │
└─────────────────────────────────────────────────────────────┘
    ∀n : nat. P(n)                       course of values induction
```

Figure 5.5

If n is itself prime, then we are done. (This also deals with the special case $n = 1$ for which there are no positive natural numbers $< n$.) If n is not prime, then we can write $n = p \times q$ for some natural numbers p and q, neither of them equal to 1. Then p and q are both less than n, so by induction each is a product of primes. Hence n is, too. □

We have actually cheated here in order to illustrate the technique in an uncomplicated way. The proof does not illustrate course of values induction on the natural numbers, but a similar principle on the *positive* natural numbers. The correct proof proves the property $P(n)$ defined by

$$P(n) \stackrel{\text{def}}{=} (n > 0 \to n \text{ is a product of primes})$$

Then there are two cases. If $n = 0$, then $P(n)$ is trivially true ('false → anything' is always true). Otherwise, $n > 0$, when we use the proof as given. When we reach $n = p \times q$, p and q must both be positive, so that from $P(p)$ and $P(q)$ we deduce that p and q are both products of primes. □

This example shows a common feature of course of values induction. It proves P for n by *reducing to simpler cases* (p and q, both smaller than n), which we assume have already been done.

5.6 Double induction — Euclid's algorithm without division

Consider the problem of finding the greatest common divisor again but this time replace the division in Euclid's algorithm by repeated subtraction:

```
gcd x y = gcd y x,       if x<y
        = x,             if y=0
        = gcd (x-y) y,   otherwise
```

y is no longer a recursion variant, because in the third clause y does not decrease: x does instead. It is still possible to concoct a recursion variant in this case, namely,

$$r(x, y) = 2 \times (x + y), \qquad \text{if } x \geq y$$

$$= 2 \times (x+y) + 1, \quad \text{if } x < y$$

However, this is somewhat artificial. The reasoning is that our notion of simplicity is not based simply on a numerical measure, but on the idea of lexicographic order:

(x', y') is simpler than (x, y) iff
$\quad y' < y$ or
$\quad y' = y$ and $x' < x$

You could say that y is almost a recursion variant, certainly it never *increases* in recursive calls (unlike x). But in the case where y remains unchanged as a variant, it must be helped by x decreasing.

There is a quite general principle of *well-founded* induction (see Appendix A) that uses this idea, but, rather than going into the generalities, here we shall show how to use a double induction.

Proposition 5.7 This definition of gcd satisfies the specification.

Proof We use course of values induction to prove $\forall y : nat. \ P(y)$, where
$P(y) \stackrel{\text{def}}{=} \forall x : nat. \ ((\text{gcd } x \ y) \text{ terminates and satisfies its post-condition})$

Therefore let us take a natural number Y, and assume that $P(y)$ holds for all $y < Y$. Having fixed our Y, we now use course of values induction again to prove $P(Y)$, that is, $\forall x : nat. \ Q(x)$, where
$Q(x) \stackrel{\text{def}}{=} (\text{gcd } x \ Y) \text{ terminates and satisfies the post-condition.}$

Therefore, let us now take a natural number X, and assume that $Q(x)$ holds for all $x < X$. We prove $Q(X)$. There are three cases, as follows, for the three alternatives in the definition of gcd:

$X < Y$: gcd $X \ Y$ = gcd $Y \ X$. By the induction hypothesis for y, $P(X)$ holds, so (gcd $Y \ X$) terminates and satisfies its post-condition. But the result z in the post-condition for (gcd $Y \ X$) is also good for (gcd $X \ Y$), so that is OK.

$X \geq Y$ and $Y = 0$: (gcd $X \ Y$) terminates immediately with value X, and we have argued before that X is the greatest common divisor for X and 0.

$X \geq Y$ and $Y > 0$: (gcd $X \ Y$) = (gcd $(X - Y) \ Y$):
$X - Y$ is a natural number less than X (because $Y > 0$), so by the induction hypothesis on x we know $Q(X - Y)$. Hence (gcd $(X - Y) \ Y$) terminates giving the greatest common divisor for $(X - Y)$ and Y, and this is also the greatest common divisor for X and Y since X and Y have the same common divisors as do $(X - Y)$ and Y.

By induction on x, we now know $\forall x : nat. \ Q(x)$, that is, $P(Y)$. Hence by induction on y we have $\forall y : nat. \ P(y)$, as required. □

5.7 Summary

- A recursive function is a function which calls itself. Functions that require the consideration of a very large number of cases (possibly infinitely many) are typically defined as recursive functions.
- Generally, a recursive function definition has a *base case* which specifies where the recursion process should end.
- When you write a recursive definition, also define a *recursion variant* for it.
- The existence of a recursion variant proves termination and allows you to reason inductively about the function.
- The *circular reasoning* is justified by mathematical induction.
- Simple induction in box proof form.

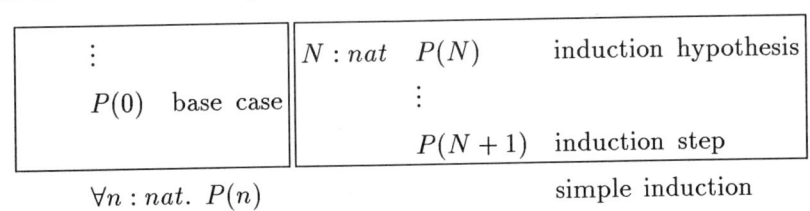

$$
\begin{array}{|ll|} \hline
\vdots & \\
P(0) & \text{base case} \\ \hline
\end{array}
\quad
\begin{array}{|ll|} \hline
N : nat \quad P(N) & \text{induction hypothesis} \\
\vdots & \\
P(N+1) & \text{induction step} \\ \hline
\end{array}
$$

$\forall n : nat.\ P(n)$ simple induction

- Course-of-values induction

$$
\begin{array}{|ll|} \hline
N : nat \quad \forall m : nat.\ (m < N \to P(m)) & \text{induction hypothesis} \\
\vdots & \\
P(N) & \text{induction step} \\ \hline
\end{array}
$$

$\forall n : nat.\ P(n)$ course of values induction

- You usually hide the induction by using the 'circular' reasoning principle for recursive definitions (once you obtain the recursion variant).
- Sometimes you need to make the induction explicit, for example, in double induction.
- Miranda's reduction strategy is called *lazy evaluation*. In lazy evaluation the evaluator evaluates an expression *only* if its result is needed.

5.8 Exercises

1. The *factorial* of a non-negative integer n is denoted as $n!$ and defined as:

$$\texttt{factorial } n \stackrel{\text{def}}{=} \times (n-1) \times (n-2) \times (n-3) \ldots \times 2 \times 1$$

   0! is defined to be 1. Write a function `factorial` to define the factorial of a non-negative integer. Ignore the possibility of integer overflow.

2. Write a function `remainder` which defines the remainder after integer division using only subtraction. Ignore the possibility of division by zero.
3. Write a function `divide` which defines integer division using only addition and subtraction. Ignore division by zero.
4. Here are some exercises with divisibility: show for all natural numbers x, y and z that

   (a) $1 \mid y$
   (b) $x \mid y \wedge x \mid z \wedge y \geq z \rightarrow x \mid (y - z)$
   (c) $x \mid 0$
   (d) $x \mid y \wedge y \mid z \rightarrow x \mid z$
   (e) $x \mid x$
   (f) $x \mid y \wedge x \mid z \rightarrow x \mid (y + z)$
   (g) $0 \mid y \leftrightarrow y = 0$
   (h) $x \mid y \wedge y \mid x \rightarrow x = y$

5. (a) Use the method of 'multiplication without multiplying' to compute exponentiation, `power` x $n = x^n$, making use of the facts that

   $$x^n = x^{n \text{ div } 2} \times x^{n \text{ div } 2} \text{ if } n \text{ is even}$$

   and

   $$x^n = x^{n \text{ div } 2} \times x^{n \text{ div } 2} \times x \text{ if } n \text{ is odd}$$

   (b) Write a Miranda function, `multiplications`, that computes the number of multiplications performed by `power(x, n)` given the value of n. How would this compare with the corresponding count of multiplications for a more simple-minded recursive calculation of x^n, using $x^{n+1} = x^n * x$?

6. (Tricky) Specify and define a function `middle` to find the middle one of three numbers. Prove that the definition satisfies its specification.

7. Prove that the principles of simple induction and course of values induction are equivalent. In other words, though course of values induction looks stronger (can prove more things), it is not.
   First, show that any simple induction proof can easily be converted into a course of values induction proof.
   Second, show that if you have a course of values induction proof of $\forall n : nat. \ P(n)$ then its ingredients can be used to make a simple induction proof of $\forall n : nat. \ (\forall m : nat. \ (m < n \rightarrow P(m)))$, and that this implies $\forall n : nat. \ P(n)$.

8. Newton's method for calculating a square root $\sqrt{x}$ works by producing a sequence $y_0, y_1, \ldots$ of better and better approximations to the answer, where

   $$y_{n+1} = \frac{1}{2}(y_n + \frac{x}{y_n})$$

   The starting approximation y_0 can be very crude — we shall use $x + 1$. We shall deem y_n accurate enough when $\mid y_n^2 - x \mid <$ `epsilon`, `epsilon` being some small number defined elsewhere in the program (for instance, `epsilon = 0.01`). Here is a Miranda definition:

```
newtonsqrt::num -> num
||pre: x >= 0 & epsilon > 0
||post: abs(r*r - x) < epsilon & r >= 0
||      where r = newtonsqrt x
newtonsqrt x = ns1 x (x+1)
ns1::num -> num -> num
||pre: x >= 0 & epsilon > 0
||      & a >= 0 & a*a >= x & (a = 0 -> x = 0)
||post: abs(r*r - a) < epsilon & r >= 0
||      where r = ns1 x a
ns1 x a = a,           if a*a - x < epsilon
        = ns1 x ((a + x/a)/2),  otherwise
```

(The last three pre-conditions of ns1 need some thought. $a \geq 0$ looks reasonable enough, $a = 0 \rightarrow x = 0$ avoids the risk of dividing by zero, and $a^2 \geq x$ is not strictly necessary but, as we shall see, it makes it easier to find a recursion variant.)

(a) Show that newtonsqrt and ns1 satisfy their specification, assuming that the recursive call in ns1 works correctly. This is easy, and the proof is finished once we have found a recursion variant; that is the difficult part!

(b) If $x \geq 0$, $a^2 \geq x$ and $b = \frac{1}{2}(a + \frac{x}{a})$ (for instance, if $a = y_n$ and $b = y_{n+1}$), show that

$$0 \leq b^2 - x = \frac{1}{4}(1 - \frac{x}{a^2})(a^2 - x) \leq \frac{1}{4}(a^2 - x)$$

(c) The basis for a recursion variant is $a^2 - x$. As this gets smaller, the approximation gets better and we are making progress towards the answer. However, as it stands it cannot be a recursion variant because it is not a natural number. (Unlike the case with natural numbers, a positive real number can decrease strictly infinitely many times, by smaller and smaller amounts.) Use (b) to show that a suitable variant is

$$max(0, 1 + entier(\log_4 \frac{a^2 - x}{epsilon}))$$

(This gives a number that — by (b) — decreases by at least 1 each time, *entier* turns it into an integer, and dividing $a^2 - x$ by *epsilon* ensures that this integer is a natural number except for the last time round, which is coped with by $max(0, 1 + \ldots)$.)

Chapter 6
Lists

6.1 Introduction

The various data types encountered so far, such as `num` and `bool`, are capable of holding only one data value at a time. However, it is often necessary to represent a number of related items of data in some way and then be able to have a single name which refers to these related items. What is required is an *aggregate type*, which is a data type that allows more than one item of data to be referenced by a single name. Aggregate types are also called *data structures* since they represent a collection of data in a structured and orderly manner.

In this chapter we introduce the list aggregate type, together with the various predefined operators and functions in Miranda that manipulate lists. We shall also see how to use lists of characters to represent strings.

6.2 The list aggregate type

Lists are used to list values (the *elements* of the list) of the same type, and they can be written in Miranda using square brackets and commas. The following are examples of lists of numbers, Booleans, other lists, and functions — notice how we also use square brackets for describing the list *types*. (In mathematics square brackets are also used for bracketing expressions, but the two uses are distinguishable by context.)

`[1,2,3]`	is of type	`[num]`
`[False,False,True]`	"	`[bool]`
`[[1,2],[],[3]]`	"	`[[num]]`
`[(+),(*)]`	"	`[num -> num -> num]`

The third example is a valid list since the elements of the list have the same type; they are all lists of numbers. The *empty* list [], which has no elements, is rather special because it could be of type [*], where the symbol * represents *any* type. (In fact, if you enter []:: in Miranda, which asks for the type of [], the system will respond [*].) Similarly, the fourth example illustrates a valid list since all its elements have the same type, namely functions that map two numbers to a number.

A list [x] with just one element is known as a *singleton* list. Two lists are equal if and only if they have the same values with the same number of occurrences in the same order. Otherwise they are different, so the lists

[1,2]   [2,1]   [1,1,2]   [1,2,1]   [2,1,1]

are all different even though they have the same elements 1 and 2.

Concatenation

The most important operator for lists is ++ (called *concatenate* or *append*), which joins together two lists of the same type to form a single composite list. For example,

[1,2,3]++[1,5] = [1,2,3,1,5]

We shall see shortly that there is another method for building up lists, called *cons*; none the less ++ is usually conceptually more natural, and it is often useful in specifications. We can formalize the condition that a value x is an element of a list xs as

$\exists us, vs. \ (xs = us$++$[x]$++$vs)$

Note that, like + and *, ++ is *associative*: the equation

xs++$(ys$++$zs) = (xs$++$ys)$++zs

always holds, and so you might as well write xs++ys++zs. In fact, there is no need for brackets for any number of lists appended together. Concatenating any list xs with the empty list [] returns the given list. This is called the *unit law* and [] is the *unit* (just like 0 for + or 1 for *) with respect to ++:

xs++$[] = []$++$xs = xs$

List deconstruction

The function hd (pronounced *head*) selects the first element of a list, and tl (pronounced *tail*) selects the remaining portion:

hd [1,2,3] = 1
tl [1,2,3] = [2,3]

Notice the type difference — the result of hd is an *element*, that of tl is *another list*. It is an error to apply either of these functions to an empty list, and so appropriate tests must be carried out (using guards or pattern matching) to avoid such errors.

Indexing and finding lengths of lists

A list can be indexed by a natural number n in order to find the value appearing at a given position using the ! infix operator:

[11,22,33] ! 1 = 22
[10,200,3000] ! 0 = 10

Note that the first element of the list has index 0: $xs!0$ = hd xs. Thus, one would use the index $n-1$ for the nth element of a list.

The prefix operator # returns the length of a list (that is, the number of elements that it contains):

#[] = 0
#[x] = 1
#[1,1,2,2,3,3] = 6
#(xs++ys) = (#xs) + (#ys)

Cons

The *cons* (for *construct*) operator : is an inverse of hd and tl. It takes a value and a list (of matching types) and puts the value in front to form a new list, for example,

1:[2,3,4] = [1,2,3,4] = 1:2:3:4:[]
x:xs = [x]++xs
hd (x:xs) = x
tl (x:xs) = xs
xs = (hd xs):(tl xs),   if xs ~= []

Some convenient notations for lists

The special form [a..b], where a and b are numbers, denotes the list of numbers [a,a+1,a+2, ...b] in increasing order from a to b inclusive. This will be [] if a > b.

Lists of characters (also called *strings*) can alternatively be denoted by using double quotation marks. For example, `"hello"`.

```
Miranda  "cow" ++ "boy"
cowboy
```
An important feature of strings is how they are printed.
```
Miranda  "cowboy"
cowboy
Miranda  ['c','o','w','b','o','y']
cowboy
Miranda  "this line has \none newline"
This line has
one newline
```
The double quotation marks do not appear in the output and special characters are printed as the character they represent. This printing convention gives programmer control over the layout of results.

Cons as constructor

From the human point of view, there is often nothing to indicate that one end of a list should be given any preference over the other. However, functional programming interpreters store the elements in a manner such that those elements from one end are much more accessible than those from the other.

Imagine a list as having its elements all parcelled up together, but in a nested way. If you unwrap the parcel you find just one element, the head, and another parcel containing the tail. (The empty list is special, of course.) The further down the sequence a value is, the more difficult it is to get out, because you have to unwrap more parcels.

From this point of view, the most accessible element in a list is the *first*, that is, the leftmost in the [...] notation.

Storing a list `[x0,x1,x2,...,xn]` in this way corresponds notationally to writing it, using *cons*, as `x0:x1:x2:...:xn:[]`; and the way the function *cons* is applied in the computer, for example to evaluate `x:xs`, does not perform any real calculations, but, rather, just puts `x` and `xs` together wrapped up in a wrapper that is clearly marked ':'. (The empty list is just a wrapper, marked '*empty*'.) A function implemented in this way is called a 'constructor' function, and there are some more examples in Chapter 7. Obviously, a crucial aspect is that you can unwrap to regain the original arguments, so it is important that : is 'one-to-one' — different arguments give different results — or, more formally,

$$\forall x, y, xs, ys.\ (x\!:\!xs = y\!:\!ys \rightarrow x = y \wedge xs = ys)$$

`++` is not one-to-one and so could never be implemented as a constructor function, but `snoc`, defined by

72 Lists

```
snoc [] = []
snoc xs x = xs++[x]
```
is one-to-one and could have been implemented as a constructor function for lists instead of :, but it is not.

Special facilities for pattern matching on lists

Because every list can be expressed in terms of [] and : in *exactly one way*, we can pattern match on lists using [] and :. For example, any of the following will match a two-element list.

```
a:b:[]    a:[b]    [a,b]
```

Figure 6.1 shows the function isempty which uses pattern matching to determine if a given list is empty or not. Of course, an easier definition is

patterns

isempty []   = True

isempty (x:xs)   = False

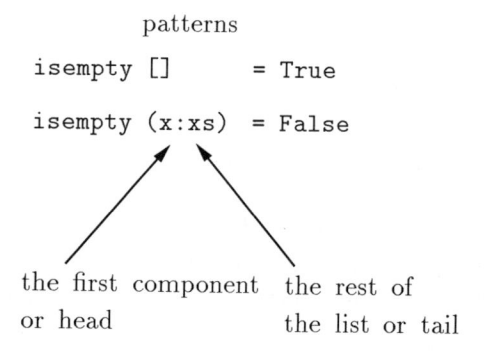

the first component   the rest of
or head   the list or tail

Figure 6.1

just `isempty x = x = []`. Similarly, we can formally define hd and tl (not that one would need to) by:

```
hd (x:xs)  =  x
tl (x:xs)  =  xs
```

Notice how pattern matching does not just express implicit tests on the actual arguments (Are they empty or non-empty? Is the wrapper marked *empty* or *cons*?) as we saw in Section 4.4; it also provides the right-hand side of the equation with names for the unwrapped contents of the arguments.

6.3 Recursive functions over lists

Because of the way in which lists are stored, recursion (and also induction) on lists is usually based on two cases: the empty list [], and lists of the form $(x\!:\!xs)$. As an example, consider the function which finds the length of a list (that is, the operator **#**):

```
length :: [num] -> num
||pre: none
||post: length xs = #xs
length [] = 0
length (x:xs) = 1 + (length xs)
```

which can be evaluated as follows:

$\underline{\texttt{length [10,20,30]}}$
$= 1+(\underline{\texttt{length [20,30]}})$ by the second equation
$= 1+(1+(\underline{\texttt{length [30]}}))$
$= 1+(1+(1+(\underline{\texttt{length []}})))$
$= 1+(1+(1+(\underline{0})))$ by the first equation
$= 3$ by built-in rules for **+**

Of course, we should ask what the recursion variant of `length` xs is; it is just **#**xs — in the recursive call, the length of the argument has gone down by 1. In fact, it is almost always the case for recursively defined list functions that the recursion variant is the length of some list.

That is pretty silly in this example. Either we are assuming that the length function **#** already exists, in which case there is no point in redefining it as `length`, or we are not, in which case we cannot use it for a recursion variant. However, there is an important lesson to be drawn regarding *infinite lists*.

Infinite lists

Some lists in Miranda can be *infinite*, such as the following examples:

```
zeros = 0:zeros              || = [0,0,0,...]
nandup n = n:(nandup (n+1))  || = [n,n+1,n+2,...]
cards = nandup 0             || = [0,1,2,3,...]
```

Some calculations using these will be potentially infinite, and you will need to press *control-C* when you have had enough. For instance, evaluating `zeros` or `cards` will start to produce an infinite quantity of output, and evaluating `#zeros` or `#cards` will enter an infinite loop.

However, the lazy evaluation of Miranda means that it will not go into infinite computations unnecessarily. For instance, `hd (tl cards)` gives 1 as its result and stops.

Now the problem is that we thought we had proved that `length` xs always terminates, because it has a recursion variant **#**xs; `length zeros` does not terminate, and this is because the variant #zeros is undefined (or infinite, which is just as bad). The moral is:

> Our reasoning principles using recursion variants only work for *finite* lists.

This is a shame because infinite lists can be useful and well-behaved; in fact research into finding the most convenient ways of reasoning about infinite lists is ongoing. However, we shall only deal with finite lists and shall make the implicit assumption — usually amounting to an implicit pre-condition — that our lists are finite. Then we can use their lengths as recursion variants, and the 'circular reasoning' technique for recursion works exactly as before.

Another example

The following is a less trivial example. It tests whether a given number occurs as an element of a given list of numbers. Note how this condition can be expressed precisely using ++ in the specification. If x is an element of xs, then xs can be split up as us++[x]++vs, where us and vs are the sublists of xs coming before and after some occurrence of x:

```
isin :: num -> [num] -> bool
||pre: none
||post: isin x xs <-> (E)us,vs:[num]. xs = us++[x]++vs
||recursion variant = #xs
isin x [] = False
isin x (y:ys) = True,      if x = y
              = isin x ys, otherwise
```

The recursion variant in `isin x xs` is #xs, and we can reason that `isin x xs` works correctly as follows.

Proposition 6.1 `isin x` meets its specification. If $xs =$ [], then we cannot possibly have $xs = us$++[x]++vs, for that would have length at least 1. Hence the result `False` is correct.

If xs has the form $(y\!:\!ys)$ then note that, from the definition, `isin x (y:ys)` $\equiv (x = y) \lor$ `isin x ys`. Hence we must prove

$$(x = y) \lor \text{isin } x \text{ } ys \leftrightarrow \exists us, vs. \ ((y\!:\!ys) = us\text{++}[x]\text{++}vs)$$

assuming that the recursive call works correctly. For the $\rightarrow$ direction, we have the following two cases:

1. If $x = y$ then $(y\!:\!ys) =$ []++[x]++ys.
2. If `isin x ys` then by induction $ys = U$++[x]++V for some U and V and so $y\!:\!ys = (y\!:\!U)$++[x]++V.

For the ← direction, we have $(y\!:\!ys) = U\texttt{++}[x]\texttt{++}V$ for some U and V (not necessarily the same as before). If $U = \texttt{[]}$ then $y = x$, while if $U \neq \texttt{[]}$ then $ys = (\texttt{tl}\ U)\texttt{++}[x]\texttt{++}V$ and so `isin x ys` by induction. □

Although this may look a little too much like hard work, something of value has been achieved. The post-condition is very much a *global* property of the function — a property of what has been calculated rather than how the calculation was done. It is tempting to think of the function definition itself as a formal description of what the intuition 'x is an element of the list xs' means, but actually the specification comes closer to the intuitive idea. You can see this if you think how you might prove such intuitively obvious facts as 'if x is in xs then it is also in $xs\texttt{++}ys$ and $ys\texttt{++}xs$ for any ys' — this is immediate from the specification, but less straightforward from the definition.

Let us note one point that will be dealt with properly in Chapter 7, but is useful already. You could replace `num` in `isin` by `char` or `bool` or `[num]` or any other type at all to give other versions of `isin`, but the actual definition would not suffer *any changes whatsoever*: it is 'polymorphic' (many formed), and it is useful to give its type 'polymorphically' as `* -> [*] -> bool`, leaving `*` to be replaced by whatever type you actually want. Indeed, Miranda itself understands these polymorphic types.

6.4 Trapping errors

The evaluator will generate a run-time error message for cases where no matching equation has been found for a particular function application. However, it is always a good idea not to rely on this. Either convince yourself that your program cannot cause a run-time error, or — for a defensive specification — traps errors at the program level. In this way it is possible to generate more meaningful error messages and to bring the execution to a graceful halt. Such program generated information may then be more useful for debugging purposes. The predefined function

```
error :: [char] -> *
```

can be used for this purpose. (The `*` means that the result of `error` — actually not a result at all because the program has aborted — can be considered formally to be of any type: it will not cause type checking errors.)

As examples, the following are defensive specifications for `hd` and `divide`. Again, the `*`s represent any type:

```
hd   :: [*] -> *
||pre: none
||post: (E)ys:[*]. xs = [hd xs]++ys
||         \/ xs = [] & error message generated
hd (x:ys) = x
hd []     = error "hd of []"
```

```
divide :: num -> num -> num
||pre:  none
||post: y ~= 0 & x = (divide x y)*y
||      \/ y = 0 & error message generated
divide x 0 = error "Sorry! divide by 0"
divide x y = x/y
```

It is good programming practice to ensure that a given function performs just one activity. So it is better if a defensive function performs the validations (the checks) and error responses itself, but calls on a separate non-defensive function to perform the actual calculations.

6.5 An example — insertion sort

Here we will consider a slightly larger problem and use a top-down design technique to arrive at a solution. We shall look at the problem of sorting data items into ascending order. There are many algorithms for doing this, and one of simplest methods — though not a very efficient one — is the *insertion* sort, which sorts a list by first sorting the tail and then inserting the head in the correct place. We shall look at a more efficient algorithm, 'quick sort', in Chapter 12.

Sortedness

Let us start by specifying when a list is sorted (in ascending order) — if $xs = [x_0, x_1, x_2, \ldots, x_n]$ then we write *Sorted(xs)* to mean that informally
$$x_0 \leq x_1 \leq x_2 \leq \ldots \leq x_n$$
This can be formalized quite straightforwardly using the subscripting operator ! but another way, using ++, is as follows:
$$Sorted(xs) \stackrel{\text{def}}{=} \forall us, vs : [\,*\,].\ \forall a, b : *.\ xs = us\text{++}[a, b]\text{++}vs \rightarrow a \leq b$$
In other words, whenever we have two adjacent elements a and b in xs (with a first), then $a \leq b$.

Note that we used a polymorphic type — we wrote * for the type of the elements, [*] for that of the lists. Of course, it only makes sense to call a list sorted if we know what $\leq$ means for its elements. It is obvious how to do this when their type is num, but Miranda understands $\leq$ for many other types. For instance, values of type char have a natural ordering (by ASCII code), and this is extended to strings (values of type [char]) by lexicographic ordering and to values of other list types by the same method. The sorting algorithm works 'polymorphically' — it does not depend on the type. We shall therefore express its type using *, but remember (as implicit pre-conditions) that * must represent a type for which $\leq$ is understood.

Let us prove some useful properties about sortedness.

Proposition 6.2

1. The empty list [] and singleton [x] are sorted.
2. [x, y] is sorted iff $x \leq y$.
3. If xs is sorted, then so is any sublist ys (that is, such that we can write $xs = xs_1$++ys++xs_2 for some lists xs_1 and xs_2).
4. Suppose xs++ys and ys++zs are both sorted, and ys is *non-empty*. Then xs++ys++zs is sorted.

Proof

1. This is obvious, because the decomposition $xs = us$++$[a, b]$++vs can only be done if #$xs \geq 2$.
2. This is obvious, too.
3. If $ys = us$++$[a, b]$++vs, then $xs = (xs_1$++$us)$++$[a, b]$++$(vs$++$xs_2)$, and so $a \leq b$ because xs is sorted.
4. Suppose xs++ys++$zs = us$++$[a, b]$++vs. It is clear that a and b are either both in xs ++ys or both in ys ++zs, and so $a \leq b$.

□

The third case, set out in full using box notation (Chapters 16 and 17), can be seen in Figure 6.2.

xs is sorted

$\forall a, b, us, vs. \ (xs = us$++$[a, b]$++$vs \rightarrow a \leq b)$

$xs = xs1$++ys++$xs2$

def of sublist
assumption

$\forall \mathcal{I} \ A, B, US, VS$		
$ys = US$++$[A, B]$++VS		
$xs = xs_1$++US++$[A, B]$++VS++xs_2		def sublist
$A \leq B$		assoc of ++ and $\forall \rightarrow \mathcal{E}$
$ys = US$++$[A, B]$++$VS \rightarrow A \leq B$		$\rightarrow \mathcal{I}$

$\forall a, b, us, vs. \ (ys = us$++$[a, b]$++$vs) \rightarrow a \leq b$ \quad $\forall \mathcal{I}$

ys is sorted \quad def

Figure 6.2

78 Lists

When we sort a list, we obviously want the result to be sorted, and this will be specified in the post-condition. The other property that we need is that the result has the same elements as the argument, but possibly rearranged — the result is a *permutation* of the argument.

Let us write $Perm(xs,ys)$ for 'ys is a permutation of xs'. We shall not define this explicitly in formal terms, but use the following facts:

- $Perm(xs,xs)$
- $Perm(xs,ys) \rightarrow Perm(ys,xs)$
- $Perm(xs,ys) \land Perm(ys,zs) \rightarrow Perm(xs,zs)$
- $Perm(us\text{++}vs\text{++}ws\text{++}xs\text{++}ys, us\text{++}xs\text{++}ws\text{++}vs\text{++}ys)$, that is, vs and xs are swapped

In fact, any permutation can be produced by a sequence of swaps of adjacent elements. We are now ready to specify the function sort:

```
sort :: [*] -> [*]
||pre:   none (but, implicitly, there is an ordering over *)
||post:  Sorted(ys) & Perm(xs,ys)
||          where ys = sort xs
```

Recall that the method of insertion sort was to sort x:xs by first sorting xs and then inserting x in the correct place. We therefore define

```
sort []      =   []
sort (x:xs)  =   insert x (sort xs)
```

The following is an example of how we intend sort to evaluate:

```
  sort [4, 1, 9, 3]
= insert 4 (sort [1, 9, 3])
= insert 4 (insert 1 (sort [9, 3]))
= insert 4 (insert 1 (insert 9 (sort [3])))
= insert 4 (insert 1 (insert 9 (insert 3 (sort []))))
= insert 4 (insert 1 (insert 9 (insert 3   [])))
= insert 4 (insert 1 (insert 9 [3]))
= insert 4 (insert 1   [3, 9])
= insert 4 [1, 3, 9]
= [1, 3, 4, 9]
```

Specifying insert

insert will be defined later — this is 'top-down programming'. However, we must *specify* insert immediately.

We want to say three things about **insert** *a xs*. First, it contains the elements of *xs*, in the same order, with *a* inserted somewhere in the middle. Imagine that *xs* is prised apart as $xs = xs_1 \text{++} xs_2$, and then *a* is inserted in the gap to give the result $xs_1\text{++}[a]\text{++}xs_2$. Next, we want to say that an *a* is inserted in the *correct* place in the middle — in other words, the result is sorted. Finally, when we use **insert** in **sort**, its second argument is always sorted and we expect this fact to make it easier to implement **insert**. This gives us a pre-condition:

```
insert :: * -> [*] -> [*]
||pre:  Sorted(xs)
||post: Sorted(ys) &
||        (E)x1s,x2s:[*]. (xs = x1s++x2s & ys = x1s++[a]++x2s)
||        where ys = (insert a xs)
```

sort is correctly implemented

That is to say, **sort** will work correctly provided that **insert** satisfies its specification. Of course, when we do get round to implementing **insert** it may have any number of errors in it and they will lead **sort** astray also, but that is not the point. We can regard **sort** now as correct and finished because our reasoning about it uses the specification of **insert**, not the implementation. The only thing that could thwart us is if we discover that the specification of **insert** as it stands cannot be implemented.

Let us now prove that **sort** is correct. First, and crucially, we have a recursion variant #*xs* for **sort** *xs*. As usual, this proves termination, at least when *xs* is finite (we could not expect that sorting an infinite list would terminate), and allows us to assume that the recursive calls all work correctly. The two alternatives in the definition cover all possible cases, so we must just check that they give correct answers.

Proposition 6.3 **sort** meets its specification.

Proof First we must check that [] is sorted and a permutation of []. This is obvious.

Next we must check **sort** *x:xs*. Let *ys* = **insert** *x* (**sort** *xs*). We can assume that **sort** *xs* is sorted and a permutation of *xs*; we deduce in particular that the pre-condition of **insert** is satisfied. The post-condition of **insert** tells us that *ys* is sorted, as required, and it remains to show that *ys* is a permutation of *x:xs*. By the post-condition of **insert**, there are lists ys_1 and ys_2 such that

$$\text{sort } xs = ys_1\text{++}ys_2$$
$$ys = ys_1\text{++}[x]\text{++}ys_2$$

Hence ys is a permutation of $x\!:\!ys_1$++ys_2 = $x\!:\!($sort $xs)$, which is a permutation of $x\!:\!xs$ because the recursive call worked correctly. □

Implementing insert

The idea in insert a xs is that we must move past all the elements of xs that are smaller than a (they will all come together at the start of xs) and put a in front of the rest. Hence there are two cases for insert a $(x\;\!:\!xs)$: the head is either a or x, according to which is bigger, and if a is bigger then it must be inserted into xs:

```
||insert was specified above
insert a [] = [a]
insert a (x:xs) = a:x:xs,          if a <= x
                = x:(insert a xs),  otherwise
```

for example,

```
insert 3 [1,4,9] = 1:(insert 3 [4,9]) = 1:3:4:[9] = [1,3,4,9]
```

insert is correctly implemented

The recursion variant for insert a xs is #xs. The three alternatives in the definition cover all possible cases, so we must just check that each one gives a satisfactory answer.

Proposition 6.4 insert meets its specification.

Proof For insert a []: we must check that $[a]$ is sorted (this is obvious), and that we can find lists xs_1 and xs_2 such that [] = xs_1++xs_2 and $[a]$ = xs_1++$[a]$++xs_2. This is easy — take $xs_1 = xs_2 =$ [].

For insert a $(x\;\!:\!xs)$ when $x\;\!:\!xs$ is sorted and $a \leq x$, the result $a\!:\!x\;\!:\!xs$ is sorted by Proposition 6.2 — for $[a]$++$[x]$ and $[x]$++xs are both sorted. To find xs_1 and xs_2 such that $x\!:\!xs = xs_1$++xs_2 and $a\!:\!x\!:\!xs = xs_1$++$[a]$++xs_2, we take $xs_1 =$ []and $xs_2 = x\!:\!xs$.

The final case is for insert $a(x\!:\!xs)$ when $x\!:\!xs$ is sorted (so xs is sorted and the pre-condition for insert is satisfied) and $a > x$; let $ys =$ insert a xs. By induction, ys is sorted and there are lists xs_1 and xs_2 such that $xs = xs_1$++xs_2 and $ys = xs_1$++$[a]$++xs_2. It follows immediately that $x\!:\!xs = (x\!:\!xs_1)$++xs_2, and the result, $x\!:\!ys$, is $(x\!:\!xs_1)$++$[a]$++xs_2.

Proposition 6.2 tells us that $x\!:\!ys$ is sorted. For either $xs_1 =$ [], in which case $x\!:\!ys = [x]$++$[a]$++xs_2 with both $[x]$++$[a]$ and $[a]$++xs_2 (that is, ys) sorted, or $xs_1 \neq$ [], in which case $x\!:\!ys = [x]$++xs_1++$(a\!:\!xs_2)$ with both $[x]$++xs_1 (a sublist of $x\!:\!xs$) and xs_1++$(a\!:\!xs_2)$ (that is, ys) sorted. □

This completes the development of `sort` and `insert`.

6.6 Another example — sorted merge

In the preceding example, insertion sort, we introduced the predicates *Sorted* and *Perm*. These are very useful in their own right, and because (at least for *Perm*) a direct formalization into logic is difficult, we used an *axiomatic* approach starting from useful properties. The example in this section uses a similar method with another useful predicate, *Merge*.

Merge(xs, ys, zs) means that the list zs is made up of xs and ys merged together. That is to say, the elements of xs and the elements of ys have been kept in the same order but interleaved to give zs. For instance,

Merge('abcd', '123', '1ab2c3d')	
¬*Merge*('abcd', '123', '1ba2c3d')	a and b used in wrong order
¬*Merge*('abcd', '1234', 'a1ab2c3d')	a used twice, 4 not used
Merge('abcd', '123', 'ab12cd3')	
Merge('1abd', '2c3', '1ab2c3d')	

We shall use the following properties:

1. *Merge*($xs, ys,$ []) iff $xs = ys =$ []
2. *Merge*($xs, ys, [z]$) iff ($xs = [z] \land ys =$ []) $\lor$ ($xs =$ [] $\land ys = [z]$)
3. *Merge*(xs, ys, zs_1++zs_2) iff $\exists xs_1, xs_2, ys_1, ys_2$.
   ($xs = xs_1$++$xs_2 \land ys = ys_1$++$ys_2 \land$ *Merge*(xs_1, ys_1, zs_1) $\land$ *Merge*(xs_2, ys_2, zs_2))

Note that the right-to-left parts can be written more simply, as

1. *Merge*([], [], [])
2. *Merge*([z], [], [z])
   Merge([], [z], [z])
3. *Merge*(xs_1, ys_1, zs_1) $\land$ *Merge*(xs_2, ys_2, zs_2) $\rightarrow$
   Merge(xs_1++xs_2, ys_1++ys_2, zs_1++zs_2)

If the left-to-right direction of (3) seems difficult to understand, think of xs_1 and ys_1 as the parts of xs and ys that go into zs_1, and xs_2 and ys_2 as the rest.

Let us now look at sorted merge. The idea is that if you have two sorted lists, then it is quite easy to merge them into a sorted result. Imagine merging two files by reading from the inputs and writing to the output. At each stage, the item to write is the smaller of the two front input items. The following is a Miranda version:

82   Lists

```
smerge :: [*] -> [*] -> [*]
||pre:  Sorted(xs) & Sorted(ys)
||post: Sorted(zs) & Merge(xs,ys,zs)
||        where zs = smerge xs ys
||recursion variant = #xs + #ys
smerge [] ys = ys
smerge (x:xs) [] = x:xs
smerge (x:xs) (y:ys) = x:(smerge xs (y:ys)),   if x <= y
                     = y:(smerge (x:xs) ys),   otherwise
```

It is easy enough to see that this works correctly in the first two cases. The fourth is just like the third, so we shall concentrate on that. We must show the following.

Suppose $x:xs$ and $y:ys$ are both sorted, and that $x \leq y$. Let $ws = ($smerge$\ xs\ (y:ys))$. The pre-conditions for this are satisfied (xs and $y:ys$ are both sorted), so we know that ws is sorted and that $Merge(xs, y:ys, ws)$. We must show that $Merge(x:xs, y:ys, x:ws)$ (this is almost immediate), and that $x:ws$ is sorted. The intuitive reason why $x:ws$ is sorted is easy enough to see; ws is sorted, and x is less than all the elements of ws — these are either from xs and are $\geq x$ because $x:xs$ is sorted, or they are from $y:ys$ and are bigger than x because y is the smallest and $x \leq y$. We could quite reasonably be satisfied with this argument, but let us also show it slightly more formally by going back to the definition of sortedness.

Suppose $x:ws$ = us++$[a,b]$++vs. If us = [] , then $x = a$ and $ws = b:vs$. Two possibilities arise because $Merge(xs, y:ys, b:vs)$, namely that b is either hd xs or y. If $b = $ hd xs, then $x:xs$, which is sorted, is []++$[x,b]$++ (tl xs) and so $x \leq b$ giving $a \leq b$. If $b = y$, then $x \leq b$ by assumption giving $a \leq b$. If us is non-empty, then ws = (tl us)++$[a,b]$++vs, and so $a \leq b$ because ws is sorted.

The formal version, written in box notation, appears in Figure 6.3

6.7   List induction

The reasoning techniques using recursion variants are usually all we need for proving that functions satisfy their specifications, but for more general properties they may break down. This is particularly the case when we want to compare the results of different calls of the same function. The following is an example with a function to reverse a list.

reverse

The **reverse** function is defined as follows:

List induction   83

	1	$x \leq y$	
	2	$Merge(xs, y{:}ys,\ ws)$	
	3	ws is sorted $x{:}xs$ is sorted	assumptions
$\forall \mathcal{I}$ US, VS, A, B	4		
	5	$x{:}ws = US\text{++}[A,B]\text{++}VS$	
	6	$US = [\,] \vee US \neq [\,]$	
	7	case 1 of $\vee\mathcal{E}$	
	8	$US = [\,]$	
	9	$x = A$	
	10	$ws = B : VS$	
	11	$B = \text{hd } xs \vee B = y$	def $Merge$
	12	$B = \text{hd } xs$	$B = y$
	13	$x{:}xs = [\,]\text{++}[x,B]\text{++}\text{tl } xs$	$x \leq y$ assumed
	14	$x \leq B$ $(x{:}xs$ sorted$)$	$A \leq B$ eqsub
	15	$A \leq B$ eqsub	
	16	$A \leq B$	$\vee\mathcal{E}(11)$
	17	case 2 of $\vee\mathcal{E}$	
	18	$US \neq [\,]$	
	19	$ws = \text{tl } US\text{++}[A,B]\text{++}VS$	
	20	$A \leq B$	$(ws$ sorted$)$
	21	$A \leq B$	$\vee\mathcal{E}(6)$
	22	$x{:}ws = US\text{++}[A,B]\text{++}VS \rightarrow A \leq B$	$\rightarrow\mathcal{I}$
	23	$x{:}ws$ is sorted	$\forall\mathcal{I}$

Figure 6.3

```
reverse :: [*] -> [*]
||pre:  none
||post: reverse xs is the reverse of xs
||recursion variant for reverse xs is #xs
reverse []     = []
reverse (x:xs) = (reverse xs)++[x]
```
It is not clear how this function ought to be specified. But bearing in

84 Lists

mind that the specification is supposed to say how we can make use of the function, and bearing also in mind our idea that ++ is more useful than *cons* in specifications because it does not prefer one end of the list to the other, let us try to elaborate the specification by giving some useful properties of the function:

- (reverse []) = []
- (reverse [x]) = [x]
- (reverse (xs++ys)) = (reverse ys)++(reverse xs)

These are enough to force the given definition, for we must have

reverse (x:xs) = reverse ([x]++xs)
   = (reverse xs)++(reverse [x])
   = (reverse xs)++[x]

There still remains the question of whether the definition does indeed satisfy these stronger properties. The first two are straightforward from the definition, but the third is trickier. It is certainly not obvious whether the recursion variant method gives a proof.

The principle of list induction

What we shall use is a new principle, the *Principle of List Induction*. It is the exact analogue of simple mathematical induction, but applied to lists instead of natural numbers.

Recall that each natural number is either 0 or $N+1$ for some N, and so simple induction requires us to prove a property P in the *base case*, $P(0)$, and also in the other cases, $P(N+1)$. But that was not all. In the other cases the principle gave us a valuable free gift, the *induction hypothesis*, by allowing us to assume $P(N)$. Proving $P(N+1)$ from $P(N)$ was the *induction step*. Using boxes, an induction proof is shown in Figure 6.4 List induction is

$$
\begin{array}{|c|c|}
\hline
\vdots & N : nat \quad P(N) \quad \text{hypothesis} \\
P(0) & \vdots \\
 & P(N+1) \\
\hline
\end{array}
$$

$\forall n : nat.\ P(n)$ simple induction

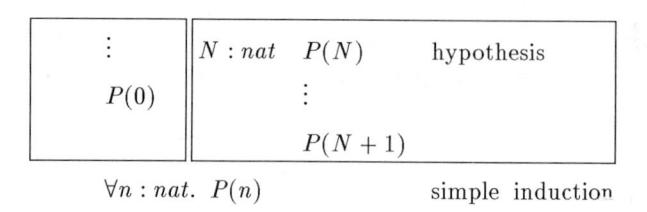

Figure 6.4

similar, but uses the fact that every list is either [] or x:xs for some x and xs. It says:

Let $P(xs)$ be a property of lists xs. To prove $\forall xs:$ [*]. $P(xs)$, it is enough to prove:

base case: $P(\texttt{[]})$.
induction step: $P(x\!:\!xs)$ on the assumption of the *induction hypothesis*, $P(xs)$.

The box proof version of list induction appears in Figure 6.5.

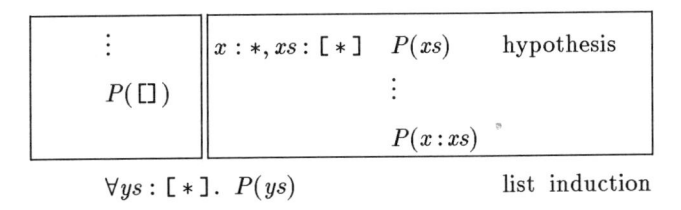

```
       ⋮          | x:*, xs:[*]   P(xs)    hypothesis
     P([])        |     ⋮
                  |   P(x:xs)

   ∀ys:[*]. P(ys)                          list induction
```

Figure 6.5

REMEMBER! All lists here are assumed to be finite. The induction principle will not tell you anything about infinite lists.

The principle can be justified in the same way as the principle of simple mathematical induction — if P does *not* hold for all lists xs, then what is a shortest possible list for which it fails? Surely not [], if we have proved the base case; and if it is $x\!:\!xs$ then xs is shorter, so $P(xs)$ holds, and the induction step tells us that P also holds for $x\!:\!xs$ — a contradiction.

Alternatively, it can be justified using simple induction — see Exercise 17. However, more important than the justification is knowing how to use the principle.

Application to reverse

Proposition 6.5 Let xs and ys be lists. Then
(reverse (xs++ys)) = (reverse ys)++(reverse xs)

Proof We use list induction on xs to prove $\forall xs:$ [*]. $P(xs)$, where
$$P(xs) \stackrel{\text{def}}{=} \forall ys:[*]. \text{ (reverse } (xs\texttt{++}ys)) = \text{(reverse } ys)\texttt{++}\text{(reverse } xs)$$

base case: $xs =$ []

LHS = (reverse ([]++ys)) = (reverse ys)
    = (reverse ys)++[]   unit law
    = (reverse ys)++(reverse []) = RHS

induction step: Assume $P(xs)$; then in the equation for $P(x\!:\!xs)$:

LHS = reverse ($x\!:\!xs$++ys)

86   Lists

$$
\begin{aligned}
&= (\texttt{reverse } (xs\texttt{++}ys))\texttt{++}[x] && \text{definition}\\
&= ((\texttt{reverse } ys)\texttt{++}(\texttt{reverse } xs))\texttt{++}[x] && \text{induction}\\
&= (\texttt{reverse } ys)\texttt{++}(\texttt{reverse } (x\!:\!xs)) && \text{definition}\\
&= \text{RHS}
\end{aligned}
$$

□

Note how although we have two lists to deal with, xs and ys, in this example we only need to use induction on one of them: xs. If you try to prove the result by induction on ys, you will find that the proof just does not come out.

To illustrate the advantage of using our stronger properties (Proposition 6.5) instead of just the definition, let us prove the intuitively obvious property that if you reverse a list twice you get the original one back. If you try to prove this directly from the definition, you will find that it is not so easy.

Proposition 6.6 Let xs be a list. Then $(\texttt{reverse }(\texttt{reverse } xs)) = xs$

Proof We use list induction on xs.

base case: $xs = \texttt{[]}$ $\texttt{reverse }(\texttt{reverse }\texttt{[]}) = (\texttt{reverse }\texttt{[]}) = \texttt{[]}$

induction step: When the list is not empty,

$$
\begin{aligned}
(\texttt{reverse } (\texttt{reverse}(x\!:\!xs))) &\\
&= (\texttt{reverse } ((\texttt{reverse } xs) \texttt{++}[x]))\\
&= (\texttt{reverse } [x])\texttt{++}(\texttt{reverse } (\texttt{reverse } xs))\\
&= [x]\texttt{++}xs && \text{by induction}\\
&= x\!:\!xs
\end{aligned}
$$

□

6.8 Summary

- A list is a sequence of values, its *elements*, all of the same type. Lists are widely used in functional languages and are provided as a built-in type in Miranda in order to provide some convenient syntax for their use, for example, `[]` (the *empty* list), `[1,3,5,7]`.
- If xs is a list whose elements are of type `*`, then xs is of type `[*]`.
- The *append* operator `++` on lists puts two lists together. For example, `[1,2,3,4]++[5,6,7,8]` = `[1,2,3,4,5,6,7,8]`. It satisfies the laws

    $xs\texttt{++}\texttt{[]} = \texttt{[]}\texttt{++}xs = xs$ unit laws
    $xs\texttt{++}(ys\texttt{++}zs) = (xs\texttt{++}ys)\texttt{++}zs$ associativity

    As a consequence of associativity, if you append together several lists, you do not need any parentheses to show in which order the appends are done.

- As long as a list xs is not empty, then its first element is called its *head*, `hd xs`, and its other elements form its *tail*, `tl xs` (another list). If

x is a value (of the right type) and xs a list, then `x:xs = [x]++xs` is a new list, 'cons of x and xs', whose head is x and whose tail is xs.
- Some other operators on lists are `#` (length) and `!` (for indexing).
- Every list can be expressed in terms of `[]` and `:` in *exactly one way*. Thus pattern matching can be performed on lists using `[]` and `:`. This makes `:` particularly useful in implementations, though `++` is usually more useful in specifications.
- The special form `[a..b]` denotes the list of numbers in increasing order from `a` to `b` inclusive.
- A list of characters (also called a *string*) can alternatively be denoted by using double quotation marks.
- For a recursively defined list function, the recursion variant is usually the length of some list.
- The principle of list induction says that to prove $\forall xs : [\,*\,]. \ P(xs)$, it suffices to prove

base case: $P(\texttt{[]})$

induction step: $\forall x : *. \ \forall xs : [*]. \ (P(xs) \to P(x : xs))$

This only works for finite lists.

6.9 Exercises

1. How would the evaluator respond to the expressions `[1]:[]` and `[]:[]`?
2. How would you use `#` and `!` to find the *last* element of a list?
3. Explain whether or not the expression `[8,'8']` is well-formed and if not why not.
4. Describe the difference between `'k'` and `"k"`.
5. Define a function `singleton` which given any list returns a Boolean indicating if the list has just one element or not. Write a function `has2items` to test if a list has exactly two items or not. Do not use guards or the built-in operator `#`.
6. Consider the following specification of the indexing function `!`:

   ```
   ||pre:   0 <= n < #xs
   ||post:  (E)us,vs:[*]. (#us = n & xs = us++[x]++vs)
   ||            where x = xs!n
   ```

   (This is not quite right — the built-in `!` has a defensive specification.) Write a recursive definition of this function, and prove that it satisfies the specification.
   A straightforward way of writing specifications for list functions is often to use the indexing function and discuss the elements of the list. For instance, you could specify `++` by

Lists

```
||pre:  none
||post: #zs = #xs+#ys
||       & (A)n:nat. ((0 <= n < #xs -> zs!n = xs!n)
||                 & (#xs <= n < #xs+#ys -> zs!n = ys!(n-#xs)))
||      where zs = xs++ys
```

Although this is straightforward, it has one disadvantage: when we appended the lists, we had to re-index their elements and it is not so terribly obvious that we did the calculations correctly.

For this reason, the specifications in this book avoid the 'indexing' approach for lists wherever possible, and this exercise shows that even indexing can be specified using ++ and #.

7. Write a definition of the function count:

```
count :: * -> [*] -> num
||pre:  none
||post: (count x ys) = number of occurrences of x in ys
```

For example (using strings), count 'o' "quick brown fox" = 2.

The specification is only informal, but try to show informally that your definition satisfies it.

8. Consider the function locate of type * -> [*] -> num, locate x ys being the subscript in ys of the first occurrence of the element x, or #ys if x does not occur in ys. (In other words, it is the length of the largest initial sublist of ys that does not contain an x.) For instance,

locate 'w' "the quick brown" = 13

Specify locate with pre- and post-conditions, write a Miranda definition for it, and prove that it satisfies its specification.

If a character c is in a string s, then you should have

$s!(\text{locate } c\ s) = c$

Check this for some values of s and c.

9. Use box notation to write the proof of Proposition 6.1.
10. Specify and write the following functions for strings.

    (a) Use count to write a function table which produces a list of the the numbers of times each of the letters in the lowercase alphabet and space appear in a string:

    table"a bad dog" = $[2, 1, 0, 2, 0, 0, 1, 0, 0, 0, \ldots, 0, 2]$

    You may find it useful to define a constant containing the characters that you are counting:

    ```
    alphabetsp = "abcdefghijklmnopqrstuvwxyz "
    ```

In writing this function you may find it helpful to define an auxiliary function which takes as an additional argument *as*. With the auxiliary function you can then step through the letters of the alphabet counting the number of times each letter appears in the string passed as an argument to `table`.

(b) Write a simple enciphering function, `cipher` that uses `locate`, `!` and `alphabetsp` to convert a character to a number, add a number to it, and convert it back to a character by indexing into `alphabetsp`. The type of `cipher` is then `num -> [char] -> [char]`. It should carry out this function on every character *separately* in the string it is given, to produce the encrypted string as its output.

$$\text{cipher } 2 \text{ "quick brown fox"} = \text{"swkembdtqypbhqz"}$$
$$\text{cipher } (-2) \text{ "swkembdtqypbhqz"} = \text{"quick brown fox"}$$

Use the function `table` on a string and the same string in enciphered form. What is the the relation between the two tables?

If you have a table generated from a large sample of typical English text how might you use this information to decipher an enciphered string. Can you think of a better enciphering method?

11. Consider the following Miranda definition:

```
scrub ::   * -> [*] -> [*]
scrub x [] = []
scrub x(y:ys) = scrub x ys,       if x=y
              = y:(scrub x ys),  otherwise
```

(a) Write informal pre- and post-conditions for `scrub`.

(b) Use list induction on *ys* to prove that for all *x* and *ys*,

```
scrub x(scrub x ys) = scrub x ys
```

(c) Prove that for all *x*, *ys* and *zs*,

$$\text{scrub } x \ (ys\text{++}zs) = (\text{scrub } x \ ys)\text{++}(\text{scrub } x \ zs)$$

Now consider the following more formal specification for `scrub`:

```
||pre:  none
||post: ~isin(x,s)
||          /\ (E)xs:[*] ((A)y:* (isin(y,xs) -> y=x)
||                         /\ Merge(xs,s,ys))
||          where s=scrub x ys
```

90   Lists

  (d) Show that the definition of scrub satisfies this.
  (e) Show by induction on s that the specification specifies the result uniquely. (In fact, it specifies both ys and xs uniquely.)
  (f) Use (e) to show (b) and (c) without induction.
12. Use the ideas of the preceding exercise to specify count more formally and prove that your definition satisfies the new specification.
13. Suppose f :: [*] -> num satisfies the following property:

$$\forall xs, ys : [\,*\,].\ f\ (xs\texttt{++}ys) = (f\ xs) + (f\ ys)$$

Prove that

$$\forall xs : [\,*\,].\ f\ (\texttt{reverse}\ xs) = f\ xs$$

14. Rewrite the proof for Proposition 6.5 using box notation.
15. Use induction on ws to show that if xs is sorted and can be written as $us\texttt{++}[a]\texttt{++}ws\texttt{++}[b]\texttt{++}vs$ then $a \leq b$. (The definition of sortedness is the special case when $ws = \texttt{[]}$.)
16. In Proposition 6.2 it is proven that if $xs\texttt{++}ys$ and $ys\texttt{++}zs$ are both sorted, and ys is *non-empty*, then $xs\texttt{++}ys\texttt{++}zs$ is sorted. Rewrite this proof in box notation.
17. Suppose that you believe simple induction on natural numbers, but not list induction. Use the box notation to show how, if you have the ingredients of a proof by list induction of $\forall xs : [\,*\,].\ P(xs)$, you can adapt them to create a proof by simple induction of $\forall n : nat.\ Q(n)$ where

$$Q(n) \stackrel{\text{def}}{=} \forall xs : [\,*\,].\ (\#xs = n \rightarrow P(xs))$$

Show that (assuming, as usual, that all lists are finite) $\forall xs : [\,*\,].\ P(xs)$ and $\forall n : nat.\ Q(n)$ are equivalent.
18. Give specifications (pre-conditions and post-conditions) in logic for the following programs.
  (a) ascending :: [num] -> bool; returns true if the list is ascending, false otherwise.
  (b) primes :: num -> [num]; primes n returns a list of the primes up to n.
  (c) unique :: [num] -> bool; returns true if the list has no duplicates, false otherwise.

Chapter 7
Types

7.1 Tuples

Recall three properties of lists of type [*] (for some type *):

1. They can be as long as you like.
2. All their elements must be of the same type, *.
3. They can be written using square brackets, [-,-,...,-].

There is another way of treating sequences that relaxes (2) (you can include elements of different types) at the cost of restricting (1) (the length becomes a fixed part of the type). They are written using parentheses and are called *tuples*.

The simplest are the *2-tuples* (length 2), or *pairs*. For instance, (1,9), (9,1) and (6,6) are three pairs of numbers. Their type is (num, num), and their elements are called *components*. A *triple* (*3-tuple*) of numbers, such as (1,2,3), has a different type, namely (num, num, num).

Note that each of the types (num,(num, num)), ((num, num), num) and (num, num, num) is distinct. The first is a pair whose second component is also a pair, the second is a pair whose first component is a pair, and the third is a triple. There is *no* concept of a one-tuple, so the use of parentheses for grouping does not conflict with their use in tuple formation. One advantage of the use of tuples is that if, for example, one accidentally writes a pair instead of a triple, then the strong typing discipline can pinpoint the error.

We can define functions over tuples by using pattern matching. For example, selector functions on pairs can be defined by:

```
fst :: (*, **) -> *
snd :: (*, **) -> **
fst (x,y) = x
snd (x,y) = y
```

Both `fst` and `snd` are polymorphic functions; they select the first and second components of any *pair* of values. Neither function works on any other tuple-type. Selector functions for other kinds of tuples have to be defined separately for each case.

The following is a function which takes and returns a tuple (the quotient and remainder of one number by another):

```
quotrem :: (num, num) -> (num, num)
quotrem (x,y) = (x div y, x mod y)
```

`quotrem` is defined to be a function of just one argument (a pair of numbers) and its definition is read as: `quotrem` takes a pair and returns a pair. Thus using tuples we can construct multiple arguments or results which are packaged up in the form of a *single* value. You can also mix the types of components, for instance the pair (10, [True]) has type (num, [bool]).

The following is an example using lists. `zip` takes two lists — which should be of the same length — and 'zips' them together, making a single list of pairs. For instance,

```
zip [1,3,5] [2,4,6] = [(1,2),(3,4),(5,6)]
```

(It does not matter if * and ** are two different types.)

```
zip :: [*] -> [**] -> [(*,**)]
||pre:  #xs = #ys   (for zip xs ys)
||post: difficult to make logical specification much
||      different from definition, but see Exercise 2
||recursion variant = #xs
zip [] [] = []        ||3 different types for [] here
zip (x:xs) (y:ys) = (x,y):(zip xs ys)
```

(Note that the pre-condition ensures that there is no need to consider cases where one argument is empty and the other is not.)

To unzip a list, you want in effect *two* results — the two unzipped parts. So the actual (single) result can be these two paired together, for example,

```
unzip [(1,2),(3,4),(5,6)] = ([1,3,5],[2,4,6])
```

```
unzip :: [(*,**)] -> ([*],[**])
||pre:  none
||post: zip xs ys = ps
||          where (xs, ys) = unzip ps
||recursion variant = #ps.
unzip [] = ([],[])
unzip (x,y):ps = (x:xs,y:ys)
                 where (xs,ys) = unzip ps
```

This illustrates in two places how pattern matching can be used to give names to the components of a pair: first in (x,y):ps, to name the components of the head pair in the argument, and second in the **where** part for the components of the result of the recursive call.

7.2 More on pattern matching

Patterns in general are built from variables and constants, using constructors. For example,
x   5   (x,4,y)
are a variable, a constant and a triple built from two variables and a constant using the (,,) constructor for triples. The components of a structured pattern can themselves be arbitrary patterns, thus allowing nested structures of any depth. The constructors which can be used in patterns include those of tuple formation (...,...), list formation [...,...], and those of user-defined types (which we will see later in this chapter). In addition we have also seen the special facilities for pattern matching on lists and natural numbers. Patterns are very useful in the left-hand side of function definitions for two reasons:

1. They provide the right-hand side with names for subcomponents of the arguments.
2. They can serve as guards.

Pattern matching can also be combined with the use of guards:

```
last (x:xs) = x,         if xs = []
            = last xs,   otherwise
last []     = error "last of empty"
```

Patterns in the above definition are disjoint. In Miranda, patterns may also contain repeated variables. In such cases identical variables implicitly express the condition that their corresponding matched expressions must also be identical. For example,

```
equal :: * -> * -> bool
equal a a = True
equal a b = False
```

Such patterns match a value *only* when the parts of the value corresponding to the occurrences of the same repeated variable are equal.

Finally, patterns can be used *in conjunction with local definitions* — **where** parts, as in **unzip** to decompose compound structures or user-defined data types. In the following example if the value of the right-hand side matches the structure of the given pattern, the variables in the pattern are bound to the corresponding components of the value. This is useful since it enables the programmer to decompose structures and name its components:

94   *Types*

```
...where
    [3,4,x,y] = [3,4,8,9]
    (a,b,c,a) = fred
    (quot,rem) = quotrem (14,3)
```

For the second definition to make sense the type of `fred` must be a 4-tuple. If the match fails anywhere, all the variables on the left will be undefined and an error message will result if you try to access those values in any way.

7.3 Currying

Now that you have seen pairs, it might occur to you that there are different ways of supplying the arguments to a multi-argument function. One is the way that you have seen repeatedly already, as in

```
cylinderV :: num -> num -> num
cylinderV h r = volume h (areaofcircle r)
```

Another is to pair up the arguments, into a single tuple argument, as in

```
cylinderV' :: (num, num) -> num
cylinderV' (h,r) = volume h (areaofcircle r)
```

You might think that the difference is trivial, but for Miranda they are quite different functions, with different types and different notation (the second must have its parentheses and comma).

To understand the difference properly, you must realize that the first type, `num -> num -> num`, is actually shorthand for `num -> (num -> num)`; `cylinderV` is really a function of one argument (h), and the result of applying it, `cylinderV h`, is *another function*, of type `num -> num`. `cylinderV h r` is another shorthand, this time for `(cylinderV h) r`, that is, the result of applying the *function* `cylinderV h` to an argument r.

This simple device for enabling multi-argument functions to be defined without the use of tuples is called *currying* (named in honour of the mathematician Haskell Curry). Therefore, multi-argument functions such as `cylinderV` are said to be *curried* functions. `cylinderV` is the curried version of `cylinderV'`.

Partial application

One advantage of currying is that it allows a simpler syntax by reducing the number of parentheses (and commas) needed when defining multi-argument functions. But the most important advantage of currying is that a curried function does not have to be applied to all of its arguments at once. Curried functions can be *partially applied* yielding a function which requires fewer arguments.

For example, the expression (cylinderV 7) is a perfectly well-formed expression which is a partial application of the function cylinderV. This expression is an anonymous function (that is, a function without a name) which maps a number to another number. Once this expression is applied to some argument, say r, then a number is returned which is the volume of a cylinder of height 7 and base radius of r.

Partial application is extremely convenient since it enables the creation of new functions which are specializations of existing functions. For example, if we now require a function, volume_cylinder100, which computes the volume of a cylinder of height 100 when given the radius of the base, this function can be defined in the usual way:

```
volume_cylinder100 :: num -> num
volume_cylinder100 radius  =  cylinderV 100 radius
```

However, the same function can be written more concisely as

```
volume_cylinder100 =  cylinderV 100
```

or indeed we may not even define it as a separate function but just use the expression (cylinderV 100) in its place whenever needed.

Even more importantly, a partial application can also be used as an actual parameter to another function. This will become clear when we discuss higher-order functions in Chapter 8.

Order of association

For currying to work properly we require function application to 'associate to the left': for example, smaller x y means (smaller x) y not smaller (x y).

Also, in order to reduce the number of parentheses required in type declarations the function type operator -> associates to the *right*. Thus num -> num -> num means num -> (num -> num) and not (num -> num) -> num. You should by now be well used to omitting these parentheses, but as always, you should put them in any cases where you are in doubt.

Partial application of predefined operators

Any curried function can be partially applied, be it a user-defined function or a predefined operator or function. Similarly, primitive infix operators can also be partially applied. We have seen how parenthesized operators can be used just like ordinary prefix functions in expressions. This notational device is extended in Miranda to partial application by allowing an argument to be also enclosed along with the operator (see Figure 7.1). For example,

```
(1/)    is the 'reciprocal'  function
(/2)      ,    'halving'       ,
(^3)      ,    'cubing'        ,
(+1)      ,    'successor'     ,
(!0)      ,    'head'          ,
```

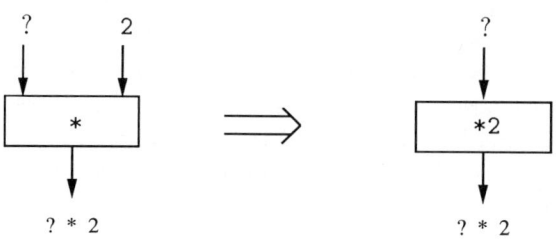

Figure 7.1

These forms can be regarded as the analogue of currying for infix operators. They are a minor syntactic convenience, since all the above functions can be explicitly defined. Note that there is one exception which applies to the use of the minus operator. (-x) is always interpreted by the evaluator as being an application of unary minus operator. Should the programmer want a function which subtracts x from numbers then a function must be defined explicitly.

More examples of such partial applications are given in Chapter 8, where simple higher-order functions are discussed.

7.4 Types

As we have seen from Chapter 4, expressions and their subexpressions all have types associated with them.

expression of type: **num**
3 * 4

operand of type: **num**   operand of type: **num**

function of type: **num -> (num -> num)**

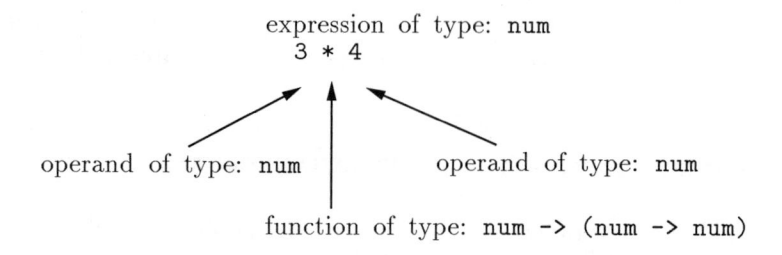

Figure 7.2

There are *basic* or primitive types (**num**, **bool** and **char**) whose values are built-into the evaluator. There are also *compound* types whose values are constructed from those of other types. For example,

- tuples of types,
- function types (that is, from one given type to another),
- lists of a given type.

Each type has associated with it certain operations which are not meaningful for other types. For example, one cannot sensibly add a number to a list or concatenate two functions.

Strong typing

Functional languages are *strongly typed*, that is, every well-formed expression can be assigned a type that can be deduced from its subexpressions alone. Thus any expression which cannot be assigned a sensible type (that is, is not well-formed) has no value and is regarded as illegal and is rejected by Miranda before evaluation. Strong typing does not require the explicit type declaration of functions. The types can be inferred automatically by the evaluator.

There are two stages of analysis when a program is submitted for evaluation: first the *syntax analysis* picks up 'grammatical' errors such as [1,)2((]; and if there are no syntax errors then the *type analysis* checks that the expressions have sensible types, picking up errors such as 9 ++ True. Before evaluation, the program or expression must pass both stages. A large number of programming errors are due to functions being applied to arguments of the wrong type. Thus one advantage of strong typing is that type errors can be trapped by the type checker prior to program execution. Strong typing also helps in the design of clear and well-structured programs. There are also advantages with respect to the efficiency of the implementation of the language. For example, because all expressions are strongly typed, the operator + knows at run-time that both its arguments are numeric it need not perform any run-time checks.

Type polymorphism

As we have already seen with a number of list functions, some functions have very general argument or result types. For example,
id x = x
The function id maps every member of the source type to itself. Its type is therefore * -> * for some suitable type *. But * suits every type since the definition does not require any particular properties from the elements of *. Such general types are said to be *generic* or *polymorphic* (many-formed) types

and can be represented by *type variables*. In Miranda there is an alphabet of type variables, written `*`, `**`, `***`, etc., each of which stands for an arbitrary type. Therefore, `id` can be declared as follows:

`id :: * -> *`

Like other kinds of variables, a type variable can be instantiated to different types in different circumstances. The expression (`id 8`) is well-formed and has type `num` because `num` can be substituted for `*` in the type of `id`. Similarly, (`id double`) is well-formed and has type `num -> num`. Similarly, (`id id`) is well-formed and has type `* -> *` because the type (`* -> *`) can be substituted for `*`. Thus, again like other kinds of variables, type-variables are instantiated consistently throughout a single function application. The following are some more examples:

```
sillysix :: * -> num
sillysix x = 6
second :: * -> ** -> **
second x y = y
```

Notice that in a type expression all occurrences of the same type variable (for example, `**`) refer to *the same* unknown type at every occurrence.

Example — comparison operators

The comparison operators `=`, `<`, `<=`, and so on, are all polymorphic: the two values being compared must be of the same type, but it does not matter what that type is. Each operator has type `* -> * -> bool`.

Having said that, not all choices of `*` are equally sensible. `id :: * -> *` is polymorphic because it genuinely does not care what type its argument is — the algorithm is always the same. The comparisons, on the other hand, have to use different algorithms for different types (such polymorphism is often called *ad hoc*). The following are the *ad hoc* methods used.

- On `num`, the comparisons are numeric in the standard way.
- On `bool`, `False < True`.
- On `char`, the comparisons are determined by the ASCII codes for characters. For instance, `'a' < 'p'` because `'a'` comes before `'p'` in the ASCII table.
- On list types `[*]`, comparisons use the lexicographic, or 'alphabetical' ordering. It does not work only with lists of type `[char]`. For instance, with lists of numbers the same idea tells you that

    $[1] < [1,0] < [1,5] < [3] < [3,0]$

- On tuple types, comparisons are similar. For instance, for pairs,

    $(a,b) < (c,d)$ iff $(a < c) \vee ((a = c) \wedge (b < d))$

- On function types, no comparisons are possible. (Consider, for example, the problems of computing f = g, that is, $\forall x.\ f\ x\ =\ g\ x$.)

Example — the empty list

As we have seen before, the empty list [] has type [*]. Being used in a particular expression may force [] to have more refined (specific) type. For instance, in [[],[1]], [] must have type [num] to match that of [1].

Type synonyms

Although it is a good idea to declare the type of all functions that we define, it is sometimes inconvenient, or at least uninformative, to spell out the types in terms of basic types. For such cases type synonyms can be used to give more meaningful names. For example,

```
name     == [char]
parents  == (name, name)
age      == num
weight   == num
date     == (num, [char], num)
```

A type synonym declaration does not introduce a new type, it simply attaches a name to a type expression. You can then use the synonym in place of the type expression wherever you want to. The special symbol == is used in the declaration of type synonyms; this avoids confusion with a value definition. Type synonyms can make type declaration of functions shorter and can help in understanding what the function does. For example,

databaseLookup :: name -> database -> parents

Type synonyms can *not* be recursive. Every synonym must be expressible in terms of existing types. In fact should the program contain type errors the type error messages will be expressed in terms of the names of the existing types and not the type synonyms.

Type synonyms can also be *generic* in that they can be parameterized by type variables. For example, consider the following type synonym declaration:

binop * == * -> * -> *

Thus binop num can be used as shorthand for num -> num -> num, for example,

smaller, cylinderV :: binop num

7.5 Enumerated types

We can define some simple types by explicit enumeration of their values (that is, explicitly *naming* every value). For example,

```
day        ::= Mon | Tue | Wed | Thu | Fri | Sat | Sun
direction  ::= North | South | East | West
switch     ::= On | Off
bool       ::= False | True         ||predefined
```

Note that the names of these values all begin with upper case letters. This is a rule of Miranda. Values of enumerated type are ordered by the position in which they appear in the enumeration, for instance

```
Mon < Tue < ...
```

These are easily used with pattern matching. For instance, suppose a point on the plane is given by two Cartesian coordinates

```
point == (num, num)
```

A function to move a point in some direction can be defined by

```
move :: direction -> num -> point -> point
move North d (x,y) = (x,y+d)
move South d (x,y) = (x,y-d)
move East  d (x,y) = (x+d,y)
move West  d (x,y) = (x-d,y)
```

It is possible to code these values as numbers, and indeed in some programming languages that is the only option. However, this is prone to error, as the coding is completely artificial — there is no natural way of associating numerical values with (for example) days of the week, so you are at risk of forgetting whether day 1 was supposed to be Sunday or Monday. A single lapse will introduce errors into your program. With enumerated types you do not have to remember such coding details, and, also, the strong typing guards against meaningless errors such as trying to add together two days of the week.

7.6 User-defined constructors

Recall the idea of constructors — 'packaging together several values in a distinctive wrapper'. The main examples that you have seen so far have been *cons* and tupling, but there are ways of defining your own.

User-defined constructors 101

You have just seen the simplest examples! Each value (for example, `Mon`, `Tue`, `Wed`, etc.) in an enumerated type is a trivial, 'nullary' constructor that is nothing but the distinctive wrapper — no values packaged inside. (You may remember that the empty list could be considered like this.) It is also easy to define non-trivial constructors.

For example, we can define a new datatype `distance` to express the fact that distances may be measured by different units. The subsequent definition of `addDistances` is designed to eliminate the possibility of a programmer attempting to mix operations on distances of different kinds. Note again that constructor names in Miranda must start with upper case letters:

```
distance ::= Mile num | Km num | NautMile num

addDistances :: distance -> distance -> distance
addDistances (Mile x) (Mile y) = Mile (x+y)
addDistances (Km x) (Km y) = Km (x+y)
addDistances (NautMile x) (NautMile y) = NautMile (x+y)
addDistances x y = error "different units of measurement!"
```

In this way it is guaranteed that adding distances of different measurement units (or attempting to multiply, divide or subtract two distances) is not performed accidentally. This is because the predefined arithmetic operators will not operate on any datatype other than `num`. Therefore, programmers are forced to think carefully about their intentions and are helped to avoid mistakes by the type checker. This style of programming is clearly much better than simply using `num`s to represent all three kinds of distance. The constructor functions (`Mile`, `Km` and `NautMile`) are essential in the datatype definitions, for otherwise there will be no way of, say, determining whether 6 has type `num` or `distance`.

Notice that the type `bool` need not be considered as primitive. It can be defined by two nullary constructors `True` and `False` (both of type `bool`). Similarly, one may argue that type `char` can also be defined using nullary constructors `Ascii0...Ascii127`. But characters, like numbers and lists, are more of a special case as they require a different, non-standard naming and printing convention.

Another example is that of *union types*. Suppose, for instance, you have mixed data, some numeric and some textual. You can use constructors to say what sort each item of data is, by

```
data ::= Numeric num | Text [char]
```

The following is an example with 2-argument constructors, representing a complex number by either Cartesian or polar coordinates:

```
complex ::= Cart num num | Polar num num

multiply :: complex -> complex -> complex
multiply (Cart u v) (Cart x y) = Cart (u*x - v*y) (u*y + v*x)
multiply (Polar r theta) (Polar s psi) = Polar (r*s) (theta+psi)
|| and two more cases for mixed coordinates
```

Finally, it is also possible to have polymorphic constructors. A standard example is pairing. Of course, this is already built into Miranda with its own special notation (-,-), but just to illustrate the technique we can define it in a do-it-yourself way:

```
diypair * ** ::= Pair * **
```

For instance, `Pair 10 [True]` (our do-it-yourself version of `(10,[True])`) has type `diypair num [bool]`. A new type can have one or more constructors. Each constructor may have zero or more fields/arguments of any type at all (including the type of the object returned by the constructor). The constructor itself also has a type, usually a function type. So *Pair* has type `* -> ** -> (diypair * **)`.

The number of fields taken by a constructor is called its *arity*, hence a constructor of arity zero is called a *nullary* constructor. Constructors (like other values) can appear in lists, tuples and definitions. Just as with ordinary functions, constructor names must also be unique. Unlike ordinary functions, constructor names must begin with a capital letter. Constructors are notionally 'applied' just like ordinary functions. However, two key properties distinguish constructors from other functions:

1. They have no rules (that is, definitions) and their application cannot be further reduced.
2. Unlike ordinary functions they can appear as patterns on the left-hand side of definitions.

It is always possible to define 'selector' functions for picking the components of such data types, but in practice, like `fst` and `snd` for pairs, this is not necessary. Pattern matching can be used instead.

7.7 Recursively defined types

The greatest power comes from the ability to use recursion in a type definition. To illustrate the principle let us define do-it-yourself lists. These really are lists implemented in the same way as Miranda itself uses, but without the notational convenience of : and the square brackets. Instead, there are explicit constructors *Emptylist* and *Cons*, and for our do-it-yourself version of [*] we write

```
diylist * ::= Emptylist | Cons * (diylist *)
```

The 'recursive call' here (of `diylist *`) is really no more of a problem than it would be in a function definition, as you should understand from your experience with lists.

The following is another do-it-yourself type, this time without polymorphism. It is for natural numbers:
diynat ::= Zero | Suc diynat
The idea is that every natural number is either (and in a unique way) Zero or 'the successor of' (one plus) another natural number, and can be represented uniquely as Zero with some number of Sucs applied to it. For instance, 5 is represented as
Suc (Suc (Suc (Suc (Suc Zero))))
It is no accident that the two examples given here are exactly the types for which you have seen induction principles: the induction is closely bound up with the recursion in the definition, and generalizes to other datatypes. We will explore this more carefully after looking at a datatype that does not just replicate standard Miranda.

Trees

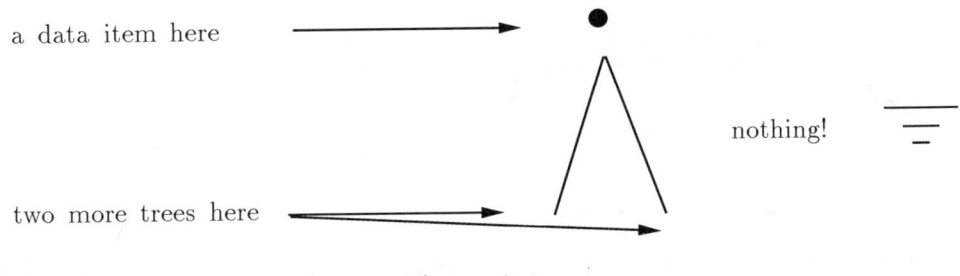

Figure 7.3

By 'tree' here, we mean some branching framework within which data can be stored. In its greatest generality, each *node* (branching point) can hold some data and have branches hanging off it (computer trees grow down!); and each branch will lead down to another node. Also, branches do not rejoin lower down — you never get a node that is at the *bottom* of two different branches. To refer to the tree as a whole you just refer to its top node, because all the rest can be accessed by following the branches down.

We are going to look at a particularly simple kind in which there are only two kinds of nodes:

- a 'tree' node has an item of data and two branches.
- a 'leaf' node has no data and no branches.

These will correspond to two constructors: the first, Node, packages together data and two trees and the second, Emptytree, packages together nothing:

104 *Types*

```
tree * ::= Emptytree | Node (tree *) * (tree *)
where * is the type of the data items.
```

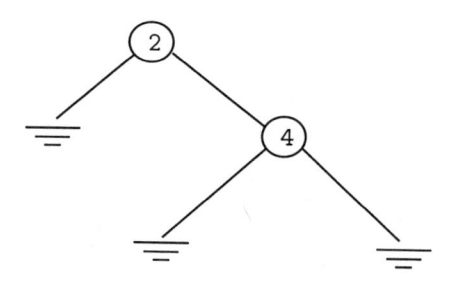

Node Emptytree 2 (Node Emptytree 4 Emptytree)

Figure 7.4

As an example (see Figure 7.4), let us look at ordered trees. Orderedness is defined as follows. First, Emptytree is ordered. Second, Node t_1 x t_2 is ordered iff

- t_1 and t_2 are both ordered;
- the node values in t_1 are all $\leq x$ (let us say 'x is an upper bound for t_1');
- the node values in t_2 are all $\geq x$ ('x is a lower bound for t_2').

Ordered trees are very useful as storage structures, storing data items (of type *) as the 'x' components of Nodes. This is because to check whether y is stored in Node t_1 x t_2, you do not have to search the whole tree. If $y = x$ then you have already found it; if $y < x$ you only need to check t_1; and if $y > x$ you check t_2.

Hence lookup is very quick, but there is a price: when you insert a new value, you must ensure that the updated tree is still ordered. The following is a function to do this. Notice that we have fallen far short of a formal logical account; there is a lot of English. But we have at least given a reasoned account of what we are trying to do and how we are doing it, so it can be considered fairly rigorous:

```
insertT :: * -> (tree *) -> (tree *)
||pre:  t is ordered
||post: insertT n  t is ordered, and its node
||      values are those of t together with n.

insertT n  Emptytree = Node Emptytree n Emptytree
insertT n (Node t1  x t2)
    = Node (insertT n t1) x t2,    if n <= x
    = Node t1  x (insertT n t2),   otherwise
```

Proposition 7.1 The definition of insertT satisfies its specification.

Proof If t is ordered, we must show that insertT $n\ t$ then terminates giving a result that satisfies the post-condition. We shall use the usual 'circular reasoning' technique, but note that it remains to be justified because we have not given a recursion variant. We shall discuss this afterwards.

If t = Emptytree (which is ordered), then insertT n Emptytree terminates immediately, giving result Node Emptytree n Emptytree. This is ordered, and its node values are those of Emptytree (none) together with n, as required.

Now suppose that t = Node $t_1\ x\ t_2$, and assume that the recursive calls work correctly. Since t is ordered, so, too, are t_1 and t_2, so the pre-conditions for the recursive calls hold. There are two cases, as follows:

Case 1, $n \leq x$: insertT $n\ t$ terminates, giving result r (say) = Node (insertT $n\ t_1$) $x\ t_2$. From the recursive post-condition, insertT $n\ t_1$ is ordered, and its node values are those of t_1 together with n. Hence the node values of r are those of t_1, n, x and those of t_2: that is, those of t together with n, as required.

Also, r is ordered, for the following reasons. insertT $n\ t_1$ and t_2 are both ordered, and x is a lower bound for t_2 because t is ordered.
x is also an upper bound for insertT $n\ t_1$ because the node values are those of t_1 (for which x is an upper bound because t is ordered) together with n (and $x \geq n$ because we are looking at that case).

Case 2, $n > x$, is similar. □

As promised, we must justify the circular reasoning, and the obvious way is to find a recursion variant. We will show how to do this, but let us stress right away that the technique that we are actually going to recommend is slightly different, and that the calculation of a recursion variant is just to give you a feel for how it works.

The recursion variant technique is really a partial substitute for induction. It is not always applicable, but when it is applicable it is very convenient and smooth and the idea is to make it as streamlined as possible. What we shall see in a while is that you should try to think of *the tree itself* as a kind of recursion variant, 'decreasing' in the recursive calls from Node $t_1\ x\ t_2$ to either

t_1 or t_2, and that it is really unnecessary to convert it to a natural number for the standard sort of recursion variant that you have already seen. But to make this idea clearer we shall first go through the unstreamlined reasoning.

We shall define a function `treesize` of type `tree * -> num`, with no pre-conditions, satisfying the properties

$$\text{treesize } t_1 < \text{treesize (Node } t_1 \ x \ t_2)$$
$$\text{treesize } t_2 < \text{treesize (Node } t_1 \ x \ t_2)$$

Then `treesize` t is a recursion variant for `insertT` n t.

```
treesize::(tree *) -> num
treesize Emptytree = 1
treesize (Node t1 x t2)
    = (treesize t1) + 1 + (treesize t2)
```

But how do we know that `treesize` t always terminates? Well, it does not! You can define infinite trees just as easily as infinite lists (for example, $t = \text{Node } t \ 0 \ t$), and for them `treesize` does not terminate. So we have only actually shown that `insertT` n t works for *finite* trees t, those for which `treesize` t gives a result. Strictly speaking, we should state the finiteness as a pre-condition for `insertT`, but just as for lists we will leave it implicit.

Now it is important not to see `treesize` as a clever trick cooked up specially for `insertT`. It works equally well for *any* function of trees whose recursive calls are on the left or right subtrees of the main argument, and this is by far the most common pattern.

What is more, the numerical value of `treesize` t is not in itself very important — there are many other functions satisfying the specification of `treesize`, all serving just as well. What you should see in the specification is the idea of the tree itself 'decreasing' to a subtree, and hence serving as a recursion variant:

$$t_1\text{'} <\text{'Node } t_1 \ x \ t_2 \text{ and}$$
$$t_2\text{'} <\text{'Node } t_1 x \ t_2$$

This kind of '<' is explored more mathematically in Appendix A, which in particular looks at what properties of '<' are needed; but for the present it is enough to remember that it gives a more general kind of recursion variant. If you are unsure about this you could always use `treesize`, but we prefer you to use the *structural induction* that is described in the following section.

7.8 Structural induction

The real purpose of this section is to show how to introduce new induction principles for recursively defined datatypes (such as `tree *`), although we are going to start off with non-recursive types that do not lead to induction. The key idea is to see a direct link between the type definition and the box proof structure of induction (and also, though we are not going to discuss it so much in this section, function definitions).

Type definition	Induction proofs	Function definitions
constructors	boxes	cases
arguments of constructor	new constants in box	variables matched in pattern
recursion	induction hypotheses	recursion

This should become clearer with the examples. We start off with a couple of non-inductive ones.

- The first example illustrates the first line only of the above table: it has four constructors (without arguments) and four corresponding boxes.
  direction ::= North | South | East | West

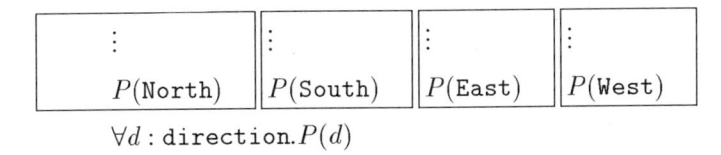

$\vdots$	$\vdots$	$\vdots$	$\vdots$
$P(\mathtt{North})$	$P(\mathtt{South})$	$P(\mathtt{East})$	$P(\mathtt{West})$

  $$\forall d : \mathtt{direction}.P(d)$$

  This is really nothing more than ∀-introduction (see Chapter 17) and ∨-elimination (Chapter 16) based on an axiom

  $$\forall d : \mathtt{direction}.(d = \mathtt{North} \vee d = \mathtt{South} \vee d = \mathtt{East} \vee d = \mathtt{West})$$

  The boxes given above are a streamlined version setting out what is needed to complete the proof (exercise — show how this works).

- The second example moves on to the second line of the table, bringing in constructors with arguments:
  distance ::= Mile num | Km num | NautMile num

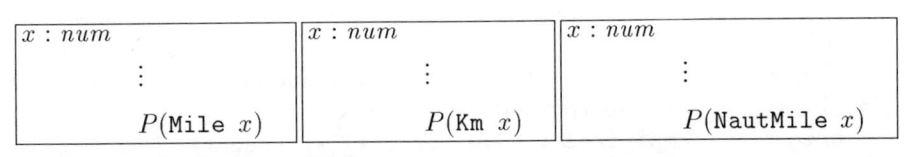

$x : num$	$x : num$	$x : num$
$\vdots$	$\vdots$	$\vdots$
$P(\mathtt{Mile}\ x)$	$P(\mathtt{Km}\ x)$	$P(\mathtt{NautMile}\ x)$

  $$\forall d : distance.\ P(d)$$

  Again (exercise) this is no more than you would obtain from logic, using ∀-introduction, ∨- and ∃-elimination Chapters 16 and 17, and an axiom

  $$\forall d : \mathtt{distance}.\ ((\exists x : \mathtt{num}.\ d = \mathtt{Mile}\ x) \\ \vee (\exists x : \mathtt{num}.\ d = \mathtt{Km}\ x) \vee (\exists x : \mathtt{num}.\ d = \mathtt{NautMile}\ x))$$

- Natural numbers (and simple induction):

```
diynat ::= Zero | Suc diynat
```

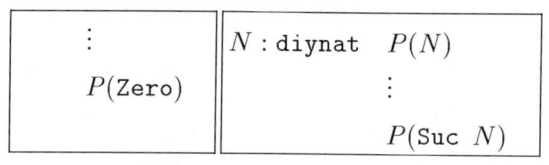

$$\frac{\vdots}{P(\text{Zero})} \qquad \frac{N : \texttt{diynat} \quad P(N)}{\vdots \\ P(\texttt{Suc } N)}$$

$$\forall n : \texttt{diynat}. P(n)$$

This is exactly the simple induction you know already, but translated into the notation for the do-it-yourself natural numbers.

Now because there is recursion in the definition of `diynat`, we have the inductive hypothesis $P(N)$, and that takes this example beyond mere logic. You could not justify the induction hypothesis solely from an axiom such as

$$\forall n : \texttt{diynat}. \, (n = \texttt{Zero} \lor \exists m : \texttt{diynat}. \, n = \texttt{Suc } m)$$

so the induction hypothesis is a free gift. (It is not completely free. The cost is the restriction to *finite* natural numbers, even though Miranda can cope with some infinite ones.)

- Lists:
```
diylist * ::= Emptylist | Cons * (diylist *)
```

$$\frac{\vdots}{P(\texttt{Emptylist})} \qquad \frac{X : * \quad XS : \texttt{diylist } * \quad P(XS)}{\vdots \\ P(\texttt{Cons } X \, XS)}$$

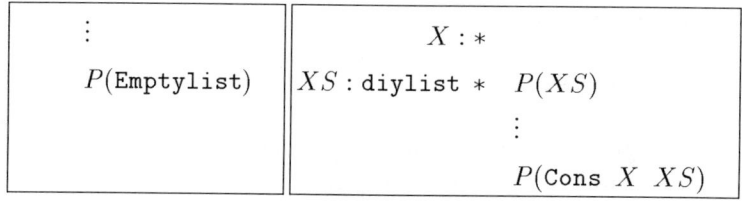

$$\forall xs : \texttt{diylist } *. P(xs)$$

Again, this is just a familiar (list) induction translated into the do-it-yourself notation.

Notice how because `cons` has two arguments, there are two new constants X and XS in the proof box. But only its second argument is recursively of type `diylist` *, so there is only one induction hypothesis, $P(XS)$.

- Finally, we come to tree induction:
```
tree * ::= Emptytree | Node (tree *) * (tree *)
```

$$\frac{\vdots}{P(\texttt{Emptytree})} \qquad \frac{t_1 : \texttt{tree } * \quad P(t_1) \\ x : * \\ t_2 : \texttt{tree } * \quad P(t_2)}{\vdots \\ P(\texttt{Node } t_1 \, x \, t_2)}$$

$$\forall t : \texttt{tree } *. P(t)$$

This is an entirely new induction principle! It says that to prove $\forall t : tree * [P(t)]$, it suffices to prove

- a base case, $P(\texttt{Emptytree})$;
- an induction step, $P(\texttt{Node } t_1 \ x \ t_2)$, assuming that $P(t_1)$ and $P(t_2)$ both hold (two induction hypotheses).

(All this is subject to the usual proviso, that it only works for finite trees — in Miranda, infinite trees are just as easy to define as infinite lists.)

Is this induction principle really valid? As it happens, it is, and it is justified in Exercise 25. But it is not so important to understand the justification as the pattern of turning a datatype definition into an induction principle.

The following is an application. (The specifications are not given formally, but you can give informal proofs that the definitions satisfy the informal specifications.)

```
flatten :: (tree *) -> [*]
||pre:  none
||post: the elements of flatten t are exactly the node values of t
flatten Emptytree = []
flatten (Node t1 x t2) = (flatten t1) ++ (x:(flatten t2))

revtree :: (tree *) -> (tree *)
||pre:  none
||post: revtree t is t "seen in a mirror"
||      (with left and right reversed)
revtree Emptytree = Emptytree
revtree (Node t1 x t2) = Node (revtree t2) x (revtree t1)
```

We can use tree induction to prove that

$\quad \forall t : tree \ *.\ $ `flatten (revtree ` t`)` $=$ `reverse(flatten ` t`)`

base case: Emptytree

$\quad$ `flatten (revtree Emptytree)` $=$ `flatten Emptytree`
$\qquad\qquad\qquad\qquad\qquad\qquad\quad = $ `[]`
$\qquad\qquad\qquad\qquad\qquad\qquad\quad = $ `reverse []`
$\qquad\qquad\qquad\qquad\qquad\qquad\quad = $ `reverse (flatten Emptytree)`

induction step: Node $t_1 \ x \ t_2$

$\quad$ `flatten (revtree (Node ` $t_1 \ x \ t_2$`))`
$\quad = $ `flatten (Node (revtree ` t_2`) ` x ` (revtree ` t_1`))`
$\quad = $ `(flatten (revtree ` t_2`))++(` x `: (flatten (revtree ` t_1`)))`
$\quad = $ `(reverse(flatten ` t_2`))++[` x `]++(reverse(flatten ` t_1`))` $\qquad$ induction

$$= \text{reverse}((\text{flatten } t_1)\text{++}[x]\text{++}(\text{flatten } t_2))$$
$$= \text{reverse}(\text{flatten } (\text{Node } t_1 \ x \ l_2))$$

The pattern works for *any* datatype `newtype` that is defined using constructors. The key points to remember are

- There is a box for each constructor.
- Within a box, there is a new constant introduced for each argument of the corresponding constructor.
- There is an induction hypothesis for each argument whose type is `newtype` used recursively.
- The property proved inductively is proved only for *finite* values of `newtype`.
- *Base cases* are those boxes with no induction hypotheses; *induction steps* are those with at least one induction hypothesis.
- The method can be extended to *mutually* recursive types, each defined using the others. Then you need separate properties for the different types and you prove them all together, using induction hypotheses where there is any kind of recursion.

We will describe the general principles, though to be honest you may see these more clearly from the examples already given.

Each alternative in a type definition corresponds to a box in the proof, so let us concentrate on one alternative:

`thing ::= ... | A s1 ... sn | ...`

A is a constructor, it has n arguments, and they are of types $s_1, \ldots, s_n$. *Some* of these types may be `thing` again, using recursion. They will give induction hypotheses:

$x_1 : s_1$

$\vdots$

$x_n : s_n$

$\quad P(x_i)$

$\quad P(x_j)$

$\quad \vdots$

$\quad P(\text{A } x_1 \cdots x_n)$

$\forall x : \text{thing}. \ P(x)$

Recursion variants

Whenever a type `newtype` is defined using constructors, there is a natural format for recursively defined functions on `newtype`, using pattern matching: for each constructor you have a separate case with a pattern to extract the arguments of the constructor, and the arguments of type `newtype` will be used as arguments for the recursive calls of the function.

As long as you keep to this format, and also as long as you restrict yourself to finite elements of `newtype`, the 'circular reasoning' will be valid and you will not need to define a recursion variant.

What is happening in effect is that the argument of type `newtype` is itself being used as a recursion variant, 'decreasing' to one of its components. This can be justified by defining a numerical recursion variant of type `newtype -> num` that counts the number of constructors used for values of `newtype`. It can also be justified using the structural induction just described.

7.9 Summary

- One way of combining types to form new ones is to form a *tuple*-type (for example, a pair, or a triple or a quadruple). Tuple-values are formed by using the constructor (,...,).
- Using tuples, functions can return more than one result by packaging their results into a single tuple.
- A *pattern* serves two purposes. Firstly it specifies the form that arguments must take before the rule can be applied; secondly it decomposes the arguments and names their components.
- Multi-argument functions (also called *curried* functions) are functions which take more than one argument (as opposed to those functions which operate on a single argument such as a tuple).
- An advantage of currying is that a curried function does not have to be applied to all of its arguments at once. Curried functions can be *partially applied*, yielding a function which is of fewer arguments.
- Every expression has a type associated with it and each type has associated with it a set of operations which are meaningful for that type.
- Functional languages are *strongly-typed*, that is, every well-formed expression can be assigned a type that can be deduced from its subexpressions alone. Any expression which cannot be assigned a sensible type (that is, is not well-typed) has no value and is rejected before evaluation.
- *Generic* or *polymorphic* (many-formed) types are represented using *type variables* *, **, *** etc., each of which stands for an arbitrary type.

Within a given type expression, all occurrences of the same type variable refer to *the same* unknown type.
- You can define a type by listing the alternative forms of its values (separated by |). Each alternative form is a constructor (whose name begins with a capital letter) applied to some number of arguments. It represents 'the arguments packaged together in a wrapper that is clearly marked with the constructor's name'.
- This method subsumes the ideas of enumerated types, union types and recursively defined types (such as trees).
- The type definition determines both a natural format for recursive definitions of functions taking arguments from the type, and an induction principle for proving properties of values of the type.
- If you restrict yourself to using the 'natural format of recursive definitions' then you can use 'circular reasoning' just as though you had a recursion variant.
- Miranda allows infinite values of the new types. The methods here apply only to the finite values.

7.10 Exercises

1. What are the types of +, ->, -, ++, #, !, >=, =, hd and tl?
2. Prove by induction on xs_1 that zip satisfies

    $$\forall xs_1, xs_2 : [\,*\,].\forall ys_1, ys_2 : [\,*\,*\,].(\#xs_1 = \#ys_1 \wedge \#xs_2 = \#ys_2 \rightarrow$$
    $$\text{zip } (xs_1\text{++}xs_2)\ (ys_1\text{++}ys_2) = (\text{zip } xs_1\ ys_1)\text{++}(\text{zip } xs_2\ ys_2))$$

3. Prove by induction on xs that unzip satisfies its specification, namely that

    $$\forall xs : [\,*\,].\forall ys : [\,*\,*\,].(\#xs = \#ys \rightarrow \text{unzip}(\text{zip } xs\ ys) = (xs, ys))$$

4. (a) Explain why the expression zip (unzip ps) is not well-typed. Can you make it well-typed by redefining zip?

    (b) Prove by induction on ps that

    $$\forall ps : [(*, **)].\forall xs : [\,*\,]\forall ys : [\,*\,*\,].$$
    $$(\text{unzip } ps = (xs, ys) \rightarrow \text{zip } xs\ ys = ps)$$

    (NOTE: box proofs will help you, but you will need to use a little extra thought to deal with the pattern matching.)

5. Let P be a property of elements of type *, and consider a function separate_P specified as follows. (How it is defined will depend on P.)

```
separate_P :: [*] -> ([*], [*])
||pre:  none
||post: (A)x:* ((isin(x,Ps) -> P(x))
||             & (isin(x,notPs) -> not P(x)))
||      & Merge(Ps,notPs,zs)
||          where (Ps,notPs) = separate_P zs
```

separate_P is supposed to 'demerge' the elements of zs into those satisfying P and those not.

Prove that this specification specifies the result uniquely.

6. (a) Recall the function scrub of Exercise 10, Chapter 6. Show that scrub satisfies the following specification:

```
scrub :: * -> [*] -> [*]
||pre:  none
||post: (E)xs:[*] (xs, scrub x ys) = separate_P ys
||          where (given x) P(u) is the property u = x.
```

(b) Specify count in a similar way.

(c) Use the uniqueness property of the specification of separate_P to prove some of the properties of scrub and count given in the exercises in Chapter 6.

7. Suppose that the names of the employees of a Department of Computing are stored as a list of pairs, for example

[("Broda","Krysia"),("Eisenbach","Susan"),
("Khoshnevisan","Hessam"),("Vickers","Steve")]

Declare and define a function display which, given the current staff list, will return a string in the following format:

K. Broda

S. Eisenbach

H. Khoshnevisan

S. Vickers

Assume that everyone has exactly one forename.

8. Define and declare the type of a function that, given any triple whose first component is a pair, returns the second component of that pair.

9. Give an example of an expression (that is, just *one* expression) that contains two occurrences of the empty list, the first occurrence having type [num] and the second type [char].

10. Discuss whether the expression smaller (quotrem (7,3)) is well-formed or not. If not explain why.

11. Given the data type tree num write a function tmax which finds the maximum element stored in a non-empty tree. (HINT: you may use a

function `largest` which returns the largest of three numbers.)

12. Define a data type `tree2_3` in which a value is either `Empty` or is a node which holds an item and has left and right subtrees, or is a node which holds two items and has a left, middle and a right subtree. All subtrees are of type `tree2_3` and all items stored in the tree have the same type.

13. For the sake of this question, take an *expression* in the variable x to be either

    - a number, for example 1
    - a variable (any character),
    - or the sum, difference or product of two expressions.

    Below is the definition of a type *expression* in Miranda using data constructors. It is recursive in that an expression can contain other expressions:
    ```
    expr::= Number num | Variable char |
            Sum expr expr |
            Difference expr expr |
            Product expr expr
    ```
    The rules for partial differentiation of simple expressions with respect to x are

    $\frac{\partial n}{\partial x} = 0$ — where n is a number

    $\frac{\partial x}{\partial x} = 1$

    $\frac{\partial y}{\partial x} = 0$ — if y is different from x

    $\frac{\partial (E_1+E_2)}{\partial x} = \frac{\partial E_1}{\partial x} + \frac{\partial E_2}{\partial x}$ — where E_1, E_2 are *any* exprs

    $\frac{\partial (E_1-E_2)}{\partial x} = \frac{\partial E_1}{\partial x} - \frac{\partial E_2}{\partial x}$

    $\frac{\partial (E_1 \times E_2)}{\partial x} = \frac{\partial E_1}{\partial x} \times E_2 + E_1 \times \frac{\partial E_2}{\partial x}$

    Define a function `differentiate` of type `char -> expr -> expr` that will perform these differentiation rules, `differentiate x e` representing $\frac{\partial e}{\partial x}$. For example,

    ```
    differentiate x (Sum e1 e2)   =
        Sum (differentiate x e1) (differentiate x e2)
    ```

    ```
    differentiate x (Number n) = Number 0
    ```

14. Show that any application of your function `differentiate` will terminate.

How might you write a simplify function to reduce such expressions to a simpler form? For example, simplifying a multiplication by 0 would result in replacing $0 \times x$ and $x \times 0$ by 0.

15. Give specifications (pre-conditions and post-conditions) in logic for the following programs.

    (a) last :: [*] -> * ; returns the last element of a list.

    (b) front :: num -> [*] -> [*] ; front n xs returns the list of the first n elements of xs if n ≤ #xs, otherwise it returns xs.

    (c) make_unique :: [*] -> [*]; make_unique xs removes the duplicates in xs. The elements need not be in the same order as in xs.

16. Define a function

    ```
    sub :: expr -> char -> expr -> expr
    ||pre:  none
    ||post: sub e1 v e2 = e2 with e1 substituted for every
    ||      occurrence of var v
    ```

    and use structural induction on e_1 to prove

    $\forall e_1, e_2, e_3 : \text{expr } \forall v : \text{char } (\text{sub } e_3\ v\ (\text{sub } e_2\ v\ e_1)$
    $= \text{sub}(\text{sub } e_3\ v\ e_2)\ v\ e_1)$

17. This exercise requires you to implement a series of Miranda functions which manage dictionarys stored as ordered binary trees. We define

    ```
    word == [char]
    dictionary ::= Empty | Node dictionary word dictionary
    ```

    Show that dictionary is equivalent to tree word. Write the following functions:

    (a) create_new_dictionary, which creates an empty dictionary.

    (b) add_word, which adds a word to a dictionary.

    (c) lookup, which returns whether a word is in the dictionary.

    (d) count_words, which returns the number of words in a dictionary.

    (e) delete_word, which deletes a word from a dictionary.

    (f) find_word, which returns the nth word in a dictionary, or returns an empty word if there is no nth word.

    (g) list_dictionary, which produces a list of all the words in a dictionary, one to a line. (Use a function such as flatten.)

18. Write coding and decoding functions for translating between *diynat* and ordinary natural numbers:

    ```
    numtonat :: num -> diynat
    nattonum :: diynat -> num
    ```

Prove that
$$\forall x : \texttt{num.nattonum(numtonat } x) = x$$
and
$$\forall n : \texttt{diynat.numtonat(nattonum } n) = n.$$

Also, write equivalents for `diynat` of the ordinary arithmetic operations and prove that they satisfy their specifications, for example,

```
add :: diynat -> diynat -> diynat
||pre:  none
||post: (nattonum (add m n))=(nattonum m)+ (nattonum n)
add Zero n=n || represents 0+n=n
add (Suc m)n= Suc (add m n) || represents (m+1)+n=(m+n)+1
```

19. Do something similar for `diylist *`.
20. Define a Miranda program to test whether a tree is ordered.
21. Specify and define a Miranda function to count how many times a given value occurs in a given ordered tree. Prove (informally but rigourously) that the definition satisfies the specification.
22. Use recursion to define some infinite trees.
23. Use `insertT` to define a function `build` to the following specification:

```
build :: [*] -> (tree *)
||pre: none
||post: build xs is ordered, and its node values are exactly
||      the elements of xs.
```

24. Show (you can use the method of 'trees as recursion variants') that if `t` is an ordered tree then `flatten t` is an ordered list.
    Hence show that the following definition satisfies the specification for sort (Chapter 6):

```
treesort :: [*] -> [*]
treesort xs = flatten (build xs)
```

25. Suppose $P(t)$ is a property of trees, and consider the following sentences:

$$Q \stackrel{\text{def}}{=} \forall t : (tree\ *).P(t)$$

$$R \stackrel{\text{def}}{=} \forall n : nat.\forall t : (tree\ *).(\texttt{treesize } t = n \to P(t))$$

Remember, as always, that we are talking only about *finite* trees.

(a) Use a box proof to show that $Q \leftrightarrow R$.

(b) Suppose you have a proof by tree induction of Q. Show how you can use its ingredients to create a proof by course of values induction of R. (Use the specification of `treesize`.)

Chapter 8

Higher-order functions

You have already seen examples of functions delivering functions as results, namely the curried functions. These were easy to understand as functions with more than one argument. Much more subtle are functions that take other functions as arguments — some examples from mathematics are differentiation and integration. These are called *higher-order* functions. The argument and result types of functions are *not* restricted to being values.

Differentiation takes one function, f, say, of type `num -> num`, and returns another, usually written f'. So there is a higher-order function `diff` of type `(num -> num) -> num -> num` such that

$$\text{diff } f \ x = f'(x) = \text{derivative of } f \text{ at } x$$

8.1 Higher-order programming

Consider the definitions in Figure 8.1. Although they define different functions, their *pattern of recursion* is the same. In all definitions a function `f` is applied to every element of a list, where `f` is `f x = x*x`, `f x = factorial x` and `f x = x mod 2 = 0` respectively.

It is possible to express such common patterns of recursion by a few higher-order functions. We begin by defining a higher-order function corresponding to the above three definitions and then discuss other patterns.

8.2 The higher-order function map

If `f` is a function of type `* -> **`, then the idea is to define a function `map f` of type `[*] -> [**]` that works by applying `f` one by one to all the elements of a list. This can be specified in an obvious way using indices. Since the first argument of `map` is a function `f`, `map` itself is a higher-order

118 Higher-order functions

```
squares          :: [num] -> [num]
||pre:           none
||post:          #ys = #xs
||               & (A) i:nat.(0 <= i< #xs->ys!i = (xs!i)^2)
||               where ys = squares xs
squares []     = []
squares (x:xs) = (x * x) : (squares xs)

factlist         :: [num] -> [num]
||pre:           none
||post:          #ys = #xs
||               & (A) i:nat. (0 <= i < #xs -> ys!i
||               = factorial(xs!i))
||               where ys = factlist xs
factlist []     = []
factlist (x:xs) = (factorial x) : (factlist xs)

iseven           :: [num] -> [bool]
||pre:           none
||post:          #ys = #xs
||               & (A) i:nat. (0 <= i < #xs ->
||               ys!i = (xs!i mod 2 = 0) )
||               where ys = iseven xs
iseven []     = []
iseven (x:xs) = (x mod 2 = 0) : (iseven xs)
```

Figure 8.1 Pattern of recursion

function.

In fact, the pattern of recursion expressed by `map` is so common in list-manipulating programs that `map` is *predefined* in many evaluators or is included in a library, for example as in Miranda.

```
map      :: (* -> **) -> [*] -> [**]
||pre:   none
||post:  #ys = #xs
||       & (A) i:nat. (0 <= i < #xs -> ys!i = f(xs!i))
||       where ys = map f xs
map f[]     = []
map f(x:xs) = (f x):(map f  xs)
```

The definitions of Figure 8.1 can now be more concisely defined in terms of map:

```
squares  = map (^2)
factlist = map factorial
iseven   = map f
           where f x = (x mod 2 = 0)
```

For example,
squares[1,3,2] = map(^2)[1,3,2] = [1,9,4]
Note that partial application is especially convenient when used in conjunction with higher-order functions, as can be seen from the new definition for squares.

Example

Integration (we mean *definite* integration) takes a function f and two limits, a and b, and returns a number. One way of calculating the definite integral is by cutting the domain of integration into equal-sized *slices*, and guessing the average height of the function in each slice. For example, if the function is to be integrated from 0 to 5 in 10 slices, the slices are: 0 to 0.5, 0.5 to 1, and so on up to 4.5 to 5. The guessed height for each slice is simply the value of the function in the centre of each slice, such as $f(4.75)$ for the last slice in the example above. This assumes that the slices are rectangular-shaped, rather than whatever curved shape the function actually has.

The guessed *area* of a slice is then the width (0.5 each, in the example) times the guessed average height. The final answer is the sum of the areas of all the slices. The type of a function integrate which calculates the area under a curve could be declared as follows:

```
function == num -> num

integrate :: function -> num -> num -> num -> num
||args are <function> <start> <finish> <no. of slices>
||pre: nat(n) & n>0
||post: (integrate f start finish n) is an estimate of the
||      integral of f from start to finish
```

This function is higher-order because it takes a function as one of its arguments. The following is a definition of integrate:

```
integrate f start finish n
  = sum (map area [1..n])
    where
      width  = (finish - start) / n
      area i = width * f(start + width * (i-0.5))
```

120   *Higher-order functions*

8.3 The higher-order function `fold`

Consider the following function again:

```
sum :: [num] -> num
||pre:  none
||post: sum xs = xs!0 + ... + xs!(#xs-1)
```

In other words, `sum xs` adds together the elements of `xs`:

```
sum [] = 0
sum (x:xs) = x + (sum xs)
```

You can imagine an exactly similar function for finding the product of the elements, replacing + by *. You also have to replace the base case result 0 by 1 — otherwise you obtain the wrong answer for singleton lists, and so by the recursion for longer lists.

These are so similar that you could imagine both specification and definition being constructed automatically once you have supplied the operator (+ or * or other possibilities) and the base case result (0 or 1). Higher-order functions allow you to do just that. We shall write `fold` f e for the function that 'folds together' the elements of a list using the operator `f` and base case result e.

The infix notation is very convenient, so in what follows we shall often use the Miranda convention that if `f` is a 2-argument function then `$f` is the same function treated notationally as an infix operator. For example, x `$gcd` y is the same as `gcd` x y.

Let us first look at the type of `fold`. It has three arguments, namely the function `f`, e for the base case and the list `xs`. We do not care what list type `xs` has. It is [*] for some type *, and then `f` must have matching types * -> * -> * and e must have the type *. (For `sum`, * was `num`.)

```
fold :: (* -> * -> *) -> * -> [*] -> *
```

For the post-condition, we require

```
||post: fold f e xs = xs!0 $f ... $f xs!(#xs-1)
```

This is a little imprecise. It does not make it at all clear what should happen when *xs* is empty, and the '...' is slightly fuzzy. We will look at these issues more closely later. For the moment, what is more important is that certain pre-conditions are implied.

First, we wrote `xs!0 $f ... $f xs!(#xs-1)` without any parentheses to show the evaluation order of the different `$f`s. We could have chosen an evaluation order and put parentheses in, for instance

```
(...(xs!0 $f xs!1)... $f xs!(#xs-1))
```
or
```
(xs!0 $f ... (xs!(#xs-2) $f xs!(#xs-1))...)
```

But rather than make such a choice, let us keep to the simple case where, as with + and *, parentheses are unnecessary.

A particular case of this is when operating on three elements: we require
$$\forall x, y, z.\ x\ \$f\ (y\ \$f\ z) = (x\ \$f\ y)\ \$f\ z$$
In fact, this particular case (the 'associativity' law) is enough to show also that parentheses are unnecessary in longer expressions — we mentioned this with ++ in Chapter 6.

Here, then, is one pre-condition: $f must be associative.

The other pre-condition concerns the interaction between $f and e. The key properties (they will appear at various points of the reasoning) of 0 and 1 in relation to + and * are that they are 'identities': $x + 0 = x$, $x * 1 = x$. We shall assume a general identity law for e:
$$\forall x.\ x\ \$f\ e = x = e\ \$f\ x$$
Finally, let us try to improve the post-condition by removing the dots. We shall use the same trick as we did with reverse, namely to give strong and useful properties (not, strictly speaking, a post-condition) of the way fold f e works, trying to relate it to ++:

```
fold :: (* -> * -> *) -> * -> [*] -> *
||pre:   (A) x,y,z:*. x $f (y $f z)
||                  = (x $f y) $f z     ($f is associative)
||       & (A) x:*. x $f e = x = e $f x  (e is an identity for $f)
||post: fold f e [] = e
||       & (A) x:*. fold f e [x] = x
||       & (A) xs,ys:[*]. fold f e (xs++ys)
||                  = (fold f e xs) $f (fold f e ys)
```

Let us note straight away that the specification specifies fold uniquely. In other words, if $f1$ and $f2$ both satisfy the specification, $f is associative, e is an identity for $f and xs is a (finite!) list, then
$$f1\ f\ e\ xs = f2\ f\ e\ xs$$
This is easily proved by induction on xs, the induction step coming from
$$f1\ f\ e\ (x:xs) = (f1\ f\ e\ [x])\ \$f\ (f1\ f\ e\ xs) = x\ \$f\ (f1\ f\ e\ xs)$$

8.4 Applications

We shall implement fold later. For the moment, let us look at some applications. sum can be defined as fold (+) 0. (Notice how a built-in infix operator can be passed as an argument to a higher-order function by placing it in parentheses.) Once you have checked that + is associative (that is, $x+(y+z) = (x+y)+z$) and 0 is an identity ($x+0 = x = 0+x$), then you know immediately that sum (xs++ys) = (sum xs)+(sum ys). You do not need to prove it by induction; the induction will be done once and for all when we implement fold and show that the specification is satisfied.

The analogous function product can be defined as `fold (*) 1`. Note that subtraction and division are not associative, and it is less obvious what one would mean by 'the elements of a list folded together by subtraction'. The function `concat` is defined as `fold (++) []`. It takes a list of lists and appends (or concatenates) them all together.

By combining `fold` and `map`, quite a wide range of functions can be defined. For instance, `count` of Exercise 7 in Chapter 6 can be defined by

```
count x xs = fold (+) 0 (map f xs)
             where f y = 1,   if y = x
                       = 0.   otherwise
```

Then we can prove the properties of `count` without using induction. For instance,

$$\begin{aligned}
\text{count } x \ (xs\text{++}ys) &= \text{fold } (+) \ 0 \ (\text{map } f \ (xs\text{++}ys)) \\
&= \text{fold } (+) \ 0 \ (\text{map } f \ xs)\text{++}(\text{map } f \ ys) \\
&= \text{fold } (+) \ 0 \ (\text{map } f \ xs)+\text{fold } (+) \ 0 \ (\text{map } f \ ys) \\
&= (\text{count } x \ xs)+(\text{count } x \ ys)
\end{aligned}$$

8.5 Implementing `fold` — `foldr`

There are two common implementations of `fold`. They have different names, `foldr` and `foldl`, and this is because they can also be used when `$f` and `e` do not satisfy the pre-conditions of `fold`, but they give different answers — actually, they correspond to different bracketings. (In fact, they even have more general types than `fold`, as you can see if you ask the Miranda system what it thinks their types are.) `foldr` and `foldl` are rather different. We shall show `foldr` here — it uses the same idea as `sum` — and leave the discussion of `foldl` to Exercise 6. `foldr f e xs` calculates

$$(xs!0 \ \$f \ldots \$f \ (xs!(\#xs-1) \ \$f \ e)\ldots)$$

```
foldr f e [] = e
foldr f e (x:xs) = x $f (foldr f e xs)
```

Proposition 8.1 `foldr` satisfies its specification. We fix an associative operator `$f` with an identity `e`, and prove the three equations of the post-condition. The first is immediate and the second is easy. For the third we use induction on xs to prove $\forall xs : [\ *\ ]. \ P(xs)$, where

$$P(xs) \stackrel{\text{def}}{=}$$
$$\forall ys : [\ *\ ]\text{foldr } f \ e \ (xs\text{++}ys) = (\text{foldr } f \ e \ xs) \ \$f \ (\text{foldr } f \ e \ ys)$$

base case: $P(\texttt{[]})$

$$\begin{aligned}\text{LHS} &= \texttt{foldr } f \ e \ (\texttt{[]++}ys) \\ &= \texttt{foldr } f \ e \ ys \\ &= e \ \texttt{\$f}(\texttt{foldr } f \ e \ ys) \qquad \text{(identity law)} \\ &= (\texttt{foldr } f \ e \ \texttt{[]}) \ \texttt{\$f} \ (\texttt{foldr } f \ e \ ys) = \text{RHS}\end{aligned}$$

induction step: assume $P(xs)$ and prove $P(x\!:\!xs)$:

$$\begin{aligned}\text{LHS} &= \texttt{foldr } f \ e \ (x\!:\!xs\texttt{++}ys) = x \ \texttt{\$f} \ (\texttt{foldr } f \ e \ (xs\texttt{++}ys)) \\ &= x \ \texttt{\$f} \ (\texttt{foldr } f \ e \ xs) \ \texttt{\$f} \ (\texttt{foldr } f \ e \ ys) \\ &= (\texttt{foldr } f \ e \ (x\!:\!xs)) \ \texttt{\$f} \ (\texttt{foldr } f \ e \ ys) = \text{RHS}\end{aligned}$$

□

Although the reasoning is more complicated, `foldr` can also be used in more general cases (for example, non-associative); note also that the definition of `foldr` has a more liberal type than `fold`:

```
foldr :: (** -> * -> *) -> * -> [**] -> *
length x   = foldr fun 0 x   where fun a acc = 1 + acc
```

Notice that built-in infix operators can be passed as arguments to higher-order functions by placing them in parentheses. Recall the function for building an ordered tree from a list:

```
build        ::  [*] -> (tree *)
build []     =   Emptytree
build (x:xs) =   insertT x (build xs)
```

A more concise and preferred definition uses `fold`:

```
build x = foldr insertT Emptytree x
```

The evaluation sequence for an application of the new definition of `build` illustrates the reduction sequence:

```
build[6,2,4]
= foldr insertT Emptytree [ 6, 2, 4 ]
= insertT 6 (insertT 2 (insertT 4 Emptytree) )
= Node (Node Emptytree 2 Emptytree) 4 (Node Emptytree 6 Emptytree)
```

8.6 Summary

- Most list-processing functions can be described using higher-order functions such as `map` and `fold` (which capture the two most common patterns of recursion over lists). The same approach can also be applied to other patterns of recursion and for user-defined types.
- A small suite of higher-order functions to iterate over each data type can be used to avoid writing many explicit recursive functions on that

type. Then an appropriately parameterized higher-order function is used to define the required function.
- The technique can be compared with polymorphism where structures (including functions, of course) of similar shape are described by a single polymorphic definition. Higher-order functions are used to describe other recursive functions with the same overall structure.
- The functional programming 'style' is to use higher-order functions since they lead to concise and abstract programs.
- It is usually easier to understand programs that avoid excessive use of explicit recursion and to use library and higher-order functions whenever possible.
- Induction proofs can be done once and for all on the higher-order functions.

8.7 Exercises

1. Prove that `integrate` terminates, assuming that the supplied function terminates.
2. Define a function `sigma`, which, given a function, say `f`, and two integers corresponding to the lower and the upper limits of a range of integers, say `n` and `m`, will capture the common mathematical notation of
$$\sum_{x=n}^{m} fx$$
3. In the imperative programming language C there is a library function called `ctoi` which converts a string to an integer. For example, `ctoi "123"` gives `123`. Declare and define `ctoi` in Miranda. Ensure that your definition is not recursive.
4. Give type declarations and definitions of functions `curry` and `uncurry`, for example, `uncurry f (x,y) = f x y`.
5. This question is about writing a function to sort lists using what is called a *merging* algorithm:
   (a) Recall `smerge`, which, given two sorted lists, merged them into a single sorted list. Show that `smerge` is associative and `[]` is an identity for it.
   (b) Write a function `mergesort` which sorts a list by converting it to a list of singletons and then applying `fold smerge []`.
6. The other implementation of `fold` is `foldl`, which calculates
$$(\ldots(e \ \$f \ xs!0) \ \$f \ldots \$f \ xs!(\#xs-1))$$

```
foldl f a [] = a
foldl f a (x:xs) = foldl f (a $f x) xs
```

Note that we have replaced e by a. This is because the parameter is passed through the recursive calls of `foldl`, so even if it starts off as an identity for `$f` it will not remain as `$f`'s identity. In general, still assuming that `$f` is associative and e is an identity for it, `foldl f a xs = a $f (foldl f e xs)`. This can be proved easily by induction on xs; but since we would still need another induction to prove the equations of the specification, it is possible to combine both induction proofs.

(a) Use induction on xs to prove that

$$\forall a : *.\ \forall xs, ys : [\,*\,].\ \texttt{foldl}\ f\ a\ (xs\texttt{++}ys)$$
$$=\ \texttt{foldl}\ f\ (a\ \$f\ (\texttt{foldl}\ f\ e\ xs))\ ys$$

(HINT: In the induction step you use the induction hypothesis *twice*, with different values substituted for a and ys. The unexpected one has $ys = \texttt{[]}$. To avoid confusion, introduce new constants for your $\forall$-introductions.)

(b) Deduce from (a) that

$$\forall a : *.\ \forall xs : [\,*\,].\ \texttt{foldl}\ f\ a\ xs\ =\ a\ \$f\ (\texttt{foldl}\ f\ e\ xs)$$

(c) Deduce from (a) and (b) that

$$\forall xs, ys : [\,*\,].\ \texttt{foldl}\ f\ e\ (xs\texttt{++}ys)$$
$$=\ (\texttt{foldl}\ f\ e\ xs)\ \$f\ (\texttt{foldl}\ f\ e\ ys)$$

and hence that `foldl` implements the specification for `fold`.

(d) Deduce that

$$\texttt{foldr}\ f\ e\ xs\ =\ \texttt{foldl}\ f\ e\ xs$$

provided that `$f` is associative, e is an identity for it (and xs is finite).

(e) Give examples to show that `foldr` and `foldl` can compute different results is `$f` is not associative or e is not an identity for it.

7. Consider the following specification:

```
filter :: (*->bool)->[*]->[*]
||filter p xs is the list xs except that the
||elements x for which p x is False have all been removed.
||pre: none
||post: (A)x:*. (Isin(x,ys) -> p x)
||        & (E)ws:[*]. (Merge(ys,ws,xs)
||        & (A)x:*. (Isin(x,ws) -> ~(p x)))
||              where ys = filter p xs
||        (ws contains the elements that were filtered out)
```

(a) Prove by induction on xs that this specification specifies `filter` uniquely.

(b) Show that `filter` is implemented by

```
filter p xs = fold (++) [] (map f xs)
              where f x= [x], if p x
                    = [], otherwise
```

8. For each of the functions given below:

    (a) Write down equations to show their values in the cases when

    $ys = $ []
    $ys = us$++vs
    $ys = [y]$

    (b) Show (by list induction) that there is at most one function that satisfies your answers to (a).

    (c) Write a similar equation for the case when $ys = y\!:\!zs$, and show how it is implied by the equations given in (a).

    (d) Use (c) to write down a recursive Miranda definition of the function.

    (e) Prove by induction that your definition satisfies the properties in (a).

    (f) Use `map` and `fold` to write a non-recursive definition of the function.

    (g) Use standard properties of `map` and `fold` to show that your definition in (f) satisfies the properties given in (a).

    Here are the functions:

    - `length: [*] -> num`, `length` ys is the length of ys.
    - `prod: [num] -> num`, `prod` ys is the product of the elements of ys. (NOTE: consider carefully what `prod` [] should be.)
    - `count: * -> [*] -> num`, `count` x ys is the number of occurrences of x in ys.
    - `split: (* -> bool) -> [*] -> ([*], [*])`. If `split` p ys=(ys_1,ys_2), then `merge`(ys_1, ys_2, ys), and for every y, if y is an element of ys_1 then $(p\ y)$, while if y is an element of ys_2 then $\neg\ (p\ y)$.
    - `all: (* -> bool) -> [*] -> bool`, (`all` p ys) iff for every element y of ys we have $(p\ y)$.
    - `some: (* -> bool) -> [*] -> bool`, (`some` p ys) iff for some element y of ys we have $(p\ y)$.
    - `sum: [*] -> num`, `sum` ys is the sum of the elements of ys.

9. Consider fold (&) True :: [bool] -> bool. (& is associative, and True is its identity.) Remember that in Miranda it is possible to have infinite lists, for instance trues where

   trues = True:trues

   (all its element are True).

   Show that if *bs* is an infinite list of type [bool], then

   foldr (&) True (False:*bs*) = False   but
   foldl (&) True (False:*bs*)   goes into an infinite loop.

10. (a) Define the polymorphic function reverse using foldr.
    (b) Define the polymorphic function reverse using foldl.
    (c) Which is more efficient and why?

11. Define the higher-order function map without explicit recursion by using the higher-order function foldr (with a non-associative argument).

12. In a version of the game Mastermind, one player thinks of a four-digit number, while the other player repeatedly tries to guess it. After each guess, player 1 scores the guess by stating the number of bulls and cows. A bull is a correct digit in the correct place and a cow is a correct digit in an incorrect place. No digit is scored more than once. For example, if the secret code is 2113, then:

    1234 scores 03
    1111 scores 20
    1212 scores 12

    Construct a function score which takes a code and a guess and returns the number of bulls and cows. (Your function score should be written using higher-order functions.)

    You may find it helpful to use the -- construct. -- is a list subtraction operator. The value of *xs*--*ys* is the list which results when, for each element *y* in *ys*, the first occurrence of *y* is removed from *xs*. For example,

    [1,2,1,3,1,3]--[1,3] = [2,1,1,3]
    "angle"--"l" ++"l" = angel
    || "xyz" is short for ['x','y','z']

13. (Advanced) This is an exercise in using both polymorphism and higher-order functions. The question investigates *predicates* on Miranda types: a predicate on type * is understood as a function from * to bool:

    pred * == (* -> bool)

Suppose `f :: bool -> bool -> bool`. Then `f` can be extended to a function on predicates by applying it *pointwise*:

```
ptwise :: (bool->bool->bool)->(pred *)->(pred *)->(pred *)
ptwise f p q x = f(p x)(q x)
```

(Experiment: define this in Miranda, and try `ptwise ::`. Miranda realizes that this definition can be used much more widely than just when `f :: bool -> bool -> bool`. Also, why does the type of `ptwise` seem to give it three arguments, whereas the definition gives it four?) If $p, q :: $ `pred *`, let us write

$$p \Rightarrow q \text{ iff } \forall x :: *((p\ x) = \text{True} \to (q\ x) = \text{True})$$

(a) Translate the following specifications into English, and write Miranda definitions for functions to implement them:

```
all :: (pred *) -> (pred [*])
||pre:  none
||post: (all p t)=True <->
||      (A)x. ((E)n. In-At(x,t,n)->(p x)=True)

some :: (pred *) -> (pred [*])
||pre:  none
||post: (some p t)=True <->
||      (E)x. ((E)n. In-At(x,t,n) & (p x)=True)
```

(b) Prove that for all $p, q :$ `pred *`,

$$\text{all(ptwise } (\backslash/)\ p\ q) \Rightarrow \text{ptwise } (\backslash/)\ (\text{all } p)\ (\text{some } q)$$
$$\text{ptwise } (\&)\ (\text{all } p)\ (\text{some } q) \Rightarrow \text{some } (\text{ptwise } (\&)\ p\ q)$$

Describe in English what these results mean.

Chapter 9

Specification for Modula-2 programs

We now move on to imperative programming, using the Modula-2 language. (This material also applies to Pascal and Ada programs.) We will not describe the features of Modula-2 here because there are already many books about it.

9.1 Writing specifications for Modula-2 procedures

The general idea is the same as for Miranda: a specification has some typing information, a pre-condition and a post-condition. These can be conveniently placed at the header of the procedure as follows:
```
PROCEDURE CardMin(x,y: CARDINAL):CARDINAL;
(*pre: none
 *post: (result = x \/ result = y) & (result <=x & result <=y)
 *)
BEGIN
  IF x<=y THEN RETURN x ELSE RETURN y END
END CardMin;
```

The principles here are exactly the same as in Miranda, with three minor points of difference. First, the typing information, that is,
`PROCEDURE CardMin(x,y: CARDINAL):CARDINAL;`
is compulsory in Modula-2. Second, comments look different: they are between (* and *), instead of being after ||. Third, we are using the word **result** in post-conditions to mean the value returned by the procedure. This means that it would be inadvisable to have a *variable* called **result** because of the confusion that would arise.

> **result** has a special meaning in post-conditions of functions: it means the value returned.

129

Variables changing

What is not apparent from this example is that there is a big difference between Miranda and Modula-2: Modula-2 has variables that *change their values*. Therefore, our reasoning must be able to cope with symbols that take different values at different times. In general, because a variable may change its value many times during the computation, there may be lots of different times at which we may wish to put our finger on the value and talk about it. There is a general technique for doing this. But in a procedure specification, there are really only two values to talk about, before (on entry to) and after (on return from) the procedure, and we use a special-purpose notation to distinguish these.

A pre-condition must only talk about the values before the procedure is executed, so when a variable is used in a pre-condition it means the value *before*. A post-condition will usually want to compare the values before and after, and this is where the special notation comes in. A variable with a *zero* (for example, x_0 or x_0) means the value *before*; an unadorned variable (for example, x or x) means the value *after*. We shall be consistent in using unadorned variables to denote the value *now* (in the pre-condition, 'now' is the time of entry; in the post-condition it is the time of return), and in using various adornments such as the zero to show the value at some *other* time.

The following are two examples:

```
PROCEDURE Swap (VAR x,y: INTEGER);
(*pre: none
 *post: x=y_0 & y=x_0
 *)
PROCEDURE Sqrt (VAR x: REAL);
(* Replaces x by an approximation to its square root.
 * epsilon is a global variable.
 * pre:   x>=0 & epsilon>0
 * post:  x>=0 & | x^2-x_0|< epsilon & epsilon = epsilon_0
 *)
```

Some variables are not expected to change

To specify that a variable does not change, you say so in the post-condition: for example, epsilon = epsilon_0 says that *epsilon* does not change (value on return = value on entry). But this could get out of hand, so let us adopt the following two conventions.

First, if a global variable is not mentioned at all in the specification, then we assume an implicit specification that it should not change.

Second, if a parameter is called by value, then, again, we assume an implicit specification that it should not change. (That is why in `CardMin` we did not bother to write x_0 or y_0.) (If you think about it, this assumption will seem pointless. Apparently, all the changes made to the parameter are local to the procedure and the caller can never notice them.)

9.2 Mid-conditions

When we implement the specifications, there is a very simple technique for reasoning. It generalizes the idea of pre- and post-conditions by using logical assertions that are supposed to hold at points in the middle of the computation, not just at the beginning or end. We call them *mid-conditions*. They are written as comments in the middle of the code.

The following is an implementation of `Swap`, with a complete set of mid-conditions:

```
PROCEDURE Swap (VAR x,y: INTEGER);
(* pre: none
*post: x=y_0 & y=x_0
*)
VAR z: INTEGER;
BEGIN          (*x=x_0 & y=y_0*)
  z:=x;        (*z=x_0 & y=y_0*)
  x:=y;        (*z=x_0 & x=y_0*)
  y:=z;        (*y=x_0 & x=y_0*)
END Swap;
```

You would not normally put in so many mid-conditions. There are just certain key positions where they are important — you have already seen two, namely entry and return (corresponding to pre- and post-conditions). With most simple straight-line sections of code such as this it is easy to omit the intermediate mid-conditions and fill them in mentally. But we can use the example to illustrate the reasoning involved.

Each mid-condition is supposed to hold whenever program control passes through that point — at least, provided that the procedure was called correctly, with the pre-condition holding. (Note that unadorned variables still denote the value 'now', that is, at the time when control passes through that point; zeroed variables denote the value on entry.) Does this work here?

The first mid-condition, $x = x_0 \wedge y = y_0$, holds by definition: we have only just entered the procedure, so the value of x has to be its value on entry, which is x_0 by definition.

Now look at the next mid-condition, $z = x_0 \wedge y = y_0$. To have arrived here, we must have started at the point where we had $x = x_0 \wedge y = y_0$, and then done the assignment $z := x$. It is not difficult to see that this is bound to

132 Specification for Modula-2 programs

set up the mid-condition we are looking at (though there are formal systems in which this can be proved — in effect they define the meaning of the assignment statement).

The next mid-condition is similar, and finally we reach the final mid-condition, which is the post-condition. By this stage we know that by the time the program returns it must have set up the post-condition.

Note the 'stepping stone' nature of the reasoning. To justify a mid-condition we do not look at *all* the computation that has gone before, but, rather, at the preceding program statement and the mid-condition just before that.

Conditionals

Here is an example with an IF statement.

```
PROCEDURE IntMax (x,y: INTEGER):INTEGER;
(*pre: none
 *post:   (result = x_0 \/ result = y_0) &
 *        (result >=x_0 &  result >=y_0)
 *)
BEGIN
  IF x>=y
  THEN (*x>=y*) RETURN x (* result = x_0 &  result >=y_0*)
  ELSE (*x<y*) RETURN y  (* result = y_0 &  result >x_0*)
  END
END IntMax;
```

There are two branches of the code, the THEN and ELSE parts, and in each we can write a mid-condition based on the condition 'IF $x \geq y$'. For instance, when we enter the THEN part, that can only be because the condition has evaluated as TRUE: so we know at that point that $x \geq y$. (This is relying on the fact that there are no side-effects when the condition $x \geq y$ is evaluated.) After RETURN x, we know that the result is x and also, because we knew $x \geq y$, that result $\geq y$. The other branch, the ELSE part, is similar. On entering it, we know that the condition evaluated as FALSE, so $x < y$.

Finally, we must show that the post-condition is set up. There are *two* return points, each with a different mid-condition. But it is a matter of logic (and properties of $\geq$) to show that

$$\text{result} = x \wedge \text{result} \geq y$$
$$\rightarrow (\text{result} = x \vee \text{result} = y) \wedge \text{result} \geq x \wedge \text{result} \geq y$$
$$\text{result} = y \wedge \text{result} > x$$
$$\rightarrow (\text{result} = x \vee \text{result} = y) \wedge \text{result} \geq x \wedge \text{result} \geq y$$

9.3 Calling procedures

When you specify a procedure, the zero convention is very convenient; and throughout that procedure you use the zeroed variables for the values on entry. But when you *call* the procedure, you must be careful about the zeroes in its specification: because you now have two contexts, the called procedure and the calling context, in which zero has different meanings.

The following is an example of a rather simple sorting algorithm. The first procedure, Order2, sorts two variables, and the second, Order3, uses Order2 to sort three variables.

```
PROCEDURE Order2 (VAR x,y: INTEGER);
(*pre: none
 *post: ((x=x_0 & y=y_0) \/ (x=y_0 & y=x_0)) & x<=y
 *)
  BEGIN              (*x=x_0 & y=y_0*)
    IF x>y
    THEN (*x_0>y_0*) Swap(x,y);     (*x=y_0 & y=x_0 & x<y*)
(* ELSE x_0<=y_0*)                  (*x=x_0 & y=y_0 & x<=y*)
    END              (*either way, x<=y*)
  END Order2;
```

Before giving the definition of Order3, let us outline the idea. We are ordering x, y and z. If we can arrange for z to be the greatest, that is, $x \leq z \wedge y \leq z$, then the rest is easy: just order x and y. So this condition becomes a key objective in our computation strategy, dividing the task into two. It appears as the second mid-condition. You can probably believe that this objective is achievable using Order2(y,z) and Order2(x,z), and we shall show this more carefully.

On this analysis, the first two mid-conditions are slightly different in character. The second is a computational objective, used to specify the task of the first part of the code. As a condition it does not express everything known at that point, but, rather, just something achievable that gives us what we need to be able to finish off the problem. The first mid-condition, on the other hand, is more to help us reason that our code, once written, really does work:

```
PROCEDURE Order3 (VAR x,y,z: INTEGER);
(*pre: none
 *post: x,y,z  are a permutation of x_0,y_0,z_0 & x<=y<=z
 *)
  BEGIN
    Order2(y,z);      (*y<=z*)
    Order2(x,z);      (*y<=z & x<=z*)
    Order2(x,y)       (*x<=y<=z*)
  END Order3;
```

How do we know that `Order3` works? (Are you actually convinced at this stage?) Let us dispose straight away of the specification that x, y and z are a permutation of x_0, y_0 and z_0 (that is, the same values, possibly rearranged). Although it is actually quite difficult to express this in pure logic, it is quite clear that each call of `Order2` just permutes the variables, so that is all the three consecutive calls can do. The real problem is knowing that the order is correct in the end.

The first call certainly sets up the first mid-condition, $y \leq z$, but how do we know that the second call does not spoil this? We must look at the specification of `Order2`, which says (after we have substituted the actual parameter z for the formal parameter y)

$$((x = x_0 \land z = z_0) \lor (x = z_0 \land z = x_0)) \land x \leq z$$

The zero here denotes the value on entry to the (second) call of `Order2`, but we are reasoning about `Order3`, trying to prove it correct: so for us the zero could also denote the value on entry to `Order3`. To avoid the conflict, you have to invent some new names: say x_1, y_1 and z_1 for the values of x, y and z between the first two `Order2`s: At that point we have, by the mid-condition, $y_1 \leq z_1$, and this is *eternally true* — because y_1 and z_1 are unchanging values not computer variables.

Now what `Order2` sees as x_0 and z_0 are — in our `Order3` context — x_1 and z_1. Hence on return from the second `Order2`, we can use its post-condition to write

$$((x = x_1 \land z = z_1) \lor (x = z_1 \land z = x_1)) \land x \leq z \land y = y_1$$

So far, although we have said a lot by way of explanation, all that has happened has been some notational manipulation and with practice you should be able to do it automatically. What comes next is real logic; Figure 9.1 contains a box proof that shows $y \leq z \land x \leq z$.

More compactly, we want to show at this point that $y \leq z$, that is, $y_1 \leq z$. Since $y_1 \leq z_1$, it is sufficient to show that $z_1 \leq z$ (that is, `Order2(x, z)` cannot decrease the value of z; you would expect this intuitively, but we can also prove it). There are two cases. If $(x = x_1 \land z = z_1)$, that is, `Order2` did not do a swap, then $z_1 = z$. In the other case, we have $(x = z_1 \land z = x_1 \land x \leq z)$, so $z_1 = x \leq z$.

We have now proved that the second mid-condition, $y \leq z \land x \leq z$, is set up correctly. For the third mid-condition, the fact that z is greater than both x and y is unaffected whatever `Order2(x, y)` does, while it also ensures $x \leq y$. Hence, finally, $x \leq y \leq z$.

You may invent new *logical* constants as names for intermediate computed values. This is like Miranda 'where ...' notation.

1. $y_1 \leq z_1$
2. $(x = x_1 \wedge z = z_1) \vee (x = z_1 \wedge z = x_1)$
3. $x \leq z$
4. $y = y_1$
5. $y \leq z_1$ eqsub in 1

6	$x = x_1 \wedge z = z_1$		$x = z_1 \wedge z = x_1$	
7	$z = z_1$	$\wedge \mathcal{E}$	$x = z_1$	$\wedge \mathcal{E}$
8	$y \leq z$	eqsub in 5	$z_1 \leq z$	eqsub in 3
9			$y \leq z$	trans $\leq$

10. $y \leq z$ $\vee \mathcal{E}(2)$
11. $y \leq z \wedge x \leq z$ $\wedge \mathcal{I}(3, 10)$

Figure 9.1 $y \leq z \wedge x \leq z$

9.4 Recursion

To deal with recursion, you use recursion variants (or induction) just as in Miranda. Recursively defined functions in Miranda translate readily into recursively defined function procedures in Modula, and the reasoning is the same in both cases. Actually, it is often more convenient to reason with the Miranda definitions, because the notation is much more economical. Consider, for instance, the Euclidean algorithm implemented recursively in Modula-2:

```
PROCEDURE gcd(x,y: CARDINAL):CARDINAL;
(*pre: none
 *post: result | x & result | y &
 *      (A)z:Cardinal. (z | x & z | y-> z | result)
 *recursion variant = y
 *)
BEGIN
  IF y=0 THEN RETURN x ELSE RETURN gcd(y,x MOD y) END
END gcd;
```

Proposition 9.1 The definition of gcd satisfies the specification.

Proof Both specification and definition are direct translations of those for the Miranda function gcd given in Chapter 5. (Note that the Miranda pre-condition $nat(x) \wedge nat(y)$ has been translated into typing information in Modula-2. Unlike Miranda, Modula-2 has special types CARDINAL and INTEGER, with CARDINALs corresponding to nat.) We have already proved that the Miranda definition satisfied the Miranda specification. □

136 *Specification for Modula-2 programs*

It is somewhat difficult at this stage to give sensible examples of recursion that genuinely use the new imperative features. The following is a rather artificial example:

```
PROCEDURE gcd1(VAR x,y: CARDINAL);
(*Replaces x by the gcd of x and y.
 *pre: none
 *post: x | x_0 & x | y_0 & (A)z:Cardinal. (z | x_0& z | y_0-> z | x)
 *recursion variant=y
 *)
VAR z: CARDINAL;
BEGIN
  IF y # 0 THEN
    z:=x MOD y;
    x:=y;
    y:=z;         (*x=y_0 & y=x_0 MOD y_0*)
    gcd1(x, y)
  END
END gcd1;
```

Proposition 9.2 The definition of `gcd1` satisfies the specification.

Proof If $y = 0$ then $x = \gcd(x, 0)$ and so nothing has to be done. If $y \neq 0$, then by the usual reasoning with recursion variants we can assume that the recursive call `gcd1`(x, y) replaces x by the gcd of y_0 and x_0 MOD y_0, which, by the same argument as given in Chapter 5, is the gcd of x and y. □

9.5 Examples

The following procedure swaps the values of two variables without using any extra variables as storage space. Mid-conditions show very clearly how the sequence of assignments works:

```
PROCEDURE Swap (VAR x,y: INTEGER);
(* pre: none
 *post: x=y_0 & y=x_0
 *)
BEGIN           (*x=x_0 & y=y_0*)
  x:=x-y;       (*x=x_0-y_0 & y=y_0*)
  y:=x+y;       (*x=x_0-y_0 & y=x_0*)
  x:=y-x        (*x=y_0 & y=x_0*)
END Swap;
```

WALKIES SQUARE

Imagine a WALKIES package with position coordinates X and Y, and procedures Up and Right for updating these:

```
VAR X,Y: INTEGER;
PROCEDURE Up(n: INTEGER);
(*pre: none
 *post: X=X_0 & Y=Y_0+n
 *)
PROCEDURE Right(n: INTEGER);
(*pre: none
 *post: X=X_0+n & Y=Y_0
 *)
```

We can use mid-conditions to show that the following procedure returns with X and Y unchanged:

```
PROCEDURE Square(n: INTEGER);
(*pre: none
 *post:   ... & X=X_0 & Y=Y_0
 *)
BEGIN              (*X=X_0 & Y=Y_0*)
  Right(n);        (*X=X_0+n & Y=Y_0*)
  Up(n);           (*X=X_0+n & Y=Y_0+n*)
  Right(-n);       (*X=X_0 & Y=Y_0+n*)
  Up(-n)           (*X=X_0 & Y=Y_0*)
END Square;
```

It is reasonably clear that these mid-conditions are correct. But to justify this more formally you need to use the specifications of Right and Up. For instance, consider the call 'Right$(-n)$'. In the specification for Right, X_0 and Y_0 mean the values of X and Y *on entry to* Right, and not, as we should like to use them in the mid-conditions, on entry to Square. But we do know (from the preceding mid-condition) that on entry to this call of Right X and Y have the values $X_0 + n$ and $Y_0 + n$ (where X_0 and Y_0 are values on entry to Square), so we can substitute these into the post-condition for Right. Also, Right is called with actual parameter $-n$, so we must substitute this for the formal parameter n in the post-condition. All in all, in $X = X_0 + n$ & $Y = Y_0$ substitute

- $-n$ for n,
- $X_0 + n$ for X_0,
- $Y_0 + n$ for Y_0,

giving $X = X_0$ & $Y = Y_0 + n$. This is the next mid-condition.

9.6 Calling procedures in general

A typical step of reasoning round a procedure call looks as follows:

$$\ldots mid1(x,y,z,\ldots) \quad P(a,b,c,\ldots) \quad mid2(x,y,z,\ldots)$$

Here $x, y, z, \ldots$ represent the relevant variables, and $a, b, c, \ldots$, expressions involving the variables, are the actual parameters in the call of P. We assume for simplicity that evaluating these actual parameters does not call functions that cause any side-effects. We have reasoned that $mid1$ holds just before entry to P (imagine freezing the computer and inspecting the variables: they should satisfy the logical condition $mid1$, and we now want to reason that $mid2$ will hold on return). We must do this by using the specification of P; however, that is written using the *formal* parameters of P, and the first step is to replace these by the actual parameters $a, b, c, \ldots$ to obtain the properties of $x, y, z, \ldots$

```
pre: preP(x,y,z,... )
post: postP(x,x_0,y,y_0,z,z_0,... )
```

(But the zeros in *postP* show values of x, y, and z *on entry to* P, and we shall have to allow for this.) Next we must show that $mid1$ entails $preP$, in other words that $mid1$ is sufficient to ensure that P works correctly. This is pure logic.

Next, we must work out what exactly we know on return from P, at the same time coping with possible notational clashes due to x_0, and so on, having different meanings in different places. Suppose x_1, y_1, z_1, ...are convenient names for the values of $x, y, z, \ldots$ before the call of P. Then the post-condition tells us that on return we have $postP(x, x_1, y, y_1, z, z_1, \ldots)$. But we also know, because x_1, and so on, are just names of values, that we have $mid1(x_1, y_1, z_1, \ldots)$. Hence, on return from P we know the following (and no more):

$$postP(x, x_1, y, y_1, z, z_1, \ldots) \wedge mid1(x_1, y_1, z_1, \ldots)$$

Our final task is to prove that this entails $mid2(x, y, z, \ldots)$. Again, this is pure logic.

To summarize, after manipulating the specification of P a little, we have two tasks in pure logic: prove —

$$mid1(x, y, z, \ldots) \rightarrow preP(x, y, z, \ldots)$$
$$postP(x, x_1, y, y_1, z, z_1, \ldots) \wedge mid1(x_1, y_1, z_1, \ldots) \rightarrow mid2(x, y, z, \ldots)$$

Thus the step between $mid1$ and $mid2$ (via P) really has the two logical steps, above, and a computational step (P) in the middle. The specification of P gets us from $preP(x, y, z, \ldots)$ to

$$postP(x, x_1, y, y_1, z, z_1, \ldots) \wedge mid1(x_1, y_1, z_1, \ldots).$$

9.7 Keeping the reasoning simple

When all the features of imperative programming are taken together, some of them can be quite complicated to reason about. There is a general useful principle:

> Keep the programming simple to keep the reasoning simple.

We have already seen some examples:

- It is simpler if you do not assign to 'call by value' parameters, even though Modula-2 allows you to (hence our default assumption that they do not change their values).
- It is simpler if functions, and hence expressions containing them, do not have side-effects. We assumed this when we were discussing IF statements — it is tricky if the condition has side-effects for the actual parameters.

When we say that these features make the reasoning more difficult, this applies even to the most superficial of reasoning. The effects they have are easy to overlook when you glance over the program. A classic source of error is careless use of global variables, because they tend to be updated in a hidden way, as a side-effect of a procedure.

9.8 Summary

- For Modula-2 the essential ideas of pre- and post-conditions (also recursion variants) are the same as for Miranda; *result* in a post-condition means the result of the procedure.
- Variables change their values, so a logical condition must always carry an idea of 'now', a particular moment in the computation. For pre- and post-conditions, 'now' is, respectively, entry to and return from a procedure.
- An unadorned variable always denotes its value 'now'.
- A zero on a variable indicates its value 'originally', that is, on entry to the procedure it appears in.
- Introduce new constant symbols (for example, variables adorned with 1s) as necessary to indicate values at other times.
- There are implicit post-conditions: variables not mentioned, and local variables, are not changed.
- Mid-conditions can be used as computational objectives ('post-conditions for parts of a procedure body') and to help reason correctness.
- In an IF statement, the test gives pre-conditions for the THEN and ELSE parts.

- When reasoning about procedure calls, there are three parts:
    1. notational manipulation to see what the pre- and post-conditions say in the calling context;
    2. logical deduction to prove the pre-condition;
    3. logical deduction to prove the next mid-condition (what you wanted to achieve by the procedure call).

9.9 Exercises

1. You have already seen the following problems for solution in Miranda:
    - `round`: round a real number to the nearest integer.
    - `solve`: solve the quadratic equation $ax^2 + bx + c = 0$.
    - `middle`: find the middle one of three numbers.
    - `newtonsqrt`: calculate a square root by Newton's method.

   Translate the Miranda solutions (specifications and definitions) directly into Modula-2.

2. The following standard procedures are defined in Niklaus Wirth's *Programming in Modula-2*: `ABS`, `CAP`, `CHR`, `FLOAT`, `ODD`, `TRUNC`, `DEC`, `INC`. Try to translate the explanations in the report into formal, logical specifications.

3. Implement the `middle` function (see Exercise 1) in Modula-2 using the `SWAP` procedure instead of recursion. Show that it works correctly.

4. Specify and define Modula-2 procedures `Order4` and `Order5` analogous to `Order3`, and using the same method, a straight-line sequence of calls of `Order2`. Prove that they work correctly. Can you show that you use the minimum number of calls of `Order2`? Is there a general argument that shows that this method works for ordering any given number of variables?

Chapter 10
Loops

An important difference between functional and imperative programming is the loop constructs (WHILE, UNTIL and FOR). They are essentially imperative (that is what DO means), and to perform analogous computations in Miranda you must use recursion. The techniques you need to reason about WHILE loops are really just a use of mid-conditions; but the mid-conditions involved are so important that they are given a special name of their own — they are *loop invariants*. Even in relatively unreasoned programming, experience shows that there is a particularly crucial point at the top of the loop where it is useful to put comments, and the method of loop invariants is a logical formalization of this idea.

10.1 The coffee tin game

This game illustrates reasoning with loop invariants. It uses a tin full of two kinds of coffee bean, Blue Mountain and Green Valley (Figure 10.1).

Rules:
WHILE at least two beans in tin DO
  Take out any two beans;
  IF they are the same colour
  THEN
    throw them both away;
    put a Blue Mountain bean back in (*you may need spare blue beans*)
  ELSE
    throw away the blue one;
    put the green one back
  END
END;

Figure 10.1 Coffee beans

> QUESTION: if you knew the original numbers of blue and green beans, can you tell the colour of the final bean?

The contents of the tin at any given moment are described by the numbers of blue and green beans. Let us write the state as $mB + nG$ for m blue beans, n green.

A transition (move) is determined by the colours of the two beans taken out: BB, BG or GG (Figure 10.2).

More generally, we have

BB: $mB + nG \to (m-1)B + nG$
BG: $mB + nG \to (m-1)B + nG$
GG: $mB + nG \to (m+1)B + (n-2)G$

The important thing to notice is the way the number of *green* beans can change. If it changes at all, it is decreased by 2, and this means that the *parity* of the number of greens — whether it is odd or even — does not change. The parity is *invariant*.

Suppose, then, there is originally an *odd* number of green beans. Then, however the game progresses (and there are lots of different possibilities), there will always be an odd number of greens. This holds true right up to the end, when there is only one bean left. So what colour is that? It must be green. Similarly, if there is originally an even number of green beans, then the final bean must be blue. So we have answered our question.

The coffee tin game 143

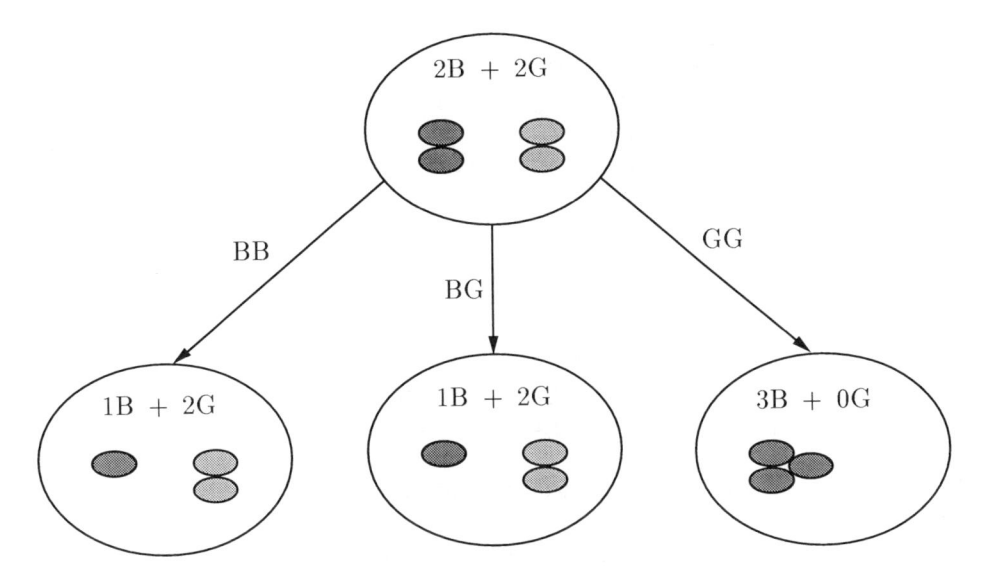

Figure 10.2 Transition

Notice how the invariant, the parity, does not in itself tell us much about the numbers of beans. It is only when we reach the end that the parity combines with that fact to give very precise information about the numbers.

Another small point. How do we know that we ever reach a state with only one bean? This is obvious, because the *total* number of beans always decreases by one at each move. This total number is called a *variant* because it varies and it works very like recursion variants.

Coffee tin game with comments

Here is a version with 'mid-conditions' written as comments. We talked before about an invariant *quantity*, the green parity (odd or even). However, what appears here is an invariant *assertion*, a logical formula, namely that the current parity is the same as the original one. Our reasoning said that if this assertion was true before the move, then it will be true afterwards as well; hence if it was true at the beginning of the game (which it was, by definition) then it will be true at the end as well.

This conversion of invariant quantity into invariant assertion might look cumbersome in this case, but it gives a very general way of formulating invariants. Henceforth, an invariant will always be a logical assertion.

The *variant*, on the other hand (the total number of beans, which we used to prove that the game would end), is always a number:

```
(*pre: green parity p is p_0 & no. of beans > 0
*post:   ( p_0 = Even & one blue left)
*        \/ ( p_0 = Odd & one green left)
*loop invariant: green parity p_0 & no. of beans > 0
*loop variant = total number of beans
*)
WHILE at least two beans in tin DO
      (* number of greens = n, say *)
   Take out any two beans;
   CASE two colours OF
      BB: replace by B      (* greens = n*)
   |  GG: replace by B      (* greens = n-2*)
   |  BG,GB: replace by G   (* greens = n*)
   END
   (* green parity = p_0 again, variant decreased *)
END;
(* green parity is still p_0 & just one bean left *)
```

10.2 Mid-conditions in loops

Now think of a real **WHILE** loop, **WHILE** *test* **DO** *body* **END**, and imagine putting mid-conditions in. There is one point in the program execution that is crucial, namely (each time round) immediately before the loop test is evaluated. What makes it special is that there are two ways of reaching this point — when control comes to the loop from higher up in the code, and when it loops back from the end of the body — so it ties different execution paths together.

A mid-condition here is called the *loop invariant*. You should write it explicitly in a comment before the loop:

```
(*loop invariant:   ...   *)
WHILE test DO
body
END
```

Because there are two ways of reaching the invariant's point, two things need to be proved to show that the invariant behaves:

1. that it holds the first time the loop is reached, in other words that the invariant is *established* initially;
2. that *if* it holds at the start of an iteration, and *if* the loop test succeeds (so that we continue looping and we know that invariant ∧ test), then the execution of the body will ensure that the invariant still holds next time round, in other words that the body *reestablishes* the invariant.

Because the loop invariant point can be reached by two routes, it is — apart from the overall specification — far and away the most important place for mid-conditions. We suggest you take every opportunity to practise the method in your programming.

For the Coffee Tin, the invariant (green parity $= p_0$ and beans > 0) is established trivially — by definition of p_0. It is the reestablishment that is important, showing that whatever move is made (and whatever happens while the move is being made), the green parity is restored to p_0 and beans remain > 0.

At the end, the payoff is that we still know that the invariant holds, but we also know that the loop test fails (that is why we have finished looping). If the invariant is a good one, this combination will allow us to deduce the post-condition (maybe with some final computation). At the end of the Coffee Tin game, we have both that the green parity is still p_0 and that there is only one bean left. This combination is strong enough to tell us exactly what colour the bean is.

10.3 Termination

If we finish looping, then we know the combination 'invariant $\wedge \neg$loop test' holds. But not all loops do terminate. Some loop for ever, and we want to rule out this possibility. The Coffee Tin Game must terminate, because each move decreases by one the total number of beans left, but this can never go negative. Therefore after finitely many moves, the game must stop.

In general, to reason with **WHILE** loops we use not only the invariant, a logical condition as above, but also a *loop variant*. This works the same way as does a recursion variant. It is a natural number related to the computer variables such that the loop body must strictly decrease it, but it can never go negative. Then only finitely many iterations are possible, so the **WHILE** loop must eventually terminate.

For the Coffee Tin, the variant is the total number of beans left.

10.4 An example

Apparently, the method of invariants and variants as presented so far is a *reasoning tool:* given a **WHILE** loop, you might be able to find a loop invariant to prove that it works. But actually, the invariant can appear much earlier than that, even before you have written any code, as a clarification of how you think the implementation will work. Let us explore this in a simple problem to sum the elements of an array of reals:

146   Loops

```
PROCEDURE AddUp(A: ARRAY OF REAL):REAL;
(*pre: none
 *post: result = Sum (i=0 to HIGH(A))A[i]
 *)
```
that is,
$$result = \sum_{i=0}^{\text{HIGH}(A)} A[i].$$
There is an obvious technique for doing this; we read through the elements of A with a variable subscript n and add them one by one into an accumulator S.

Now imagine freezing the computation at the point when we have read exactly n elements and added them all into S. Diagrammatically, the state of the computer can be seen in Figure 10.3

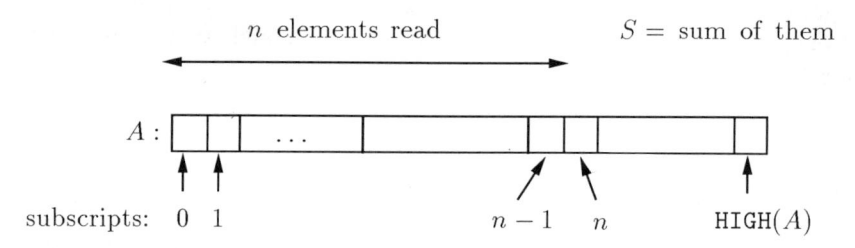

Figure 10.3

This diagram includes quite a lot. Importantly, it says exactly what values we intend to have in our variables n and S. An enormous number of programming errors are caused by imprecise ideas of what values variables are supposed to have. For instance, is $A[n]$ the last element read, or the next one to be read? Our diagram tells us. It also shows us that n varies from 0 (no elements read, at start) to $\text{HIGH}(A) + 1$ (all the elements read, at finish). *Most important of all*, there is an easy link from the diagram to the post-condition. If we can ever get n to be $\text{HIGH}(A) + 1$, then S must be the answer we want and all we need to do is RETURN S.

What the diagram is expressing is a *computational objective* — we intend to write the program so that after each iteration of the loop we have achieved a state as pictured by the diagram. At the same time, we want to push n up to $\text{HIGH}(A) + 1$. We do not have to draw this diagram in a program comment; we can translate it into logic:
$$0 \leq n \leq \text{HIGH}(A) + 1 \land S = \sum_{i=0}^{n-1} A[i]$$
This is the loop invariant. It also guides our programming:

- Initially (no elements read) we want $n = 0$ and $S = 0$ ($\sum_{i=0}^{-1} A[i]$, the empty sum).

- If $n = \text{HIGH}(A) + 1$, then S is the result we want and we can just return it.
- If $n \leq \text{HIGH}(A)$ then we want to read $A[n]$, add it to S, and increment n.

Thus the very act of formulating the invariant has subdivided our original problem into three smaller ones: initialization, finalization, and reestablishing the invariant. This is a very important aspect of the method.

And the variant? A natural number that decreases each time is the number of elements left to be read: this is $\text{HIGH}(A) + 1 - n$.

In effect we have now proved that the algorithm works, but we have not written the program yet! For the sake of our idiot computer, we must implement the algorithm in Modula-2:

```
PROCEDURE AddUp (A: ARRAY OF REAL):REAL;
(*pre: none
 *post: result = Sum (i=0 to HIGH(A))A[i]
 *)
VAR n: CARDINAL;
  S: REAL;
BEGIN
  S:=0.0;
  n:=0.0;
(* Loop invariant:
 *0<=n<= HIGH(A)+1 & S= Sum(i=0 to n-1) A[i]
 *Variant = HIGH(A)+1-n
 *)
  WHILE n<= HIGH(A) DO
    S:=S+A[n];
    n:=n+1
  END;
  RETURN S
END AddUp;
```

This is exactly the quantity of comments you should use in practice: the specification and the invariant and variant. Once you have actually written down the invariant, it is relatively easy — for you or for anyone else who needs to look at your code — to check the minor details. For instance,

- Is the invariant established initially? Yes, easy.
- Is the post-condition set up at the end? Yes. When the loop has terminated, we know both that $0 \leq n \leq \text{HIGH}(A) + 1$ (from the invariant) and that $n > \text{HIGH}(A)$ (because the loop test failed). Hence n must be

exactly $\text{HIGH}(A) + 1$. Then the other part of the invariant tells us that S is the required result, and all we have to do is return it.
- When $A[n]$ is read, is n within range as an array subscript? Yes. We know at that point that the loop test succeeded, so $n \leq \text{HIGH}(A)$: it is in range.
- Does the loop body reestablish the invariant? Yes, this is fairly easy to see.
- Does the loop body decrease the variant? Yes, n is increased (by 1), so $\text{HIGH}(A) + 1 - n$ is decreased.
- Can the loop variant go negative? No. When the loop body is entered, we know $n \leq \text{HIGH}(A)$, so the variant is at least 1. After that iteration, it has decreased by exactly 1, so it is still at least 0.

These are all specific questions that can be asked about the correctness of the program, and for all of them the answer depends on the loop invariant. No other possible mid-condition in this program plays such a crucial role.

10.5 Loop invariants as a programming technique

The whole technique comes into operation as soon as you decide to use a loop structure. First, ask what the computer is supposed to look like at intermediate stages. Do not think about the dynamics of this (a common trap for beginners is to try to make a loop invariant by forcing the loop body into a logical notation); you must imagine freezing the computation at a crucial point and giving a static description of the internal state. There is already a vague picture at the back of your mind, and that is what you must bring out. Diagrams are absolutely invaluable here.

Also remember that you must understand *at that exact point in the computation* what the value of each computer variable signifies. If you do not know what values they are supposed to be storing, you will never be able to use those values correctly.

A critical test of the diagram is that under certain conditions (for example, $n = \text{HIGH}(A) + 1$ in the AddUp example) you must be able to use the information carried by the diagram to arrive at the post-condition. The loop test should be the negation of these conditions (because you continue looping WHILE the conditions fail). At this point it is often easy to see a loop variant — the loop test is often equivalent to $variant > 0$.

Next, formalize the picture in logic to obtain a loop invariant. Perhaps your picture is incomplete; you will realize this later because you will find you do not quite understand how the program is supposed to be working. Then you fill in more details in the picture and refine the invariant. You now have an incomplete implementation:

```
PROCEDURE ...;
(*pre: ...
 *post: ...
 *)
VAR ... ;
BEGIN
  Initialize; (* Remains to be written *)
(*loop invariant: ...
 *variant =
 *)
  WHILE loop test DO
    Loop Body (* Remains to be written *)
  END;
  Finalize (* Remains to be written *)
END ... ;
```

There are three pieces of code that remain to be written: the initialization, the loop body and the finalization. (You probably saw fairly clearly how the finalization would work when you formulated the invariant.) Hence the original programming problem has been divided into three. Moreover, because you have formulated the invariant and variant, each of these three pieces has a precise job to do, a 'subcontract' of the contract (specification) for the overall procedure. These subcontracts can be specified with 'local' pre- and post-conditions.

Piece of code	*Local pre-condition*	*Local post-condition*
Initialize	Overall pre-condition	Invariant
Loop body	Invariant ∧ Loop test	Invariant ∧ variant < variant$_0$
Finalize	Invariant ∧¬Loop test	Overall post-condition

(We assume as usual that there are no side-effects when you evaluate the Loop test.) If you can implement Initialize, Loop body and Finalize to satisfy these local specifications, then you know they will automatically fit together in the WHILE loop to implement the overall specification correctly.

10.6 FOR loops

FOR loops are obviously very similar to WHILE loops, and you may well be used to seeing our WHILE loop examples coded as FOR loops (for instance this is quite easy for AddUp). In fact every FOR loop can be translated into a WHILE loop (see Exercise 6), and it follows that one way to reason with FOR loops is to give loop invariants and variants for the corresponding WHILE loops.

However, we are not going to recommend this here. One reason is that, for the purposes of reasoning, the control variable, for example, the i in FOR `i := ...`, is often still needed after the last iteration, whereas its value in the computer has evaporated by then and is no longer accessible from the program. This has the effect that the `FOR` loops fit uncomfortably with the loop invariant reasoning, and in this book you will see `FOR` loops used less often than you might expect.

Nevertheless, there are some applications where `FOR` loops are particularly natural, namely when the different iterations of the body are more or less independent of each other and could even be done in parallel. You might think of the `WHILE` loop as being good for temporal iteration ('this then this then this, etc.') and the `FOR` loop as more spatial, less ordered ('do all these').

Here is a typical example:

```
CONST Size = ...;
TYPE Matrix = ARRAY [1..Size],[1..Size] OF INTEGER;

PROCEDURE ZeroMatrix (VAR A: Matrix);
(*pre: none
 *post: (A)i,j:CARDINAL. (1<=i<=Size & 1<=j<=Size -> A[i,j]=0)
 *)
VAR i,j: CARDINAL;
BEGIN
  FOR i := 1 TO Size DO
    FOR j := 1 TO Size DO
      A[i,j] := 0
    END
  END
END ZeroMatrix;
```

(NOTE: The logical variables i and j in the post-condition, bound by the $\forall$, are formally quite different from the computer variables `i` and `j`. However, the structure of the post-condition — $Size^2$ checks of zeroness — is so similar to that of the code — $Size^2$ assignments to 0 — that it seems fussy to insist on different symbols.)

It is possible to translate the `FOR` loops into `WHILE` loops and give an invariant for each. If you try this, you will see how clumsy it is. It is much simpler to argue as follows. To show that the post-condition holds at the end, let I and J be natural numbers between 1 and `Size`; we must show that at the end $A[I,J] = 0$. This is so, because

1. there was an iteration of the `FOR` loops (namely with $i = I$ and $j = J$) in which $A[I, J]$ became 0; and
2. once that was done, none of the other iterations would ever undo it.

The pattern is quite general. You reason that everything necessary was done, and then (because the iterations are independent) never undone. Note that no special argument is needed to show termination. `FOR` loops are bound to terminate unless you have a `BY` part of 0, for example,

```
FOR i := 1 TO 2 BY 0 DO ... END
```
As a general rule of thumb, if the iterations are fixed in number and independent of each other, then try to find a simple argument such as the one above and use a `FOR` loop. Otherwise, use a loop invariant and `WHILE` loop.

10.7 Summary

- The method of loop invariants is the method of mid-conditions applied to `WHILE` loops.
- The invariant is a mid-condition that should always be true immediately before the loop test is evaluated.
- Do not confuse the loop invariant with the loop test. They are both logical conditions, but
    1. the loop invariant is a mid-condition, used in reasoning, not evaluated by the computer, and intended to be true right through to the end;
    2. the loop test is a Boolean expression, evaluated by the computer, and is bound to be false after the last iteration.
- The invariant arises first (in your reasoned programm*ing*) as a computational objective, often after drawing a diagram; when the reasoned program is completed, the invariant is used to give a correctness proof.
- The invariant is used to divide the overall problem into three: initialization, loop body, and finalization.
- The loop variant, a number, is like a recursion variant and is used to prove termination.
- `FOR` loops are best reserved for simpler problems in which the iterations are independent of each other.

10.8 Exercises

1. The problem is to implement the following specification:
   ```
   PROCEDURE Negs(A: ARRAY OF INTEGER):CARDINAL;
   (*pre: none
   *post: no. of subscripts for which A[i]<0
   *)
   ```
   The idea is to inspect the elements starting at $A[0]$ and working up to $HIGH(A)$:

   (a) Draw a diagram to illustrate the array when n elements have been inspected — make it clear what are the subscripts of the

last element to have been inspected and the next element to be inspected.

(b) What values will n take as the program proceeds?

(c) Write down the implementation (Modula-2 code), including the loop invariant and variant as comments in the usual way. The invariant should in effect translate the diagram of (a) into mathematical form.

(d) Use the invariant and the failure of the loop test to show that the post-condition is set up.

(e) Show that whenever an array element is accessed, the subscript is within bounds.

NOTE: (c) contains the ingredients that you should write down in your practical programming.

2. Develop reasoned Modula-2 programs along the lines of Exercise 1 to solve the following problems about arrays:

(a) Find the minimum element in an array of integers.

(b) Find whether an array of integers is in ascending order.

(c) Find the length of an array of CHARs, on the understanding that if it contains the character NUL (assumed predefined as a constant), then that and any characters after it are not to be counted. (In other words, NUL is understood as a terminator.)

(d) Find the median of an array of reals, that is, the array value closest to the middle in the sense that as many array elements are smaller than it as are greater than it. Is the problem any easier if the array is known to be sorted?

3. Develop the procedure Search:

```
PROCEDURE Search(A: ARRAY OF INTEGER; x:INTEGER):CARDINAL;
(*pre: Sorted(A)
 *post:   result <= HIGH(A)+1
 &(A)i:CARDINAL
       ((i< result ->A[i]<x)
 &(result <=i<= HIGH(A)->A[i]>=x))*)
```

Use a 'linear' search, inspecting the elements of A one by one starting at A[0].
Explain how the post-condition is deduced at the end (this is where sortedness is needed).

4. Implement the procedure IsIn, using a call of Search (Exercise 3):

```
PROCEDURE IsIn(x: INTEGER; A:ARRAY OF INTEGER):BOOLEAN;
(*pre: Sorted(A)
*post:   result <->(E)i:Cardinal (i<= HIGH(A) & A[i]= x)
*)
```

Using the pre- and post-conditions of Search (not the code), prove that your implementation of IsIn works correctly. What this means is that in every place where a result is returned, you must show that it is the correct result.

5. Give FOR loop implementations of the following:

   (a) IsIn

   (b) Copy

   ```
   PROCEDURE Copy(A: ARRAY OF INTEGER;
           VAR B: ARRAY OF INTEGER);
   (* Copies A to B
   *pre: HIGH(A) = HIGH(B)
   *post: B=A
   *)
   ```

6. Show how a FOR loop
   ```
   FOR i := a TO b BY c DO
       S
   END
   ```
   can be translated into a WHILE loop. There are some tricky points:

   (a) If c is negative the translation is different.

   (b) The intention is that b and c should be evaluated *only once*, at the beginning. Hence you must be careful if they are expressions containing variables (actually, Modula-2 forbids this for c).

7. Consider the following problem:

   ```
   PROCEDURE Copy (n,Astart,Bstart: CARDINAL; A:ARRAY OF INTEGER;
               VAR B: ARRAY OF INTEGER);
   (*copies n elements from A, starting at A[Astart],to B,
   *starting at B[Bstart].
   *)
   ```

   (a) Give a FOR loop implementation of this, including pre- and post-conditions. Give your reasoning to show that it works.

   (b) If the array A is large, you might be tempted to call A as a VAR parameter, since then a local copy of it would not be made for use by the Copy procedure. If you did that, what might go wrong in the case where A and B are the same array? Can you give a sensible specification that allows for this possibility?

Chapter 11

Binary chop

How do you look up a word, 'binary', say, in a dictionary? What you *do not* do is to look through all the words in order, starting at page 1, until you find the word you want. If the dictionary had 1170 pages, you might have to check all of them before you found your word (if it was 'zymurgy'). Instead, you open the dictionary about half way through, at 'meridian', and you see that 'binary' must be in one of the pages in your left hand. You divide those about half way through, at 'drongo', and again you see that 'binary' must come before that. Each time, you halve the number of pages in which your word might be:

Stage:	0	1	2	3	4	5	6	7	8	9	10	11
Pages left:	1170	585	293	147	74	37	19	10	5	3	2	1

Hence, you have only to check eleven pages before you find your word. This method is called the 'binary chop algorithm', and it relies crucially on the fact that the entries in the dictionary are in alphabetical order. It is a very important algorithm in computing contexts, and, what is more, it is a good example of an algorithm that is very easy to get wrong if you try to write the code without any preliminary thought.

There is another important lesson in this algorithm, namely that the natural order of writing a procedure is not necessarily from top to bottom. (This is similar to the way you write a natural deduction proof.) You know already that the loop invariant should generally be worked out before the code; here the most important piece of code to be fixed is the finalization part.

11.1 A telephone directory

To explore different possible ways in which the algorithm might be used, imagine a telephone directory stored on a computer as an array of records, each record comprising a name, an address and a telephone number. The records are stored in alphabetical order of names, but for different records under the same name it is perhaps not worth ordering them any more precisely.

To look up a record, you supply a name and apply the binary chop algorithm. Although it is possible to use the algorithm simply to tell you *whether* the name is present in the directory, clearly in this case you need to know *where* it is so that you can then read the telephone number. Also, it is necessary to remember that there may be more than one record under the same name. It is most convenient if the algorithm tells you the subscript of the first one, so that you can then inspect the addresses one by one.

Now suppose that there is *no* record under the name you supplied. You might think that it is sufficient for the algorithm to tell you that, but consider the problem of updating the array. Any new record must be inserted in exactly the right place (after prising open a gap by shifting a lot of records up one place), and the binary chop algorithm can tell you where that right place is. (Note the payoffs here: lookup is very cheap, but update is expensive.)

Thus the algorithm apparently has many different situations to consider. It is an indication of the power of the algorithm that the cases are actually handled in a very uniform way.

11.2 Specification

Purely for the sake of example, let us take A to be an array of integers, its elements appearing in ascending order: if $i \leq j$, then $A[i] \leq A[j]$. (The method works not just for integers, but for any kind of data with an understood ordering — for instance, the telephone records described above, ordered alphabetically by name.) If x is an integer, the problem is to search for x in A. We can divide A into two blocks, one on the left where the elements are $< x$, and one on the right where they are $\geq x$. The answer is to be the subscript of the first element on the right:

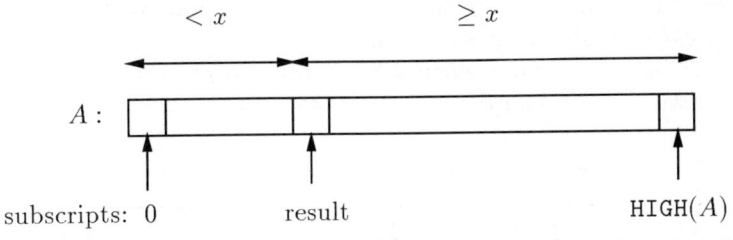

We can translate this into logic. First, all elements with subscripts between 0 and $result-1$ inclusive are $< x$:

$$\forall i : nat \ (i < result \rightarrow A[i] < x) \tag{11.1}$$

156   *Binary chop*

Second, all elements with subscripts between result and HIGH(A) inclusive are $\geq x$:
$$\forall i : nat \ (result \leq i \leq \text{HIGH}(A) \rightarrow A[i] \geq x) \tag{11.2}$$
Third, we should say what range the result will lie in. The extremes are when all the elements of the array are $\geq x$, when the result should be 0, and when all the elements are $< x$, when the result should be HIGH(A) + 1 (notice how in this case $A[result]$ is undefined):
$$0 \leq result \leq \text{HIGH}(A) + 1 \tag{11.3}$$
These three conditions will form the post-condition.

If x is present at all in the array, then we must have $A[result] = x$. (We shall prove that this holds a little later.) If x is absent, then either $A[result] > x$ or $result = \text{HIGH}(A) + 1$.

11.3   The algorithm

The algorithm uses two natural number variables *Left* and *Right*, which represent your two hands holding the dictionary: what you know at each stage is that the answer must be between *Left* and *Right*. At each iteration, you find the midpoint between *Left* and *Right* (call it *Middle*), and use that as a new *Left* or *Right*. Now this intuition is relatively simple, but it is tricky to say exactly what it means. Some points to be resolved are as follows:

- Should the answer be strictly between *Left* and *Right*, or not? Or strict at one end but not at the other? (Four possibilities here.) This is very important. If your ideas are not consistent throughout the program, then errors will arise.
- It is tempting to say something like $A[Left] < x$ and $A[Right] \geq x$, but might we ever want *Left* or *Right* to be HIGH(A) + 1, that is, not a valid subscript for A?

The key is to notice that *result* is used twice in the post-condition, once to show where the elements $< x$ are, and once to show where those $\geq x$ are. *Left* and *Right* can divide these two tasks between them: elements before *Left* are known to be $< x$, and elements at or after *Right* are known to be $\geq x$. In between, we do not know:

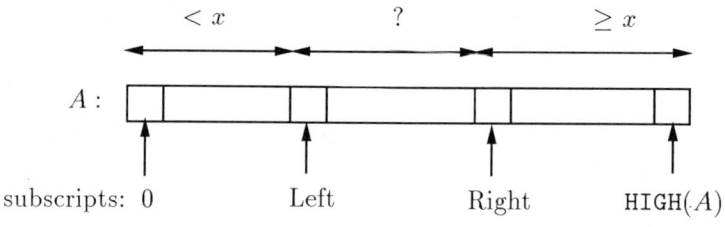

(Middle does not appear — it is used only for calculating within the loop body.)

We are trying to eliminate the '?' region, that is, to make *Left* and *Right* equal. Then we have essentially the same diagram as before, and *Left* (= *Right*) is the required result.

Initially, on the other hand, everything is '?' and so we want *Left* = 0 and *Right* = HIGH(A) + 1.

Actually, this idea, that when *Left*=*Right* we stop and return *Left* as result, is a fundamental design decision that strongly influences the rest: our initial decision is how to finalize! — though that should not come as a surprise by now. So the first program fragments we can write down are

```
(*loop invariant: ??? (formalizes picture)
 *variant = Right-Left  *)
WHILE Left < Right DO
  :
END;
RETURN Left
END Search;
```

There are different ideas, for instance 'when `Right = Left+1 return Right`'; which we could have chosen but we did not and, as it turns out, the method we have chosen is simpler.

Next, let us formulate the invariant. We have a picture already, but we also know that we are choosing <'s or ≤'s precisely to make the *Left* and *Right* parts of the invariant match parts 11.1 and 11.2 of the post-condition. Therefore, it has to be

$Left \leq Right \leq \text{HIGH}(A) + 1$
$\wedge \forall i : nat. ((i < Left \rightarrow A[i] < x) \wedge (Right \leq i \leq \text{HIGH}(A) \rightarrow A[i] \geq x))$

Let us also take the opportunity to say that the variant is *Right* − *Left*.

We have already dealt with the finalization; what next? The initialization is easy — we want *Left* = 0 and *Right* = HIGH(A) + 1. All that remains is the loop body.

The idea is to find *Middle* between *Left* and *Right* and update either *Left* or *Right* depending on the value of *A*[*Middle*]. How should we do that? Let us be very careful to use the information precisely.

If *A*[*Middle*] < *x*, then *Middle* is in the '< *x*' area of the array; so *Left*, which is to be in the '?' area, can safely be set to *Middle* + 1. On the other hand, if [*Middle*] ≥ *x*, then we must set *Right* to *Middle* (why not *Middle* − 1?). We have not said exactly what *Middle* is, but we have made a start on the loop body:

158   Binary chop

```
Middle := ?;
IF A[Middle] < x THEN
  Left := Middle+1
ELSE
  Right := Middle
END
```

It remains to assign a value to *Middle*, and it is important to see what precisely are the requirements here — all we know so far is that *Middle* should be (about) half way between *Left* and *Right*, or at least somewhere between them. Consider how the invariant *Left* $\leq$ *Right* is reestablished. The new *Left* may be *Middle* $+ 1$, so we want *Middle* $+ 1 \leq$ *Right*, that is, *Middle* $<$ *Right*. In the other case, the new *Right* is *Middle*, so we want *Left* $\leq$ *Middle*. We can use a mid-condition to express these requirements as a computational objective:

```
Middle := ?;     (* Left <= Middle < Right *)
```

It is not difficult to see that *if* we can achieve this, then the rest of the loop body will reestablish the invariant and decrease the variant as well. We shall see soon that we can assign $(Left + Right)$ DIV 2, the rounded-down average of *Left* and *Right*, to *Middle*. That is probably what you expected anyway, but more care is needed here than you might think. In Exercise 1 you will see a use of essentially the same algorithm in a different context where it is more natural to require *Left* $<$ *Middle* $\leq$ *Right*, and there it is necessary to use $((Left + Right)$ DIV $2) + 1$ — the problem comes when *Right* $=$ *Left* $+ 1$, so that *Middle* $=$ *Left*.

11.4   The program

The program appears in Figure 11.1 Notice the order in which the parts appear:

1. The procedure heading, with specification and the fragments `BEGIN` and `END Search;`.
2. The framework for the loop: `WHILE Left < Right DO` and `END; RETURN Left;` also the slots for the invariant and variant (we have filled in the variant), and the `VAR` declarations.
3. The invariant, carefully formulated to match 2, and the post-condition.
4. The initialization.
5. Pieces of the loop body: an incompleted assignment statement `Middle := ?;`, and all of the `IF` statement.
6. The comment `(* Left <= Middle < Right *)`.
7. The assigned value `(Left+Right) DIV 2`.

At each stage, the choices to be made depended in a natural way on preceding choices, so the development had a certain logical inevitability.

```
PROCEDURE Search( A: ARRAY OF INTEGER; x: INTEGER) : CARDINAL;
(*pre: Sorted(A),
*      i.e. (A)i,j:nat. ( i<=j<= HIGH(A) -> A[i]<=A[j] )
*post: result <= HIGH(A)+1 & (A)i:nat.
*      ( ( i<result -> A[i]<x ) & ( result<=i<=HIGH(A) -> A[i]>=x ) )
*)
VAR Left,Right,Middle: CARDINAL;
BEGIN
  Left := 0;
  Right := HIGH(A)+1;
(*Loop invariant: Left <= Right <= HIGH(A)+1 & (A)i:nat.
*          ( ( i< Left -> A[i]<x ) & ( Right<=i<= HIGH(A) -> A[i]>=x ) )
*variant = Right-Left
*)
  WHILE Left < Right DO
    Middle := (Left+Right) DIV 2;   (* Left <= Middle < Right *)
    IF A[Middle]<x
    THEN Left := Middle+1
    ELSE Right := Middle
    END
  END;
  RETURN Left
END Search;
```

Figure 11.1

As an experiment, try to write the program code straight down from the top without thinking of invariants. You will probably find (everyone else does) that it is not easy to get it right.

11.5 Some detailed checks

We have already covered most of the important aspects of the invariant: that it is established correctly initially, that it is reestablished on each iteration, and that at the end it can be used to deduce the post-condition. The following are some small remaining questions.

At the end of each iteration, do we still have $Left \leq Right$? After the assignment to *Middle*, do we indeed have $Left \leq Middle < Right$? Because we are still looping, we know that $Left < Right$, that is, $Left \leq Right - 1$. Hence,

$$Middle = (Left + Right) \text{ DIV } 2 \geq (2 \times Left) \text{ DIV } 2 = Left$$
$$Middle = (Left + Right) \text{ DIV } 2 \leq (2 \times Right - 1) \text{ DIV } 2 = Right - 1 < Right$$

NOTE: the equality $(2 \times Right - 1)$ DIV $2 = Right - 1$ is correct according to the definition of Modula-2, given that $Right \geq 1$ (which we know because $Right > Left$): the fractional answer $(Right - 0.5)$ is *truncated* to $Right - 1$. But it is possible to imagine an integer division that might round the fractional answer $Right - 0.5$ up to $Right$. Therefore, if you translate this algorithm to languages other than Modula-2, you should check that their integer divisions behave as expected. Dijkstra and Feijen ('A Method of Programming') give a treatment that does not depend on the rounding method. However, their program only checks whether x is present in A and some elegance is lost when the method is extended to return the position — extra checking is needed to make up for the doubts about the integer division. In truth, the point of integer arithmetic is that it should be *exact*, and an inadequately specified integer division is a blunt instrument.

When A is subscripted, is the subscript within bounds? The only place is in 'IF A[$Middle$] ...'. Can we guarantee that $Middle \leq$ HIGH(A)? Yes, because (as above) $Middle < Right$, and, by the invariant, $Right \leq$ HIGH$(A) + 1$.

Does the variant definitely decrease each time round? If $Right$ is replaced by $Middle$, then it has definitely decreased; if $Left$ is replaced by $Middle + 1$, then it has definitely increased. Either way, the variant has decreased.

11.6 Checking for the presence of an element

Suppose we only want to check whether x is present in A. If we calculate

```
r:= Search(A,x);
```

how can we use A, x and r to perform our check? Just to be sure, let us write down what we know about r solely from the post-condition for Search:

$r \leq$ HIGH$(A) + 1$
$\wedge \forall i : nat.\ ((i < r \rightarrow A[i] < x) \wedge (r \leq i \leq$ HIGH$(A) \rightarrow A[i] \geq x))$ $(*)$

If $A[r] = x$, then x must be present; while a quick look at one of the diagrams above makes it fairly clear that if $A[r] > x$ then x is absent. But wait! Is $A[r]$ defined? Not necessarily. r might be equal to HIGH$(A) + 1$; in this case, x is absent because all the elements are $< x$.

> Check that array subscripts are in bounds when you write the program, not when you run it.

The following is the program:

```
PROCEDURE IsIn(x: INTEGER; A: ARRAY OF INTEGER):BOOLEAN;
(*pre: (A)i,j:nat. (i<=j<= HIGH(A)->A[i] <=A[j])
*post:  result <->(E)i:nat. (i<= HIGH(A) & A[i]= x)
*)
VAR r: CARDINAL;
BEGIN
  r:= Search(A,x);
  RETURN r<= HIGH(A) AND A[r] = x
END IsIn;
```

The code above relies on Modula-2's short circuit evaluation. That is, A[r] = x will not be evaluated if r > HIGH(A). In other languages, such as Pascal, Boolean expressions are evaluated completely even if the result is known after the first subexpression has been evaluated. The code after the RETURN would then need to be written as the following:

```
IF r <= HIGH(A)
THEN RETURN A[r] = x
ELSE RETURN FALSE
END
```

Let us show as rigourously as possible that the code for IsIn satisfies its specification: that if the returned Boolean value is TRUE then x is indeed present in A (that is, $\exists i : nat. \ (i \leq \text{HIGH}(A) \wedge A[i] = x)$), and that if FALSE is returned then x is absent (that is, $\neg \exists i : nat.(i \leq \text{HIGH}(A) \wedge A[i] = x)$).

- [first case:] $r > \text{HIGH}(A)$, so FALSE is returned. We know that r is a natural number and that $r \leq \text{HIGH}(A) + 1$, so $r = \text{HIGH}(A) + 1$. Then from $(*), \forall i : nat.(i \leq \text{HIGH}(A) \rightarrow A[i] < x)$, in other words all the elements of A are $< x$ — so x must be absent. Note that the invalid array access $A[r]$ is not attempted here because of the way in which Modula-2 evaluates AND.
- [second case:] $r \leq \text{HIGH}(A), A[r] = x$, so TRUE is returned. Certainly x is present, with subscript r.
- [third case:] $r \leq \text{HIGH}(A), A[r] \neq x$, so FALSE is returned. Because $r \leq \text{HIGH}(A), (*)$ tells us that $A[r] \geq x$, so we must have $A[r] > x$. Now consider any subscript $i \leq \text{HIGH}(A)$. If $i < r$, then $(*)$ tells us that $A[i] < x$, while if $i \geq r$, then (using orderedness) $A[i] \geq A[r] > x$. Either way, $A[i] \neq x$, so $\neg \exists i : nat. \ (i \leq \text{HIGH}(A) \wedge A[i] = x)$.

11.7 Summary

- Binary chop is an important and efficient search algorithm if the elements are arranged in order. You should know it.
- The algorithm has many uses, but to use it effectively it is important to understand exactly what the result represents (that is, to have a clear

specification).
- There is a particular train of reasoning that leads to the algorithm easily; otherwise it is easy to get into a mess.

11.8 Exercises

1. What happens if you replace the assignment `Left := Middle+1` in `Search` by `Left := Middle`? (HINT: the invariant is still reestablished.) A common belief is that the problem can be corrected by stopping early, looping `WHILE Left+1 < Right`. Follow through this idea and see how it gives more complicated code.

2. The following is another version of `intsqrt` by the binary search algorithm:

```
intsqrt::num->num
||pre: x >= 0
||post: n = entier (sqrt x)
||      i.e. nat(n) & n^2 <= x & (n+1)^2 > x
||      where n = intsqrt x
intsqrt x = f x 0 (entier x)
            where f x l r = l,          if l = r
                          = ?,          if m*m <= x
                          = ?,          otherwise
                      where m = ?
  ||m satisfies some conditions
```

Specify f precisely and in full, and complete the definition. (Beware! m is not $(l+r) \, div \, 2$, as you will see if you follow the method properly.)

3. Show that the specification of `Search` specifies the result uniquely. In other words, if there are two natural numbers r and r' that are both valid results, then $r = r'$.

   Use this to deduce the following. Suppose that in A there is exactly one index, i, for which $A[i] = x$. Then $i = Search(A, x)$.

4. There are other ways of giving the post-condition for `Search`. Here is one that translates the informal specification much more directly:

```
post1: (result <= HIGH(A) & A[result]>=x
         & (A)i:nat. (i<=HIGH(A) & A[i]>=x->i>=result))
       \/(result=HIGH(A)+1
         & (A)i:nat. (i<=HIGH(A)->A[i]<x))
```

Use natural deduction (together with standard properties of arithmetic) to prove that

$$pre \vdash (post \leftrightarrow post1)$$

where *pre* and *post* are the pre- and post-conditions for Search as originally specified, and *post*1 is as given above.
Can you think of any other equivalent post-conditions?

5. This question examines how you might use Search to update an ordered array.

First, a function Search1 is intended to work in the same way as Search, but with a 'soft HIGH' called High1 to allow for variable length lists of integers within a fixed length array. (We actually use a soft version of $HIGH(A) + 1$. This allows us to specify an empty list by setting High1 $= 0$.)

```
PROCEDURE Search1(A: ARRAY OF INTEGER;
  High1: CARDINAL; x: INTEGER):CARDINAL;
(*pre: High1<= HIGH(A)+1 & Sorted(A[0 to High1-1])
 *post: result <= High1  & (A)i:nat.
 *      ((i< result ->A[i]<x)
 *      & (result <=i< High1->A[i]>=x))
 *)
```

(It is obvious how to implement this: just initialize *Right* to High1 instead of $HIGH(A) + 1$ in the implementation for Search. Note that this works even in the case where High1 $= 0$.)

Implement the following procedures, giving invariants and variants for all loops. The notation A[i to j] is introduced in Section 12.3.

```
PROCEDURE OpenUp(VAR A: ARRAY OF INTEGER; VAR High1: CARDINAL;
 NewGap: CARDINAL);
(*pre: NewGap <= High1<= HIGH(A)
 *post:   (E)x:Integer.
 *    A[0 to High1-1] =
 *       A_0[0 to NewGap-1]++[x]++A_0[NewGap to High1_0-1]
 *)

PROCEDURE Insert(VAR A: ARRAY OF INTEGER; VAR High1: CARDINAL;
 x:INTEGER);
(*pre: High1<= HIGH(A)  & Sorted(A[0 to High1-1])
 * post:  Sorted(A[0 to High1-1])
 *    & (E)s,t:[Integer]
 *       (A_0[0 to High1_0-1]=s++t
 * &A[0 to High1-1]=s++[x]++t)
 *)
```

(HINT: implement Insert using *Search*1 and *OpenUp*.)

6. Redo the proof that IsIn satisfies its specification using box proofs.

Chapter 12

Quick sort

12.1 Quick sort

Donald Knuth, in his book *Sorting and Searching*, gives an estimate of over 25 per cent for the proportion of computer running time that is spent on sorting. Whether this estimate is still accurate, we do not know, but his conclusion is still valid: whether (i) there are many important applications of sorting, or (ii) many people sort when they should not, or (iii) inefficient sorting algorithms are in common use, or something of all three, sorting is worthy of serious study as a practical matter.

As a general principle, if a program is used a lot then it is worth making it run quickly. In this chapter we present *quick sort,* an efficient sorting algorithm due to Tony Hoare. It is a good example of a combination of different kinds of argument. It is recursive, and the framework of the algorithm is very conveniently discussed as a Miranda function working on lists. However, when it is transferred to Modula-2 working on arrays, a significant improvement becomes possible using the 'Dutch national flag' algorithm, and this can be discussed using loop invariants — in fact it is a rather good example of a loop invariant that is a logical translation of a diagram.

12.2 Quick sort — functional version

The problem is, given a list, to sort it into order. We start off in Miranda. Since in Miranda datatypes have natural orderings, we do not need to say what our lists are lists of:

```
sort:: [*]->[*]
||pre: none
||post: Sorted(sort xs) & Perm(sort xs,xs)
```

Quick sort — functional version

Idea: partition

It is so much easier to sort short lists than long ones that it helps to do a preliminary crude sort, a *partition* with respect to some key k (Figure 12.1).

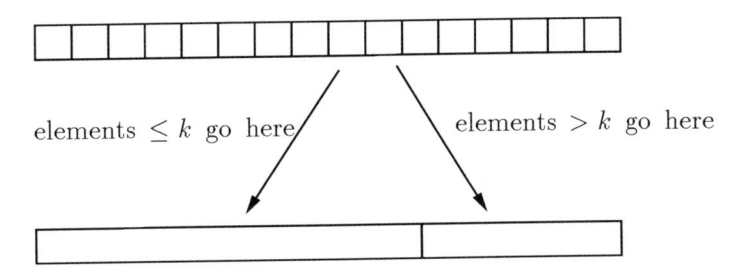

Figure 12.1

```
partition:: *->[*]->([*],[*])
||pre: none
||post: Perm(xs,ys++zs)
||  all elements of ys are <=k
||  all elements of zs are >k
||       where (ys,zs) = (partition k xs)
```

Note that the specification does not uniquely determine the function. If (ys, zs) is a possible result, so is (ys', zs') where ys', zs' are any permutations of ys and zs. It is simple to implement **partition** in Miranda, but we do not need to — it is the specification that is important, and in the end we will implement it by a totally imperative method. A pure functional quick sort is not terribly quick and uses lots of space.

Implementing quick sort

The idea is to do a partition first and then sort the two parts separately; they can be sorted using the same method, recursively. The head of the list can be the key:

```
qsort:: [*]->[*]
||pre: none
||post: Sorted(qsort (xs)) & Perm((qsort (xs)),xs)
||recursion variant = #xs
qsort []     = []
qsort (x:xs) = (qsort ys)++[x]++(qsort zs)
               where (ys,zs) = partition x xs
```

This is the essence of the recursion in the quick sort algorithm. To prove that it works, note first that #*xs* really is a recursion variant. The recursion is unusual in that the recursive calls work not on *xs*, but on *ys* and *zs*. However, we know that these are strictly shorter than $x:xs$. For instance, #*ys* $\leq$ (#*ys* ++ #*zs*) = #*xs* < #*x:xs* so we do have a recursion variant.

Proposition 12.1 qsort terminates and satisfies its specification.
Proof qsort [] clearly works correctly.

Now consider qsort $x:xs$. The result, (qsort *ys*) ++ [x] ++ (qsort *zs*), is sorted, because

- (qsort *ys*) is sorted (the recursive calls can be assumed to be satisfactory);
- (qsort *ys*) is a permutation of *ys*, and by the specification of Partition every element of *ys* is $\leq x$, so every element of (qsort *ys*) is $\leq x$;
- similarly, (qsort *zs*) is sorted and all its elements are $> x$.

Also, it is a permutation of *ys*++[x]++*zs*, hence of $x:(ys{++}zs)$, and hence (by specification of partition) of $x:xs$. □

12.3 Arrays as lists

Miranda is a much simpler notation than Modula-2 and it is often helpful to be able to reason first in terms of Miranda and then transfer the reasoning to Modula-2. The most important properties of an array are its elements, together with their order: in other words, abstractly, the list or sequence of elements. For example, suppose we have

```
A: ARRAY [La..Ha] OF REAL;
B: ARRAY [Lb..Hb] OF REAL;
```
Then

A represents the list $[A[La], A[La+1], \ldots, A[Ha]]$
B represents the list $[B[Lb], B[Lb+1], \ldots, B[Hb]]$
$A{+}{+}B$ represents the list $[A[La], \ldots, A[Ha], B[Lb], \ldots, B[Hb]]$

(Note how we can sensibly talk about the append $A{+}{+}B$, even though in Modula-2 it is quite difficult to construct it.) Also, $\text{hd}(A) = A[La]$, $\text{hd}(B) = B[Lb]$.

For computing purposes, we must also know how the elements are subscripted: hence the need for the bounds in the declarations. But the numerical values of the subscripts may be quite irrelevant to our original problem, and are just a computational necessity forced on us by the way Modula-2 accesses arrays. Then it is better to try to reason without them as much as possible — in fact, specifications that put too great a reliance on subscripts are said to suffer from 'indexitis'.

That said, we can of course put a subscript structure onto a list and thus treat it as an array. The conventional way in both Modula-2 (for open array parameters) and Miranda (for the ! operation) is to say that the first element has subscript 0. Thus a Miranda list
$$t = [t!0, t!1, \ldots, t!(\#t - 1)]$$
can be understood as an array with bounds $[0..(\# \; t-1)]$. (But of course you cannot assign to the elements in Miranda.)

Let us also introduce some notation — *not* part of Modula-2 — for sublists. Suppose A has been declared as $A: ARRAY[m..n] OF \ldots$. We write $A[i \text{ to } j]$ to mean, essentially, the list
$$[[A[i], A[i+1], \ldots, A[j]]]$$
This is provided that $m \leq i \leq j \leq n$. It is also useful to define $A[i \text{ to } j]$ to be empty if $j < i$. Recursively,

```
A[i to j] = [],              if j<i
          = A[i]:A[i+1 to j], otherwise
```

Some properties of this notation are

- As lists, $A = A[m \text{ to } n]$.
- $A[i \text{ to } j]$ is defined iff $(i > j) \vee (m \leq i \leq j \leq n)$. Use induction on $j - i$.
- If $A[i \text{ to } j]$ is defined and non-empty, then its length is $j - i + 1$.
- If $m \leq i \leq j \leq k \leq n$ then $A[i \text{ to } k] = A[i \text{ to } j-1] \texttt{++} A[j \text{ to } k]$
  $= A[i \text{ to } j] \texttt{++} A[j+1 \text{ to } k]$.
- $A[i \text{ to } i] = [A[i]]$.
- $A[0 \text{ to } \text{HIGH}(A)] = A$.

12.4 Quick sort in Modula-2

A Miranda version would waste space by creating lots of new lists all the time. In Modula-2, with arrays (of INTEGERs, say), we can instead try for an *in-place* sort, rearranging the elements within the original array. The recursive calls of `qsort` will now work on regions within the original array, so the procedure must have extra parameters to specify the region. Let us say that QuickSort(A, *Start*, *Rest*) is to sort $A[Start \text{ to } Rest\text{-}1]$. (The -1 lets us specify empty regions by taking *Start=Rest*, even if *Start* $= 0$.)

```
PROCEDURE QuickSort (VAR A: ARRAY OF INTEGER; Start,Rest: CARDINAL);
(*pre: 0<= Start <= Rest <= HIGH(A)+1
 *post: Perm(A, A_0)
 *      & A[0 to Start-1] = A_0[0 to Start-1]
 *      & A[Rest to HIGH(A)] = A_0[Rest to HIGH(A)]
 *      & Sorted(A[Start to Rest-1])
 *)
```

168 Quick sort

Partition will also work in-place:
```
PROCEDURE Partition (VAR A: ARRAY OF INTEGER;
            Start, Rest: CARDINAL;
                K: INTEGER): CARDINAL;
(*pre: 0<= Start <= Rest <= HIGH(A)+1
 *post: Start <= result <= Rest
 *      & Perm(A, A_0)
 *      & A[0 to Start-1] = A_0[0 to Start-1]
 *      & A[Rest to HIGH(A)] = A_0[Rest to HIGH(A)]
 *      & (A[Start to result-1], A[result to Rest-1])
 *        satisfies the Miranda specification for
 *        (partition K   A_0[Start to Rest-1])
 *)
```
Let us leave the implementation of Partition until after the Dutch national flag problem; but note that we do not need Partition to compute the same function as partition (which, in any event, we have not defined yet), only to satisfy its specification.

The functional qsort can now be translated into Modula-2, using a call of Partition:
```
PROCEDURE QuickSort (* specified above *);
(* recursion variant = Rest-Start *)
  VAR n: CARDINAL;
      x: INTEGER;
BEGIN
  IF Start < Rest
  (* region is nonempty,
   *(qsort A_0[Start to Rest-1]) =
   *       (qsort ys)++[A_0[Start]]++(qsort zs)
   * where (ys,zs) =
   *       partition A_0[Start] A_0[Start+1 to Rest-1]-from Miranda
   *)
  THEN
    n:=Partition(A, Start+1, Rest, A[Start]);
    Swap(A[Start], A[n-1]);
    (*(A[Start to n-2], A[n to Rest-1])
     *is a valid result for
     *(partition A_0[Start] A_0[Start+1 to Rest-1])
     *)
    QuickSort(A, Start, n-1);
    QuickSort(A, n, Rest)
(*ELSE Start = Rest, region is empty. *)
  END
END QuickSort;
```

This really is just a translation of the Miranda qsort, though you might not think it at first glance. (That is why we suggest that it is a good idea to see the algorithm clearly in Miranda first.)

Think of the call qsort$(x:xs)$. In the Modula-2 context, x is $A_0[Start]$, and xs is $A_0[Start+1$ to $Rest-1]$. After n := Partition(...) we have a satisfactory result for Partition x xs, namely $(A[Start+1$ to n-1$]$, $A[n$ to $Rest$-1$])$ $(= (ys_1, zs_1)$, say). However, this is not quite yet the (ys,zs) that is used for the recursive call of qsort, the reason being that we want x in the middle instead of at the left-hand end where it is at the moment. What we do next is to swap $A[Start]$ with $A[n$-1$]$, so that instead of having the equivalent of $[x]$++ ys_1 ++ zs_1 we have ys++ $[x]$++ zs where ys is a permutation of ys_1 — its last element has been moved to the head — and zs is just zs_1 renamed. (ys,zs) is still a satisfactory result for Partition x xs, so if we apply the sorting algorithm recursively in place to ys and to zs we obtain (qsort ys) ++ $[x]$ ++ (qsort zs), as required.

12.5 Dutch national flag

This algorithm, due to the Dutch computer scientist Dijkstra, solves the sorting problem in the very simple case where there are only three possible values of the elements to be sorted.

The Dutch national flag is a tricolour, red (at the top), white and blue (Figure 12.2). For the problem imagine that (a computer representation of)

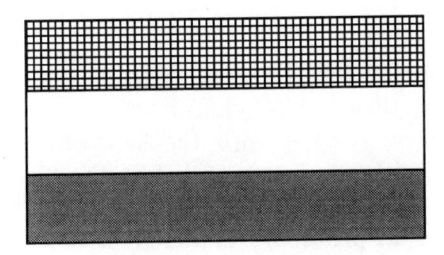

Figure 12.2

the flag gets scrambled (Figure 12.3), the stripes being cut up horizontally and rearranged: It is desired to correct this in one pass, that is, inspecting each stripelet once only. We are not told whether the three stripes are cut into the same number of stripelets. The only permitted way of rearranging stripelets is by swapping them, two at a time:

Quick sort

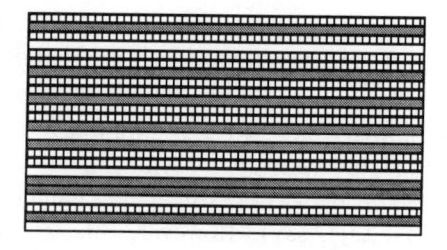

Figure 12.3

```
TYPE Colour = (red, white, blue);

PROCEDURE Restore (VAR A: ARRAY OF Colour);
(*pre: none
 *post:  Perm(A, A_0) & Sorted(A)
 *)
```
The idea is to track through the stripelets and put each one in 'the right area'. Part way through, let us have the stripelets arranged as in Figure 12.4. We shall need to keep pointers to the boundaries between the four areas.

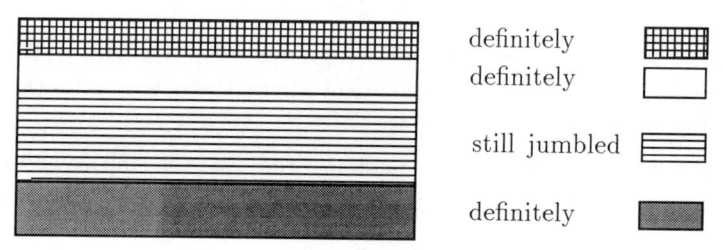

definitely
definitely

still jumbled

definitely

Figure 12.4

At each iteration, we inspect the first, that is, the top, grey (uninspected) stripelet. If it is *white*, then it is already in the right place and we can move on. If it is *red*, then we swap it with the first white and move on. If it is *blue*, then we swap it with the last grey before the blues but do not move on because we have now fetched another grey to inspect. Finally, when there are no greys left, then the stripelets are in the right order.

If we invent names for the pointers, then we can improve the diagram (Figure 12.5). We have adopted a convention here: there are three boundaries to be marked (red–white, white–grey and grey–blue), and the corresponding variable is always the index of the element just *after* the boundary. If two adjacent markers are equal, it shows that that region is empty. In particular, when *GreyStart=BlueStart* then there are no greys left and the flag is in order.

This diagram is essentially the loop invariant. At the appropriate points in the computation, we can imagine freezing the computer, inspecting the

Dutch national flag

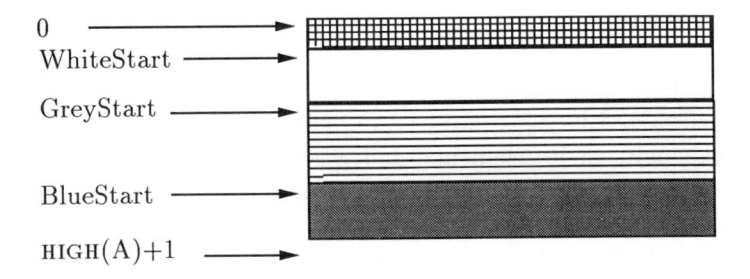

Figure 12.5

variables and the array, and asking whether the stripelets from, for instance *WhiteStart* to *GreyStart*−1, are indeed all white, as the diagram suggests. In other words, the diagram suggests a statement about the computer's state, and our next task is to translate this into logic as the invariant. You will see this in the implementation.

The variant, which is a measure of the amount of work left to be done, is the size of the jumbled (grey) area: *BlueStart*−*GreyStart*. Progress is made by reducing it:

```
PROCEDURE Restore(VAR A: ARRAY OF Colour);
VAR WhiteStart,GreyStart,BlueStart: CARDINAL;
BEGIN
  WhiteStart := 0; GreyStart := 0;
  BlueStart := HIGH(A)+1;
(* loop invariant:
*   Perm(A,A_0)
*   & WhiteStart <= GreyStart <= BlueStart <= HIGH(A)+1
*   & (A)i:nat. ((0 <= i < WhiteStart -> A[i] = red)
*   & (WhiteStart <= i < GreyStart -> A[i] = white)
*   & (BlueStart <= i <= HIGH(A) -> A[i] = blue))
* variant = BlueStart-GreyStart
*)
  WHILE GreyStart < BlueStart DO
    CASE A[GreyStart] OF
        red:   Swap(A[WhiteStart],A[GreyStart]);
               WhiteStart := WhiteStart+1;
               GreyStart := GreyStart+1
      |white:  GreyStart := GreyStart+1
      |blue:   Swap(A[GreyStart],A[BlueStart-1]);
               BlueStart := BlueStart-1
    END
  END
END Restore;
```

172   *Quick sort*

Sample reasoning

Let us us look at just two examples of how to verify parts of the procedure. First, why is `Perm` (A, A_0) always true? This is because all we ever do to the array is swap pairs of its elements, and a sequence of swaps is a permutation.

Next, why does the *red* part of the `CASE` statement reestablish the invariant? Let us write *WS*, *GS*, *BS* and A_1 for the values of *WhiteStart*, *GreyStart*, *BlueStart* and A when the label *red* is reached.

We know that $0 \leq WS \leq GS < BS \leq \text{HIGH}(A) + 1$, so after the update, when *WhiteStart* $= WS + 1$, *GreyStart* $= GS + 1$ and *BlueStart* $= BS$, we have $0 \leq$ *WhiteStart* $\leq$ *GreyStart* $\leq$ *BlueStart* $\leq \text{HIGH}(A) + 1$, as required. To check that the colours are correct after the update, let i be a natural number.

If $0 \leq i <$ *WhiteStart*, then $0 \leq i \leq WS$. We must show that $A[i]$ is *red*. If $i = WS$, this follows from the specification of `Swap`:

- $A[WS] = A_1[GS] = red$ by the `CASE` switch.
- If $i < WS$, which is $\leq GS$, then i is neither *WS* nor *GS*. Hence $A[i]$ was unaffected by the `Swap`, so $A[i] = A_1[i] = red$ by the loop invariant.

Next, suppose *WhiteStart* $\leq i <$ *GreyStart*, that is, $WS + 1 \leq i \leq GS$. Note in this case that $A_1[WS] = white$ by the loop invariant, for $WS < WS + 1 \leq GS$. (The point is that the situation where $WS = GS$, and so $A_1[WS]$ is *grey*, is impossible given the i that we are considering.) Hence for $i = GS$, the specification of `Swap` tells us that $A[GS] = A_1[WS] = white$.

If $i < GS$, then i is neither *WS* nor *GS*. Hence from the specification of *Swap*, $A[i]$ is unchanged, and by the loop invariant it was white. For the third case, take *BlueStart* $\leq i \leq \text{HIGH}(A)$. Again, $A[i]$ is unchanged, and by the loop invariant it was *blue*.

12.6 Partitions by the Dutch national flag algorithm

Suppose, given a key integer K, you think of all integers as being coloured:
  integers $< K$ are *red*
K is *white*
  integers $> K$ are *blue*
Then the Dutch national flag algorithm, applied to an integer array, can do a crude sort. The *white* region is likely to be small or non-existent, so it is reasonable to merge it with the *red* region to make *pink*. The two regions correspond to those that `Partition` discovers: one for $\leq K$, one for $> K$.

We can therefore implement `Partition` by simplifying the Dutch national flag algorithm to cope with the flag of the Royal College of Midwives (pink and blue stripes). `QuickSort` will then look as in Figure 12.6, with recursive calls to sort the pink and blue regions. To implement `Partition` by adapting

Partitions by the Dutch national flag algorithm 173

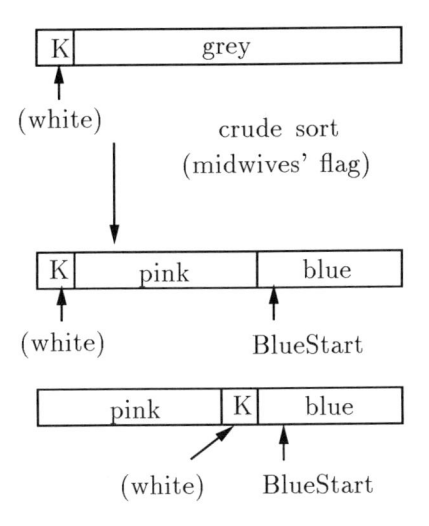

Figure 12.6

the `Partition` from the Dutch national flag, we must:

1. Simplify `Restore` to do the Midwives' sort (drop the 'red' case and *WhiteStart*; we can also turn the `CASE` statement to an `IF` statement).
2. Return the final *BlueStart* as a result in order to show the boundary of the partition.
3. Convert the colours to arithmetic inequalities ($\leq$ or $>$ the key K).
4. Allow for partitioning regions, rather than the whole array.

There should be no need to reason that the implementation is correct because we have done all the reasoning for `Restore`. But the loop invariant allows us to check, in case of doubt:

```
PROCEDURE Partition(VAR A: ARRAY OF INTEGER; Start, Rest: CARDINAL;
                    K: INTEGER): CARDINAL;
(*specification as before *)
VAR GreyStart, BlueStart: CARDINAL;
    x: INTEGER;
BEGIN
  GreyStart := Start; (* no pinks *)
  BlueStart := Rest; (* no blues *)
(* loop invariant:
 * Perm(A, A_0)
 * & Start <= GreyStart <= BlueStart <= Rest
 * & (A)i:nat.
 * ((Start <=i< GreyStart -> A[i]<=K)
```

174   *Quick sort*

```
 *  &(BlueStart <=i< Rest -> A[i]>K))
 *  variant = BlueStart-GreyStart
 *)
   WHILE GreyStart < BlueStart DO
     IF A[GreyStart]<=K(*pink*)
     THEN GreyStart := GreyStart+1
     ELSE
       x:=A[GreyStart];
       A[GreyStart] := A[BlueStart-1];
       A[BlueStart-1] := x;
       BlueStart := BlueStart-1
     END
   END;
   RETURN BlueStart
 END Partition;
```

12.7 Summary

- Functional definitions can be useful reasoning tools even if the final implementation is to be imperative.
- Sometimes a diagram is the real loop invariant.
- The method of introducing logical constants to name the values of computer variables is often (as in `Restore`) indispensable when you show that the loop body reestablishes the invariant.

12.8 Exercises

1. For the Dutch national flag algorithm show the following:

    (a) the invariant is established by the initialization;

    (b) the invariant is reestablished by each iteration (that is, do the *blue* and *white* cases corresponding to the *red* case above);

    (c) when looping stops, the post-condition has been set up;

    (d) the variant strictly decreases on each iteration, but never goes negative;

    (e) for every array access or `Swap`, the subscripts are within bounds (that is, $\leq \text{HIGH}(A)$).

2. Consider the following idea for the Dutch national flag problem. The

white stripelets are to be put at the other end of the grey area:

[Red |Grey |White |Blue]
          ↑   ↑   ↑
          GreyStart   WhiteStart   BlueStart

(a) Show that this is unsatisfactory for two reasons:
- on average, more swaps are done than are necessary;
- this method can give wrong answers.

(b) Two other sequences of two swaps are possible; is either of them correct?

3. Can the Dutch national flag method be generalized to work with more than three colours?
4. Implement **partition** in Miranda.
5. Modify the Miranda **partition** and **qsort** so that the order relation used does not have to be $\leq$, but is supplied as a parameter *lte*, a 'comparison function' which takes two elements as arguments and gives a Boolean result:

```
partition1::(*->*-> bool)->* ->[*]->([*],[*])
qsort1::(*->*-> bool)->[*]->[*]
```

(The comparison function can be thought of as a two-place predicate, or as a relation.) Give implementations for these, ensuring that **qsort** and **partition** are (qsort1 ($\leq$)) and (partition1 ($\leq$)). To obtain a *downward* ordered list, you would use (qsort1($\geq$)).

Chapter 13

Warshall's algorithm

Warshall's algorithm is an example of an algorithm that is difficult to understand at all without some kind of reasoning based on a loop invariant. The problem is to find the transitive closure of a relation. We shall first look at an algorithm that is relatively clear, and then go on to one (Warshall's algorithm) that is clever, and more efficient, but more difficult to understand.

13.1 Transitive closure

Warshall's algorithm computes transitive closures, a notion that comes from the theory of *relations*. To keep the discussion here simple, we shall explain this in terms of graphs, such as the one in Figure 13.1. A graph has a

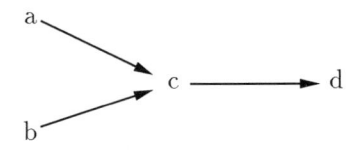

Figure 13.1

number of *nodes* (a, b, c and d here), and some *edges* (the arrows). In the sort of graph that we shall be using, for any pair (x, y) of nodes, there will be at most one edge from x to y (but possibly also one from y to x). Let us write "$x \to y$" if there is an edge from x to y. In our example,

$$a \to c,\ b \to c \text{ and } c \to d$$

but not $\quad a \to b,\ a \to a,\ c \to b,$ nor $a \to d$.

We shall interest ourselves in the problem of finding composite *paths* through the graph, made by joining edges up, head to tail, like elephants on parade.

Let us write "$x \to^+ y$" if there is a path from x to y; so here we have
$$a \to^+ c,\ b \to^+ c,\ c \to^+ d,\ a \to^+ d \text{ and } b \to^+ d$$
but not $\quad a \to^+ b,\ a \to^+ a$ or $c \to^+ b$.

Formally, $x \to^+ y$ iff we can find a sequence $z_1, \ldots, z_n$ with
$$x \to z_1 \to \ldots \to z_n = y$$
$\to^+$ is the *transitive closure* of $\to$.

The *length* of the path is the number of *edges*, which is n here. We write $x \to^r y$ if there is a path of length r from x to y. Then

- $x \to^+ y$ iff $\exists n$:nat. $(1 \leq n \land x \to^n y)$
- $x \to y$ iff $x \to^1 y$

The following are some applications of finding the transitive closure:

- Suppose the nodes and edges represent airports and direct air flights. The paths are composite trips that can be made by plane alone.
- Suppose that nodes represent procedures in some program, and an edge from a to b means that a *calls* b. Then a path from a to b means that a calls b, though possibly indirectly (via some other procedures). A path from a to *itself* shows that a is potentially recursive. It may be useful for a compiler to be able to discover this because non-recursive procedures can be optimized to store return addresses, parameters and local variables in fixed locations instead of on a stack.

Computer representation

The graph can also be thought of as a *matrix*, or *array*, and this is the basis of the computer representation. If you give each node a number, then the whereabouts of the edges can be described by a square array of Boolean values:
$$Edge[a, b] = \begin{cases} \text{TRUE} & \text{if there is an edge from } a \text{ to } b, \text{ that is, } a \to b \\ \text{FALSE} & \text{otherwise} \end{cases}$$
This array, or matrix, is called the *adjacency matrix* of the graph. The transitive closure can be described the same way:
$$Path[a, b] = \begin{cases} \text{TRUE} & \text{if there is a path from } a \text{ to } b, \text{ that is, } a \to^+ b \\ \text{FALSE} & \text{otherwise} \end{cases}$$

Let us give some suitable declarations, and also specify the transitive closure procedure:

178   Warshall's algorithm

```
CONST Size = ...;(*number of nodes*)

TYPE
  Node = 1..Size;
  AdjMatrix = ARRAY Node,Node OF BOOLEAN;

PROCEDURE TransClos(Edge: AdjMatrix; VAR Path: AdjMatrix);
(*pre: none
 *post: Path represents transitive closure of Edge
 *)
```

You might decide to have `Edge` a `VAR` parameter, to avoid any possible copying. Then you would need a pre-condition to say that `Edge` and `Path` are different arrays, and an extra post-condition to say that `Edge` = `Edge`$_0$.

13.2   First algorithm

We shall look at three algorithms, and all of them will use the same basic idea. Some paths are more complicated than others; the simplest ones are the single edges, and they can be put together to make more complicated ones. The loop invariant will always say 'the TRUE entries in *Path* all represent paths, and all paths up to a certain degree of complication have been registered as TRUEs in *Path*'. More formally,

$\forall a, b: Node. \ ((Path[a,b] \to (a \to^+ b))$
$\wedge((a \to^+ b)$ by a path of degree of complication $\leq N \to Path[a,b]))$

The invariant will always be established initially by copying *Edge* to *Path* (thus registering the simplest paths), and each algorithm terminates when the degree of complication is sufficient to cover all possible paths. One difference between the algorithms lies in the measure of complication.

For the first two algorithms, we equate complication of a path with its *length*.

Suppose *Path* has registered all the paths of length $\leq n$, and we now want to find all paths of length $\leq n+1$: the new ones that we must find are those of length exactly $n+1$. But such a path from a to b splits up as a path of length n (from a to c_n, say), which is already registered in *Path*, and then an edge from c_n to b. Hence we shall be able to recognize it by the fact that $Path[a, c_n] = Edge[c_n, b]$ = TRUE. Our method is to look at all possible combinations for a, b and c, and assign TRUE to $Path[a, b]$ if either it was TRUE already or we have $Path[a, c] = Edge[c, b]$ = TRUE.

Paths can be of arbitrary length, so we must find a way of stopping. Actually, we can stop when we have registered all paths of length $\leq Size$, for longer ones do not tell us anything new. To see this, suppose we have a path from a to b of length $n > Size$:

$$c_0 \to c_1 \to \ldots \to c_{n-1} \to c_n \quad \text{where } c_0 = a \text{ and } c_n = b$$

Consider $c_0, \ldots, c_n$. There are at least $Size + 1$ of these symbols, but there are only $Size$ possible nodes. Therefore, one node appears twice — $c_i = c_j$ where $i < j$. But this path can now be collapsed to a shorter path from a to b:

$$a \to c_1 \to \ldots \to c_i = c_j \to \ldots \to c_n = b$$

(See Exercise 1 for a more rigorous induction proof.)

Detailed reasoning

initialization: This follows because $a \to^1 b$ iff $Edge[a, b]$.

finalization: This follows because at the end $N = Size$, and $a \to^+ b$ iff $a \to^r b$ for some $r \leq Size$, as reasoned above.

reestablishing the invariant: Let us split the invariant I_1 into two parts:

$$I_1 1 \equiv_{def} \forall a, b : Node. \ (Path[a, b] \to (a \to^+ b))$$

$$I_1 2 \equiv_{def} \forall a, b : Node. \ (\forall r : nat. \ (a \to^r b) \land 1 \leq r \leq N \to Path[a, b])$$

The first thing to notice is that nothing ever spoils the truth of $I_1 1$. In particular, suppose it holds just before the assignment in the FOR loop. The only possible change is if $Path[i, j]$ becomes TRUE because we already have $Path[i, k]$ and $Edge[k, j]$; but then from $I_1 1$ we know $(i \to^+ k)$ and $(k \to j)$, so $(i \to^+ j)$, as required, and $I_1 1$ still holds afterwards. Hence $I_1 1$ holds right through the program.

Turning to $I_1 2$, this involves N so we must take care to allow for the increment $N := N + 1$. Let us write N_1 for the old value of N; after the increment, $N = N_1 + 1$. Before the FOR loops, $I2$ told us that if $a \to^r b$ with $r \leq N_1$ then $Path[a, b]$ and this much is never spoiled because $Path[a, b]$ never changes from TRUE to FALSE. Now suppose afterwards that $a \to^{N_1+1} b$, so there is a path of length $N_1 + 1$ from a to b. The last step of this path goes from c (say) to b, so we know $a \to^{N_1} c$ and $Edge[c, b]$; by the previous invariant we know $Path[a, c]$. Now consider the FOR loop iteration when $i = a$, $j = b$ and $k = c$: because $Path[a, c] = Edge[c, b] =$ TRUE, this sets $Path[a, b]$ to TRUE and it stays TRUE for ever, as required.

This is a good example of the reasoning style for FOR loops that was suggested in Section 10.6

180 *Warshall's algorithm*

Implementation

```
PROCEDURE TransClos(Edge: AdjMatrix; VAR Path: AdjMatrix);
(*pre: none
*post:     Path represents transitive closure of Edge
*notation: write - a-> b   iff Edge[a,b] = true
*          (there is an edge from a to b)
*          a-> +b   iff a is related to b by the transitive closure
*          of Edge (there is a path from a to b);
*          a-> ^n   b   iff there is a path from a to b  of length n
*)
VAR N: CARDINAL;
  i,j,k: Node;
BEGIN
  CopyAdjMatrix(Edge,Path);
  N:=1;
(*loop invariant - call it I1:
*N<= Size
* & (A)a,b:Node.
*   ((Path[a,b]-> (a-> +b))
* & (A)r:nat. ((a-> ^r b) & 1<=r<=N -> Path[a,b]))
* variant = Size-N
*)
  WHILE N < Size DO
    FOR i:=1 TO Size DO
      FOR j:=1 TO Size DO
        FOR k:=1 TO Size DO
          Path[i,j] := Path[i,j] OR (Path[i,k] AND Edge[k,j])
          (*NB Path[a,b] never changes from true to false *)
        END
      END
    END;
    N:=N+1
  END
END TransClos;

PROCEDURE CopyAdjMatrix(From: AdjMatrix; VAR To: AdjMatrix);
(*pre: none
*post:  From = To
*)
BEGIN
(*exercise*)
END CopyAdjMatrix;
```

Efficiency

There are four nested loops, controlled by N, i, j and k. Each is executed roughly $Size$ times.

($Size - 1$ times for N, $Size$ each for i, j, k. $Total = Size^4 - Size^3$.) Hence, the total number of iterations is of the order of $Size^4$. (For large graphs the $Size^3$ term is insignificant compared with $Size^4$.)

This measures the *complexity* of the algorithm. $Size$ measures how big the problem is: so the execution time increases roughly as the fourth power of the size of the problem. Thus big problems (lots of nodes) will really take quite a long time. Can we improve on this?

The first improvement is obvious but good. Suppose all paths of length N or less are recorded in $Path$. Then any path of length $2 * N$ or less can be decomposed into two parts, each of length N or less: if $a \to^r b$ with $r \leq 2 * N$, then we can write $r = s + t$ with $s, t \leq N$, and $a \to^s c \to^t b$ for some node c. Therefore, we have already registered $Path[a, c] = Path[c, b] = \text{TRUE}$.

By this means, we can double N at each stage (that is, replace the assignment $N := N + 1$ by $N := 2 * N$) by using the innermost statement

```
Path[i,j] := Path[i,j] OR (Path[i,k] AND Path[k,j])
```

The outermost (N) loop is now executed approximately $log_2 Size$ times, so the total number of iterations is of the order of $log_2 Size \times Size^3$. This is good. $log_2 Size$ increases much more slowly than $Size$. Can we do better still?

13.3 Warshall's algorithm

The path relation that we are building up is *transitive:*

$$\forall a, b, c : Node.\ ((a \to^+ c) \land (c \to^+ b) \to (a \to^+ b))$$

(This is proved by joining paths together.) One way of understanding Warshall's algorithm is through the idea that part way through the calculation, $Path$ will not be completely transitive but will be 'partially' transitive in that only certain values of c, not too big, will work in the above formula:

$$\forall a, b, c : Node.\ (Path[a, c] \land Path[c, b] \land c \leq N \to Path[a, b])$$

Now suppose we have achieved this partial transitivity, and we have a path

$$a \to c_1 \to c_2 \to \ldots \to c_n \to b$$

The partial transitivity tells us that provided the nodes $c_1, \ldots, c_n$ (let us call these the *transit nodes* of the path, as distinct from the endpoints a and b) are all $\leq N$, then we have $Path[a, b]$.

Warshall's algorithm

This leads to a new idea of how complicated a path is:

A *simple* path is one whose transit nodes (no matter how many) are all small — they have numerically small codes.

A *complicated* path is one whose transit nodes (no matter how few) include big ones.

The simplest paths from a to b have no transit nodes at all: they are just edges $a \to b$.

The next simplest are the paths that use node 1 as a transit node. These are of the form $a \to 1 \to b$.

Next, with node 2 also as a transit node, we have the possible forms

$$a \to 2 \to b,\ a \to 1 \to 2 \to b,\ a \to 2 \to 1 \to b$$

We quantify this numerically by defining the *transit maximum* of a path to be the maximum numerical code of its transit nodes (or 0 if there are none). Let us write $a \to_N b$ if there is a path from a to b with transit maximum $\leq N$.

Suppose we have already determined where there are paths of transit maximum $\leq N$, in other words we have computed the relation $\to_N$. Any path from a to b of transit maximum $N+1$ must use node $N+1$ in transit, and by much the same argument as before we do not need to consider such paths that use node $N+1$ more than once in transit (find the first and last transit occurrences of $N+1$ and cut out all the path in between them). Then we have

$$a \to \ldots \to (N+1) \to \ldots \to b$$

where the two sections of this have transit maximum at most N and so have already been found. To reiterate, once we know about all the paths of transit maximum $\leq N$, then all the paths of transit maximum $N+1$ from a to b can be recognized by the pattern $a \to_N (N+1) \to_N b$, the two sections of this being paths that we already know about.

Detailed reasoning

initialization: This follows because $a \to_0 b$ iff $a \to b$.
finalization: Because $a \to_{Size} b$ iff $a \to^+ b$.
reestablishing the invariant: Let N_1 be the value of N before the increment, and let J be the following, which follows from the invariant I_2:

$$\forall a, b : Node.\ (Path[a,b] \to (a \to^+ b)) \wedge ((a \to_{N_1} b \to Path[a,b]))$$

No iteration of the FOR loops ever spoils the truth of J so it is still true after the FOR loops. However, the invariant will say something stronger than J because of the increment of N, and we must check this.

Suppose $a \to_N b$, so there is a path from a to b with transit maximum $\leq N$ (which is now $N_1 + 1$). If all its transit nodes are actually $\leq N_1$, then $a \to_{N_1} b$ and so by J we know $Path[a, b]$. The only remaining case is when some transit node is equal to N. Then by splitting up the path we see that $a \to_{N_1} N \to_{N_1} b$, so by J we know that $Path[a, N]$ and $Path[N, b]$. The FOR loop iteration when $i = a$ and $j = b$ makes $Path[a, b]$ equal to TRUE and it remains so for ever.

Implementation

```
PROCEDURE TransClos(Edge: AdjMatrix; VAR Path: AdjMatrix);
(*pre: none
 *post:  Path represents transitive closure of Edge
 *notation: a-> n   b  means there is some path
 *            a-> c1-> c2-> ... -> cr -> b(r>=0)
 *         where c1, ... , cr are all <=n,i.e. its transit maximum is <=n.
 *         Hence a-> +b   iff a-> Size b.
 *)
VAR N: CARDINAL;
    i,j: Node;
BEGIN
  CopyAdjMatrix(Path,Edge);
  N:=0;
(*loop invariant I2:
 * N<= Size
 * & (A)a,b:Node.
 *   ((Path[a,b]-> (a-> +b))
 * & ((a-> N b)-> Path[a,b]))
 *variant = Size-N
 *)
  WHILE N < Size DO
    N:=N+1;
    FOR i:=1 TO Size DO
      FOR j:=1 TO Size DO
        Path[i,j] := Path[i,j] OR (Path[i,N] AND Path[N,j])
      END
    END
  END
END TransClos;
```

Efficiency

There are now three nested loops (for N, i and j), each one being executed $Size$ times, so the total number of iterations is of the order of $Size^3$. This is the best of our three algorithms.

We could optimize this further. For instance, we could replace the `FOR` loops by

```
FOR i:=1 TO Size DO
  IF Path[i,N]
  THEN
    FOR j:=1 TO N  DO
      Path[i,j] := Path[i,j] OR Path[N,j]
    END
  END
END
```

(QUESTION: can you prove that this has the same result as the preceding version?) However, this is local fine tuning. The step from the original version to Warshall's was a fundamental change of algorithm, with a new Invariant.

13.4 Summary

- We have given three algorithms to compute transitive closures, each one fundamentally more efficient than the previous one.
- The most efficient is Warshall's algorithm. It would be difficult to see clearly why it works without the use of loop invariants.
- The reasoning about `FOR` loops was essentially different from the loop invariant technique used for `WHILE` loops.

13.5 Exercises

1. Given a graph with $Size$ nodes, show that for any nodes a and b, if $a \to^+ b$ then $a \to^r b$ for some $r \leq Size$. HINT: use course of values induction on n to show $\forall n : nat.\ P(n)$, where

$$P(n) \equiv (a \to^n b) \to \exists r : nat.\ (r \leq Size \land (a \to^r b)).$$

2. Use Warshall's algorithm 'in place' to implement the following procedure (without using any array other than $Graph$):

```
PROCEDURE TransClos(VAR Graph: AdjMatrix);
(*pre: none
*post: Graph represents transitive closure of Graph_0
*)
```

3. Modify the detailed reasoning of the first algorithm to justify the second.
4. Warshall's algorithm can be modified to compute shortest paths between nodes in a graph. Here is the specification:

```
TYPE Matrix = ARRAY Node, Node OF CARDINAL;

PROCEDURE ShortPaths(Edge: AdjMatrix; VAR SP: Matrix);
  (*pre: none
  *post: (A)i,j:Node. (A)r:nat.
  *         (1 <= SP[i,j] <= Size+1
  *         & (SP[i,j] = r & r <= Size -> (i -> ^r j))
  *     & ((i -> ^r j) & r >= 1 -> SP[i,j] <= r))
  *)
```

The idea is that if there is any path at all from i to j then there is one of length $Size$ or less, and $SP[i,j]$ is to be the shortest such length. If there is no path, then $SP[i,j]$ is to be $Size + 1$.

Show how to modify the invariant and code of Warshall's algorithm to solve this new problem. You will probably need to use the relation $\rightarrow_N^r$, defined by $(i \rightarrow_N^r j)$ iff there is a path of length r from i to j, with transit nodes all $\leq N$.

Chapter 14
Tail recursion

It is often convenient to do a lot of reasoning in Miranda because the language has a more elegant notation that is more directly related to mathematical ideas. For instance, the properties of list functions such as append and reverse came out fairly simply in Miranda. However, in practice, you will often want to use an imperative language for its greater efficiency and so it would be nice somehow to reuse that reasoning in the context of Modula-2. We saw an example in Chapter 12. While on the subject of efficiency, it is worth mentioning that efficiency is usually less important than clarity. This is because *any* unclear piece of program can hide a fatal error, while it is only in frequently used parts that inefficiencies make a significant difference.

The feature that we now address is the transfer from the *recursive* definitions of Miranda to the *iterative* (looping) definitions of Modula-2. Of course, one can also give recursive definitions in Modula-2, but it is generally less efficient to do so.

There is a general method by which a particular special kind of definition in Miranda, the so-called *tail recursive* definition, can be converted automatically into a WHILE loop implementation in Modula-2; and even though not all recursive definitions are tail recursive, there is still a chance of finding equivalent tail recursive definitions — ones that define the same function.

14.1 Tail recursion

A definition of a function f is *tail recursive* iff the results of any recursive calls of f are used immediately as the result of f, without any further calculation. Therefore in a tail recursive definition, the recursion is used simply to call the same function but with different arguments.

The reason for this name is that the recursion occurs right at the end, the tail, of the calculation, and there is no more to do afterwards. For instance, the following definition of isin (to test whether a list t contains an element x) is tail recursive. The result of the recursive call, (isin x ys), is used directly as the result of what was being defined (isin x (y :ys)).

```
isin x []= False
isin x(y:ys)= True,      if y=x
            = isin x xs, otherwise
```

The following example, on the other hand, is *not* a tail recursive definition. The result of the recursive call (append xs ys) is used in a further calculation: it has x *cons*-ed on the front.

```
append [] ys = ys
append (x:xs) ys = x:(append xs ys)
```

Figure 14.1 contains some function definitions. Which are tail recursive? ANSWERS: the definitions of rev1, gcd, f1 and listcomp are tail recursive. What is (f1 a n) for general a, not necessarily 1?

```
reverse [] = []
reverse (x:xs) = (reverse xs)++[x]

||reverse xs = rev1 [] xs
rev1 as []      = as
rev1 as (x:xs)  = rev1 (x:as) xs

gcd x y = x,             if y=0
        = gcd y(x mod y),   otherwise

fact n = 1,              if n=0
       = n*(fact (n-1)),   otherwise

||fact n=f1 1 n
f1 a n = a,              if n=0
       = f1 (a*n) (n-1),   otherwise

order ::= Before | Same | After
listcomp [ ] [ ]   = Same
listcomp [ ] (y:t) = Before
listcomp (x:s) [ ] = After
listcomp (x:s) (y:t) = Before,        if x < y
                     = After,          if x > y
                     = listcomp s t, otherwise
```

Figure 14.1 Assorted Miranda definitions

Tail recursion and WHILE loops

Think of the tail recursion as meaning 'do the same computation again, but with new arguments'. In Modula-2, you could keep variables for the arguments, and then tail recursion means 'update the variables, and repeat'. This is just looping.

To express this more precisely, we use the method of loop invariants:

> The loop invariant says: the answer you originally wanted is the same as if you calculated it starting with the variables you have got now.

For instance, for `isin` the loop invariant would be

isin x ys_0 (`isin` calculated with original ys)
    = isin x ys (`isin` calculated with current ys)

14.2 Example: gcd

It is easy to imagine Euclid's algorithm set out in a table. For instance, to calculate the gcd of 26 and 30, you could write

x	y
26	30
30	26
26	4
4	2
2	0 answer is 2

At each stage, you replace x and y by y and x mod y, because the method says that (gcd x y) = (gcd y (x mod y)) if $y \neq 0$. The crucial property is that in each line, (gcd x y) = (gcd x_0 y_0), where x_0 and y_0 are the original values of x and y (26 and 30 here). This is our loop invariant. Note also that the loop variant y is the same as the recursion variant for gcd x y.

```
PROCEDURE GCD(x,y: CARDINAL):CARDINAL;
(*pre: none
 *post: result = (gcd x_0 y_0) where gcd is as defined in Miranda.
 *)
VAR z: CARDINAL ;
BEGIN
(* loop invariant: (gcd x y)=(gcd x_0 y_0)
 * variant = y
 *)
  WHILE y#0 DO z := x MOD y ; x := y ; y := z END ;
  RETURN x
END GCD ;
```

Justification

initialization: initially by definition $x = x_0$ and $y = y_0$, so the invariant holds without any initialization being necessary.

loop test and finalization: we stop looping when $y = 0$, for then the first clause in the Miranda definition tells us that $(\text{gcd } x\ y) = x$, and by the loop invariant this is the answer we want. So we just return it.

reestablishing the invariant: when $y \neq 0$, then

$$(\text{gcd } x\ y) = (\text{gcd } y\ (x \text{ mod } y)).$$

Hence by replacing x and y by y and $x \text{ mod } y$ (which is what the sequence of assignments does), we leave $(\text{gcd } x\ y)$ unchanged and hence reestablish the invariant. Also, we have decreased the variant, y. (NOTE: $(x \text{ mod } y)$ has a pre-condition, namely that $y \neq 0$. This holds in this part of the program.)

To be slightly more formal, let x_1 and y_1 be the values of x and y at the start of the iteration. The invariant tells us that $\text{gcd } x_1\ y_1 = \text{gcd } x_0\ y_0$. It is easy to see that after the loop body we have $x = y_1$, $y = x_1 \text{ mod } y_1$ (EXERCISE: prove this with mid-conditions). Thus we have reestablished the invariant for

$$\text{gcd } x\ y = \text{gcd } y_1\ (x_1 \text{ mod } y_1) = \text{gcd } x_1\ y_1 = \text{gcd } x_0\ y_0.$$

Recall that in general we resolved not to assign to variables that were called by value. This was to make the reasoning easier. However, with this method it is particularly convenient and natural to break this resolution — after all, the informal justification was that we change the arguments of the function. Therefore, we put in an explicit disclaimer to say that the call-by-value parameters might change. In this example, of course, the only effects of this are local to the procedure — the change cannot be detected in the outside world.

14.3 General scheme

In general, a tail recursive definition in Miranda looks as follows:

```
f x = a1,    if c1
    = a2,    if c2
    = ...            || more non-recursive cases
    = an,    if cn
    = f x1,  if d1
    = f x2,  if d2
    = ...            || more recursive cases
```

$a_1, a_2, \ldots, a_n$ are expressions giving the answers in the non-recursive cases. $x_1, x_2, \ldots$ are the new parameters used in the tail recursive cases. $a_1, a_2, \ldots, a_n, x_1, x_2, \ldots$, as well as the guards $c_1, c_2, \ldots, c_n, d_1, d_2, \ldots$, are all calculated simply, without recursion. There is no difficulty in making this work when f has more than one parameter.

Translation using WHILE loop

```
PROCEDURE f(x: ... ): ...;
(* NB Value parameter x  may be changed
 *pre: any pre-conditions needed for f
 *post: result = (f x_0) where f is as defined above in Miranda
 *)
BEGIN
(* loop invariant: (f x) = (f x_0)
 * variant: recursion variant for Miranda f
 *)
  WHILE NOT c1 AND NOT c2 AND ... NOT cn  DO
    IF d1 THEN x:=x1
    ELSIF d2 THEN x:=x2
    ELSIF ...
    END
  END;
  IF c1 THEN RETURN a1
  ELSIF c2 THEN RETURN a2
  ELSIF ...
  END
END f;
```

EXERCISE: how does gcd fit this pattern? Note that the invariant and the variant come automatically.

14.4 Example: factorial

The following is the obvious recursive definition of the factorial function, but it is not tail recursive:

```
fact :: num -> num
||pre: nat(n)
||post: fact n = n!
fact n = 1,                if n=0
       = n*(fact (n-1)),  otherwise
```

Example: factorial

After the recursive call (fact($n-1$)), there is still a residual computation ($n * \ldots$). However, these can be 'accumulated' into a single variable:

```
f1 a n = a,              if n=0
       = f1(a*n)(n-1),   otherwise
```

and then (fact n) = (f1 1 n) (but we shall have to prove this). a is the *accumulator parameter* in f1. f1 *is* tail recursive, so you can convert it into a WHILE loop. But in fact, we do not need to implement f1 separately in Modula-2; we can put its WHILE loop into the implementation for fact, with an extra local variable for the accumulator parameter:

```
PROCEDURE fact(n: CARDINAL):CARDINAL;
(* NB may change n
 *pre: none
 *post: result = (fact n_0)
 *     where fact is as defined in Miranda
 *)
VAR a: CARDINAL;
BEGIN
  a := 1;
(*loop invariant: (fact n_0) = (f1 a n) where f1 as defined in Miranda
 *variant = n
 *)
  WHILE n#0 DO a := a*n; n := n-1 END;
  RETURN a
END fact;
```

Justification

initialization: this relies on the property, promised but not yet proved, that $(fact\ n) = (f1\ 1\ n)$.
loop test and finalization: when $n = 0$, we know that $(f1\ a\ n)$ is just a; but this is the answer we require, so we can just return a as the result.
reestablishing the invariant: when $n \neq 0$ then $(f1\ a\ n) = (f1\ (a*n)(n-1))$, so we reestablish the invariant by replacing a and n by $a*n$ and $n-1$.

It still remains to be shown that $fact\ n = f1\ 1\ n$. The method to use is induction, but some care is needed. Suppose we try to use simple induction on n to prove $\forall n : nat.\ P(n)$, where

$P(n) \equiv fact\ n = f1\ 1\ n$

For the induction step we assume $P(n)$, and prove $P(n+1)$:
$$fact\ (n+1) = (n+1) \times (fact\ n) = (n+1) \times (f1\ 1\ n)$$
$$= f1\ 1\ (n+1) = f1\ (n+1)\ n$$

How can we bridge the gap and prove $(n+1) \times (f1\ 1\ n) = f1\ (n+1)\ n$? The answer is that we cannot. The inductive hypothesis only tells us about the behaviour of $f1$ when its accumulator parameter is 1. We actually have to prove something more general and this involves understanding what $(f1\ a\ n)$ calculates for the general a: it is $a \times n!$, so we want to prove it equal to $a \times (fact\ n)$.

Proposition 14.1 : $\forall n : nat.\ fact\ n = f1\ 1\ n$

Proof We first prove by induction on n that $\forall n : nat.\ P(n)$ where
$$P(n) \equiv \forall a : nat.\ a * (fact\ n) = f1\ a\ n$$

base case: $f1\ a\ 0 = a = a * 1 = a * (fact\ 0)$

induction step: Assume $P(n)$, and prove $P(n+1)$. Let a be a natural number. Then

$$
\begin{aligned}
f1\ a\ (n+1) &= f1(a * (n+1))n \\
&= a * (n+1) * (fact\ n) \text{ by induction} \\
&= a * (fact\ (n+1)) \\
\text{Hence } 1 * (fact\ n) &= fact\ n = f1\ 1\ n.
\end{aligned}
$$

□

For functions with accumulating parameters, you may need to first understand how the accumulator works, and then formulate a stronger statement to prove.

14.5 Summary

- A recursive function is said to be *tail* recursive if in each recursive clause of the definition the entire right-hand side of its equation consists of a call to the function itself. A tail recursive function is similar to a loop.
- A general technique for transforming recursive Miranda definitions into WHILE loop Modula-2 definitions is as follows:
    1. Find an obvious solution in Miranda.
    2. Find a (perhaps less obvious) tail recursive solution in Miranda.
    3. Prove that they both give the same answers.
    4. Translate the tail recursive version into Modula-2 with WHILE loops.
    5. Write down the loop invariant in terms of the Miranda function.
    6. The loop variant is the recursion variant.

14.6 Exercises

1. Write Modula-2 code for the tail recursive Miranda functions in Section 14.1. Prove that reverse xs=rev1 xs as claimed.

2. One way of viewing integer division x div y is that the result is how many times you can subtract y from x (and the remainder x mod y is what is left). The following is an implementation of that idea:

```
divmod::num->num->(num,num)
||pre: nat(m) & nat(n) & n >= 1
||post: divmod m n = (m div n, m mod n)
||i.e. nat(q) & nat(r) & r < n
||        & m = q*n + r
||           where (q,r) = divmod m n
divmod = f 0
         where f a m n = (a,m),       if m < n
                       = f (a+1) (m-n) n, otherwise
```

How does this work? (HINT: using n as recursion variant for $f\ a\ m\ n$, show that if a, m and n are natural numbers with $n \geq 1$, then $f\ a\ m\ n$ satisfies the post-condition for divmod (m + a*n) n.)

Use the fact that f is tail recursive to implement the method iteratively in Modula-2.

3. Define a recursive function add in Miranda for the addition of two *diynat* (as defined in Chapter 7) natural numbers. Rewrite your function in tail recursive style.

4. The Fibonacci sequence is
   0, 1, 1, 2, 3, 5, 8, 13, 21, 34, 55, ...
   Each number is the sum of the preceding two, and this can be defined in Miranda by

```
fib :: num -> num
||pre: nat(n)
||post: fib n is the nth Fibonacci number
||      (starting with "zeroth"=0, "first"=1)
fib n=0,                         if n=0
    = 1,                         if n=1
    = (fib (n-2))+(fib (n-1)),  otherwise
```

This is *terribly* inefficient. Try fib 25. Why does it take so long?
A more efficient method is to calculate the *pair* ($fib\ n$, $fib\ (n+1)$):

```
twofib :: num -> (num,num)
||pre: nat(n)
||post: twofib n = (fib n, fib(n+1))
twofib n=(0,1),          if n=0
       =(y,x+y),         otherwise
          where (x,y) = twofib (n-1)
fib1 n=x
       where (x,y) = twofib n
```

Prove (by induction on n) that

$$\forall n : nat.\ twofib\ n = (fib\ n\ fib\ (n+1))$$

5. Let us define the *generalized* Fibonacci numbers ($gfib\ x\ y\ n$) by

```
gfib :: num -> num -> num -> num
||pre:nat(n)
||post: g fib x y n is the nth generalized Fibonacci number
||      (starting with "zeroth"=x, "first"=y)
gfib x y n=x,   if n=0
         =y,   if n=1
         =(gfib x y(n-2))+(gfib x y(n-1)), otherwise
```

They are generated by the same recurrence relation (the 'otherwise' alternative) as the ordinary Fibonaccis, but starting off with x and y instead of 0 and 1.

(a) Prove by induction on n that

$$\forall n : nat.\ fib\ n = gfib\ 0\ 1\ n$$

(b) Now the sequence ($gfib\ y\ (x+y)$) (as n varies) is the same as the sequence ($gfib\ x\ y$) except that the first term x is omitted: ($gfib\ x\ y\ (n+1)) = (gfib\ y\ (x+y)\ n)$. Prove this by induction on n.

Let us therefore define

```
gfib1 x y n = x,                  if n=0
            = gfib1 y(x+y)(n-1),  otherwise
```

(c) Prove by induction on n that

$$\forall n : nat.\ \forall x,y : num.\ gfib1\ x\ y\ n = gfib\ x\ y\ n$$

Part II

Logic

Chapter 15

An introduction to logic

15.1 Logic

In this part of *Reasoned Programming* we investigate *mathematical logic*, which provides the formal underpinnings for reasoning about programming and is all about formalizing and justifying arguments. It uses the same rules of deduction which we all use in drawing conclusions from premisses, that is, in reasoning from assumptions to a conclusion. The rules used in this book are *deductive* — if the premisses are believed to be true, then the conclusions are bound to be true; acceptance of the premisses forces acceptance of the conclusion.

A program's specification can be used as the premiss for a logical argument and various properties of the program may be deduced from it. These are the conclusions about the program that we are forced to accept given that the specification is true.

```
A :: num -> num
|| pre: none
||post: returns (x+1)^2
```

For example, in the program above, it can be deduced from the specification of A that, for whatever argument (input) x that A is applied to, it delivers a result ≥ 0. We cannot deduce, however, that it will always deliver a result $\geq x^2$ unless the pre-condition is strengthened, for example to $x \geq 0$.

Examples of applications of correct, or valid, reasoning are 'I wrote both program A and program B so I wrote program A', 'if the machine is working I run my programs; the machine is working so I run my programs', 'if my programs are running the machine is working; the machine is not working so my programs are not running', etc.

It is not difficult to spot examples of the use of invalid reasoning; political debates are usually a good source. Some examples are 'if wages increase

198 *An introduction to logic*

too fast then inflation will get worse; inflation does get worse so wages are increasing too fast', 'some people manage to support their elderly relatives; so all people can'.

In this Chapter we introduce the language in which such deductions can be expressed.

15.2 The propositional language

An example

In order to see clearly the logical structure of an English sentence we translate it into a special logical notation which is unambiguous. This is what we mean by 'translating into logic'. For example, consider the sentence

> If Humphrey is over 21 and either he has previously been sentenced to imprisonment or non-imprisonment is not appropriate then a custodial sentence is possible.

We can translate this into logical notation in stages, by teasing out the logical structure layer by layer. First, we may write

> If Humphrey is over 21 ∧ (he has previously been sentenced to imprisonment ∨ non-imprisonment is not appropriate) then a custodial sentence is possible.

Next,

> (Humphrey is over 21 ∧ (he has previously been sentenced to imprisonment ∨ non-imprisonment is not appropriate)) → a custodial sentence is possible.

Then,

$$\begin{pmatrix} over21(Humphrey) \land \\ (already\text{-}sentenced(Humphrey)) \lor non\text{-}imprisonment\text{-}is\text{-}not\text{-}appropriate) \end{pmatrix}$$
$$\to possible\text{-}custodial\text{-}sentence(Humphrey)$$

and, finally,

$$\begin{pmatrix} over21(Humphrey) \land \\ (already\text{-}sentenced(Humphrey)) \lor \neg non\text{-}imprisonment\text{-}is\text{-}appropriate) \end{pmatrix}$$
$$\to possible\text{-}custodial\text{-}sentence(Humphrey).$$

In this example we have introduced the connectives ∨ (*or* or *disjunction*), ∧ (*and* or *conjunction*), → (*implies* or *if* ⋯ *then*), and ¬ (*not*). We also used parentheses to disambiguate sentences. Without parentheses we cannot tell whether $A \land B \to C$ is really $A \land (B \to C)$ or $(A \land B) \to C$.

Eventually, the analysis reaches statements, or propositions, such as 'Humphrey is over 21', where we do not wish to analyze the logical structure any further. These are called *atoms* (atomic means indivisible), that is, not made up using connectives. The connectives then connect atoms to make *sentences*. We have also introduced a structure for the atoms. Propositions usually have a subject (a thing) and then describe a property about that thing. For example, 'Humphrey' is a thing and 'over 21' is a property, or predicate, about it. Atoms are usually written as *predicate*(*thing*). We distinguish between *terms*, which are things, and *predicates*, which are the properties.

As another example, consider 'Jane likes logic and (she likes) programming'. The logical meaning is two sentences connected by 'and'. In each one, Jane is the subject, so the translation is

$$likes(Jane, logic) \land likes(Jane, programming)$$

Notice how Jane appears twice in the logical structure, although only once in English. The English 'and' is more flexible because it can conjoin noun phrases (logic and programming) as well as sentences (Jane likes logic and Jane likes programming).

The use of parentheses to express priority can sometimes be avoided by a convention analogous to that used in algebraic expressions:

$\rightarrow$ binds less closely than $\land$ or $\lor$ and $\neg$ binds the closest of all.

Thus $P \land Q \rightarrow R$ is shorthand for $(P \land Q) \rightarrow R$, not for $P \land (Q \rightarrow R)$ and $\neg A \land B$ is not the same as $\neg(A \land B)$. Also, (as in English) we do not need parentheses for $P \land Q \land R \land \ldots$ or $P \lor Q \lor R \lor \ldots$, but we do need them if the $\land$ and $\lor$ are mixed, as in $(P \land Q) \lor R$.

The language of atoms and connectives is called *propositional logic*.

Atoms

An atom, or a proposition, is just a statement or a fact expressing that a property holds for some individual or that a relationship holds between several individuals, for example 'Steve travels to work by train'. Sometimes, the atoms are represented by single symbols such as *Steve-goes-by-train*. More usually, the syntactic form is more complex. For instance, 'Steve goes by train' might be expressed as *goesbytrain*(*Steve*) or as *travels*(*Steve, train*).

The *predicate* symbol *travels*(,) requires two *arguments* in order to become an *atom*. *Steve-goes-by-train* (or *SGT* for short) is called a *proposition symbol*, or a predicate symbol that needs no arguments. The predicate symbol *goesbytrain* needs one argument to become an atom. The two arguments of *travels* used here are *Steve* and *train* and the argument of *goesbytrain* is *Steve*. Adjectives are translated into predicate symbols and nouns into arguments, which is why, for example 'programming is fun' is translated into $fun(programming)$ rather than into $programming(fun)$.

You may come across the word *arity*, which is the number of arguments a predicate symbol has. Predicate symbols with no arguments are called propositional, predicate symbols of arity one express properties of individuals and predicate symbols of arity two or more express relations between individuals.

In English, predicates often involve several words which are distributed around the nouns, or in front of or behind the nouns, but when translating, a convention is used that puts the predicate symbol first followed by the arguments in parentheses and separated by commas. In case the predicate has just two arguments it is sometimes written between the arguments in *infix* form. Whenever a predicate symbol is introduced a description of the property or relation it represents should be given. For example, $travels(x, y)$ is read as 'x travels by y'.

The arguments of predicate symbols are called *terms*. Terms can be simple constants, names for particular individuals, but you can also build up more complex ones using a structured or *functional term* which is a function symbol with one or more arguments. For example, whereas an empty list may be denoted by the constant [ ], a non-empty list is usually denoted by a functional term of the form $(head : tail)$, where $head$ is the first element and $tail$ is the list consisting of the rest of the elements. Thus the list $[cat, dog]$ is represented by the term $(cat : (dog : [\ ]))$. Here : is an infix function symbol.

An example of the use of a prefix function symbol is $s(0)$. Just as predicates may have arities of any value ≥ 0, so can function symbols and each argument of a functional term can also be a functional term. So functional terms can be nested, as in $mum(mum(Krysia))$ or $+(*(2,2), 3)$.

15.3 Meanings of the connectives

In English, words such as 'or' may have several slightly different meanings, but the logical connectives $\vee$, $\wedge$, etc., have a fixed unambiguous meaning.

$A \wedge B$ means A and B are both true.
$A \vee B$ means at least one of A and B is true.
$A \rightarrow B$ means if A then B (or A implies B, or B if A)
$\neg A$ means not A (or it is not the case that A is true).
$A \leftrightarrow B$ means A implies B and B implies A (or either both A and B are true or both A and B are not true).

Figure 15.1 Meanings of the connectives

The meanings can be described using a *truth table*, shown in Figure 15.2. It is possible for each atom to be either true (*tt*) or false (*ff*) so for two atoms there are exactly four possibilities: $\{tt,tt\}$, $\{tt,ff\}$, $\{ff,tt\}$, $\{ff,ff\}$. Each row of the truth table gives the meaning of each connective in one situation.

A	B	$A \wedge B$	$A \vee B$	$A \to B$	$A \leftrightarrow B$
tt	tt	tt	tt	tt	tt
tt	ff	ff	tt	ff	ff
ff	tt	ff	tt	tt	ff
ff	ff	ff	ff	tt	tt

Figure 15.2 A truth table

From this truth table it can be seen that $A \wedge B$ is only true when both A and B are true.

Determining whether a sentence is true or not in some situation is analogous to calculating the value of an arithmetic expression. To find the value of the expression $2 + (x * y)$ when x and y have the values 3 and 6, respectively, you calculate $2 + (3 * 6) = 20$. Similarly, to find the value of $A \vee (B \wedge C)$ when A, B and C are *ff*, *tt* and *ff*, respectively, you calculate $ff \vee (tt \wedge ff) = ff$.

So, in order to decide if a complex sentence is true you need to look at its atoms, decide if they are true, and then use the unambiguous meanings of the connectives to decide whether the sentence is true. For example, consider again the sentence

> If Humphrey is over 21 and either he has previously been sentenced to imprisonment or non-imprisonment is not appropriate then a custodial sentence is possible.

which was written in logic as

$$\begin{pmatrix} over21(Humphrey) \wedge \\ (already\text{-}sentenced(Humphrey) \vee \neg non\text{-}imprisonment\text{-}is\text{-}appropriate) \end{pmatrix}$$
$$\to possible\text{-}custodial\text{-}sentence(Humphrey).$$

Suppose that Humphrey is over 21, that he has not been sentenced to imprisonment before and that non-imprisonment is appropriate, then the condition of the implication is false — although the first conjunct is true the second is not as each of the disjuncts is false. In this case, then, the whole sentence is true, for an implication is true if its condition is false. You can use this method for any other situation.

Some comments on the meanings of connectives

The truth tables give the connectives a meaning that is quite precise, more precise in fact than that of their natural language counterparts, so care is sometimes needed in translation.

The meaning of $\wedge$ is just like the meaning of 'and' but notice that any involvement of time is lost. Thus A and (then) B is simply $A \wedge B$ and, for example, both 'Krysia fell ill and had an operation' and 'Krysia had an operation and fell ill' are translated the same way. 'A but B' is also translated as $A \wedge B$, even though in general it implies that B is not usually the case, as in 'Krysia fell ill but carried on working'. To properly express these sentences you need to use the quantifier language of Section 15.4.

$A \vee B$ means 'A or B or both'. The stronger, 'A or B but not both', can be captured by the sentence $(A \vee B) \wedge \neg(A \wedge B)$. The stronger meaning is called *exclusive or*. For example, consider 'donations to the cause will be accepted in cash or by cheque' and 'you can have either coffee or tea after dinner'. (Which of these is using the stronger, exclusive or?)

Consider the meaning of

$$diets(Jack) \rightarrow lose\text{-}weight(Jack)$$

that is,

'If Jack diets then he will lose weight'.

The only circumstance under which one can definitely say the statement is false is when

Jack diets but stays fat.

In other circumstances, for example

Jack carries on eating, but gets thin
Jack carries on eating, and stays fat

there is no reason to doubt the original statement as the condition of that statement is not true in these situations.

Natural language also uses other connectives, such as 'only if' and 'unless', which can be translated using the connectives given already.

A unless B is usually translated as 'A if $\neg B$' (that is, $\neg B \rightarrow A$), in which B occurs rather like an escape clause. A unless B can also can be translated as $B \vee A$. All of the sentences 'Jack will not slim unless he diets', 'either Jack diets or he will not slim' and 'Jack will not slim if he does not diet' can be translated in the same way as $diets(Jack) \vee \neg slims(Jack)$.

'A only if B' is usually translated as $A \to B$, as in 'you can enter only if you have clean shoes', which would be 'if you enter then you (must) have clean shoes'. The temptation to translate A only if B as $B \to A$ instead of $A \to B$ is very strong. To see the problem, consider

I shall go only if I am invited (A only if B)

Logically, it is $A \to B$ — if you start from knowledge about A then you can go on to deduce B (or that B must have happened). Temporally it is the other way around — B (the invitation) comes first and results in A. But A is not inevitable (I might fall ill and be unable to go) so there is *no* logical $B \to A$.

The sentence $A \leftrightarrow B$, is often defined as $A \to B \wedge B \to A$, which is A only if B and A if B, or A if and only if B, which is often shortened to A iff B.

15.4 The quantifier language

The logic language covered so far is not sufficiently expressive to fully analyze sentences such as 'all students enjoy themselves' or 'Jack will always be fat' — we need the use of generalizations.

Consider the sentence 'the cat is striped', or, in logical notation, $striped(cat)$. Before you can understand this sentence or consider whether it is true or not *cat* needs to be defined so that you know exactly which cat is meant.

Now compare this with 'something is striped'. 'Something' here is rather different from 'cat'. To test the truth of this sentence you do not need to know beforehand exactly what 'something' is; you just need to know the range of acceptable possibilities and then you go through them one by one to find at least one that is striped. If you succeed then 'something is striped' is true.

In line with this distinction, we do not write $striped(something)$ in logic, but, instead, write $\exists x.\ striped(x)$. This is read literally as 'for some x, x is striped', but we are sure that you can see this is equivalent to 'something is striped'.

The meaning of this sentence is

there is some value, which when substituted for x in $striped(x)$, yields a true statement.

This is even more clear if you consider 'the cat is striped and hungry', $striped(cat) \wedge hungry(cat)$; since the meaning of *cat* is fixed beforehand both occurrences of 'the cat' refer to the same thing. On the other hand, in 'something is striped and something is hungry', $\exists x.\ striped(x) \wedge \exists y.\ hungry(y)$, the two somethings could be different.

It is also possible to say 'something is both striped and hungry', as in $\exists x.\ [striped(x) \wedge hungry(x)]$. This time there is only one something referred to and, whatever it is, it is hungry as well as striped.

Now, unlike *cat*, which was a *constant*, x has the potential to vary and is called a *variable*. The x in $\exists x$ announces that x is a variable and applies to all of the following formula that follows the '.'. For non-atomic formulas parentheses (square or round) are needed to show the scope of the x. For example, $\exists x. [P(x) \vee Q(x)]$. The occurrence of $\exists$ is said to *bind* the occurrences of x in that formula.

$\exists$ is called a *quantifier* (and $\exists x$ is called a *quantification*). Another quantifier is $\forall$, the *universal quantifier*, which can be read as 'for all' or 'every'. For example, in 'Fred likes everyone', we do not write *likes*(*Fred*, *everyone*), but $\forall x.\ likes(Fred, x)$. To see if this sentence is true you need to check that Fred likes all values in a specified range. The meaning of this sentence is

for all values substituted for x, $likes(Fred, x)$ is a true statement.

Something that is rather important is that when you have two occurrences of the same variable bound by the same quantification they must denote the same value. For instance, the xs in $\exists x.\ [striped(x) \wedge hungry(x)]$ must denote the same value; to make the sentence true you must find a value for x that is both striped and hungry. On the other hand, in $\exists x.\ striped(x) \wedge \exists x.\ hungry(x)$ the two xs are bound by different quantifications and you just need to find something that is striped and something that is hungry — the same or different, it does not matter — for the sentence to be true.

$\forall x.\ [likes(x, Fred) \vee likes(x, Mary)]$ is true if every value tried for x makes either $likes(x, Fred)$ or $likes(x, Mary)$ true. Compare this with $\forall x.\ likes(x, Fred) \vee \forall x.\ likes(x, Mary)$, which is true if either $\forall x.\ likes(x, Fred)$ is true, or $\forall x.\ likes(x, Mary)$ is true. In the second case the two xs are bound by different quantifications and again are really two different variables.

In the sentence 'someone likes everyone', which is $\exists x.\ \forall y.\ likes(x,y)$ the two variables of the nested quantifiers are different. It would be asking for trouble if they were the same and so we shall forbid it.

Quantifiers which are of the *same* sort can be placed *in any order*. For example,

$\forall x.\ \forall y.\ [mother(x,y) \to parent(x,y)]$

is no different from

$\forall y.\ \forall x.\ [mother(x,y) \to parent(x,y)]$.

They both mean that, for any x and y, if x is a mother of y then x is a parent of y. Similarly, $\exists x.\ \exists y.\ \cdots$ means the same as $\exists y.\ \exists x.\ \cdots$.

For quantifiers of *different* sorts the order is important. For instance,

$\forall x.\ \exists y.\ mother(y,x)$

does not mean the same as

$\exists y.\ \forall x.\ mother(y,x)$

The first says that everyone has a mother, literally, for all x there is some y such that y is the mother of x and you know this is true when x and y vary over people. The second says that there is *one single person* who is the mother of everyone; literally, there is some y such that for all x, y is the mother of x. This is a much stronger statement which you know is not true when x and y can vary over people.

15.5 Translation from English

You have already seen how to translate from English to logic in the propositional case, teasing out the logical structure connective by connective. The same principles apply when you have quantifiers and variables, but there are also some specific new issues to consider.

There are several useful rules of thumb which aid the process of translation.

Pronouns

Pronouns, words such as 'he', 'it' or 'nothing', do not in themselves refer to any specific thing but gain their meaning from their context. You have already seen how the words 'something' and 'everyone' are translated using quantifiers and 'nothing' is similar — 'nothing is striped' becomes $\neg \exists x.\ striped(x)$.

Words such as 'she' or 'it' are used specifically as a reference to someone or something that has already been mentioned, so they inevitably correspond to two or more references to the same value. When you come across a pronoun such as this you must work out exactly what it does refer to. If that is a constant then you replace it by the constant: so 'Chris adores Pat who adores her' becomes $adores(Chris, Pat) \wedge adores(Pat, Chris)$.

That is easy, but when the pronoun refers to a variable you must first set up a quantification and ensure that it applies to them both.

For instance, consider 'something is spotted and it is hungry'. An *erroneous* approach is to translate the two phrases 'something is spotted' and 'it is hungry' separately. This is wrong because the 'something' and 'it' are linked across the connective 'and' and you must set up a variable to deal with this linkage:

$\exists x.\ [x$ is spotted and x is hungry$]$

and *then* deal with the 'and':

$\exists x.\ [spotted(x) \wedge hungry(x)]$

The rule of thumb is:

> If pronouns are linked across a connective, deal with the pronouns before the connective.

Qualifiers and types

Often, a phrase that is to be translated using a universal quantifier is about a certain type of thing rather than about all things and so you want to *qualify* the quantifier. In the case of a universal quantifier this is done using an *implication*. For instance, 'all rational people abhor violence', or 'a rational person abhors violence', first becomes

$\forall(\text{rational})x.\ [x\text{ abhors violence}]$

where 'rational' is called a *qualifier*. This translates to

$\forall x.\ [rational(x) \rightarrow abhors\text{-}violence(x)]$

If the quantification is existential then a *conjunction* is used to link the main part with the qualifying part. For example if you want to make it certain that Mary likes people in 'Mary likes someone who likes logic', you could first write

$\exists(\text{person who likes logic})y.\ likes(Mary, y)$

and then

$\exists y.\ [person(y) \wedge likes(y, logic) \wedge likes(Mary, y)]$

Notice the way 'who' links the conjuncts together.

Another rule of thumb is therefore

> Get the structure of the sentence correct before dealing with the qualifiers.

Qualifiers can always be translated using $\rightarrow$ or $\wedge$ as appropriate. However, their use is quite convenient and so we will introduce a notation for them and write $\forall x : typename.\ [\cdots]$ or $\exists x : typename.\ [\cdots]$ and call the quantifiers *typed quantifiers*.

The notation is most often used for standard qualifiers, sometimes referred to as 'types', and sentences using it can always be rewritten with the type property made explicit. *Standard qualifiers* include persons, numbers (integers, reals, etc.) strings, times, lists, enumerated sets, etc.

For example,

$\forall x : time.\ \forall y : time.\ [x \geq y \rightarrow after(x, y)]$

would be shorthand for

$\forall x \forall y.\ [time(x) \wedge time\ (y) \rightarrow (x \geq y \rightarrow after(x, y))]$

Standard types are used extensively in writing program specifications, and they correspond to the various data structures such as list, num, etc., used in programs.

Earlier, we indicated that a sentence $\forall x.\ P[x]$ is true iff *every* sentence $P[t]$ that can be obtained from $P[x]$ by substituting a value t for every occurrence of x in $P[x]$ is true.

For example, 'all programs that work terminate', which in logic is

$$\forall x.\ [program(x) \rightarrow (works(x) \rightarrow terminates(x))]$$

is true if each sentence obtained by substituting a value for x is true. It is true if all sentences of the kind

$$program(quicksort) \rightarrow (works(quicksort) \rightarrow terminates(quicksort))$$
$$program(quacksort) \rightarrow (works(quacksort) \rightarrow terminates(quacksort))$$
$$program(Hessam) \rightarrow (works(Hessam) \rightarrow terminates(Hessam))$$

etc., are true. If the value t substituted is a program, so that $program(t)$ is true, the resulting sentence

$$program(t) \rightarrow (works(t) \rightarrow terminates(t))$$

is true if $works(t) \rightarrow terminates(t)$ is true. If the value t makes $program(t)$ false (that is, is not a program) then the resulting sentence is also true. In practice, we evaluate the truth of a sentence in a situation in which the values to be substituted for x are fixed beforehand. For example, they could be {all programs written by me}, {programs} or even {names of living persons}.

When qualified quantifiers are used they are suggestive of the range of values that should be substituted in order to test the truth of a sentence. The sentence 'All programs that work terminate' would become

$$\forall x : program.\ [works(x) \rightarrow terminates(x)].$$

and it is suggestive that the only values we should consider for x are those that name programs. As our analysis above showed, these are exactly the values that are useful in showing that the sentence is true.

Similarly, if instead the sentence had been 'Some programs that terminate work', which in logic is

$$\exists x.\ [program(x) \wedge works(x) \wedge terminates(x)]$$

then it would be true as long as *at least one* of the sentences obtained by substituting terms t for x were true. There is no point in trying values of t for which $program(t)$ is false for they cannot make the sentence true. This is suggested by the typed quantifier version

$$\exists x : program.\ [works(x) \wedge terminates(x)].$$

Even so, a difficulty may arise. Consider the statement

'Every integer is smaller than some natural number.'

which in logic is

$$\forall x : integer.\ \exists u : nat.\ [x < u].$$

This time there are an infinite number of sentences to consider, one for each integer. How can you check them all? Of course, you cannot check them all individually *and* finish the task. Instead, you would consider different cases. For example, you may consider two cases here, $x < 0$ and $x \geq 0$. Then, all negative integers are considered *at once*, as are all natural numbers. For the first case the sentence is true by taking $u = 0$, for 0 is a natural number and it is greater than any negative integer; in the second case $x+1$ is a natural number and will do for u. Sometimes, therefore, we have to use a proof to justify the truth of a sentence; we look at proof in the next two chapters.

Some paradoxes

Generally, the need for a universal quantifier is indicated by the presence of such words as all, every, any, anyone, everything, etc., and the words 'someone', 'something' indicate an existential quantifier, but it can happen that 'someone' corresponds to $\forall$. This phenomenon is most likely in connection with $\rightarrow$.

To see how this might happen, consider 'if someone is tall then the door frame will be knocked', which translates to

$$[\exists x.\ tall(x)] \rightarrow door\text{-}knocked.$$

'Someone' has become $\exists$ here, just as you would expect. But note that there is an equivalent translation using $\forall$. The original sentence could be rephrased as 'for anyone, if they are tall then the doorframe will be knocked', which becomes

$$\forall x.\ [tall(x) \rightarrow knocked(doorframe)]$$

Hence, in this example, 'someone' can possibly become $\forall$.

Now consider 'if someone is tall then he will bump his head'. This time the pronoun is linked to 'someone' across the implication and you have to deal with the quantification first. The only translation is

$$\forall x.\ [tall(x) \rightarrow bumphead(x)]$$

so that 'someone' has to become $\forall$.

15.6 Introducing equivalence

Often, English sentences can be translated into more than one equivalent formula in logic. For example, 'if Steve is a vegetarian then he does not eat chicken' might be translated directly as $vegetarian(Steve) \rightarrow \neg eat(Steve, chicken)$ but it could also be paraphrased as 'Steve is not both a vegetarian and a chicken-eater', which translates to $\neg(vegetarian(Steve) \wedge eat(Steve, chicken))$. The two logic sentences are *equivalent* and any conclusion that follows from using one form also follows from using the other. You will come across many useful equivalences and a selection is presented in Appendix B. We write $A \equiv B$ if A and B are equivalent. Two sentences are said to be *equivalent* ($\equiv$) iff they are both true in exactly the same situations. An important property of equivalent sentences is that they may safely be substituted for each other in any longer sentence without affecting the meaning of that sentence.

For example, if $A = S \vee T$ and $B = T \vee S$ then A is equivalent to B. If $E[A]$ is the sentence $S \vee T \to U$ ($=A \to U$) then we can substitute B for A giving the sentence $E[B] (= B \to U)$, or $T \vee S \to U$. We have $E[A] \equiv E[B]$. S and T can themselves be any sentence; for example, if $S = P \wedge Q$ and $T = R \vee \neg P$ then $(P \wedge Q) \vee (R \vee \neg P) \equiv (R \vee \neg P) \vee (P \wedge Q)$.

In general, then, if $A \equiv B$ then $E[A] \equiv E[B]$, where A, B, E are any sentences with no variable occurrences. $E[A]$ denotes that A occurs in E and $E[B]$ denotes the result of substituting B for A in none or more of those occurrences. This is so because if A evaluates to $t\!t$ in a situation then so will B as they are equivalent, and the $E[A]$ and $E[B]$ have the same value. In particular, $E[A]$ could be just the sentence A, so $E[B]$ is the sentence B and B can be used in place of A.

Equivalences are frequently used, as it may be that one form of a sentence is more convenient than another in some derivation. More discussion can be found in Section 18.4, where we consider relaxing the condition on A and B.

Equivalences can be used in 'algebraic reasoning'. For example,

$(P \wedge Q) \wedge R$
$\equiv \neg\neg((P \wedge Q) \wedge R)$, since $\neg\neg X \equiv X$
$\equiv \neg(\neg(P \wedge Q) \vee \neg R)$, since $\neg(X \wedge Y) \equiv \neg X \vee \neg Y$
$\equiv \neg(\neg P \vee \neg Q \vee \neg R)$

that is, $(P \wedge Q) \wedge R \equiv \neg(\neg P \vee \neg Q \vee \neg R)$.

As another example, the two sentence forms $A \vee (S \vee T)$ and $(A \vee S) \vee T$ are equivalent; that is, $\vee$ is an *associative* operator and hence the parentheses can be omitted. The operator $\wedge$ behaves similarly. Using this fact you can show easily that any number of sentences all disjoined by $\vee$, or all conjoined by $\wedge$, can be freely parenthesized; for example, $Q \vee R \vee S \vee T \equiv Q \vee (R \vee S \vee T) \equiv (Q \vee R) \vee (S \vee T) \equiv (Q \vee R \vee S) \vee T$.

If a sentence has a form which makes it always true it is called a *tautology*; for example $A \vee \neg A$ is a tautology. A sentence that is always false is called a *contradiction*, or falsehood, for example $A \wedge \neg A$. Both tautologies and contradictions will play an important role in the reasoning steps that we shall be introducing.

15.7 Some useful predicate equivalences

In this section we look briefly at some useful equivalences using quantified sentences.

The equivalences in Appendix B are schemes in which the constituents represent sentence forms. For example, $F(x)$ indicates a constituent sentence in which x occurs, whereas S (without an x) indicates a constituent sentence in which x does not occur. An instance of a scheme such as

$\forall x.\ [S \wedge F(x)] \equiv S \wedge \forall x.\ F(x)$ is obtained by replacing all occurrences of S and $F(x)$ by appropriate sentences, for example S could be $\exists y.\ G(y)$ and $F(x)$ could be $P(x,a) \vee Q(x,b)$, where a and b are constants. The variables x and y are like formal parameters and can be renamed. So $\neg \forall u.\ F(u,a)$ is an instance of the scheme $\neg \forall x.\ F(x)$ and rewrites to $\exists u.\ \neg F(u,a)$.

NOTE: $\exists x.\ \forall y.\ F(x,y)$ is *not* equivalent to $\forall y.\ \exists x.\ F(x,y)$. In order to help you to remember this one, find an interpretation for F that distinguishes clearly, for you, between the two sentences. For example, you could interpret F as 'father', so that the first sentence translates into 'there is some x that is the father of everyone' and the second into 'for each person y there is some x that is the father of y'.

An instance of the important equivalence $\exists x.\ F(x) \to B \equiv \forall x.\ [F(x) \to B]$ is used in the following:

$\exists c.\ mother(Pam, c) \to parent(Pam)$
$\equiv \forall c.\ [mother(Pam, c) \to parent(Pam)]$

The occurrence of $\exists x.\ F(x)$ is $\exists c.\ mother(Pam, c)$, in which the bound variable x is renamed to c, and of B is $parent(Pam)$. Notice that c does not occur in $parent(Pam)$.

It is also true that equivalent forms of sentences involving variables and quantifiers can be substituted for one another in any context as in the following example. After reading Section 18.4 you will be able to prove this.

In the following example the equivalences used and the scheme occurrences are not given. It is left as an exercise to list the equivalences at each step.

No student works all the time $\equiv$ All students fail to work some of the time.
$\neg \exists s.\ [student(s) \wedge \forall t.\ [time\text{-}period(t) \to works\text{-}at(s,t)]]$
$\equiv \forall s.\ [\neg student(s) \vee \neg \forall t.\ [time\text{-}period(t) \to works\text{-}at(s,t)]]$
$\equiv \forall s.\ [\neg student(s) \vee \exists t.\ [time\text{-}period(t) \wedge \neg works\text{-}at(s,t)]]$
$\equiv \forall s.\ [student(s) \to \exists t.\ [time\text{-}period(t) \wedge \neg works\text{-}at(s,t)]]$

The equivalences also hold if the quantifiers are typed. The above example then becomes
$\neg \exists s : student.\ \forall t : time\text{-}period.\ [works\text{-}at(s,t)] \equiv$
$\forall s : student.\ \exists t : time\text{-}period.\ [\neg works\text{-}at(s,t)]$
and the transformation is simpler.

15.8 Summary

- Logic uses connectives to express the logical structure of natural language.
- The syntax and meanings of propositional logic follow the principles of algebra.

- Atoms consist of predicates which have arguments called terms. Terms can be constants, or function symbols and their arguments.
- For reference, the meanings can be summarized using a *truth table*. For two propositions there are four different classes of situation: $\{tt, tt\}$, $\{tt, ff\}$, $\{ff, tt\}$, $\{ff, ff\}$. Each row of the truth table gives one situation.

A	$\neg A$
tt	ff
ff	tt

A	B	$A \wedge B$	$A \vee B$	$A \rightarrow B$	$A \leftrightarrow B$
tt	tt	tt	tt	tt	tt
tt	ff	ff	tt	ff	ff
ff	tt	ff	tt	tt	ff
ff	ff	ff	ff	tt	tt

For example, from this truth table it can be seen that $A \vee B$ is true unless both A and B are false.
- To facilitate translation from English into logic, typed quantifiers are introduced.
- The informal meaning of a sentence involving a quantifier is

  $\forall x.\ P[x]$ is true iff every sentence $P[t]$ obtained by substituting t for x, where t is taken from a suitable range of values, is true.
  $\forall x.\ P[x]$ is false if some $P[t]$ is false.

  $\exists x.\ P[x]$ is true iff some sentence $P[t]$ obtained by substituting t for x, where t is taken from a suitable range of values, is true.
  $\exists x.\ P[x]$ is false if no sentence $P[t]$ is true.

- Equivalent sentences can be substituted for one another.

15.9 Exercises

1. Suggest some predicate and function symbols to express the following propositions: Mary enjoys sailing; Bill enjoys hiking; Mabel is John's daughter; Ann is a student and Ann is Mabel's daughter
2. Translate the following sentences into logic. First get the sentence structure correct (where the $\wedge$, $\vee$, etc., go) and then structure the atoms, for example Frank likes grapes could become *likes(Frank, grapes)*.
    (a) If there is a drought, standpipes will be needed.
    (b) The house will be finished only if the outstanding bill is paid or if the proprietor works on it himself.
    (c) James will work hard and pass, or he belongs to the drama society.
    (d) Frank bought grapes and either apples or pears.
    (e) Janet likes cricket, but she likes baseball too.
    (f) All out unless it snows!

3. Translate the following into logic as faithfully as possible:
   (a) All red things are in the box.
   (b) Only red things are in the box.
   (c) No animal is both a cat and a dog.
   (d) Anyone who admires himself admires someone.
   (e) Every prize was won by a chimpanzee.
   (f) One particular chimpanzee won all the prizes.
   (g) Jack cannot run faster than anyone in the team.
   (h) Jack cannot run faster than everyone in the team.
   (i) A lecturer is content if she belongs to no committees.
   (j) All first year students have a programming tutor.
   (k) No student has the same mathematics tutor and programming tutor.
   (l) A number is a common multiple of two numbers if each divides it.
   (m) Mary had a little lamb, its fleece was white as snow. And everywhere that Mary went her lamb was sure to go!

4. (a) Let A be tt, B be tt, C be ff. Which of the following sentences are true and which are false?
   i. $((A \to B) \to \neg B)$
   ii. $((\neg A \to (\neg B \land C)) \lor B)$
   iii. $((((A \lor \neg C) \land \neg B) \to A) \to (\neg B \land \neg C))$

   (b) If A is ff, B is ff and C is tt, which of the sentences in part (a) are true and which are false?
   (c) If A is ff, B is tt and C is tt, which of the sentences in part (a) are true and which are false?

5. We mentioned, but did not prove, that associativity allows you to omit parentheses if all the connectives are $\lor$ or $\land$. Explain how associativity is used to show the equivalence of $((Q \lor R) \lor S) \lor T$ and $Q \lor (R \lor (S \lor T))$.

6. Show that the following are equivalent forms by considering all different situations and showing that the pairs of sentences have the same truth value in all of them. For example, for the equivalence $P \land f\!f \equiv f\!f$ there are two situations to consider — $P = tt$ and $P = f\!f$. When $P = f\!f$, $P \land f\!f = f\!f \land f\!f = f\!f$, and when $P = tt$, $P \land f\!f = tt \land f\!f = f\!f$. In both cases the sentence is $f\!f$. For the example $P \land Q \equiv \neg(P \to \neg Q)$ there are four situations to consider which can be tabulated as

P	Q	$P \land Q$	$P \to \neg Q$	$\neg(P \to \neg Q)$
tt	tt	tt	$f\!f$	tt
tt	$f\!f$	$f\!f$	tt	$f\!f$
$f\!f$	tt	$f\!f$	tt	$f\!f$
$f\!f$	$f\!f$	$f\!f$	tt	$f\!f$

You can see that the two sentences have the same value in all four situations and so are equivalent.

(a) $P \vee Q \equiv (P \to Q) \to Q$
(b) $P \wedge Q \equiv \neg(P \to \neg Q)$
(c) $P \leftrightarrow Q \equiv Q \leftrightarrow P$ (that is, $\leftrightarrow$ is commutative)
(d) $P \leftrightarrow (Q \leftrightarrow R) \equiv (P \leftrightarrow Q) \leftrightarrow R$ (that is, $\leftrightarrow$ is associative)
(e) $P \leftrightarrow Q \equiv \neg P \leftrightarrow \neg Q$
(f) $\neg(P \leftrightarrow Q) \equiv \neg P \leftrightarrow Q$
(g) $P \to (Q \to R) \equiv P \wedge Q \to R$
(h) $P \to (Q \wedge R) \equiv (P \to Q) \wedge (P \to R)$

7. Show that $R \equiv S$ iff $R \leftrightarrow S$ is a tautology. (HINT: consider the possible classes of situations for $R \leftrightarrow S$).
8. Discuss how you would decide the truth or falsity of the sentences below in the given situations. Also decide which are true in the given situations and which are false (if feasible). The situation indicates the possible values that can be substituted for the bound variables.

  (a) All living creatures, animal or not:
      i. $\forall x.\ [animal(x) \to \exists y.\ [animal(y) \wedge (eats(x,y) \vee eats(y,x))]]$
      ii. $\exists u.\ [animal(u) \wedge \forall v.\ [animal(v) \to eats(v,u)]]$
      iii. $\forall y.\ \forall x.\ [animal(x) \wedge animal(y) \to (eats(x,y) \leftrightarrow eats(y,x))]$
      iv. $\neg \exists v.\ [animal(v) \wedge \forall u.\ [animal(u) \to (\neg eats(u,v))]]$

  (b) There are three creatures Cat, Bird and Worm. Cat eats all three, Worm is eaten by all three and Bird only eats Worm. Use the sentences (i) through (iv) of part (a) of this question.

  (c) The universe of positive integers:
      i. $\exists x.\ [x$ is the product of two odd integers$]$
      ii. $\forall x.\ [x$ is the product of two odd integers$]$
      iii. $\forall x.\ \exists y.\ [y > x]$
      iv. $\forall x.\ \forall y.\ [x \times y \geq x]$

9. By using the appropriate equivalences and translation of $\forall x : T.\ P[x]$ into $\forall x.\ [is\text{-}T(x) \to P[x]]$ and $\exists x : T.\ P[x]$ into $\exists x.\ [is\text{-}T(x) \wedge P[x]]$, show that $\forall x : T.\ [P[x] \to S] \equiv (\exists x : T.\ P[x]) \to S$.
10. Show that the following pairs of sentences are equivalent by using equivalences. State the equivalences you use at each step:

  (a) $\forall x.\ [\neg \forall y.\ [woman(y) \to \neg dislikes(x,y)] \to dislikes(Jane, x)]$
      and $\forall x.\ [\exists y.\ [woman(y) \wedge dislikes(x,y)] \to dislikes(Jane, x)]$
  (b) $\neg \exists x.\ [Martian(x) \wedge \neg dislikes(x, Mary) \wedge age\text{-}more\text{-}than\text{-}25(x)]$
      and $\forall x.\ [Martian(x) \wedge age\text{-}more\text{-}than\text{-}25(x) \to dislikes(x, Mary)]$

Chapter 16

Natural deduction

16.1 Arguments

Now that you can express properties of your programs in logic we consider how to reason with them to form *correct* proofs. Initially, we will look at reasoning with sentences that do not include any quantifiers.

The method we use is called natural deduction and it formalizes the approach to reasoning embodied in the 'argument form'

> 'This is so, that is so, so something else is so and hence something else, and hence we have shown what we wanted to show.'

An argument leads from some statements, called the premisses, to a final statement, called the conclusion. It is valid if whenever circumstances make the premisses true then they make the conclusion true as well. The only way in which the conclusion of a *valid* argument can be rejected is by rejecting the premisses (a useful way out).

We justify a potential argument by putting it together from small reasoning steps that are all known to be valid. We write $A \vdash B$ (pronounced 'A proves B') to indicate that B can be derived from A using some correct rules of reasoning. So, if we can find a derivation, then $A \vdash B$ is true.

Schematically:

$$P_1 \vdash P_2, \quad \{P_1, P_2\} \vdash P_3 \quad \cdots \quad \{P_1, P_2, \ldots, P_{n-1}\} \vdash P_n.$$

The steps are supposed to be so simple that there is no doubting the validity of each one.

The following is a valid argument:
1. If Hessam's program is less than 10 lines long then it is correct.
2. Hessam's program is not correct.
3. Therefore Hessam's program is more than 10 lines long.

The first two lines are the premisses and the last the conclusion. A derivation of the conclusion in this case is the following: suppose Hessam's program is less than 10 lines long; then it is correct. But this contradicts the second premiss so we conclude that Hessam's program is more than 10 lines long. These reasoning steps mean that $1, 2 \vdash 3$.

Sometimes, we may be tempted to use invalid reasoning steps, in which the conclusion does not always have to be the case even if the premises are true. Any justification involving such steps will not be correct.

The following is an invalid argument:

> If I am wealthy then I give away lots of money.
> I give away lots of money.
> Therefore I am wealthy.

The reasoning is not valid because from the premises you cannot derive the conclusion; the premises could be true and yet I could be poor and generous.

If $A \vdash B$ then the sentence $A \rightarrow B$ is a tautology because whenever A is true B must be true also. The various tautologies such as $A \wedge B \rightarrow A$ each give rise to simple and valid arguments. This one yields the valid argument $A \wedge B \vdash A$.

An informal example

The natural deduction rules to be introduced in this chapter are quite formal. This is a good thing for it enables a structure to be imposed on a proof so that you can be confident it is valid. When you are quite sure of the structure imposed by the rules it is possible to present proofs in a more relaxed style using English. Typical of such an English proof is the following proof of the valid argument:

> If Chris is at home then he is working.
> If Ann is at work then she is working.
> Ann is at work or Chris is at home.
> Therefore someone is working.

A justification of this argument might follow the steps: to show someone is working, find a person who is working — there are two cases to consider: if Ann is at work, she is working and if Chris is at home, he is working. Either way, someone is working.

16.2 The natural deduction rules

About the rules

There are two kinds of rule. The first kind tells us how to reason using a sentence with a given connective, that is, how to exploit a premiss. For example, from $A \wedge B$ we can deduce each of A and B. The second kind tells us how to deduce a sentence with a given connective, that is, how to prove a conclusion. For example, to deduce $A \wedge B$ we must prove both A and B. The first kind are called *elimination rules* and the second are called *introduction rules*. They are labelled $\wedge \mathcal{E}$ (pronounced *and elimination*), $\vee \mathcal{E}$, $\wedge \mathcal{I}$ (pronounced *and introduction*), $\vee \mathcal{I}$, etc.

If a formula is derived using the rules, the notation

$\vdash \langle formula \rangle$

will be used. When initial data is needed to prove a formula the notation is

$\langle assumptions \rangle \vdash \langle formula \rangle$.

$S \vdash C$ is called a *sequent* and can be read as:

A proof exists of goal sentence C from data sentences S.

The initial data sentences S are placed at the top of the proof and the conclusion C is placed at the bottom. The actual proof goes in the middle. Frequently, a proof will consist of subproofs, which will be written inside boxes.

As you read a proof from top to bottom, you see more and more consequences of the earlier sentences. However, that is not the way in which a proof is constructed in the first place. As you will see, when proving something we can work both forwards from the data and backwards from the conclusion so that the middle part is not usually filled in straight from data to conclusion. When a proof is written 'in English' it is written to reflect this 'construction order' of the proof.

Each of the rules will be presented in the following style:

$$\frac{\text{one or more antecedents}}{\text{a conclusion} \qquad \text{(rule name)}}$$

'Antecedent' just means 'something that has gone before'.

Often, it is just an earlier sentence, though sometimes it is a bigger chunk of proof. The rules can either be read *downwards* — from the antecedents the conclusion can be derived, or *upwards* — to derive the conclusion, you must derive the antecedents. We will frequently omit the line between the antecedents and the conclusion.

∧-introduction (∧$\mathcal{I}$) and ∧-elimination (∧$\mathcal{E}$) rules

The two rules of this section, $\wedge \mathcal{I}$ and $\wedge \mathcal{E}$, correspond closely to everyday deduction.

The first rule is $\wedge\mathcal{I}$:

> From each of $P_1, \ldots, P_n$ as data or derived sentences, conclude $P_1 \wedge \ldots \wedge P_n$ or, to give a proof of $P_1 \wedge \ldots \wedge P_n$, derive proofs for $P_1, \ldots, P_n$

The proof is structured using *boxes*:

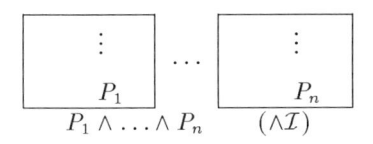

$$\begin{array}{c} \boxed{\begin{array}{c} \vdots \\ P_1 \end{array}} \quad \ldots \quad \boxed{\begin{array}{c} \vdots \\ P_n \end{array}} \\ \hline P_1 \wedge \ldots \wedge P_n \quad (\wedge\mathcal{I}) \end{array}$$

The boxes are introduced to contain the proofs of $P_1, \ldots, P_n$ prior to deriving $P_1 \wedge \ldots \wedge P_n$. The vertical dots indicate the proof that is to be filled in. There is one box to contain the proof for each of P_1 to P_n. The use of the $\wedge\mathcal{I}$ rule is automatic — there is a standard plan which you always use when proving $P_1 \wedge \ldots \wedge P_n$.

When a proof is presented, it is usually read from the top to the bottom, but when you are actually proving something, you may work backwards from the conclusion. So, in a proof, you will probably read an application of $\wedge\mathcal{I}$ downwards, but when you have to prove $P \wedge Q$, you ask 'how do I do it?', and the answer is by proving P and Q separately. We can say that you work backwards from the conclusion, deriving a new conclusion to achieve.

The second rule is $\wedge\mathcal{E}$:

> from data or derived sentences $P_1 \wedge \ldots \wedge P_n$ conclude any of $P_1, \ldots, P_n$, or

$$\frac{P_1 \wedge \ldots \wedge P_n}{P_i} \quad (\wedge\mathcal{E})$$

for each of P_i, $i = 1, \ldots, n$.

This time the rule is used exclusively in a forward direction, deriving new data.

Figure 16.1 contains the first steps in a proof of $A \wedge B \vdash B \wedge A$. If we need to refer to lines in proofs then each row in the proof will be labelled for reference. In the diagram, the given sentence $A \wedge B$ is initial data and is placed at the start of the deduction, and the conclusion, or goal, is $B \wedge A$, which appears at the end. Our task is to fill in the middle.

There are now two ways to proceed — either forwards from the data or backwards from the goal. In general, a natural deduction derivation involves working in both directions. Here, as soon as you see the $\wedge$ in the conclusion,

218 Natural deduction

```
1   A ∧ B
2   ⋮
3   B ∧ A
```

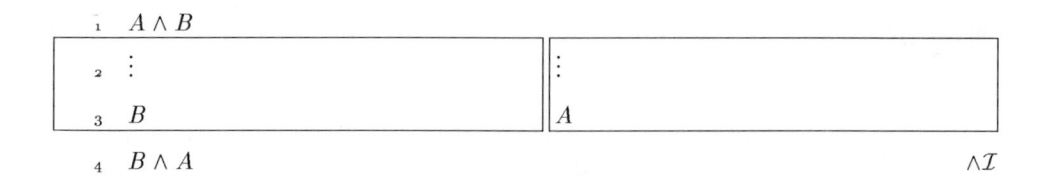

Figure 16.1

```
1   A ∧ B
┌─────────────────────┐  ┌─────────────────────┐
│ 2   ⋮               │  │ ⋮                   │
│ 3   B               │  │ A                   │
└─────────────────────┘  └─────────────────────┘
4   B ∧ A                                           ∧ℐ
```

Figure 16.2

think (automatic step) ∧ℐ and prepare for it by making *the preparation* as in Figure 16.2. Working backwards from the conclusion is generally applicable when introduction rules are to be used. This example will require the use of the ∧ℐ rule. The boxes are introduced to contain the subproofs of A and B. It needs a tiny bit of ingenuity to notice that each of the subgoals can now be derived by ∧ℰ from the initial data $A \wedge B$ by working forwards. The completed proof appears in Figure 16.3. Lesson — the ∧ℐ step is automatic

```
1   A ∧ B
┌─────────────────────┐  ┌─────────────────────┐
│ 2   B      ∧ℰ(1)    │  │ A        ∧ℰ(1)      │
└─────────────────────┘  └─────────────────────┘
3   B ∧ A                                           ∧ℐ
```

Figure 16.3 $A \wedge B \vdash B \wedge A$

— to prove $A \wedge B$ you must prove A and B separately. But to use ∧ℰ requires ingenuity — which conjunct should you choose?

An alternative proof construction for $A \wedge B \vdash B \wedge A$ is shown in Figure 16.4. It works forwards only — first derive each of A and B from $A \wedge B$ and then derive $B \wedge A$.

You can see that these two rules are valid, from the definition of true sentences of the form $P \wedge Q$ given in Chapter 15. For if $P \wedge Q$ is true then so must each of P and Q be (∧ℰ), and vice versa (∧ℐ).

1. $A \wedge B$
2. A $\wedge \mathcal{E}(1)$
3. B $\wedge \mathcal{E}(1)$
4. $B \wedge A$ $\wedge \mathcal{I}$

Figure 16.4 Another proof of $A \wedge B \vdash B \wedge A$

∨-elimination (∨$\mathcal{E}$) and ∨-introduction (∨$\mathcal{I}$) rules

The ∨-elimination rule is frequently used in everyday deduction and is often called a case analysis — a disjunction $P_1 \vee P_2$ (say) represents two possible cases and in order to conclude C, C should be proven from both cases, so that it is provable whichever case actually pertains. It can be generalized to $n > 2$ arguments and is

∨$\mathcal{E}$ If C can be derived from each of the separate cases $P_1, \ldots, P_n$, then from $P_1 \vee \ldots \vee P_n$, derive goal C.

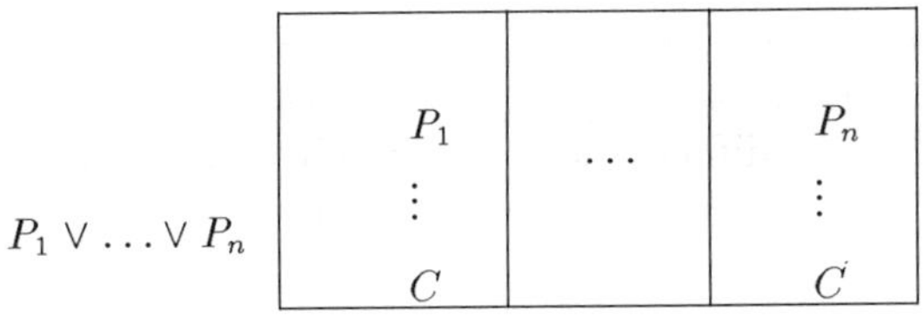

There is one box for each of P_i, $i = 1, n$.

Each box that is part of the preparation for the ∨$\mathcal{E}$ step represents a subproof for one of the cases, and contains as an additional assumption the disjunct P_i that represents its case. The assumptions P_i are only available inside the box and their use corresponds to the English phrase 'suppose that $P_i \ldots$'. Once the proof leaves the box we forget our supposition. Hence the box says something significant: P_i is true in here.

The ∨$\mathcal{I}$ rule is

∨$\mathcal{I}$ From any one of $P_1, \ldots, P_n$ derive $P_1 \vee \ldots \vee P_n$

$$\frac{P_i}{P_1 \vee \ldots \vee P_n} \quad (\vee \mathcal{I})$$

for each of P_i, $i = 1, \ldots, n$.

The ∨-introduction rule is usually used in a backward direction — in order to show $P \vee Q$ one of P or Q must be shown. In the forward direction the rule

220   *Natural deduction*

is rather weak — if P is known then it does not seem very useful to derive the weaker $P \vee Q$ (unless such a deduction is needed to obtain a particular desired sentence, as in the next example). This rule, too, can be generalized to $n > 2$ arguments.

This time, the $\vee \mathcal{E}$ rule is automatic, whereas the $\vee \mathcal{I}$ rule is the one that requires ingenuity — when proving $P_1 \vee \ldots \vee P_n$ which disjunct should we choose to prove?

In the next example, a proof of $A \wedge (B \vee C) \vdash (A \wedge B) \vee (A \wedge C)$, we illustrate how a proof might be found. The first step is to place the initial assumption at the top and the conclusion at the bottom as in Figure 16.5. Now, where

$A \wedge (B \vee C)$
$\vdots$

$(A \wedge B) \vee (A \wedge C)$

Figure 16.5

do we go from here? There are no automatic steps — $\wedge \mathcal{E}$, and $\vee \mathcal{I}$ need ingenuity. Can we obtain the conclusion by $\vee \mathcal{I}$? Does either of the sentences $A \wedge B$ or $A \wedge C$ follow from the premiss? A little insight says *no*, so try $\wedge \mathcal{E}$ on $A \wedge (B \vee C)$ — it is not so difficult and the result is given in Figure 16.6. Now an automatic step is available — exploit $B \vee C$ by $\vee \mathcal{E}$ (case analysis).

$A \wedge (B \vee C)$
A $\qquad\qquad\qquad\qquad\qquad\qquad\qquad\qquad\qquad\qquad\qquad\qquad\qquad$ $\wedge \mathcal{E}$
$B \vee C$ $\qquad\qquad\qquad\qquad\qquad\qquad\qquad\qquad\qquad\qquad\qquad\qquad$ $\wedge \mathcal{E}$
$\vdots$

$(A \wedge B) \vee (A \wedge C)$

Figure 16.6

The preparation is given in Figure 16.7. Look at the left-hand box. There are no automatic steps, but look, we can prove $A \wedge B$ by using B and then use $\vee \mathcal{I}$ to show $(A \wedge B) \vee (A \wedge C)$. Similarly in the right-hand box, proving $A \wedge C$. The complete proof is given in Figure 16.8. It is often the case that a disjunctive conclusion can be derived by exploiting a disjunction in the data. Sometimes, an inspired guess can yield a result, as inside the boxes of the example.

The natural deduction rules

$A \wedge (B \vee C)$

A $\wedge \mathcal{E}$

$B \vee C$ $\wedge \mathcal{E}$

B	C
$\vdots$	$\vdots$
$(A \wedge B) \vee (A \wedge C)$	$(A \wedge B) \vee (A \wedge C)$

$(A \wedge B) \vee (A \wedge C)$ $\vee \mathcal{E}$

Figure 16.7

1. $A \wedge (B \vee C)$
2. A $\wedge \mathcal{E}(1)$
3. $B \vee C$ $\wedge \mathcal{E}(1)$

4. B		4. C	
5. $A \wedge B$	$\wedge \mathcal{I}(2,4)$	5. $A \wedge C$	$\wedge \mathcal{I}(2,4)$
6. $(A \wedge B) \vee (A \wedge C)$	$\vee \mathcal{I}(5)$	6. $(A \wedge B) \vee (A \wedge C)$	$\vee \mathcal{I}(5)$

7. $(A \wedge B) \vee (A \wedge C)$ $\vee \mathcal{E}(3)$

Figure 16.8 $A \wedge (B \vee C) \vdash (A \wedge B) \vee (A \wedge C)$

As an example of how a box proof is translated into English, we will give the same proof in its more usual form.

Proposition 16.1 $A \wedge (B \vee C) \vdash (A \wedge B) \vee (A \wedge C)$

Proof Since $A \wedge (B \vee C)$, then A and $B \vee C$. Consider $B \vee C$: suppose B, then to show $(A \wedge B) \vee (A \wedge C)$ we have to show either $A \wedge B$ or $A \wedge B$. In this case we can show $A \wedge B$. On the other hand, suppose C. In that case we can show $A \wedge C$ and hence $(A \wedge B) \vee (A \wedge C)$. So in both cases we can show $(A \wedge B) \vee (A \wedge C)$. □

From now on you will have to work through the examples in order to see how they are derived, as only the final stage will usually be given.

It is easy to see that the $\vee \mathcal{I}$ rule is valid; for $X \vee Y$ is true as long as either X or Y is. If $X \vee Y$ is true then we know only that either X is true or Y is true, but we cannot be sure which one is true. For the $\vee \mathcal{E}$ case, therefore, we must be able to show C from both so as to be sure that C must be true.

It is tempting to try to ignore the $\vee\mathcal{E}$ rule because it looks complicated. But you must learn it by heart! It is automatic — as soon as you see $\vee$ in a premiss you should consider preparing for $\vee\mathcal{E}$. Writing the conclusion in $n+1$ places seems odd at first, but this is what you must do. Each occurrence has a different justification; it is $\vee\mathcal{E}$ outside the boxes and other reasons inside.

There is a special case of $\vee\mathcal{E}$ in which the number of disjuncts is zero. A disjunction of n sentences says 'at least one of the disjuncts is true', but if $n = 0$ that is impossible. To represent an impossible sentence, a *contradiction*, we use the symbol $\bot$, which is pronounced *bottom* and is always false. If you look at $\vee\mathcal{E}$ when $n = 0$ you see that there are no cases to analyze and all you are left with is

$$\frac{\bot}{C} \quad (\bot\mathcal{E})$$

$\rightarrow$-elimination ($\rightarrow\mathcal{E}$) and $\rightarrow$-introduction ($\rightarrow\mathcal{I}$) rules

The first rule is

$\rightarrow\mathcal{E}$ (pronounced *arrow elimination*)
      from P and $P \rightarrow Q$ derive Q.

$$\frac{P \quad P \rightarrow Q}{Q} \quad (\rightarrow\mathcal{E})$$

It can be used both forwards from data and backwards from the conclusion. To work backwards, suppose the conclusion is Q, then any data of the form $P \rightarrow Q$ can be used to derive Q if P can be derived. So P becomes a new conclusion. In neither direction is the rule completely automatic — some ingenuity is needed. The $\rightarrow\mathcal{E}$ rule is commonly used in everyday arguments and is also referred to as *Modus Ponens*.

The second rule is

$\rightarrow\mathcal{I}$ from a proof of Q using the additional assumption P, derive $P \rightarrow Q$.

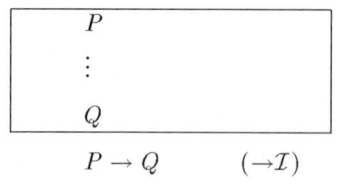

$$\boxed{\begin{array}{c} P \\ \vdots \\ Q \end{array}}$$
$$P \rightarrow Q \quad (\rightarrow\mathcal{I})$$

The $\rightarrow\mathcal{I}$ rule appears at first sight to be less familiar. In common with other introduction rules $\rightarrow\mathcal{I}$ requires preparation — in this case, to derive

$P \to Q$, a box is drawn to contain the assumption P and the subgoal Q has to be derived in this box. The English form of $P \to Q$, 'if P then Q', indicates the proof technique exactly: if P holds then Q should follow, so assume P and show that Q does follow. Note that the box shows exactly where the temporary assumption is available. $\to\mathcal{I}$ is an automatic rule and is always used by working backwards from the conclusion.

The next example is to prove $A \wedge B \to C \vdash A \to (B \to C)$. The first steps in this example are automatic. First, a preparation is made to prove $A \to (B \to C)$, and then a second preparation is made to prove $B \to C$, both by $\to\mathcal{I}$. These result in Figure 16.9. There are then two possibilities —

$A \wedge B \to C$

A	
B	
$\vdots$	
C	
$B \to C$	$\to\mathcal{I}$
$A \to (B \to C)$	$\to\mathcal{I}$

Figure 16.9

you can either use A and B to give $A \wedge B$ and hence C, or you can use $A \wedge B \to C$ to reduce the goal C to the goal $A \wedge B$.

The final proof is given in Figure 16.10. How might this proof appear in

1	$A \wedge B \to C$	
2	A	
3	B	
4	$A \wedge B$	$\wedge\mathcal{I}(2,3)$
5	C	$\to\mathcal{E}(1,4)$
6	$B \to C$	$\to\mathcal{I}$
7	$A \to (B \to C)$	$\to\mathcal{I}$

Figure 16.10 $A \wedge B \to C \vdash A \to (B \to C)$

English?

Proposition 16.2 $A \wedge B \to C \vdash A \to (B \to C)$

Proof To show $A \to (B \to C)$, assume A and show $B \to C$. To do this, assume B and show C. Now, to show C, show $A \wedge B$. But we can show $A \wedge B$ since we have assumed both A and B. □

The next three examples illustrate the use of the $\to \mathcal{E}$ and $\to \mathcal{I}$ rules. They also use the useful ✓ rule — if you want to prove A, and A is in the data, then you can just 'check' A.

$$\frac{A}{A \ (\checkmark)}$$

Show $\vdash A \to A$

There is only one real step in this example, and no initial data (Figure 16.11).

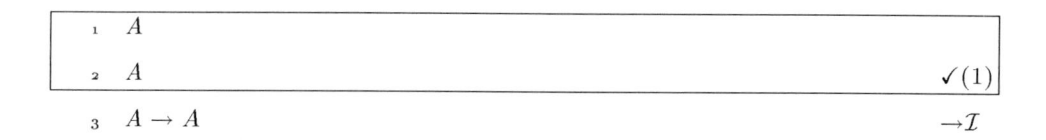

```
1   A
2   A                                    ✓(1)
─────────────────────────────────────────────
3   A → A                                 →I
```

Figure 16.11 $\vdash A \to A$

Show $A \vdash B \to A$

```
1   A
2   B
3   A                                    ✓(1)
─────────────────────────────────────────────
4   B → A                                 →I
```

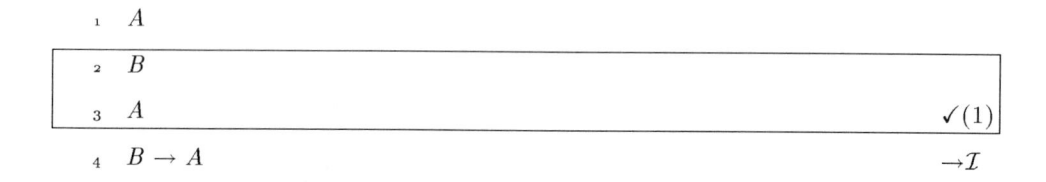

Figure 16.12 $A \vdash B \to A$

Notice that the assumption B is not used inside the box (Figure 16.12).

Show $P \vee Q \vdash (P \to Q) \to Q$

In Figure 16.13 the preparation for $\to \mathcal{I}$ is made before that for $\vee \mathcal{E}$. If the preparation for using $P \vee Q$ were made before the preparation for the conclusion, then the latter preparation would have to be made twice within each of the boxes enforced by the preparation for $\vee \mathcal{E}$.

```
1   P ∨ Q
2   │ P → Q
3   │ │ P          │ Q
4   │ │ Q  →ℰ(2,3) │ Q            ✓(3)
5   │ Q                            ∨ℰ
6   (P → Q) → Q                    →ℐ
```

Figure 16.13 $P \vee Q \vdash (P \to Q) \to Q$

The validity of →ℰ is easy to see, for the truth of $P \to Q$ and P force Q to be true by the definition of →. For the →ℐ rule, remember that $P \to Q$ is true if P is false, *or* if P and Q are both true. So, in case P is true we have to show Q as well.

Rules for negation

There are three rules for negation, two of which are special cases of earlier rules, whereas the third is new and does not conform to the introduction/elimination pattern. The rules are

¬ℐ If the assumption of P leads to a contradiction (written as ⊥) then conclude ¬P
¬ℰ From P and ¬P derive ⊥
¬¬ From ¬¬P derive P

with formats

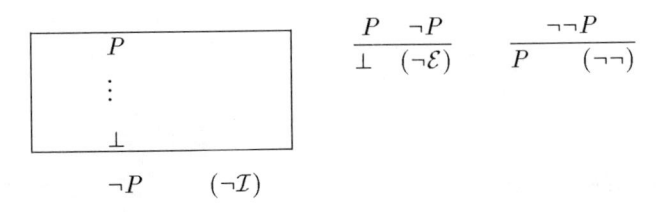

```
┌─────────┐
│ P       │         P  ¬P          ¬¬P
│ ⋮       │         ─────          ────
│ ⊥       │         ⊥  (¬ℰ)        P   (¬¬)
└─────────┘
  ¬P  (¬ℐ)
```

The ¬ℐ rule is very commonly used and is another example of an automatic rule:

to show ¬P show that the assumption of P leads to a contradiction.

The ¬ℰ rule can be used in a straightforward way in a forward direction, in which case it simply 'recognizes' that a contradiction is present amongst the derived sentences. It is also often used in a backward direction, in which case some ingenuity is needed. Suppose a sentence $\neg P$ is already derived, and $\bot$ is required, for example to use $\neg \mathcal{I}$, then the $\neg \mathcal{E}$ rule requires P to be derived in order to obtain $\bot$. Thus P becomes the new conclusion.

$\neg A$ can be equivalently written as $A \to \bot$, and then the $\neg \mathcal{I}$ and $\neg \mathcal{E}$ rules become special cases of the $\to \mathcal{I}$ and $\to \mathcal{E}$ rules.

In the next example all three negation rules are used!

Show $\vdash A \vee \neg A$

1	$\neg (A \vee \neg A)$	
2	A	
3	$A \vee \neg A$	$\vee \mathcal{I}(2)$
4	$\bot$	$\neg \mathcal{E}(1,3)$
5	$\neg A$	$\neg \mathcal{I}$
6	$A \vee \neg A$	$\vee \mathcal{I}(5)$
7	$\bot$	$\neg \mathcal{E}(1,6)$
8	$\neg\neg(A \vee \neg A)$	$\neg \mathcal{I}$
9	$A \vee \neg A$	$\neg\neg(8)$

Figure 16.14 $\vdash A \vee \neg A$

In Figure 16.14 the crucial step is to realize that $A \vee \neg A$ will follow from $\neg\neg(A \vee \neg A)$. Some ingenuity is again needed at lines 5 and 6 in deciding that to prove $A \vee \neg A$ it is appropriate to show $\neg A$.

The $\neg\neg$ rule is obviously valid. For $\neg \mathcal{E}$, notice that a proof of P and of $\neg P$ gives $P \wedge \neg P$, which is always false. For $\neg \mathcal{I}$, we have to show that P must be false — well, it must be if P leads to a contradiction, $\bot$, for otherwise $\bot$ would have to be true, which it cannot be.

Using boxes to structure proofs

Boxes are used in the natural deduction rules to structure a proof; initially, any data that is given is placed at the top of the proof and the conclusion is placed at the bottom. As a proof progresses, the gap in between is gradually filled up, sometimes working downwards from the top as in $\wedge \mathcal{E}$, $\to \mathcal{E}$ or $\vee \mathcal{E}$, and sometimes working upwards from the bottom as in $\wedge \mathcal{I}$, $\vee \mathcal{I}$ or $\neg\neg$. Many of the steps are automatic, for example, $\to \mathcal{I}$, and only require some preparation, in the form of some more boxes perhaps. Non-automatic steps, for example, $\vee\mathcal{I}$, cause more problems as they require insight and if the correct step is not seen the proof may not be found.

As boxes are introduced, the available sentences within each box will vary. Initially, only the initial data are available. Inside boxes additional sentences are also available if they are assumptions made when the box is formed; for example, in $\to\mathcal{I}$ to show $A \to B$, A is such an assumption. The structure imposed by boxes also means that any derived sentences that occur in a proof above a box X may be used within X, for their proof only required assumptions that are also available within X.

The system of box deductions is a very formal way of writing proofs; the finished product can be read from top to bottom but it gives no clue as to how the proof was derived. Doing the proof with proof boxes allows you to be more confident that your argument is correct. Eventually, you will be able to derive correct arguments every time and dispense with the explicit use of proof boxes, as is done in the majority of proofs in this book.

Derived rules

A tautology, such as $P \vee \neg P$, is a sentence that is always true. It can be derived as in Figure 16.14 using no data, and is also called a *theorem*. Theorems can be used anywhere in a proof if they are needed. Suppose you have derived the theorem $\neg(A \vee B) \to \neg A \wedge \neg B$, then, if the sentence $\neg(A \vee B)$ appears in a proof, the theorem can be used to derive, by $\to\mathcal{E}$, $\neg A \wedge \neg B$, which may be a more useful form.

When $\vdash \neg(A \vee B) \to \neg A \wedge \neg B$ is derived, A and B can be any sentences and the theorem is a *scheme* — any instance of the form of the scheme, obtained by substituting any sentences throughout for A and B, is also a theorem. If you become stuck in finding a derivation, you may find that using a theorem in order to transform a particular sentence makes everything easy again. Equivalences are especially useful for this purpose; for example, $\vdash \neg(A \wedge B) \leftrightarrow (\neg A \vee \neg B)$ — so from $\neg(A \wedge B)$ and one half of the equivalence you can derive $\neg A \vee \neg B$.

Proving theorems and then including them in a proof can make finding derivations much easier than starting from first principles and using just the given rules. Using *derived rules* can also simplify derivations. As an example, consider the following scheme, which is a typical sequence of steps for deriving S by contradiction. The derived rule in this case will be called PC for *proof by contradiction*:

228 *Natural deduction*

```
1   ¬S
2   ⋮
3   ⊥
```
4   ¬¬S   ¬ℐ
5   S   ¬¬(4)

The steps can be contracted into a new proof rule:

```
    ¬S
    ⋮
    ⊥
```
    S   PC

It is not *essential* to make use of any derived rules, for the preceding rules are enough for any proof; but they can be used to shorten a proof. The following are some more derived rules:

    contrapositive   from $A \to B$ and $\neg B$ derive $\neg A$
    simple resolution 1   from $A \vee B$ and $\neg A$ derive B
    simple resolution 2   from $\neg A \vee B$ and A derive B
    resolution   from $A \vee B$ and $\neg A \vee C$ derive $B \vee C$

As an example, the derivation of the resolution rule is given in Figure 16.15.

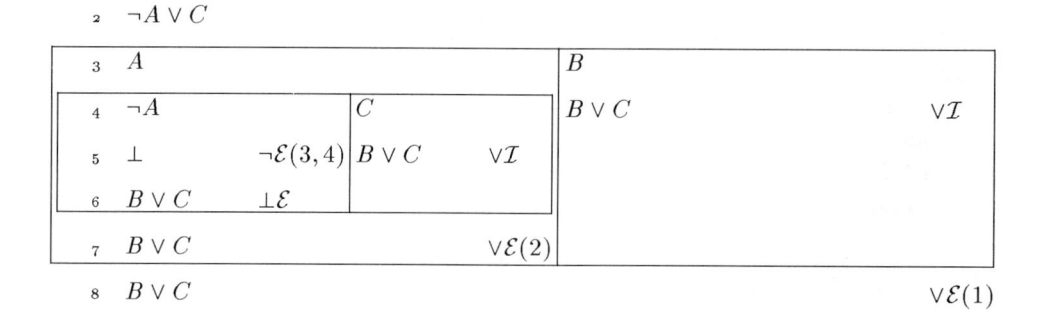

1   $A \vee B$
2   $\neg A \vee C$

```
3   A                              │ B
4     ¬A          C                │ B ∨ C                              ∨ℐ
5     ⊥    ¬ℰ(3,4) B ∨ C    ∨ℐ     │
6     B ∨ C      ⊥ℰ                │
7   B ∨ C                          ∨ℰ(2)
```
8   $B \vee C$ ∨ℰ(1)

Figure 16.15

Some hints for deriving natural deduction proofs

You have put the assumptions at the top of a proof and the conclusion at the bottom — what do you do next? You might be able to use some automatic steps, $\rightarrow\mathcal{I}$ for example, which yield a requirement for deriving various subproofs. Or, you might be able to use some insight, for example to prove $C \vee D$ using $\vee\mathcal{I}$, prove C. Since introduction rules produce conclusions they are usually used when filling in a proof from the bottom upwards — their use is dictated by the form of the conclusion. Elimination rules work on the data and so these are usually used when filling in a proof from the top downwards.

In addition to these guidelines there are many useful tactics which you will discover for yourself. We describe an assortment of such tactics next.

- $\rightarrow$ as 'if' — If there is a sentence of the form $D \rightarrow C$ and the conclusion is C then try to show D. C follows using $\rightarrow\mathcal{E}$. $D \rightarrow C$ can be read as C if D, from which the tactic gets its name.
- make use of $\neg S$ — If the conclusion is $\bot$, then perhaps there is a negative sentence $\neg S$ that is available which could be used in a $\neg\mathcal{E}$ step once S had been proved.
- $\bot\mathcal{E}$ anywhere — If you cannot see what to do next perhaps you can derive $\bot$ and then use $\bot\mathcal{E}$. This often happens in some branches of a $\vee\mathcal{E}$ box, in those branches which 'are not what the argument is about' (for example, in the left-hand inner box of Figure 16.15).
- combined $\vee$ rules — The $\vee\mathcal{I}$ and $\vee\mathcal{E}$ rules often go together — first use $\vee\mathcal{E}$ and then $\vee\mathcal{I}$. Suppose the data is $X \vee Y$ and the conclusion is $C \vee D$. $\vee\mathcal{E}$ will force two subproofs, one using X and one using Y, and perhaps in one you can prove C and in the other D. In both cases $\vee\mathcal{I}$ will yield $C \vee D$, as you required.
- equivalence — Any sentence can be rewritten using an equivalence. When filling in a proof downwards, data can be rewritten into new data and when filling in a proof upwards, conclusions can be rewritten into new conclusions.
- theorem — Remember that it is possible to use theorems anywhere in a proof, for these are previously proved sequents that do not depend on any data and so could be used anywhere.
- lemma — In some cases a large proof can best be tackled by breaking it down into smaller steps. If your problem is to show $Data \vdash Conclusion$ then maybe you could show $Data \vdash Lemma$ and then make use of $Lemma$ to show $Conclusion$ — $(Data$ and $Lemma) \vdash Conclusion$. The choice of which lemma to prove is often called a 'Eureka' step for it sometimes requires considerable ingenuity.
- excluded middle — If there are no negative sentences, then perhaps you can introduce a theorem of the form $Z \vee \neg Z$ and immediately use $\vee\mathcal{E}$.

230   *Natural deduction*

Of course, some ingenuity is needed to choose a suitable Z, but it is worth trying Z as the conclusion you are trying to prove.
- *PC* — Perhaps you can use the proof by contradiction derived rule.
- If all else fails, use *PC*, or excluded middle.
And if all else does not fail then *do not* use *PC* — the negated assumptions it introduces often make the proof more difficult to understand.

Most practical proofs make use of three of the tactics on a large scale; they are the *lemma*, *equivalence* and *theorem* tactics:

- The lemma tactic is used to break the proof into smaller steps.
- The equivalence tactic is used to rewrite the data into the most appropriate form for the problem.
- The theorem tactic is used to make large steps in one go by appealing to a previous proof.

In practice, we make use of hundreds of theorems, some of which are exercises in this book and some of which you will discover for yourself. So watch out for them!

16.3 Examples

The various rules and tactics of this chapter are illustrated in the following examples.

Show $\neg P \vdash P \to Q$

$$
\begin{array}{lll}
1 & \neg P & \\
\hline
2 & P & \\
3 & \bot & \neg\mathcal{E}(1,2) \\
4 & Q & \bot\mathcal{E}(3) \\
\hline
5 & P \to Q & \to\mathcal{I}
\end{array}
$$

Figure 16.16 $\neg P \vdash P \to Q$

The derivation in Figure 16.16 is a useful one to remember. It is used in the following example which derives a famous law called 'Pierce's law' after the logician Charles Pierce.

Show ⊢ $((P \to Q) \to P) \to P$

Two proofs are given (in Figures 16.17 and 16.18) — the first uses $P \vee \neg P$ and the second uses PC. They both illustrate the benefit of planning in a proof. In the first proof it is clear that the sentence $(P \to Q) \to P$ will yield P, the conclusion, if $P \to Q$ can be proven. Also, the sentence $P \vee \neg P$ means that since P can be derived from P, $P \to Q$ will have to be proven from $\neg P$. And we have shown this in Figure 16.16. In the second proof a useful technique is used — 'use PC if all else fails'. Applying it in this example leads to the goal of $\bot$ — the necessary $\neg \mathcal{E}$ step will require a sentence and its negation to be derived. $\neg P$ is already an assumption so consider deriving P. This can be done by deriving $P \to Q$, which follows from $\neg P$, again as in Figure 16.16. Notice that here we have had to use some insight in order to

1	$(P \to Q) \to P$			
2	$\neg P \vee P$			(Th)
3	$\neg P$		P	
4	$P \to Q$	(Fig. 16.16)	P	✓ (3)
5	P	$\to \mathcal{E}(1,4)$		
6	P			$\vee \mathcal{E}(2)$
7	$((P \to Q) \to P) \to P$			$\to \mathcal{I}$

Figure 16.17 ⊢ $((P \to Q) \to P) \to P$

1	$(P \to Q) \to P$	
2	$\neg P$	
3	$P \to Q$	(Fig. 16.16)
4	P	$\to \mathcal{E}(1,3)$
5	$\bot$	$\neg \mathcal{E}(2,4)$
6	P	PC
7	$((P \to Q) \to P) \to P$	$\to \mathcal{I}$

Figure 16.18 ⊢ $((P \to Q) \to P) \to P$

apply the heuristics in the correct order. If you tried to use '$\to$ as if' before PC, that is, tried to prove $P \to Q$ without obtaining $\neg P$, you would fail.

232 Natural deduction

Show $A \wedge B \to C, \neg D \to \neg(E \to F), C \to (E \to F) \vdash A \to (B \to D)$

The derivation for this example (in Figure 16.19) proves, and then uses, the lemma $E \to F$ to help fill in the proof between lines 5 and 12. That is, $E \to F$ can be proved first and then it can be used to prove D. If the proof

1	$A \wedge B \to C$	
2	$\neg D \to \neg(E \to F)$	
3	$C \to (E \to F)$	
4	A	
5	B	
6	$A \wedge B$	$\wedge\mathcal{I}(4,5)$
7	C	$\to\mathcal{E}(6,1)$
8	$(E \to F)$	$\to\mathcal{E}(3,7)$(a lemma)
9	$\neg D$	
10	$\neg(E \to F)$	$\to\mathcal{E}(2,9)$
11	$\bot$	$\neg\mathcal{E}(10,8)$
12	D	PC
13	$B \to D$	$\to\mathcal{I}$
14	$A \to (B \to D)$	$\to\mathcal{I}$

Figure 16.19 $A \wedge B \to C, \neg D \to \neg(E \to F), C \to (E \to F) \vdash A \to (B \to D)$

were to be written in English it might look as follows.

Proposition 16.3 $A \wedge B \to C, \neg D \to \neg(E \to F), C \to (E \to F) \vdash A \to (B \to D)$

Proof To show $A \to (B \to D)$ assume A and show $B \to D$. So assume B and try to show D. (Next a little bit of ingenuity is required. You notice that to show D it would suffice to show that $E \to F$, as the assumption of $\neg D$ then leads to a contradiction.) So, try to show $E \to F$. From A and B derive C and hence $E \to F$. Finally, D can be shown by using proof by contradiction. $\neg D$ leads to $\neg(E \to F)$, which gives a contradiction with the lemma $E \to F$. □

A specification example

One of the Miranda programs considered earlier was `min :: num -> num -> num` with specification: $\forall x \forall y \forall z. [z \leq x \wedge z \leq y \wedge (z = x \vee z = y)]$, where `z = min x y`. This can be used to define a function `min3` that yields the smallest

Examples 233

value of three numbers. What is the specification of such a function min3? The result must certainly be one of the three numbers and should also be $\leq$ each number. A suitable program is

```
min3 :: num -> num -> num -> num
min3 x y z = min ( min x y) z
```

That is, find the minimum of the first two numbers and then the minimum of this result and the third number. To show that the program meets the specification, we must show that:

$$\forall x \forall y \forall z. \ [\text{min3} \leq x \land \text{min3} \leq y \land \text{min3} \leq z \land (\text{min3} = x \lor \text{min3} = y \lor \text{min3} = z)]$$

that is

$$\forall x, y, z. \begin{bmatrix} \text{min (min } x \ y) \ z \leq x \land \text{min (min } x \ y) \ z \leq y \land \\ \text{min (min } x \ y) \ z \leq z \land \\ (\text{min (min } x \ y) \ z = x \lor \text{min (min } x \ y) \ z = y \lor \\ \text{min (min } x \ y) z = z) \end{bmatrix}$$

To show that a sentence is true for all x, y, z we should show that it is true for any arbitrary values in place of x, y, z. (See Section 17.2.) Suppose X, Y, Z are arbitrary values for x, y, z. Then we have to show

min (min X Y) $Z \leq X \land$ min (min X Y) $Z \leq Y \land$ min (min X Y) $Z \leq Z \land$
(min (min X Y) $Z = X \lor$ min (min X Y) $Z = Y \lor$ min (min X Y)$Z = Z$)

First, what are the initial assumptions? The specification of min for a start. Any other assumptions can be added as the proof progresses. A look at the sentence to be proved reveals that it is a conjunction of four sentences, so each one has to be proved.

The first is min (min X Y) $Z \leq X$. Use the specification of min — write min X Y as u, then min u $Z \leq u \land$ min u $Z \leq Z$. (Since the result of min X Y is a num, it satisfies the implicit pre-condition for the first argument of min in min (min X Y) Z.) Also, $u \leq X \land u \leq Y$. Hence, after using the fact that $\leq$ is transitive, min u $Z \leq X$, min u $Z \leq Y$, min u $Z \leq Z$. This gives the first three parts. The fourth is a disjunction.

One way to prove a disjunction is to use another. From the specification of min, $u = X \lor u = Y$, and min u $Z = u \lor$ min u $Z = Z$. Take the second of these: min u $Z = Z$ will yield the result after $\lor \mathcal{I}$. Assuming now that min u $Z = u$, from the first disjunction there are two cases: $u = X$ for one case, and $u = Y$ for the other. Together, $u = X$ and min u $Z = u$ give min u $Z = X$, which again yields the result. The other case is similar. The box proof is shown in Figure 16.20. (Notice that lines 7, 8, 9 and 10—14 give the derivations of the four conjuncts in line 16.)

234 Natural deduction

1. $\min u\ Z = u \lor \min u\ Z = Z$
2. $u = X \lor u = Y$
3. $u \leq X \land u \leq Y$
4. $u \leq X,\ u \leq Y$ $\land\mathcal{E}(3)$
5. $\min u\ Z \leq u \land \min u\ Z \leq Z$
6. $\min u\ Z \leq u,\ \min u\ Z \leq Z$ $\land\mathcal{E}(5)$

---
7. $\min u\ Z \leq X$
   by transitivity of $\leq$ (4, 6)

---
8. $\min u\ Z \leq Y$
   by transitivity of $\leq$ (4, 6)

---
9. $\min u\ Z \leq Z$ $\checkmark (6)$

---

10. $\min u\ Z = u$ | | $\min u\ Z = Z$
11. $u = X$ | $u = Y$ | $\min u\ Z = X \lor$
12. $\min u\ Z = X$ (10, 11) | $\min u\ Z = Y$ (10, 11) | $\min u\ Z = Y \lor$ $\lor\mathcal{I}(10)$
    (by equality) | (by equality) | $\min u\ Z = Z$
13. $\min u\ Z = X \lor$ $\lor\mathcal{I}(12)$ | $\min u\ Z = X \lor$ $\lor\mathcal{I}(12)$
    $\min u\ Z = Y \lor$ | $\min u\ Z = Y \lor$
    $\min u\ Z = Z$ | $\min u\ Z = Z$

14. $\min u\ Z = X \lor \min u\ Z = Y \lor$ $\lor\mathcal{E}(2)$
    $\min u\ Z = Z$

15. $\min u\ Z = X \lor \min u\ Z = Y \lor \min u\ Z = Z$ $\lor\mathcal{E}(1)$

16. $\min uZ \leq X \land \min u\ Z \leq Y \land \min u\ Z \leq Z \land$ $\land\mathcal{I}$
    $\min u\ Z = X \lor \min u\ Z = Y \lor \min u\ Z = Z$

Figure 16.20

16.4 Summary

- A valid argument consists of a collection of premises and a conclusion such that if the premises are true then the conclusion must be true, too.
- The basic natural deduction rules for propositional sentences are given in Appendix C.
- The $\vee \mathcal{I}$, $\wedge \mathcal{E}$, $\to \mathcal{E}$, $\neg \mathcal{E}$ rules require some ingenuity, choosing which rules to apply and when, whereas the $\wedge \mathcal{I}$, $\vee \mathcal{E}$, $\to \mathcal{I}$, $\neg \mathcal{I}$ rules are all automatic, requiring just some preparation, and should be applied as soon as you realize that they can be applied.
- Derived rules can be useful, especially the rule PC, proof by contradiction.
- Boxes are useful for structuring proofs and to show where assumptions hold.
- There are various tactics for finding derivations:

    $\to$ as 'if'

    making use of $\neg S$

    use $\bot \mathcal{E}$ anywhere

    PC

    excluded middle

    combined $\vee$ rules

    equivalence

    theorem

    lemma

16.5 Exercises

1. Show

    (a) $\vdash P \wedge Q \to P$
    (b) $P \vdash Q \to (P \wedge Q)$
    (c) $P \to Q, \neg Q \vdash \neg P$
    (d) $\neg P \vdash P \to Q$
    (e) $\neg P, P \vee Q \vdash Q$
    (f) $\neg I \wedge \neg F \vdash \neg (I \vee F)$
    (g) $\vdash P \to (Q \to P)$
    (h) $P \to S, (P \to Q) \to S \vdash S$
    (i) $F \to (B \vee W), \neg(B \vee P), W \to P \vdash \neg F$
    (j) $P \to Q, \neg P \to R, Q \to S, R \to S \vdash S$
    (k) $(C \wedge N) \to T, H \wedge \neg S, H \wedge \neg(S \vee C) \to P \vdash (N \wedge \neg T) \to P$
    (l) $R \to \neg I, I \vee F, \neg F \vdash \neg R$
    (m) $P \to (Q \to R) \vdash (P \to Q) \to (P \to R)$

2. For each of the equivalences $A \equiv B$ show $A \vdash B$ and $B \vdash A$.
   (a) $P \wedge (P \vee Q) \equiv P$
   (b) $P \vee (P \wedge Q) \equiv P$
   (c) $P \rightarrow Q \equiv \neg Q \rightarrow \neg P$
   (d) $P \rightarrow Q \equiv \neg P \vee Q$
   (e) $\neg(P \wedge Q) \equiv \neg P \vee \neg Q$
   (f) $\neg(P \vee Q) \equiv \neg P \wedge \neg Q$
   (g) $(P \wedge Q) \rightarrow R \equiv P \rightarrow (Q \rightarrow R)$
   (h) $P \vee Q \equiv \neg(\neg P \wedge \neg Q)$
   (i) $P \vee Q \equiv (P \rightarrow Q) \rightarrow Q$
   (j) $\neg(\neg P \wedge \neg Q) \equiv P \vee Q$
   (k) $P \vee (Q \wedge R) \equiv (P \vee Q) \wedge (P \vee R)$
   (l) $(P \vee Q) \rightarrow R \equiv (P \rightarrow R) \wedge (Q \rightarrow R)$
   (m) $(P \rightarrow Q) \wedge (Q \rightarrow P) \equiv (P \wedge Q) \vee (\neg P \wedge \neg Q)$

3. Derive an introduction and elimination rule for $\leftrightarrow$ based on the equivalences $A \leftrightarrow B \equiv (A \rightarrow B) \wedge (B \rightarrow A)$ and $A \leftrightarrow B \equiv (A \wedge B) \vee (\neg A \wedge \neg B)$. Use your new rules to show:
   (a) $\neg(P \leftrightarrow Q) \equiv \neg P \leftrightarrow Q$
   (b) $P \leftrightarrow (P \wedge Q) \equiv P \rightarrow Q$
   (c) $P \leftrightarrow (P \vee Q) \equiv Q \rightarrow P$
   (d) $P \leftrightarrow Q \equiv Q \leftrightarrow P$
   (e) $P \leftrightarrow (Q \leftrightarrow R) \equiv (P \leftrightarrow Q) \leftrightarrow R$

4. Many tautologies of the form $\vdash A \rightarrow B$ give rise to derived rules of the form $A \vdash B$. Explain how.

5. Formulate a derived natural deduction rule for *if-then-else* $\mathcal{I}$ and *if-then-else* $\mathcal{E}$. The first will be based on the rules $\wedge \mathcal{I}$ and $\rightarrow \mathcal{I}$, the second on $\wedge \mathcal{E}$ and $\rightarrow \mathcal{E}$. (HINT: *if-then-else*(x, y, z) is equivalent to $x \rightarrow y \wedge \neg x \rightarrow z$.)
   Use the rules to show
   (a) *if-then-else*$(A, B, C) \vdash$ *if-then-else*$(\neg A, C, B)$
   (b) *if-then-else*$(A,$ *if-then-else*$(D, B, C), C)$
       $\vdash$ *if-then-else*$(D,$ *if-then-else*$(A, B, C), C)$

6. (a) Derive the rules 'contrapositive', 'simpler resolution 1' and 'simpler resolution 2'.
   (b) Prove the rule $\neg\neg$ as a derived rule using the schema $Q \vee \neg Q$.
   (c) Prove the inverse of $\neg\neg$ (that is, from Q derive $\neg\neg Q$) as a derived rule.

Chapter 17

Natural deduction for predicate logic

In the preceding chapter we looked at natural deduction rules for the various logical connectives. Each connective was associated with an introduction rule for use in deriving a sentence involving the connective, and an elimination rule for deriving further sentences from a sentence using the connective.

There are six more natural deduction rules to be introduced in this chapter. Four of them cover the quantifiers, which also have elimination and introduction rules — $\forall \mathcal{I}$, $\forall \mathcal{E}$, $\exists \mathcal{I}$, $\exists \mathcal{E}$. The other two are for reasoning with equality, which is an important predicate that has its own rules: *eqsub*, which acts rather like an equality elimination rule, and *reflex*, which acts like an equality introduction rule.

17.1 ∀-elimination (∀ℰ) and ∃-introduction (∃ℐ) rules

The rules

$\forall \mathcal{E}$ From a sentence $\forall x.\ P[x]$ you may derive $P[t]$ for any ground term t that is available, where t is substituted for x everywhere that it occurs in $P[x]$.

$$\frac{\forall x.\ P[x]}{P[t]} \quad (\forall \mathcal{E})$$

$\exists \mathcal{I}$ A sentence $\exists x.\ P[x]$ can be derived from $P[b]$, where b is any available ground term and x is substituted for one or more occurrences of b in $P[b]$, or to show $\exists x.\ P[x]$ try to show $P[b]$ for some available ground term b:

$$\frac{P[b]}{\exists x.\ P[x]} \quad (\exists \mathcal{I})$$

A *ground term* is one that contains no variables. In addition, the terms t or b may only involve constants and/or function symbols that are already *available* in the current context.

Function symbols and constants appearing in proofs cannot be invented as the fancy takes you; rather, they must:

- either be occurring in sentences in the overall problem (that is, sentences which are mentioned in the premises or conclusion);
- or be implicit because a particular interpretation of the predicates is known (for example, various numbers);
- or be introduced when using the rules $\forall \mathcal{I}$ or $\exists \mathcal{E}$ (see Section 17.2).

This means that at different places in a proof different constants may be available for substitution in the use of $\forall \mathcal{E}$ or $\exists \mathcal{I}$.

The $\forall \mathcal{E}$ rule is frequently used and allows a general sentence about all individuals to become a particular sentence about some individual t. The $\exists \mathcal{I}$ rule is mostly used when filling in a proof from the conclusion upwards. That is, to show $\exists x.\ P[x]$, first a particular b is chosen (using some ingenuity) and then an attempt to show $P[b]$ is made.

Notice that the term t in an application of $\forall \mathcal{E}$ must be substituted for *all* occurrences of the bound variable, for otherwise the resulting sentence would not be properly formed.

The $\exists \mathcal{I}$ rule can also be used forwards, for if a sentence $P[b]$ has been derived then certainly $\exists z.\ P[z]$ is true, too. In that case, any number of occurrences (≥ 1) of the selected term b can be replaced by the bound variable x. In order that the resulting sentence $\exists x.\ P[x]$ is properly formed the bound variable x should be new to $P[b]$.

Quite a bit of ingenuity is necessary in using these rules; in the use of the $\forall \mathcal{E}$ rule you need to prevent too many particular sentences being generated that are not going to be useful to the proof; in the backward use of the $\exists \mathcal{I}$ rule you need to pick an individual b for which $P[b]$ can indeed be proved.

The notation using typed quantifiers is widely used in specifying programs, especially for qualifiers such as 'person', 'lists', 'numbers', etc. The $\forall \mathcal{E}$ and $\exists \mathcal{I}$ rules each have a typed counterpart that is derived from the translations

$\forall x : type.\ P[x]$ translates to $\forall x.\ [\textit{is-type}(x) \rightarrow P[x]]$

and

$\exists x : type.\ P[x]$ translates to $\exists x.\ [\textit{is-type}(x) \wedge P[x]]$

The typed rules are

$$\frac{\textit{is-type}(t) \quad \forall x : type.\ P[x]}{P[t]} \ (\forall \mathcal{E}) \qquad \frac{\textit{is-type}(b) \quad P[b]}{\exists x : type.\ P[x]} \ (\exists \mathcal{I})$$

For $\forall \mathcal{E}$ the term t must be of the correct type and satisfy $\textit{is-type}(t)$ in order for an implicit $\rightarrow \mathcal{E}$ step to be made to derive $P[t]$. For the $\exists \mathcal{I}$ rule the term b must satisfy $\textit{is-type}(b)$ so that an implicit $\wedge \mathcal{I}$ step can be made. These conditions mean that an additional check must be made on the terms being substituted. Suppose, as an example, that a term of type 'integer' was required in a $\forall\mathcal{E}$ step. The derivation so far may not mention any numbers explicitly, but implicitly the data includes a whole theory about integers, including all the facts we know about numbers such as $2 \neq 3$, 5 is prime, and so on. Any integer can be used as a substitute for t. Similarly, before using $\exists\mathcal{I}$ to derive $\exists x : int.\ P(x)$ from $P(2)$, say, you must check that $is\text{-}int(2)$ is true, which of course it is.

The $\forall\mathcal{E}$ rule is often used together with $\rightarrow\mathcal{E}$ or $\neg\mathcal{E}$ to form combined rules called, respectively, $\forall\rightarrow\mathcal{E}$ and $\forall\neg\mathcal{E}$. In both of these cases the $\forall\mathcal{E}$ step is implicit. Moreover, just as $\rightarrow\mathcal{E}$ and $\neg\mathcal{E}$ can be used backwards as well as forwards, so, too, can the combinations be used backwards as well as forwards. We will see several examples of this in the next section.

The formats are

$$\frac{\forall x.\ [P[x] \rightarrow Q[x]] \qquad P[c]}{Q[c]} \ (\forall\rightarrow\mathcal{E}) \quad \text{and} \quad \frac{\forall x.\ \neg P[x] \qquad P[c]}{\bot} \ (\forall\neg\mathcal{E})$$

The $\forall\neg\mathcal{E}$ rule can be used to show a contradiction by showing some sentence $P[c]$ and then implicitly using $\forall\mathcal{E}$ to derive $\neg P[c]$ and the contradiction.

Some examples

In our first example, shown in Figure 17.1, we give a proof of $tired(lenny) \wedge lion(lenny) \rightarrow does(lenny, sleep)$. The initial data appears in lines 1—3 and, after the automatic step of $\rightarrow\mathcal{I}$, several non-automatic steps are made in lines 4—8. The $\forall\rightarrow\mathcal{E}$ rule is used several times. For example, at line 7 $\forall\mathcal{E}$ is first (implicitly) applied to line 1, to derive $lion(lenny) \rightarrow does(lenny, hunt) \vee does(lenny, sleep)$ and then $\rightarrow\mathcal{E}$ is applied to derive $does(lenny, hunt) \vee does\ (lenny, sleep)$. After that, another automatic step is made to prepare for $\vee\mathcal{E}$.

The second example, shown in Figures 17.2 and 17.3, is a proof of an existentially quantified sentence $\exists x.\ \neg shot(x, Diana)$. The initial data given in lines 1—4 can be used to show the conclusion in two different ways. The simpler way is given first. This example is typical of real situations when more data than is required to prove the given goal is available, making ingenuity even more necessary in finding the proof.

The first derivation proves that Diana did not shoot herself, and the second that Janet did not shoot Diana. The combined rule $\forall\neg\mathcal{E}$ is used in the second derivation at line 8 — the new conclusion $inhouse(Janet) \wedge ingarden(Janet)$ is derived because if this is proved then $\forall\mathcal{E}$ using line 3 will give a contradiction. All uses of $\forall\mathcal{E}$ and $\exists\mathcal{I}$ require some insight into which substitutions for the bound variable will prove suitable. In this case there are two names, *Janet* and *Diana*, and either might be appropriate.

240 Natural deduction for predicate logic

1	$\forall x.\ [lion(x) \to does(x, hunt) \lor does(x, sleep)]$	
2	$\forall x.\ \forall y.\ [does(x, y) \to can(x, y)]$	
3	$\forall x.\ [tired(x) \land lion(x) \to \neg can(x, hunt)]$	
4	$tired(lenny) \land lion(lenny)$	
5	$tired(lenny)$	$\land\mathcal{E}(4)$
6	$lion(lenny)$	$\land\mathcal{E}(4)$
7	$does(lenny, hunt) \lor does(lenny, sleep)$	$\forall{\to}\mathcal{E}(1,6)$
8	$\neg can(lenny, hunt)$	$\forall{\to}\mathcal{E}(3,4)$
9	$does(lenny, hunt)$ | $does(lenny, sleep)$	
10	$can(lenny, hunt)$ $\forall{\to}\mathcal{E}(9,2)$ | $does(lenny, sleep)$ $\checkmark(9)$	
11	$\bot$ $\neg\mathcal{E}(10, 8)$	
12	$does(lenny, sleep)$ $\bot\mathcal{E}$	
13	$does(lenny, sleep)$	$\lor\mathcal{E}(7)$
14	$tired(lenny) \land lion(lenny) \to does(lenny, sleep)$	$\to\mathcal{I}$

Figure 17.1 Proof of $tired(lenny) \land lion(lenny) \to does(lenny, sleep)$

1	$\forall x.\ \neg shot(x, x)$	
2	$inhouse(Janet)$	
3	$\forall x.\ \neg(inhouse(x) \land ingarden(x))$	
4	$\forall x.\ [shot(x, Diana) \to ingarden(x)]$	
5	$\neg shot(Diana, Diana)$	$\forall\mathcal{E}(1)$
6	$\exists x.\ \neg shot(x, Diana)$	$\exists\mathcal{I}(5)$

Figure 17.2 Proof of $\exists x.\ \neg shot(x, Diana)$

Show $P(a) \lor P(b), \forall x.\ [P(x) \to Q(x)] \vdash \exists x.\ Q(x)$

Figure 17.4 illustrates a feature of the $\exists\mathcal{I}$ rule. Many problems are straightforward in that there is a particular term that makes $\exists x.\ A[x]$ follow from the current data. (For example, if the data had been $\forall x.\ [P(x) \to Q(x)], P(a)$ then $\exists x.\ Q(x)$ would follow because of $Q(a)$.) Sometimes, this is not the case, and although $\exists x.\ A[x]$ follows from the

∀-elimination (∀ℰ) and ∃-introduction (∃𝓘) rules   241

1   $\forall x.\ \neg shot(x,x)$
2   $inhouse(Janet)$
3   $\forall x.\ \neg(inhouse(x) \wedge ingarden(x))$
4   $\forall x.\ [shot(x, Diana) \rightarrow ingarden(x)]$

5	$shot(Janet, Diana)$	
6	$ingarden(Janet)$	$\forall{\rightarrow}\mathcal{E}(4,5)$
7	$inhouse(Janet) \wedge ingarden(Janet)$	$\wedge\mathcal{I}(2,6)$
8	$\bot$	$\forall\neg\mathcal{E}(7,3)$

9   $\neg shot(Janet, Diana)$ $\neg\mathcal{I}$
10 $\exists x.\ \neg shot(x, Diana)$ $\exists\mathcal{I}(9)$

Figure 17.3 Another proof of $\exists x.\ \neg shot(x, Diana)$

1   $P(a) \vee P(b)$
2   $\forall x.\ [P(x) \rightarrow Q(x)]$

3	$P(a)$		$P(b)$		
4	$Q(a)$	$\forall{\rightarrow}\mathcal{E}(2,3)$	$Q(b)$		$\forall{\rightarrow}\mathcal{E}(3,2)$
5	$\exists x.\ Q(x)$	$\exists\mathcal{I}$	$\exists x.\ Q(x)$		$\exists\mathcal{I}$

6   $\exists x.\ Q(x)$ $\vee\mathcal{E}(1)$

Figure 17.4 $P(a) \vee P(b), \forall x.\ [P(x) \rightarrow Q(x)] \vdash \exists x.\ Q(x)$

available data there may be uncertainty as to which term makes it do so.

Typically, this occurs when there is a disjunction in the data and one 'witness' (substitution for x) is appropriate in the context of one disjunct and another in the context of a second. Our example has a disjunction in its data which is applied before the application of $\exists\mathcal{I}$. On the other hand, in the proof of $\forall x.\ [P(x) \rightarrow Q(x)], \neg P(b) \rightarrow P(a) \vdash \exists x.\ Q(x)$, shown in Figure 17.5, the disjunction $P(b) \vee \neg P(b)$ is added as a theorem. This is a common technique, but you may need several attempts before you find the correct disjunction to introduce. The one used here is not the only possibility for either of $P(a) \vee \neg P(a)$ or $\exists x.\ Q(x) \vee \neg \exists x.\ Q(x)$ could have been used instead.

242   *Natural deduction for predicate logic*

1    $\neg P(b) \to P(a)$
2    $\forall x.\ [P(x) \to Q(x)]$
3    $\neg P(b) \lor P(b)$ (Th)

4	$\neg P(b)$		$P(b)$	
5	$P(a)$	$\to\mathcal{E}(1,4)$	$Q(b)$	$\forall\to\mathcal{E}(2,4)$
6	$Q(a)$	$\forall\to\mathcal{E}(2,5)$	$\exists x.\ Q(x)$	$\exists\mathcal{I}(5)$
7	$\exists x.\ Q(x)$	$\exists\mathcal{I}(6)$		

8    $\exists x.\ Q(x)$ $\lor\mathcal{E}(3)$

Figure 17.5 $\forall x.\ [P(x) \to Q(x)], \neg P(b) \to P(a) \vdash \exists x.\ Q(x)$

1    $\forall x : num.\ P(x)$
2    $P(25)$ $\forall\mathcal{E}(1)$
3    $\exists x : num.\ P(x)$ $\exists\mathcal{I}(2)$

Figure 17.6 $\forall x : num.\ P(x) \vdash \exists x : num.\ P(x)$

Show $\forall x : num.\ P(x) \vdash \exists x : num.\ P(x)$ (Figure 17.6)

Here, in order to show the conclusion an assumption has to be made that there are some numbers, so suppose that there are. Two checks then have to be made — that '25' is a number in deriving line 2 from line 1, and that '25' is a number in deriving line 3.

17.2 $\forall$-introduction ($\forall\mathcal{I}$) and $\exists$-elimination ($\exists\mathcal{E}$) rules

$\forall$-introduction

The next rule that we consider is $\forall\mathcal{I}$, and *its* use introduces a new constant into the proof. The rule is

> A proof of $\forall x.\ P[x]$ can be obtained from a proof of $P[c]$ for some *new* constant c.

$\forall$-introduction ($\forall\mathcal{I}$) and $\exists$-elimination ($\exists\mathcal{E}$) rules

```
┌─────────────────┐
│ c  ∀𝓘           │
│   ⋮             │
│    P[c]         │
└─────────────────┘
     ∀x. P[x]        (∀𝓘)
```

or typed

```
┌────────────────────────┐
│ c  ∀𝓘   is-t(c)        │
│   ⋮                    │
│    P[c]                │
└────────────────────────┘
```

The 'new' means that c is introduced for the first time inside the box that contains the subproof of $P[c]$; c is only available within that box and it cannot be mentioned outside it. So, in particular, c cannot occur in $\forall x.\ P[x]$. The $c\ \forall\mathcal{I}$ in the left-hand corner is a reminder that c must be new.

The version using a typed quantifier is derived from the untyped version and $\to\mathcal{I}$ using the translation of $\forall x : t.\ P[x]$ into $\forall x.\ [\textit{is-t}(x) \to P[x]]$.

The $\forall\mathcal{I}$ rule is completely automatic and is used in a backwards direction from goal to subgoal. The motivation behind this rule is the commonly quoted law:

> If one can show $P[u]$ for an arbitrary u, then $\forall x.\ P[x]$ holds.

The use of a new term for c implements the 'arbitrary' part of the law.

The following is an informal explanation of why the rule 'works': in order to derive $\forall x.\ P[x]$, the derivation should work for whatever value v could be substituted for x and should not depend on properties of a particular v. Since c is new, any data that is used to prove $P[c]$ will not mention c and the derivation cannot rely on special properties of c (apart from that it is of type t), as there are none. Properties are either not relevant or are completely general, of the form $\forall \cdots$, in which case they apply to any value.

A very common pattern used in quantified sentences is $\forall x.\ [P[x] \to Q[x]]$. If this sentence is a conclusion then two automatic steps are immediately applicable — first a $\forall\mathcal{I}$ step and then a $\to\mathcal{I}$ step. These can be combined into one step, $\forall{\to}\mathcal{I}$, that requires just one box instead of two, as is done implicitly in deriving a typed version of the $\forall\mathcal{I}$ rule.

Remember that in Chapter 15 we encountered a difficulty in checking whether a universal sentence was true when there was an infinite number of values to check? Well, now we have an alternative approach. The sentence is checked for one or more arbitrary values which between them cover all the possible cases. For example, to show that $\forall x : int.\ P[x]$, we might try to show that $P[c]$ for an arbitrary integer c. Now, any integer is either < 0, $= 0$ or > 0, so we could try to show that $P[c]$ is true in each of the three cases. (Alternatively, any integer is also prime or non-prime, so we could try to show that $P[c]$ is true in those two cases.)

∃-elimination

The $\exists\mathcal{E}$ rule is another completely automatic rule that introduces a new constant into a proof. It may seem a little difficult at first sight and you should thus learn it by heart and understand why it appears as it does.

> To derive Q using $\exists x.\ P[x]$, derive Q using $P[c]$, where c is a new constant.

The format for the $\exists\mathcal{E}$ rule is:

$$\exists x.\ P[x]$$
$$\boxed{\begin{array}{ll} c\exists\mathcal{E} & P[c] \\ & \vdots \\ & Q \end{array}}$$
$$Q \qquad (\exists\mathcal{E})$$

or typed

$$\exists x : t.\ P[x]$$
$$\boxed{\begin{array}{ll} c\exists\mathcal{E} & P[c] \\ & \textit{is-t}(c) \\ & \vdots \\ & Q \end{array}}$$
$$Q \qquad (\exists\mathcal{E})$$

The version using a typed quantifier is derived from the untyped version and $\wedge\mathcal{E}$ using the translation of $\exists x : t.\ P[x]$ into $\exists x.\ [\textit{is-t}(x) \wedge P[x]]$.

Again, c must be a new constant and the box is used to indicate where c is available. In particular, the conclusion Q must not mention c. Notice that the conclusion appears twice; outside the box it is justified by $\exists\mathcal{E}$ and inside by something else. The rule is best applied as soon as possible in a proof so that the new constant c is available as soon as possible.

An informal explanation of why the rule works is as follows: in order to use $\exists x.\ P[x]$ a name has to be given to fix the 'x that makes $P[x]$ true'. Although it would be possible to keep referring to this value as 'the x that makes $P[x]$ true', this is a very cumbersome name and also one that could be ambiguous if there were more than one such x, so a new constant c is introduced. c must be new since all that is known about it is that $P[c]$ is true (and if the quantifier is typed that c is of type t). If c were not a new constant, then the proof of Q might inadvertently use some additional properties that were true of some values but not all, and it could be that the 'x that makes $P[x]$ true' was one of those values for which these additional properties were not true.

∀-*introduction* (∀𝓘) *and* ∃-*elimination* (∃𝓔) *rules* 245

Some more examples

In this section we look at some typical examples involving sentences with quantifiers.

Show $\exists y. \forall x. P(x,y) \vdash \forall u. \exists v. P(u,v)$ (Figure 17.7)
'If there is some y that makes $P(x,y)$ true for all x, then for every u there is some v (the same one for each case) that makes $P(u,v)$ true.'

The first two steps, ∀𝓘 and ∃𝓔, are automatic but could easily have been in the opposite order. Once a and b have been introduced there are enough clues in the proof so far (lines 1—3 and 5—7) to fill in the gap. Notice that the reverse deduction is not valid:

$\forall u. \exists v. P(u,v) \nvdash \exists y. \forall x. P(x,y)$

	1	$\exists y. \forall x. P(x,y)$	
b∀𝓘	2		
a∃𝓔	3	$\forall x. P(x,a)$	
	4	$P(b,a)$	∀𝓔(3)
	5	$\exists v. P(b,v)$	∃𝓘(4)
	6	$\exists v. P(b,v)$	∃𝓔(1)
	7	$\forall u. \exists v. P(u,v)$	∀𝓘

Figure 17.7 $\exists y. \forall x. P(x,y) \vdash \forall u. \exists v. P(u,v)$

In the next example, shown in Figure 17.8, lines 1—3 form the initial data. The data include a commonly occurring pattern of quantifiers — $\forall x. \exists y$. Each time the ∀𝓔 rule is applied to a sentence such as $\forall x. \exists y. likes(x,y)$, the ∃𝓔 rule can be applied to generate a new constant. In turn, the new constant can be used in another application of ∀𝓔, which generates yet another new constant, and so on. In this case only one round is needed. Also, note that as B must be new it cannot be A. After that, the rest can be filled in fairly easily. NOTE: If a sentence has the form $Qx.Qy.\ [\cdots]$, where Q is either ∀ or ∃, then, usually, you will want to eliminate both the quantifiers in one elimination step or introduce them in one introduction step. This is quite acceptable and the two steps together are still labelled by ∀𝓔, ∃𝓔, ∃𝓘 or ∀𝓘 (and not by ∀∀𝓔, for example!)

Show $\forall x. \forall y : num.\ [(\exists z : num.\ x^z = y) \to R(x,y)] \vdash \forall w : num.\ R(w,w)$
(Figure 17.9). Here, there are two lines where checks must be made that the terms being substituted are of the correct type. The information at line

246 Natural deduction for predicate logic

$\quad_1\ \forall x.\ \exists y.\ likes(x, y)$

$\quad_2\ \forall x.\ \forall y.\ [likes(x, y) \rightarrow likes(y, x)]$

$\quad_3\ \forall u.\ \forall v.\ [\exists w.\ [likes(u, w) \wedge likes(w, v)] \rightarrow likes(u, v)]$

$A\forall\mathcal{I}$	4		
	5	$\exists y.\ likes(A, y)$	
$B\exists\mathcal{E}$	6	$likes(A, B)$	
	7	$likes(B, A)$	$\forall{\rightarrow}\mathcal{E}(2)$
	8	$likes(A, B) \wedge likes(B, A)$	$\wedge\mathcal{I}(7, 6)$
	9	$\exists w.\ [likes(A, w) \wedge likes(w, A)]$	$\exists\mathcal{I}$
	10	$likes(A, A)$	$\forall{\rightarrow}\mathcal{E}(3)$
	11	$likes(A, A)$	$\exists\mathcal{E}(5)$

$\quad_{12}\ \forall x.\ likes(x, x) \qquad\qquad\qquad\qquad\qquad\qquad \forall\mathcal{I}$

Figure 17.8 Proof of $\forall x.\ likes(x, x)$

$\quad_1\ \forall x, y : num.\ [(\exists z : num.\ x^z = y) \rightarrow R(x, y)]$

$A\forall\mathcal{I}$	2	$is\text{-}num(A)$	
	3	$is\text{-}num(1)$	(arithmetic)
	4	$A^1 = A$	(arithmetic)
	5	$\exists z : num.\ A^z = A$	$\exists\mathcal{I}$
	6	$R(A, A)$	$\forall{\rightarrow}\mathcal{E}$

$\quad_7\ \forall w : num.\ R(w, w) \qquad\qquad\qquad\qquad\qquad \forall\mathcal{I}$

Figure 17.9 Proof of $\forall w : num.\ R(w, w)$

that *is-num*(A) is part of the preparation for $\forall\mathcal{I}$. Since we only want to show $R(w, w)$ for all numbers, A can be an arbitrary number. In turn, to use the sentence at line 1 requires a check that the terms substituted for x, y are both numbers. They are, for both x, y are replaced by A. At line 5 a check must be made that 1 is a number before applying $\exists\mathcal{I}$. Finally, all the rules of arithmetic apply.

Does $\forall x.\ P(x) \vdash \exists x.\ P(x)$? (Figure 17.10)
If you try to show this using natural deduction you will find that you cannot get started because you have no knowledge that any individuals exist and so cannot make any substitutions in the $\forall \mathcal{E}$ or $\exists \mathcal{I}$ rules. In order to show the conclusion you must add to the data the sentence $\exists z.\ \top$, where $\top$ is the sentence that is always true. If you think about it, it is no real surprise that

	1	$\forall x.\ P(x)$	
	2	$\exists z.\ \top$	
$I \exists \mathcal{E}$	3	$\top$	I exists
	4	$P(I)$	$\forall \mathcal{E}$
	5	$\exists y.\ P(y)$	$\exists \mathcal{I}$
	6	$\exists y.\ P(y)$	$\exists \mathcal{E}$

Figure 17.10 $\forall x.\ P(x),\ \exists z.\ \top \vdash \exists y.\ P(y)$

the proof does not work without the extra sentence. For it could be that a situation exists in which there are no individuals. In such a situation, certainly $\forall x.\ P(x)$ is true, for there is nothing to check, but, equally, $\exists y.\ P(y)$ is false.

$\exists z.\ \top$ is often taken for granted, but not in this book.

17.3 Equality

The equality relation '=' is a predicate that is very commonly used and everyone has a fairly good idea of what $a = b$ is supposed to mean — that a and b denote the same element or individual. This in turn means that whatever properties are possessed by a will also be possessed by b. So, for example, if

   Dr Jekyll = Mr Hyde
   Mr Hyde killed someone

then it can be deduced that Dr Jekyll killed someone. For, if the sentence $\exists x.\ killed(Mr\ Hyde, x)$ is satisfied by Mr Hyde, then it is also satisfied by Dr Jekyll, that is, $\exists x.\ killed(Dr\ Jekyll, x)$. The example illustrates the main rule for reasoning with equality — the rule of equality substitution — which allows one side of an equation to be substituted for the other. An equality atom such as $Susan = Sue$ is often called an *equation*.

Using equality in translation

Let us look first at how equality can be used in sentences to express sameness, uniqueness and functionhood.

Consider the following short propositions:

1. Tig eats vegetables
2. Tig only eats vegetables
3. Tig dances with Jig
4. Tig only dances with Jig

The straightforward translations of the first two into logic are

1. $\forall x.\ [vegetable(x) \rightarrow eats(\mathit{Tig}, x)]$
2. $\forall x.\ [eats(\mathit{Tig}, x) \rightarrow vegetable(x)]$

If the third and fourth sentences are paraphrased in a similar way then they become

$\forall x.\ [x = \mathit{Jig} \rightarrow \mathit{dances\text{-}with}(\mathit{Tig}, x)]$

and

$\forall x.\ [\mathit{dances\text{-}with}(\mathit{Tig}, x) \rightarrow x = \mathit{Jig}]$

An equation is used to express the proposition that 'x is Jig', that is, $x = \mathit{Jig}$. The third sentence can be rewritten equivalently and more naturally as $\mathit{dances\text{-}with}(\mathit{Tig}, \mathit{Jig})$.

Equality is also used to express uniqueness. For example, suppose we wanted to express in logic the sentence

There is exactly one green bottle.

This sentence says the following:

1. There is at least one green bottle.
2. There is at most one green bottle.

And in logic we have

$\exists x.\ greenbottle(x) \land \neg \exists u.\ \exists v.\ [greenbottle(u) \land greenbottle(v) \land u \neq v]$

An alternative and equivalent expression is obtained by paraphrasing the sentence as

There is a greenbottle x and all greenbottles are the same as x

which in logic is

$\exists x.\ [greenbottle(x) \land \forall u.\ [greenbottle(u) \rightarrow u = x]\ ]$

The first approach can be generalized for $n \geq 1$ greenbottles:

$$\exists x_1 \ldots x_n \begin{bmatrix} greenbottle(x_1) \land \ldots \land greenbottle(x_n) \\ \land\, x_1 \neq x_2 \land \ldots \land x_n \neq x_{n-1} \end{bmatrix} \land$$

$$\neg \exists u_0, \ldots, u_n \begin{bmatrix} greenbottle(u_0) \land \ldots \land greenbottle(u_n) \land \\ u_0 \neq u_1 \land u_0 \neq u_2 \land \ldots \land u_1 \neq u_2 \land \ldots \\ \land \ldots \land u_n \neq u_{n-1} \end{bmatrix}$$

The second approach can also be generalized:

$$\exists x_1 \ldots x_n \left[\begin{array}{l} greenbottle(x_1) \wedge \ldots \wedge greenbottle(x_n) \wedge \\ x_1 \neq x_2 \wedge \ldots \wedge x_n \neq x_{n-1} \wedge \\ \forall u. \: [greenbottle(u) \rightarrow u = x_1 \vee \ldots \vee u = x_n] \end{array} \right]$$

It is not always necessary to use equality to express 'sameness'. For example, 'a and b have the same parents' might be written as

$$\forall x. \: [parent\text{-}of(x, a) \leftrightarrow parent\text{-}of(x, b)]$$

Actually, the logic only says that 'if a and b have any parents then they have the same ones', and to express that a and b have *some* parents (as implied by the English) we must add

$$\wedge \exists x. \: [parent\text{-}of(x, a)]$$

Equality is also used in expressing that a particular relation is a function. For example, the relation $mother\text{-}of(x, y)$ is a function of y — for each y there is just one x that is related to it. This is expressed as

$$\forall y. \: \forall x. \: \forall z. \: [mother\text{-}of(x, y) \wedge mother\text{-}of(z, y) \rightarrow z = y]$$

If, in addition, we state that 'everyone has a mother'

$$\forall y. \: \exists x. \: mother\text{-}of(x, y)$$

then it is possible to simplify sentences such as

$$\forall u. \: [mother\text{-}of(u, Ann) \leftrightarrow mother\text{-}of(u, Jeremy)]$$

to

$$\exists u. \: [mother\text{-}of(u, Ann) \wedge mother\text{-}of(u, Jeremy)]$$

See Exercise 9.

17.4 Substitution of equality

Equality is such a frequently used predicate that there are built-in natural deduction rules to deal with it. The main natural deduction rule for making use of equations is the *rule of substitution*:

$$\frac{a = b \quad S[a]}{S[b]} \quad (eqsub)$$

where $S[a]$ means a sentence S with one or more occurrences of a identified and $S[b]$ means those occurrences replaced by b. (There is no need to identify all occurrences of a in S.)

Any ground equation of the form $a = a$ can be introduced into a proof by the *reflex rule*

$$\overline{a = a} \quad (reflex)$$

The *reflex* rule is usually used in a backwards direction — a conclusion $a = a$ (say) can always be derived by using it.

250 *Natural deduction for predicate logic*

Any equation $a = b$ means the same as the equation $b = a$. This is a consequence of the *Symmetry law of equality* which is derivable using the two new rules *eqsub* and *reflex*. See Figure 17.11. Line 3 is obtained by

$a, b \forall \mathcal{I}$ 1 $a = b$

     2   $a = a$ *reflex*

     3   $b = a$ *eqsub*

     4   $\forall x. \forall y. [x = y \rightarrow y = x]$ $\forall{\rightarrow}\mathcal{I}$

Figure 17.11 Proof of symmetry law

substituting b for the first a of line 2. The symmetry property means that $a = b$ and $b = a$ can be treated as the same equation, for although *eqsub* using $a = b$ is defined as substituting b for an occurrence of a, the use of symmetry allows $b = a$ to be derived and hence a can be substituted for an occurrence of b. The symmetry is not usually made explicit, equalities being used in whichever direction is most appropriate. Transitivity of $=$ ($\forall x. \forall y. \forall z. [x = y \land y = z \rightarrow x = z]$) can similarly be shown.

The symmetry of equations enables the *eqsub* rule to make sense whether it is used forwards (as described already) or backwards. In that case, we can use it to show $S[b]$ if we are given $b = a$, which is the same as being given $a = b$, and can show $S[a]$. The effect is to transform the current goal $S[b]$ (say) into a new goal $S[a]$ as at line 4 in the fragment shown in Figure 17.12.

1   $\vdots$

2   $a = b$

3   $\vdots$

4   $S[a]$

5   $S[b]$ *eqsub*

Figure 17.12

Show $P(a) \leftrightarrow \forall x. [x = a \rightarrow P(x)]$ (Figure 17.13)
This example illustrates the use of the *eqsub* and *reflex* rules. The final line of Figure 17.13 is derived by $\land\mathcal{I}$ followed by the use of the definition of $A \leftrightarrow B$ as $A \rightarrow B \land B \rightarrow A$. The first half of this proof is very useful as it shows how equality conditions of a particular kind can be eliminated. This is

Figure 17.13

1	$\forall x.\ [x = a \to P(x)]$	
2	$a = a \to P(a)$	$\forall \mathcal{E}(1)$
3	$a = a$	reflex
4	$P(a)$	$\to \mathcal{E}(2,3)$
5	$\forall x.\ [x = a \to P(x)]$ $\to P(a)$	$\to \mathcal{I}$
6	$P(a) \leftrightarrow \forall x.\ [x = a \to P(x)]$	

$P(a)$	
$t\forall \mathcal{I} \quad t = a$	
$P(t)$	eqsub
$\forall x.\ [x = a \to P(x)]$	$\forall \to \mathcal{I}$
$P(a) \to$ $\forall x.\ [x = a \to P(x)]$	$\to \mathcal{I}$
	(defn)

Figure 17.13

always the case for sentences of this sort which have conditions involving an equation with at least one variable argument. For example,

$\forall x, y.\ [x = a \wedge y = b \wedge P(x, y) \to Q(x, y)]$

will yield the simpler $P(a, b) \to Q(a, b)$.

In a similar way, $\exists x.\ [x = a \wedge P(x)] \leftrightarrow P(a)$ is also true.

Rewrite proofs

A method of showing that an equation is true, familiar from school mathematics, is to use rewriting. That is, to show $a_0 = b$, a_0 is rewritten into

1	$\forall xs, ys.\ [\text{rev } xs\text{++}ys = \text{rev } ys\text{++rev } xs]$	
2	$(z\!:\!zs) = [z]\text{++}zs$	
3	$\text{rev } (z\!:\!zs)$	
4	$= \text{rev } ([z]\text{++}zs)$	(2)
5	$= \text{rev } zs\text{++rev } [z]$	$\forall \mathcal{E}(1)$
6	$= \text{rev } zs\text{++}[z]$	prop of rev

Figure 17.14 A rewrite proof

a_1, and then a_1 is rewritten into a_2, and so on, until b is obtained. Each step implicitly uses the *eqsub* rule. A typical proof using this technique is used to derive $\text{rev } (z\!:\!zs) = \text{rev } zs\text{++}[z]$, shown in Figure 17.14.

A rewrite proof can be seen as a contraction of a more cumbersome sequence of equations in which each follows from the next by the *eqsub* rule. The corresponding full proof of Figure 17.14 is given in Figure 17.15. The

252 *Natural deduction for predicate logic*

1. $\forall xs, ys.\ [\text{rev } xs\text{++}ys = \text{rev } ys\text{++}\text{rev } xs]$
2. $(z\mathop{:}zs) = [z]\text{++}zs$ defn of :
3. $\text{rev } [z] = [z]$ property of **reverse**
4. $\text{rev } zs\text{++}[z] = \text{rev } zs\text{++}[z]$ *reflex*
5. $\text{rev } zs\text{++}\text{rev } [z] = \text{rev } zs\text{++}[z]$ *eqsub*(3)
6. $\text{rev } ([z]\text{++}zs) = \text{rev } zs\text{++}[z]$ $\forall\mathcal{E}(1),\ eqsub$
7. $\text{rev } (z\mathop{:}zs) = \text{rev } zs\text{++}[z]$ *eqsub*(2)

Figure 17.15

proof uses some properties of **rev**, one occurrence of the *reflex* rule and several applications of *eqsub*. It has the general pattern shown in Figure 17.16, where at each step *eqsub* is used to rewrite either the left or right side of an equation. (So either a_i is identical to a_{i-1} or b_i is identical to b_{i-1}.) The proof given in Figure 17.16 is naturally formed by working backwards from the conclusion, at each step applying *eqsub* to some term until the two sides are identical, when the *reflex* rule is used. It can quite naturally be contracted into the rewrite proof given in Figure 17.17.

various equations
$\vdots$

$a_n = a_n$ *reflex*
$a_{n-1} = b_{n-1}$ *eqsub*
$\vdots$

$a_1 = b_1$ *eqsub*
$a_0 = b_0$ *eqsub*

Figure 17.16

Delete

We will illustrate the various features of natural deduction by proving that the **del** program meets its specification (that is, it deletes the first occurrence

various equations
$$\vdots$$
$$a_0 = a_1$$
$$= a_2$$
$$\vdots = a_n$$
$$= b_{n-1}$$
$$\vdots = b_0$$

Figure 17.17

of c from l). First of all the program and specification:

```
del ::    * -> [* ]-> [* ]
||pre:   c belongs to l
||post:  (E)m,n:[* ][z=m++n & l=m++[c ]++n &
||       not(c belongs to m)]
||  where z= del c l
del c (h:t) = t,  c=h
        = (h:  del c t), c ≠ t
```

Now the proof — the outline structure is given in Figure 17.18 and the two cases for the induction step are given in Figures 17.19 and 17.20. In the proof we use the following abbreviations:
$$P(l) \equiv \forall c : *. \ [c \in l \to Q(l)]$$
and
$$Q(l) \equiv \exists m, n : [\,*\,][\text{del } c \ l = m\text{++}n \wedge l = m\text{++}[c]\text{++}n \wedge \neg c \in m]$$
We also give the proof in English for comparison.

Proposition 17.1 del satisfies its specification. We have to show $\forall l : [*]. \ P(l)$ and we use induction on l and show $P(\texttt{[]})$ and $P(h\!:\!t)$.

The base case $P(\texttt{[]})$ is vacuously true because $c \in \texttt{[]}$ is always false. For the induction step we can assume as hypothesis $P(t)$:
$$\forall c. \ [c \in t \to \exists m, n : [\,*\,][\text{del } c \ t = m\text{++}n \wedge t = m\text{++}[c]\text{++}n \wedge \neg c \in m]]$$
So, fix c as a constant C and suppose $C \in h\!:\!t$. There are two cases: either $C = h$ or $C \neq h$. If $C = h$ then $l = \texttt{[ ]}\text{++}[C]\text{++}t$ with $C \notin \texttt{[ ]}$, and by definition $\text{del } C \ l = t = \texttt{[ ]}\text{++}t$. Hence we can take $m = \texttt{[ ]}, n = t$. If $C \neq h$ then notice that because $C \in h\!:\!t$ we must have $C \in t$ and hence by the hypothesis there is some $m1$ and $n1$ such that
$$[\text{del } C \ t = m1\text{++}n1 \wedge t = m1\text{++}[C]\text{++}n1 \wedge \neg C \in m1]$$

254   *Natural deduction for predicate logic*

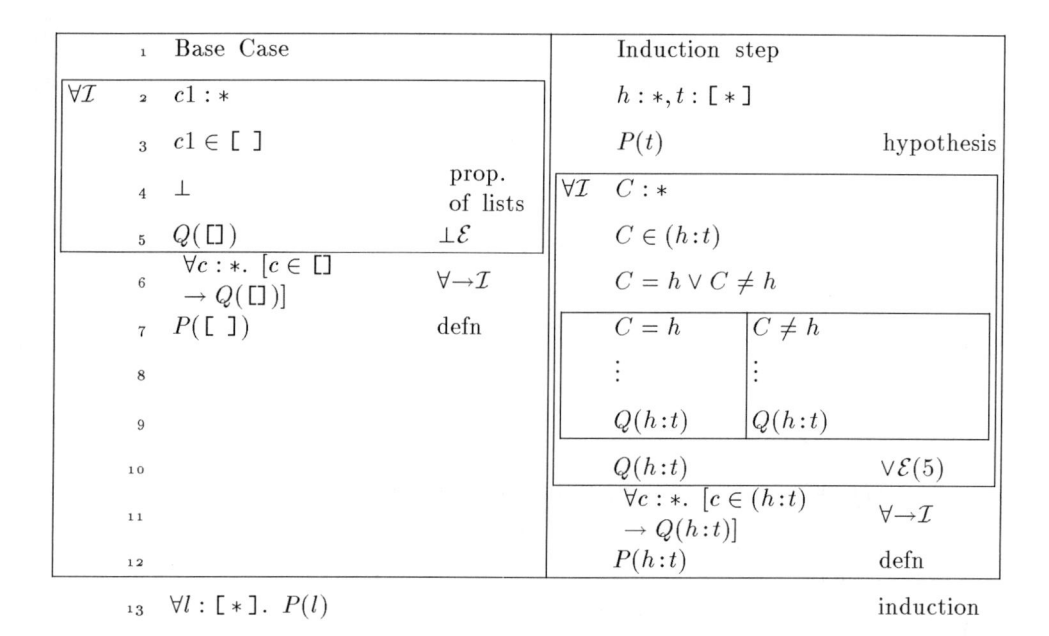

	1	Base Case			Induction step	
$\forall\mathcal{I}$	2	$c1:*$			$h:*, t:[\,*\,]$	
	3	$c1 \in [\ ]$			$P(t)$	hypothesis
	4	$\bot$	prop. of lists	$\forall\mathcal{I}$	$C:*$	
	5	$Q(\square)$	$\bot\mathcal{E}$		$C \in (h\!:\!t)$	
	6	$\forall c:*.\ [c \in [\,]\ \to Q(\square)]$	$\forall{\to}\mathcal{I}$		$C = h \vee C \neq h$	
	7	$P([\ ])$	defn		$C = h$ \hspace{1em} $C \neq h$	
	8				$\vdots$ \hspace{2em} $\vdots$	
	9				$Q(h\!:\!t)$ \hspace{1em} $Q(h\!:\!t)$	
	10				$Q(h\!:\!t)$	$\vee\mathcal{E}(5)$
	11				$\forall c:*.\ [c \in (h\!:\!t)\ \to Q(h\!:\!t)]$	$\forall{\to}\mathcal{I}$
	12				$P(h\!:\!t)$	defn
	13	$\forall l:[\,*\,].\ P(l)$				induction

Figure 17.18 Outline proof of delete

1. First part of $\vee\mathcal{E}$
2. $C = h$
3. $\texttt{del}\ C\ (C\!:\!t) = [\ ]\!+\!\!+\!t \wedge$
   $(C\!:\!t) = [\ ]\!+\!\!+\![C]\!+\!\!+\!t \wedge \neg C \in [\ ]$ \hspace{2em} $\wedge\mathcal{I}$ ($\texttt{del}\ C\ (C\!:\!t) = t$)
4. $\texttt{del}\ C\ (h\!:\!t) = [\ ]\!+\!\!+\!t \wedge$
   $(h\!:\!t) = [\ ]\!+\!\!+\![C]\!+\!\!+\!t \wedge$
   $\neg C \in [\ ]$ \hspace{2em} eqsub(2)
5. $\exists m, n:[\,*\,]\ \begin{bmatrix} \texttt{del}\ C\ (h\!:\!t) = m\!+\!\!+\!n \wedge \\ (h\!:\!t) = m\!+\!\!+\![C]\!+\!\!+\!n \wedge \\ \neg C \in m \end{bmatrix}$ \hspace{2em} $\exists\mathcal{I}(m = [\,],\ n = t)$

Figure 17.19

Since $\texttt{del}\ C\ (h\!:\!t) = (h\!:\!\texttt{del}\ C\ t) = (h\!:\!m1)\!+\!\!+\!n1$ and $h\!:\!t = (h\!:\!m1)\!+\!\!+\![C]\!+\!\!+\!n1$ with $C \notin h\!:\!m1$, we can take $m = h\!:\!m1, n = n1$ to satisfy the conclusion. $\square$

In Exercise 10 you are asked to identify the corresponding steps in the formal and informal proofs.

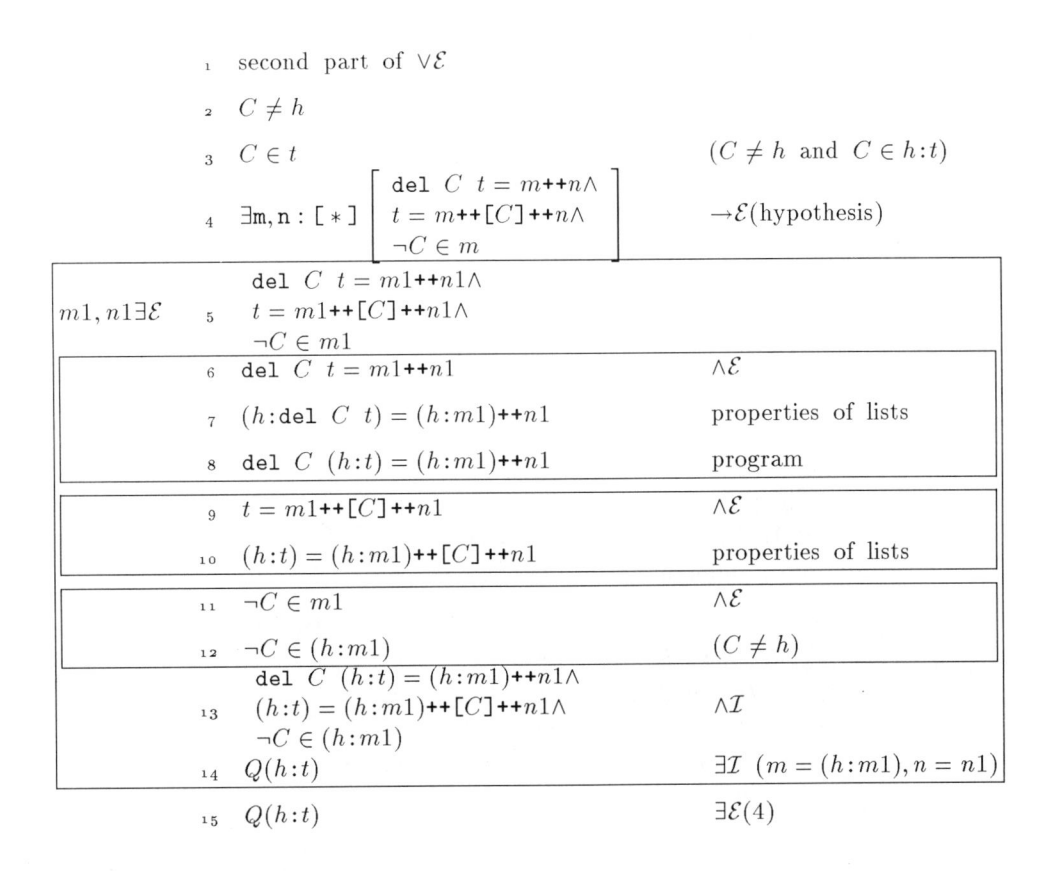

	1	second part of $\vee\mathcal{E}$	
	2	$C \neq h$	
	3	$C \in t$	$(C \neq h$ and $C \in h{:}t)$
	4	$\exists\mathtt{m,n} : [\,*\,] \begin{bmatrix} \mathtt{del}\ C\ t = m\mathtt{++}n \wedge \\ t = m\mathtt{++}[C]\mathtt{++}n \wedge \\ \neg C \in m \end{bmatrix}$	$\rightarrow\mathcal{E}$(hypothesis)
$m1, n1 \exists\mathcal{E}$	5	$\begin{array}{l}\mathtt{del}\ C\ t = m1\mathtt{++}n1 \wedge \\ t = m1\mathtt{++}[C]\mathtt{++}n1 \wedge \\ \neg C \in m1\end{array}$	
	6	$\mathtt{del}\ C\ t = m1\mathtt{++}n1$	$\wedge\mathcal{E}$
	7	$(h{:}\mathtt{del}\ C\ t) = (h{:}m1)\mathtt{++}n1$	properties of lists
	8	$\mathtt{del}\ C\ (h{:}t) = (h{:}m1)\mathtt{++}n1$	program
	9	$t = m1\mathtt{++}[C]\mathtt{++}n1$	$\wedge\mathcal{E}$
	10	$(h{:}t) = (h{:}m1)\mathtt{++}[C]\mathtt{++}n1$	properties of lists
	11	$\neg C \in m1$	$\wedge\mathcal{E}$
	12	$\neg C \in (h{:}m1)$	$(C \neq h)$
	13	$\begin{array}{l}\mathtt{del}\ C\ (h{:}t) = (h{:}m1)\mathtt{++}n1 \wedge \\ (h{:}t) = (h{:}m1)\mathtt{++}[C]\mathtt{++}n1 \wedge \\ \neg C \in (h{:}m1)\end{array}$	$\wedge\mathcal{I}$
	14	$Q(h{:}t)$	$\exists\mathcal{I}\ (m = (h{:}m1), n = n1)$
	15	$Q(h{:}t)$	$\exists\mathcal{E}(4)$

Figure 17.20

17.5 Summary

- The natural deduction rules for quantifiers are collected in Appendix C.
- The rules $\forall\mathcal{I}$ and $\exists\mathcal{E}$ are automatic, whereas $\forall\mathcal{E}$ and $\exists\mathcal{I}$ are not and require some ingenuity in their use. A useful tactic for dealing with quantifiers is

    Apply the automatic $\forall\mathcal{I}$ and $\exists\mathcal{E}$ rules as soon as possible for they will yield constants that can be used in $\exists\mathcal{I}$ and $\forall\mathcal{E}$ steps later.

- It can be helpful to apply equivalences to quantified sentences so that the quantifiers qualify the smallest subsentences possible. For example, $\forall x.\ [(\exists y.\ Q(x,y)) \rightarrow P(x)]$ might be easier to deal with than $\forall x.\ \forall y.\ [Q(x,y) \rightarrow P(x)]$.
- The *eqsub* and *reflex* natural deduction rules are also listed in Appendix C.

17.6 Exercises

1. Show:

    (a) $dragon(Puff), \forall x. [dragon(x) \rightarrow fly(x)] \vdash \exists x. fly(x)$

    (b) $\forall x. \neg(man(x) \land woman(x)),$
    $man(tom), woman(jill), woman(sophia) \vdash \exists x. \neg man(x)$

    (c) $\forall x, y. [arc(x, y)] \rightarrow path(x, y),$
    $\forall x, y. [\exists z. [arc(x, z) \land path(z, y)] \rightarrow path(x, y)],$
    $arc(A, B), arc(B, D), arc(B, C), arc(D, C) \vdash \exists u. path(u, C)$

    How many different proofs are there?

    (d) $\forall x, y, z. [R(x, y) \land R(y, z) \rightarrow R(z, x)], \forall w. R(w, w)$
    $\vdash \forall x, y. [R(x, y) \rightarrow R(y, x)]$

    (e) $On(A, B), On(B, C),$
    $\forall x. \neg(Blue(x) \land Green(x)), \quad Green(A), \quad Blue(C),$
    $\forall x, y. [On(x, y) \land Green(x) \land \neg Green(y) \rightarrow Ans(x, y)]$
    $\vdash \exists x. \exists y. Ans(x, y)$

    (f) $\forall x, y. [\forall z[z \in x \rightarrow z \in y] \rightarrow x \subseteq y],$
    $\forall x. \neg(x \in \emptyset), \forall y. y \in U \vdash \forall r. \emptyset \subseteq r \land \forall s. s \subseteq U \land \forall t. t \subseteq t$

2. Show

    $\forall x, y, z. [less(x, z) \land less(z, y) \rightarrow between(x, y, z)],$
    $\forall x. less(x, s(x)), \forall x, y. [less(x, y) \rightarrow less(x, s(y))]$
    $\vdash$ (a) $\land$ (b) $\land$ (c)

    where

    (a) $= between(s(0), s(s(s(0))), s(s(0)))$

    (b) $= \exists x. [between(0, x, s(0)) \land between(s(s(0)), s(s(s(s(0)))), x)]$

    (c) $= \exists x. \exists y. [between(0, x, y) \land between(s(0), s(s(s(0))), x)]$

3. Use Natural Deduction to show:

    (a) $\forall x. \neg P(x) \vdash \neg \exists x. P(x)$

    (b) $\neg \exists x. P(x) \vdash \forall x. \neg P(x)$

    (c) $\forall x. [F(x) \land G(x)] \vdash \forall x. F(x) \land \forall x. G(x)$

    (d) $\forall x. F(x) \lor \forall x. G(x) \vdash \forall x. [F(x) \lor G(x)]$

(e) $\exists x. \ [F(x) \wedge G(x)] \vdash \exists x. \ F(x) \wedge \exists x. \ G(x)$

(f) $\exists x. \ F(x) \vee \exists x. \ G(x) \vdash \exists x. \ [F(x) \vee G(x)]$

(g) $\forall x, y. \ F(x, y) \vdash \forall u, v. \ F(v, u)$

(h) $\exists x. \ \exists y. \ F(x, y) \vdash \exists u. \ \exists v. \ F(v, u)$

(i) $\exists x. \ \forall y. \ G(x, y) \vdash \forall u. \ \exists v. \ G(v, u)$

(j) $\forall x, y. \ [S(y) \to F(x)] \vdash \exists y. \ S(y) \to \forall x. \ F(x)$

(k) $\forall x. \ \neg P(x) \vdash \neg \exists x. \ P(x)$

(l) $\neg \forall x. \ P(x) \vdash \exists x. \ \neg P(x)$
   (HINT: assume that $\neg \exists x. \ \neg P(x)$ and derive a contradiction; this time the only way to use the negated premiss.)

(m) $P \to \forall x. \ Q(x) \vdash \forall x. \ [P \to Q(x)]$

(n) $\exists x. \ [P \to Q(x)] \vdash P \to \exists x. \ Q(x)$

(o) $P \to \exists x. \ Q(x) \ , \ \exists z. \ \top \vdash \exists x. \ [P \to Q(x)]$

(p) $(\exists x. \ P(x)) \to Q \vdash \forall x. \ [P(x) \to Q]$

(q) $\exists x. \ [P(x) \to Q] \vdash (\forall x. \ P(x)) \to Q$

(r) $\forall x. \ P(x) \to Q, \ \exists z. \ \top \vdash \exists x. \ [P(x) \to Q]$

(s) $\forall x. \ [F(x) \vee G(x)] \vdash \forall x. \ F(x) \vee \exists y. \ G(y)$.
   (HINT: use $\forall x. F(x) \vee \neg \forall x. \ F(x)$.)

(t) $\forall x. \ \exists y. \ [F(x) \vee G(y)], \ \exists z. \ \top \vdash \exists y. \ \forall x. \ [F(x) \vee G(y)]$
   (HINT: use the theorem $X \vee \neg X$ where X is the conclusion $\exists y. \ \forall x. \ [F(x) \vee G(y)]$.)

4. Show by natural deduction

   (a) $\forall x. \ P(a, x, x), \forall x, y, z. \ [P(x, y, z) \to P(f(x), y, f(z))] \vdash P(f(a), a, f(a))$

   (b) $\quad \forall x. \ P(a, x, x), \forall x, y, z. \ [P(x, y, z) \to P(f(x), y, f(z))]$
       $\vdash \exists z. \ [P(f(a), z, f(f(a)))]$

   (c) $\forall y. \ L(b, y), \forall x, z. \ [L(x, y) \to L(s(x), s(y))] \vdash \exists z. \ [L(b, z) \wedge L(z, s(s(b)))]$

5. One of the convenient ideas incorporated in Natural Deduction is that it is possible to use 'derivation patterns' (or derivation schemes); for example, the pattern $\neg A, A \vee B \vdash B$ can be derived. Such schemes enable larger steps to be taken in a proof than are possible using only the basic rules. If the scheme is very common it is sometimes called a derived rule and given a name. (The benefit lies in the fact that any sentence can be substituted throughout the scheme for A or B (for example) and the scheme remains true. For example, in (a) below we could have $\forall x. \ [P(b, x) \to Q(x, x)], P(b, a) \vdash Q(a, a)$.)

Some useful schemes are given below; in each case give a Natural Deduction proof of the scheme. The notation $P[x]$ means that x occurs in the arguments of P if P is a predicate, or, more generally, in P if it is a sentence:

(a) $\forall x.\ [P[x] \to Q[x]], \exists x.\ P[x] \vdash \exists x.\ Q[x]$ or $\forall x.\ [P[x] \to Q[x]], P[a] \vdash Q[a]$, where a is a constant

(b) $\forall x.\ [P[x] \land R[x] \to Q[x]], P[a], R[a] \vdash Q[a]$, where a is a constant. Why doesn't $\forall x.\ [P[x] \land R[x] \to Q[x]], \exists x.\ P[x], \exists x.\ R[x] \vdash \forall x.\ Q[x]$ work?

Collecting lots of these schemes together enables more concise derivations to be obtained that are still sure to be correct. There are lots of schemes for arguing about arrays, too. For example,

(c) If $n > 0$ then $\forall i[0 < i < n+1 \to P[i]] \vdash \forall i[0 < i < n \to P[i]] \land P[n]$ holds in both this direction and the opposite one and is useful for dealing with situations when $P[i]$ is a sentence about array values.

6. Use natural deduction to show the following:

   (a) $\forall x.\ [x = a \lor x = b]\ ,\ \neg P(b),\ Q(a) \vdash \forall x.\ [P(x) \to Q(x)]$
   (HINT: Use the $\lor\mathcal{E}$ and $\bot\mathcal{E}$ rules.)

   (b) (1) $\forall x.\ \neg B(x,x) \vdash \forall x.\ \forall y.\ [B(x,y) \to x \neq y]$
   (2) $\forall x.\ \forall y.\ [B(x,y) \to x \neq y] \vdash \forall x.\ \neg B(x,x)$

   (c) KB is either at home or at college, KB is not at home $\vdash$ home $\neq$ college.

   (d) Everyone likes John, John likes no-one but Jack $\vdash$ John = Jack.

   (e) S is green, S is the only thing in the box $\vdash$ Everything in the box is green.

   (f) $\forall x.\ \forall y.\ \forall z.\ [R(x,y) \land R(x,z) \to z = y], R(a,b), b \neq c \vdash \neg R(a,c)$.

   (g) $a = b \lor a = c,\ a = b \lor c = b,\ P(a) \lor P(b) \vdash P(a) \land P(b)$

   (h) $\vdash \forall x.\ \exists y.\ y = f(x)$

   (i) $\vdash \forall y.\ [y = f(a) \to \forall z.\ [z = f(a) \to y = z]]$

   (j) $\forall x.\ [x = a \lor x = b], g(a) = b,$
   $\forall x.\ \forall y.\ [g(x) = g(y) \to x = y] \vdash g(g(a)) = a$
   (HINT: You will need to use $\forall\mathcal{E}$ in the first sentence with $g(b)$ substituted for x.)

7. Express in logic:

   (a) For each x there is at most one y such that $y = f(x)$.
   (b) For each x there is exactly one y such that $y = f(x)$.

8. Show (a) (1) ⊢ (2), (b) (2) ⊢ (3) and (c) (3) ⊢ (1) by natural deduction:
   (1) $\exists x.\ [g(x) \wedge \forall z.\ [g(z) \rightarrow z = x]]$
   (2) $\exists x.\ \forall z.\ [g(z) \leftrightarrow z = x]$
   (3) $\exists x.\ [g(x)] \wedge \forall z.\ \forall y.\ [g(z) \wedge g(y) \rightarrow z = y]$

9. Show by natural deduction that
$$\vdash \begin{array}{l} \forall y.\ \forall x.\ \forall z.\ [\textit{mother-of}(x,y) \wedge \textit{mother-of}(z,y) \rightarrow z = y] \\ \forall y.\ \exists x.\ \textit{mother-of}(x,y) \\ \forall u.\ [\textit{mother-of}(u, Ann) \leftrightarrow \textit{mother-of}(u, Jeremy)] \leftrightarrow \\ \exists u.\ [\textit{mother-of}(u, Ann) \wedge \textit{mother-of}(u, Jeremy)] \end{array}$$

10. Identify the corresponding steps between the English and box proofs in Section 17.4, in which it was shown that del meets its specification.

11. Give Miranda programs for the functions given below and then use box proofs to prove, using induction if appropriate, that the functions meet their specifications. That is, show that the specification follows from any assumed pre-conditions and the execution and termination of the program. (Show that the program terminates as well.)

    (a) last :: [char] -> char; last x is the last character of x
    $$\forall x : [\ast].\ [x \neq [\,]\, \rightarrow \exists y : [\ast].\ x = y \mathtt{++} [\mathtt{last}\ x]\ ]$$

    (b) odd:: num -> num; odd x is the least odd number larger than x
    $$\forall x : num \left[\begin{array}{l} odd(\mathrm{odd}\ x) \wedge x < \mathrm{odd}\ x \wedge \\ \neg \exists y : num.\ [odd(y) \wedge y > x \wedge y < \mathrm{odd}\ x] \end{array} \right]$$

    (c) prime:: num → Bool; prime x is true iff x is prime
    $$\forall x : num.\ [\mathrm{prime}\ x \leftrightarrow \neg \exists z : num.\ [divisor(z, x) \wedge z \geq 1 \wedge z < x]]$$

    (d) uni:: [char] -> Bool: uni x is true iff x has no duplicates
    $$\forall x : [char] \left[\begin{array}{l} \mathrm{uni}\ x \leftrightarrow \neg \exists y : char. \\ \exists m : [char].\ \exists n : [char].\ \exists p : [char]. \\ [x = m\mathtt{++}[y]\mathtt{++}n\mathtt{++}[y]\mathtt{++}p] \end{array} \right]$$

Chapter 18

Models

18.1 Validity of arguments

So far, we have used natural deduction to justify that a conclusion C follows from some premises P and when we successfully derive C from P we write $P \vdash C$.

We justified the natural deduction rules from an informal idea of meaning: $P \vdash C$ is intended to capture the fact that in any situation where P holds, C must hold, too. But the relation $P \vdash C$ that we ended up defining — 'C can be proved from P by natural deduction' makes no mention of 'situations' or of sentences 'holding' and is purely formal: to apply the rules correctly (though to do it successfully and reach the desired conclusion is another matter) you just need to manipulate the syntactic structure of the sentences, the symbols used to write them down. So how do we know that $P \vdash C$ means what we intended? To give any kind of answer we need a more mathematical account of the meanings of the symbols, and this will enable us to give a precise definition of an independent relation $P \models C$ that more plainly says 'in any situation where P holds then C holds, too'. Our question, then, is whether $\vdash$ and $\models$ are equivalent:

- If we prove $P \vdash C$ by natural deduction, do we really know $P \models C$? (that is, is natural deduction *sound*?)

- If $P \models C$ is it possible to prove $P \vdash C$ by natural deduction? (that is, is natural deduction *complete*?)

We call the relationship $\models$ *logical implication* or *logical entailment*. When $P \models C$ is true, we say that it is a *valid* statement or argument.

Informal predicate structures

When you write a set of sentences in logic, you usually have in mind some interpretations which can be attached to the symbols used. For example, in writing *lives(John, Fort William)* → *likes(John, climbing)* you might have in mind that *John* referred to a particular person called John, *Fort William* referred to the place in Scotland, *climbing* referred to a sport, and *lives* and *likes* were predicates with their usual interpretations. But this need not be so. Perhaps the sentence is secret code for something else, and *John* refers to a place, *Fort William* and *climbing* to a time, *lives* to the predicate 'good weather at' and *likes* to the predicate 'will smuggle at'. Then the sentence could be saying that if the weather at some place and time is predicted to be good, that place and another time will be used for smuggling! The reader of such a sentence can only understand it if a precise interpretation of the symbols is given.

More usually, we indicate the particular interpretation we have in mind by using standard notation. For instance, a constant called 0 would suggest the number zero, a binary function called + and written infix $(x + y)$ would suggest numeric addition and a binary predicate called $\leq$ and written infix would suggest numeric comparison. Moreover, these implicitly introduce a domain of objects (the numbers) that the sentences are about.

If you are writing your sentences about numbers, you would certainly expect ordinary facts about numbers such as $\forall x.\ x \leq x$ to be available for use without being explicitly written down. But for the moment we are going to look at what pure logic can do on its own, without knowing any implicit premisses. The idea behind logical implication is to be able to forget about intended meanings and to focus on the logical structure instead.

Formal predicate structures

Logic itself provides us with connectives and quantifiers, but the predicates, functions and constants used in sentences are 'extralogical' — outside logic. Hence to know exactly what sentences we are allowing, we need to know what extralogical symbols we are using and how they are used — whether they are predicates, functions or constants, and (for predicates and functions) what their *arities* are. A specification of this extralogical information is called a *signature*. For instance, the sentence $\forall x.\ [P(x) \to \exists y.\ Q(x, f(y))]$ uses a signature that comprises (at least) a unary (unary means one argument — of arity 1) function $f(\ )$ and two predicates, $P(\ )$ and $Q(\ ,\ )$.

To find the meaning of a sentence we need to know both the range of possible values over which variables can vary, and the meanings, or *interpretations*, of the extralogical symbols. We provide these through the idea of a *structure* for a signature: the structure comprises

- a set D, known as the *domain*;
- for each constant in the signature, a corresponding element of the domain;
- for each function symbol in the signature, an actual function from D^n to D (where n is the arity of the function); and
- for each predicate P, an n-ary relation on D, that is, a subset of D^n (where n is the arity of P).

D^n here is the set of n-tuples of elements from D: so in Miranda notation, D^2, the set of pairs, is (D,D), D^3 is (D,D,D), and so on. Also, D^1 is D and D^0 has only one element, the unique '0-tuple' ( ).

The idea for the predicates is that $P(u,v,\ldots)$ should be true if and only if the tuple $(u,v,\ldots)$ is in the corresponding subset of D^n. Note that if $n=0$ (the predicate has no arguments — it is a proposition) then P is interpreted either as true (the subset is $\{(\ )\}$) or false (the subset is $\{\ \}$).

Example 18.1 of Signatures

1. Suppose we have a signature with predicates $P(\ )$ and $Q(\ ,\ )$, no functions, and a constant A. Two possible structures are

    (a) The Domain is the set of authors of this book
    $P(v)$ means 'v is female'
    $Q(u,v)$ means 'u lives further away from College than v'
    A is the first in alphabetical order (that is, *hessam*)

    (b) Domain is the set of positive integers
    $P(v)$ means 'v is even'
    $Q(u,v)$ means '$u < v$'
    A is the number 1

2. Suppose the signature has predicate $P(\ ,\ ,\ )$, function $s(\ )$ and constant a then two different structures are

    (a) Domain is the set of positive or zero integers
    $P(x,y,z)$ means $x+y=z$
    $s(n)$ means $n+1$
    a is the number 0

    (b) Domain is the set of integers ≥ 1
    $P(x,y,z)$ means $x \times y = z$
    $s(n)$ means $2 \times n$
    a is the number 1

Once we have a structure for a sentence S, that is to say a structure for a signature that includes all the extralogical symbols used in S, then we can determine the truth or falsity of S by using the rules given earlier and repeated in Figure 18.1.

- $\forall x.\ S$ is true iff for each d in D, $S(d/x)$ is true, where $S(d/x)$ means d replaces every occurrence of x in S that is bound by $\forall x$.
- $\exists x.\ S$ is true iff for some d in D, $S(d/x)$ is true
- $A \wedge B$ is true iff both A and B are true.
- $A \vee B$ is true iff at least one of A or B is true.
- $A \rightarrow B$ is true iff A is false or both A and B are true.
- $\neg A$ is true iff A is false.
- $A \leftrightarrow B$ is true if A and B are both true or both false.
- $t = u$ is true iff they are identified with the same element in the domain.

Figure 18.1 Determining the truth value of a sentence

Example 18.2

1. Find the truth or falsity of $P(A) \wedge \forall x.\ \exists y.\ [P(x) \rightarrow Q(y,x)]$ using the first pair of structures of Example 18.1.

    (a) $P(A)$ means 'hessam is female', which is false, hence the whole sentence is false. But let us find the truth value of the other constituent $\forall x.\ \exists y.\ [P(x) \rightarrow Q(y,x)]$ anyway. It means $\forall x.\ \exists y.\ [female(x) \rightarrow lives\text{-}further\text{-}from\text{-}college(y,x)]$ and its truth value will depend on the value for each x in the domain, that is, for $x = hessam$, $x = krysia$, $x = steve$ and $x = susan$.

    $x = hessam$: $\exists y.\ [female(hessam) \rightarrow lives\text{-}further\text{-}from\text{-}college(y, hessam)]$ is true for any y as $female(hessam)$ is false.
    Similarly for $x = steve$.

    $x = krysia$: $\exists y.\ [female(krysia) \rightarrow lives\text{-}further\text{-}from\text{-}college(y, krysia)]$ is true as $female(krysia) \rightarrow lives\text{-}further\text{-}from\text{-}college(steve, krysia)$ is true, as $lives\text{-}further\text{-}from\text{-}college(steve, krysia)$ is true.
    Similarly for $x = susan$.

    Thus $\forall x.\ \exists y.\ [P(x) \rightarrow Q(y,x)]$ is true in this structure.

    (b) After interpreting the symbols P, A, Q we have

    $even(1) \wedge \forall x.\ \exists y.\ [even(x) \rightarrow y < x]$ is again false since 1 is not an even integer.
    However, $\forall x.\ \exists y.\ [even(x) \rightarrow y < x]$ is true:

    even integers $x \geq 2$: $\exists y.\ [even(x) \rightarrow y < x]$ is true, for y can always be $x - 1$.

    odd integers $x \geq 1$: $\exists y.\ [even(x) \rightarrow y < x]$ is true for any choice of y, for $even(x)$ is false.

2. Find a structure with Domain = {*james,edward*} that makes both (i) and (ii) true.

   (i) *Dr Jekyll* = *Mr Hyde*

   (ii) $\exists x.\ killed(Mr\ Hyde,\ x)$

   Either both Dr Jekyll and Mr Hyde must be *edward* or both must be *james* in order to satisfy (i). Say they are both interpreted as *edward*. To make (ii) true, at least one of *killed(edward,edward)* or *killed(edward,james)* must be true.

At last we come to the important notion of *model*: a model for a sentence S is a structure in which S is true. We can now say that

$A \models B$ is true if each structure of $\{A, B\}$ that is a model of A is also a model of B.

and

$A \models B$ is false if some structure of $\{A, B\}$ that is a model of A is not a model of B.

In general, it is rather difficult to test directly whether $A \models B$ is true for there are very many structures to check. Natural deduction allows us to circumvent this difficulty. The two relations $\models$ and $\vdash$ between a set of sentences S and a conclusion T are the same. That is, if you want to show $S \models T$ you can show $S \vdash T$ instead, that is, if $S \vdash T$ then $S \models T$. It is also the case that if $S \models T$ then $S \vdash T$ so that natural deduction is an adequate alternative to checking models.

These properties are, respectively, called *soundness* and *completeness* of natural deduction and their proofs are discussed in Sections 18.6 and 18.7.

18.2 Disproving arguments

By now you will have tried to prove all sorts of arguments by natural deduction and may well be finding that sometimes it is just not possible to find a proof. In other words, for some problem to show $P \vdash C$, there seems no way to derive C from premises P by natural deduction. In this case, what can you conclude? Can you conclude that $P \nvdash C$? Well, no, you cannot. For in any proof that appears to be stuck you can, for example, go on introducing theorems of the form $X \lor \neg X$ for all kinds of exotic formulas X and one of them just might lead to a proof of C — you never can tell. Instead, you might try to show that, after all, $P \nvdash C$ does not hold. You can do that by finding a counter-example interpretation of $\{P, C\}$ which makes P true but C false. We might call this the 'failed natural deduction by counter-example' technique.

Certainly, if $P \not\models C$ then it will not be possible to show $P \vdash C$, for if it were, $P \models C$ *would* hold (by soundness, which we shall prove in Section 18.6). The next few examples show some typical situations in derivations that cannot be completed successfully. Very often, the apparent impasse provides some help as to what the counter-example interpretation might be.

Try to show $\forall x.\ P(x,x) \vdash \forall u.\ \forall y.\ P(u,y)$

```
                1   ∀x. P(x,x)
┌─────────────────────────────────────────────────────────┐
│ a∀I            2                                        │
├─────────────────────────────────────────────────────────┤
│ b∀I            3   ⋮                                    │
│                4   {cannot show P(a,b)}                 │
│                5   P(a,b)                               │
│                6   ∀y. P(a,y)                        ∀I │
└─────────────────────────────────────────────────────────┘
                7   ∀u. ∀y. P(u,y)                    ∀I
```

Figure 18.2 Failure to prove $\forall x.\ P(x,x) \vdash \forall u.\ \forall y.\ P(u,y)$

The failure in Figure 18.2 occurs because no instances of $\forall x.\ P(x,x)$ will yield $P(a,b)$. When b is introduced, it is in a context that now includes a and so b cannot be the same as a. In this case, from the failed derivation a counter-example situation can be found:

Let the domain be the set of constants $\{a,b\}$ and suppose $P(a,a)$ and $P(b,b)$ are true and other atoms are false; then this is a situation in which $\forall x.\ P(x,x)$ is true but $\forall u.\ \forall y.\ P(u,y)$ is false.

Try to show $\exists x.\ P(x) \vdash \forall x.\ P(x)$

Here, a is introduced in a context which includes b and so a must be different from b and no successful derivation can be found. If instead of using a $\forall \mathcal{I}$ step first a $\exists \mathcal{E}$ step using $\exists x.\ P(x)$ is made, a similar difficulty arises. A counter-example situation can be found here as well — suppose that the domain is again $\{a,b\}$ and take $P(a)$ to be true (as assumed in the proof attempt) and $P(b)$ to be false. Then $\exists x.\ P(x)$ is true but $\forall x.\ P(x)$ is not.

Try to show $\{\exists z.\ \top, \forall x.\ \exists y.\ P(x,y)\} \vdash \exists u\ \forall v.\ P(u,v)$

(see Figures 18.4 and 18.5). In Figure 18.4, after c has been introduced at line 3 it is natural to use it in a $\forall \mathcal{E}$ step and then in a corresponding $\exists \mathcal{I}$ step, in order to try and make $P(c,d)$ and $P(u,v)$ match. But the term used in place of v in the $\forall \mathcal{I}$ step has to be new and so cannot be the same as d. It is easy to see that a counter-example situation must have a domain of

266   Models

```
   1  ∃x. P(x)
┌─────────────────────────────────────────────┐
│ b∀𝓘  2                                       │
│┌────────────────────────────────────────────┤
││a∃𝓔  3  P(a)                                │
││     4  ⋮                                    │
││     5  {cannot complete proof}              │
││     6  P(b)                                 │
│└────────────────────────────────────────────┤
│     7  P(b)                            ∃𝓔(1)│
└─────────────────────────────────────────────┘
     8  ∀x. P(x)                           ∀𝓘
```

Figure 18.3 Failure to show $\exists x.\ P(x) \vdash \forall x.\ P(x)$

```
   1  ∃z. ⊤
   2  ∀x. ∃y. P(x,y)
┌─────────────────────────────────────────────┐
│c∃𝓔  3  ⊤                                     │
│     4  ∃y. P(c,y)                      ∀𝓔(2)│
│┌────────────────────────────────────────────┤
││d∃𝓔  5  P(c,d)                              │
││┌───────────────────────────────────────────┤
│││e∀𝓘  6                                      │
│││     7  ⋮                                    │
│││     8  {cannot fill gap}                   │
│││     9  P(c,e)                              │
││└───────────────────────────────────────────┤
││    10  ∀v. P(c,v)                        ∀𝓘│
││    11  ∃u. ∀v. P(u,v)                    ∃𝓘│
│└────────────────────────────────────────────┤
│    12  ∃u. ∀v. P(u,v)                 ∃𝓔(4) │
└─────────────────────────────────────────────┘
    13  ∃u. ∀v. P(u,v)                   ∃𝓔(1)
```

Figure 18.4 Failure to show $\{\exists z.\ \top, \forall x.\ \exists y.\ P(x,y)\} \vdash \exists u.\ \forall v.\ P(u,v)$

at least two elements — say $\{c,d\}$ with $P(c,d)$ and $P(d,c)$ both true and $P(c,c)$ and $P(d,d)$ both false. Then the premises are true but the conclusion is false.

On the other hand, after line 5 has introduced d we can use it to deduce $\exists y.\ P(d,y)$, which leads to another $\exists$ to eliminate and so on. The alternative proof attempt is shown in Figure 18.5. We can write down the constants that

$$
\begin{array}{lll}
_1 & \exists z.\ \top & \\
_2 & \forall x.\ \exists y.\ P(x,y) & \\
\hline
c\exists\mathcal{E} \quad _3 & \top & \\
_4 & \exists y.\ P(c,y) & \forall\mathcal{E}(2) \\
\hline
d\exists\mathcal{E} \quad _5 & P(c,d) & \\
_6 & \exists y.\ P(d,y) & \forall\mathcal{E}(2) \\
\hline
e\exists\mathcal{E} \quad _7 & P(d,e) & \\
_8 & \vdots & \\
_9 & \{\text{cannot fill gap}\} & \\
_{10} & \exists u.\ \forall v.\ P(u,v) & \\
\hline
_{11} & \exists u.\ \forall v.\ P(u,v) & \exists\mathcal{E}(6) \\
_{12} & \exists u.\ \forall v.\ P(u,v) & \exists\mathcal{E}(4) \\
_{13} & \exists u.\ \forall v.\ P(u,v) & \exists\mathcal{E}(1)
\end{array}
$$

Figure 18.5 Failure to show $\{\exists z.\ \top, \forall x.\ \exists y.\ P(x,y)\} \vdash \exists u.\ \forall v.\ P(u,v)$

arise in Figure 18.5, with an arrow from x to y whenever $P(x,y)$:

$c \to d \to e \to \cdots$

This suggests an infinite model:

Domain = set of natural numbers $\{0, 1, 2, 3, \cdots\}$
$P(x, y)$ means that $y = x + 1$

It is indeed a counter-example. You cannot possibly choose u so that $\forall v.\ P(u,v)$, for you never obtain $P(u,0)$.

18.3 Intended structures

There is often, implicitly, an intended interpretation for the extralogical symbols. For example, the writer of '$\forall x : nat.\ less(zero, s(x))$' quite probably had in mind the interpretation in which the domain is the set of natural numbers, *less* is $<$, s is the successor function and *zero* is the number 0. Intended interpretations allow the possibility of domain-specific deductions that go beyond logic. In Part I of this book most of the arguments were not pure logic — they had intended structures (for example, numbers, lists, etc.)

in mind and freely used known properties of those structures. For instance, in the specific domain of lists we can reason that if $c \in (h:t)$ and $c \neq h$ then $c \in t$. Now, this deduction could be made by making the particular facts about lists explicit, such as

$$\forall u, v : *. \ \forall t : [*]. \ [u \in (v:t) \to u = v \lor u \in t]$$

Or, we may think of the fact as being part of our stock of information about lists and quote it as the 'reason' for our deduction. The restricted interpretation gives us more powerful deductions.

In the case of program specifications, the pre- and post-conditions usually make clear what is the intended domain and interpretation. So if our specification indicated that the domain was integers, say, we might make use of sentences such as $\forall x : num. \ [x = 0 \lor x < 0 \lor x > 0]$.

We could in principle axiomitize (add extra premisses to constrain the structures to be sufficiently like the intended one) so that the arguments are pure logic, and this is often a good thing to do — it lays bare the logical structure of the mathematics — but we are not so formal. Hence we have used a 'mixture of logic and mathematics'. Natural deduction still helps one to get through the purely logical aspects of the argument.

Of course, any proof we make in pure logic is correct for any interpretation that satisfies the various sentences we have used, not just the particular one we had in mind. And this is really all we can expect, for when trying to show $S \models T$ by showing $S \vdash T$, the natural deduction rules know nothing of interpretations and so cannot be specific about any particular one.

18.4 Equivalences

In Chapter 15 we defined two sentences S and T to be equivalent ($S \equiv T$) if they had the same truth-value as each other in every situation. What we meant, was that

$S \equiv T$ iff
in each structure for $\{S, T\}$ S and T are either both true or both false
that is, $S \leftrightarrow T$ is true in every structure (it is a tautology)
that is, $S \models T$ and $T \models S$

The last property holds, since, if it is not possible to have S true in any structure of $\{S, T\}$ and T false, or T true and S false, then in any structure which makes S true T must be true, too, and in any structure which makes T true then S must be true, too. Hence $S \models T$ and $T \models S$.

We now take a second look at some quantifier equivalences and see how the important property of equivalent sentences, that they can be substituted for each other in any context, is affected.

In many cases, the same principles as before apply. A constituent of a sentence can be replaced by any other equivalent sentence. For example,

$\neg \forall x. \ P(x) \equiv \exists x. \ \neg P(x)$ and any occurrence of the first sentence can be replaced by the second, or vice versa. So from $S \lor \neg \forall x. \ P(x)$ we can obtain $S \lor \exists x. \ \neg P(x)$. This applies as long as there is no nested reuse of variables, for example, $\forall x. \ \exists x \cdots$, but remember we said we would not allow such forms. (They can always be avoided by renaming variables.)

If you cannot remember a useful equivalence it does not matter, for you can always derive it each time you need it. The only disadvantage is the extra time taken! Several useful quantifier equivalences are given in Appendix B and although most of the equivalences were stated for unqualified quantifiers, qualified quantifiers present no problem and behave quite well. For example, the equivalence above also holds in the form $\neg \forall x : N. \ P(x) \equiv \exists x : N. \ \neg P(x)$.

In any quantifier-free sentence S any subsentence may be replaced by an equivalent sentence without affecting the meaning of S. This is very useful as one form of a sentence may be more convenient than another. For example, $\neg(P \lor Q)$ may not be as useful a sentence form in a natural deduction proof as the equivalent $\neg P \land \neg Q$, which can be broken into two smaller pieces, $\neg P$ and $\neg Q$, and $\forall x. \ \neg P(x)$ is almost always more useful than $\neg \exists x. \ P(x)$. Many equivalences, such as those given in Appendix B, once instantiated by replacing F, G etc., by particular sentences, can be used as they stand to replace one side of the equivalence by the other.

The quantifiers $\forall$ and $\exists$ also respect equivalences:
   if $F(a) \equiv G(a)$ then
      $\forall x. \ F(x) \equiv \forall x. \ G(x)$, and
      $\exists x. \ F(x) \equiv \exists x. \ G(x)$
(Exercise 9 asks you to prove this.)

For example, since $(F(a) \land G(b)) \equiv (G(b) \land F(a))$, $\exists y. \ [F(a) \land G(y)] \equiv \exists y. \ [G(y) \land F(a)]$ and $\forall x. \ \exists y. \ [F(x) \land G(y)] \equiv \forall x. \ \exists y. \ [G(y) \land F(x)]$.

In Sections 18.6 and 18.7 we show that $A \models B$ iff $A \vdash B$ and hence we have $A \equiv B$ iff $A \vdash B$ and $B \vdash A$. An equivalence proof is therefore a good way to show $A \vdash B$ — show instead the stronger $A \equiv B$ using equivalences. Reasoning using equivalences can also be a useful way of making progress in a proof. That is, from
   $S \equiv S_1$ and $S_1 \equiv S_2$ and $\cdots$ and $S_{n-1} \equiv S_n$
you can deduce $S \equiv S_n$ and hence that $S \vdash S_n$ and $S_n \vdash S$.

Example 18.3 As an example of the use of equivalences we show
   $\exists y. \ \forall x. \ [F(x) \land G(y)] \equiv \forall x. \ \exists y. \ [F(x) \land G(y)]$
and
   $\forall x. \ \exists y. \ [F(y) \land (G(x) \to H(y))] \equiv \exists y. \ \forall x. \ [F(y) \land (G(x) \to H(y))]$
In the proofs the particular equivalences used are left to the reader to supply as an exercise.

   $\exists y. \ \forall x. \ [F(x) \land G(y)] \equiv \exists y. \ [\forall x. \ F(x) \land G(y)] \equiv \forall x. \ F(x) \land \exists y. \ G(y)$
   $\equiv \forall x. \ [F(x) \land \exists y. \ G(y)] \equiv \forall x. \ \exists y. \ [F(x) \land G(y)]$

270   Models

$$\forall x.\exists y.[F(y) \wedge (G(x) \to H(y))] \equiv \forall x.\exists y.[F(y) \wedge (\neg G(x) \vee H(y))]$$
$$\equiv \forall x.\exists y.[(F(y) \wedge \neg G(x)) \vee [(F(y) \wedge H(y))]$$
$$\equiv \forall x.[\exists y.[F(y) \wedge \neg G(x)] \vee \exists y.[F(y) \wedge H(y)]]$$
$$\equiv \forall x.\exists y.[F(y) \wedge \neg G(x)] \vee \exists y.[F(y) \wedge H(y)]]$$
$$\equiv \exists y.\forall x.[F(y) \wedge \neg G(x)] \vee \exists y.[F(y) \wedge H(y)]$$
$$\equiv \exists y.[\forall x.[F(y) \wedge \neg G(x)] \vee (F(y) \wedge H(y))]$$
$$\equiv \exists y.\forall x.[(F(y) \wedge \neg G(x)) \vee (F(y) \wedge H(y))]$$
$$\equiv \exists y.\forall x.[F(y) \wedge (G(x) \to H(y))]$$

Equivalence proofs are very helpful within natural deduction proofs for they allow premises and conclusions to be rewritten to more useful forms. There are many useful 'half-equivalences', that is, true sentences of the form $A \models B$, and some are shown in Figure 18.6.

1	$\exists x.\ \forall y.\ F(x,y) \models \forall y.\ \exists x.\ F(x,y)$
2	$\forall x.\ F(x) \vee \forall y.\ G(y) \models \forall x.\ [F(x) \vee G(x)]$
3	$\exists x.\ [F(x) \wedge G(x)] \models \exists x.\ F(x) \wedge \exists x.\ G(x)$
4	$\forall x.\ [F(x) \to G(x)] \models \forall x.\ F(x) \to \forall x.\ G(x)$
5	$\forall x.\ [F(x) \to G(x)] \models \exists x.\ F(x) \to \exists x.\ G(x)$
6	$\forall x.\ [F(x) \leftrightarrow G(x)] \models \forall x.\ F(x) \leftrightarrow \forall x.\ G(x)$
7	$\forall x.\ [F(x) \leftrightarrow G(x)] \models \exists x.\ F(x) \leftrightarrow \exists x.\ G(x)$

Figure 18.6 Useful implications

In particular, if the data contains ϕ, and $\phi \models \varphi$, then φ can be added to the data. Using half-equivalences to replace subsentences is possible but there are some dangers. Exercise 10 considers this.

A natural deduction view of equivalence
Natural deduction gives another view of equivalences. For example, the proof obligations of the two sentences $\forall x.\ [F(x) \to S]$ and $\exists x.\ [F(x) \to S]$, which are shown in Figure 18.7, are essentially the same. Here, the proof obligation is to show S from the data $F(c)$, where c is a new constant in the proof. Hence either of the original sentences behaves as a conclusion in a proof essentially in the same way. If you try a similar exercise for other equivalences you will often see that they exhibit the same kind of pattern — the proof obligation for a pair of equivalent sentences is rather similar.

Equivalent sentences, however, also operate in essentially the same way when used as data. For example, if the two sentences $\forall x.\ [F(x) \to S]$ and $\exists x.\ [F(x) \to S]$ were part of the data their use would lead to the fragments shown in Figure 18.8. Here, the proof obligations amount to showing $F(a)$ for some a in the current context. These examples, although not a proof, should help to convince you that equivalent sentences often 'behave in a natural deduction proof in the same kind of way'.

Soundness and completeness of natural deduction   271

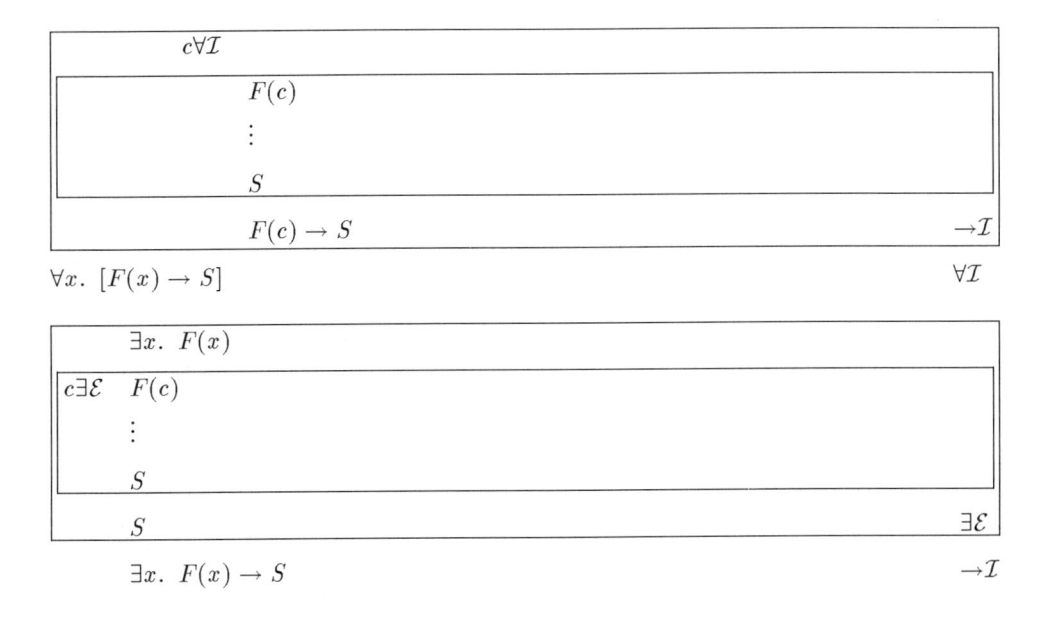

```
| c∀I                              |
| ┌──────────────────────────────┐ |
| │    F(c)                      │ |
| │     ⋮                        │ |
| │    S                         │ |
| └──────────────────────────────┘ |
|      F(c) → S              →I    |
∀x. [F(x) → S]                    ∀I
```

```
|    ∃x. F(x)                      |
| c∃E  F(c)                        |
|       ⋮                          |
|      S                           |
|      S                      ∃E   |
  ∃x. F(x) → S                →I
```

Figure 18.7

```
|     ⋮                            |
|   ∀x. [F(x) → S]                 |
|     ⋮                            |
|   F(a)                           |
|   S                        ∀→E   |
|   ∃x. F(x) → S                   |
|     ⋮                            |
|   F(a)                           |
|   ∃x. F(x)                  ∃I   |
|   S                         →E   |
```

Figure 18.8

18.5 Soundness and completeness of natural deduction

In this section we consider the two important properties of natural deduction, *soundness* and *completeness*.

One of the uses of natural deduction is as a technique for showing that $S \models T$ for sentences S and T. It is successful mainly because natural deduction is *sound*:

If $S \vdash T$ then $S \models T$

This is obviously a necessary property, otherwise all manner of sentences T might be shown to be proven from S regardless of any semantic relationship, and natural deduction would be useless.

At least, therefore, we can be sure that natural deduction proofs are correct. But there could still be a problem. Perhaps, for a particular pair of sentences $S1$ and $S2$, we cannot seem to find a proof. We may ask whether we have enough natural deduction rules to make a deduction. Well, in fact we do, because of *completeness*:

If $S \models T$ then $S \vdash T$

So we know there should be a proof.

Since we probably do not happen to know whether or not $S1 \models S2$, and hence whether or not a deduction should be possible or not, then it might be worth looking for a counter-example model if our proof attempts were floundering. Completeness is not such a crucial property as soundness — for it might be good enough in practice to be able to find a proof in most of the cases for which we expect to find one.

Natural deduction is just one method that can be used to answer the problem 'does $P \models C$'; and there are other methods which are not considered in this book. But natural deduction cannot be used to answer the question 'does $P \not\models C$'.

We say that a problem with the property that there is some method which can always decide correctly between 'yes' and 'no' answers is *decidable*. In our problem is there some method that, given P and C, always tells you 'yes' when $P \models C$ and 'no' when $P \not\models C$? In this case, there is no method that will *always* give the correct answer. Some methods may, like natural deduction, always answer *yes* correctly, and may even be able to answer *no* correctly for some cases, but no method can answer correctly in all cases. The problem, then, of checking whether $P \models C$ is called *semi-decidable*. A *decidable* problem would be one for which a method existed which correctly 'answered' both yes and no type questions.

The problem of checking whether $P \models C$ when P and C are propositional *is* decidable, for then a method that checks all interpretations for the symbols in $\{P, C\}$ is possible and is essentially the method of truth tables.

18.6 Proof of the soundness of natural deduction

In this section the important soundness property of Natural Deduction is proved:

$$\text{if } A \vdash B \text{ then } A \models B \qquad \textit{soundness}$$

that is, if a conclusion B is derivable from premisses A then it *should be* — the argument is valid.

The underlying idea is quite simple: when you read a proof from top to bottom (*not* jumping backwards and forwards in the way that it was constructed) you see a steady accumulation of true sentences. Each new one is justified on the basis that the preceding ones used as premisses by the rule you are applying have themselves already been proved and so are true. (This is an induction hypothesis! It uses induction on the length of the proof, because the earlier sentences were proved using shorter proofs. Also, disregard the fact that some parts of the proof are written out side by side — rearrange them one after the other.)

For instance: consider $\wedge\mathcal{E}$. If you have already proved $A \wedge B$, by induction you know that it is true (given the premisses) and it follows — check the truth tables if you are really in doubt — that the A delivered by $\wedge\mathcal{E}$ is also true.

This is the basic idea, but it is all made much more complicated by the boxes. The problem is that 'true' here means 'true in every model of the premisses', but the class of models varies throughout the proof. Each sentence A appearing in the proof is proved in a *context* of constants and premisses: the constants are not only those posed in the question (by being mentioned in the overall premisses and conclusion), but are also those introduced by $\forall\mathcal{I}$ or $\exists\mathcal{E}$ at the tops of boxes containing A; and the premisses are not only the overall premisses but are also the assumptions introduced for $\vee\mathcal{E}$, $\rightarrow\mathcal{I}$, $\neg\mathcal{I}$ or $\exists\mathcal{E}$ at the tops of boxes containing A.

What you introduce as a new constant or a new assumption at the top of a box is part of the context of everything inside the box.

To take proper account of both premisses and context, we shall, for the time being, use more refined notions of models and semantic entailment ($\models$). A model for a *context* (S, P) (S the set of constants, P the set of premisses; the constants in sentences in P must all be in S) is a model for P with interpretations given for all constants in S. Then we write $P \models_S C$ to mean that C is true in every model of (S, P).

Note the following: if (S', P') is a *bigger* context than (S, P) — all the constants and premisses from (S, P) and possibly some more — then any model of (S', P') is also a model of (S, P). (EXERCISE: prove this.) It follows that if $P \models_S C$ then $P' \models_{S'} C$. This is a technical explanation of why in a proof we are allowed to import sentences into boxes (smaller context to bigger), but not to export them out of boxes.

274   Models

The basic result, proved by induction on the length of the proof, is this:

if natural deduction proves C in context (S, P), then $P \models_S C$.

A proof of length 0 is one that simply repeats an assumption (that is, the conclusion C is in P) and we have shown that this is always allowed from a smaller context into a larger one. Clearly, $P \models_S C$ in that case.

Let us see first how the $\wedge \mathcal{I}$ rule works, as it is typical of the rules that do not involve boxes (the boxes used for it are purely decorative, because they do not introduce new assumptions or constants). Suppose $A \wedge B$ is proved in the context (S, P). The rule relies on having proved A and B earlier, possibly in smaller contexts (and imported), so by induction we have $P \models_S A$ and $P \models_S B$. We want to prove $P \models_S A \wedge B$, so consider any model of (S, P). In it we know that both A and B are true, so $A \wedge B$ must be as well (again, use the truth tables if you do not believe this).

The reasoning is really just the same for $\wedge \mathcal{E}$, $\vee \mathcal{I}$, $\rightarrow \mathcal{E}$, $\neg \mathcal{E}$, $\bot \mathcal{E}$, $\neg \neg$, $\forall \mathcal{E}$ and $\exists \mathcal{I}$. We can safely leave most of these as exercises, but let us look at a few of the more subtle ones.

$\bot \mathcal{E}$ Suppose A is proved in the context (S, P) by $\bot \mathcal{E}$, so we already have $P \models_S \bot$. This means that in any model of (S, P), false is true — but that is impossible, so we conclude that there are *no* models of (S, P). Hence in *all* of them A is true, so $P \models_S A$.

$\forall \mathcal{E}$ We have $\forall x.\ A(x)$ in the context (S, P), and also t is a term in the context — that is to say it is built up from the function symbols provided and the constants in S. In any model of (S, P), those ingredients are all interpreted, and so t is interpreted as a value of the model. But $\forall x.\ A(x)$ is true in the model, that is, $A(v)$ is true for all possible values v, and in particular the $A(t)$ delivered by the rule is true.

$\exists \mathcal{I}$ This case is rather similar to $\forall \mathcal{E}$ and is left as an exercise.

We now turn to those rules that really do use boxes.

$\vee \mathcal{E}$ The rule gives C in a context (S, P), and we have already proved $A \vee B$ so we know $P \models_S A \vee B$. We have also already proved C twice *but in larger contexts*: once in a box headed by the assumption A — so the context is $(S, P \cup \{A\})$ — and once with B. From these what we know is that $P, A \models_S C$ and $P, B \models_S C$. We want $P \models_S C$, so consider a model of (S, P). $A \vee B$ is true in it, so we have either A true or B true. It follows that the model is also a model either of $(S, P \cup \{A\})$ or of $(S, P \cup \{B\})$, and in either case we can deduce that C is true. (Of course, this argument is just a formalization of the idea of case analysis by which we originally justified the rule.)

$\rightarrow \mathcal{I}$ The rule gives $A \rightarrow B$ in a context (S, P) when we have already proved B in the larger context $(S, P \cup \{A\})$ and hence know $P, A \models_S B$. Consider a model of (S,P). If A is false in it, then $A \to B$ is certainly true, whilst if A is true then it is also a model of $(S, P \cup \{A\})$ so that B, and hence also $A \to B$, are true.

$\neg\mathcal{I}$ The rule gives $\neg A$ in context (S,P) when we have already proved $\bot$ in a context $(S, P \cup \{A\})$ and hence know $P, A \models_S \bot$; in other words, there are no models of $(S, P \cup \{A\})$. A model of (S,P) cannot be a model of $(S, P \cup \{A\})$, so A must be false — $\neg A$ is true.

$\forall\mathcal{I}$ The rule gives $\forall x.\ A(x)$ in a context (S,P) when we have already proved $A(c)$ in a context $(S \cup \{c\}, P)$ and hence know that $P \models_{S \cup \{c\}} A(c)$. Consider a model of (S,P): we want to know that $A(v)$ is true for every possible v. But for any particular value v we can make the model into one for $(S \cup \{c\}, P)$ by interpreting c as v (note that c had to be a *new* constant, for otherwise c would already be interpreted as something else): then we know that $A(c)$, that is, $A(v)$, is true.

$\exists\mathcal{E}$ The rule gives B in a context (S,P) when we have already proved $\exists x.\ A(x)$ in the same context and have proved B in the context $(S \cup \{c\}, P \cup \{A(c)\})$. In any model of (S,P) we know that there is at least one value v such that $A(v)$ is true; if we pick one, then we can make the model into one of $(S \cup \{c\}, P \cup \{A(c)\})$ by interpreting c as v (again, c must be new); but then we deduce that B is true.

□

18.7 Proof of the completeness of natural deduction

In this section we give a proof of the completeness property for propositional sentences and outline the changes needed for quantifier sentences.

Our method is a traditional one but, as you will see, it does not seem to be fully in the spirit of Natural Deduction, for although it shows that a deduction of B from A exists when $A \models B$, the method does not show how to construct such a proof. Moreover, the proof that *is* guaranteed to exist is also rather contrived. There are other, constructive, methods, but they are beyond the scope of this book.

Theorem 18.4 *completeness* If $A \models B$ then $A \vdash B$, that is, if an argument is valid then the conclusion *can* be derived from the premisses.

Proof: First some definitions:

A set of sentences A is *inconsistent* iff $A \vdash \bot$.
A set of sentences A is *consistent* iff it is not inconsistent.

To show $A \vdash B$, we have to show Proposition 18.5:

if A is a consistent set of sentences then A has a model.

276   Models

We can then argue:

> If $A \models B$ then $A \cup \{\neg B\}$ has *no* models. (Why?)
> Hence $A \cup \{\neg B\}$ cannot be consistent (by Proposition 18.5).
> Hence $A \cup \{\neg B\}$ is inconsistent.
> Hence $\{A, \neg B\} \vdash \bot$.
> Hence $A \vdash B$ by $\neg I$ and $\neg\neg$.

$\square$

Notice that in the penultimate step the existence of a natural deduction proof is asserted but there are no means given to help you to find it.

We will first deal with a simple case in which the only logical symbols allowed in A are $\wedge, \vee$ and $\neg$ (called $\wedge$-$\vee$-$\neg$ form) and all negations are immediately before a proposition symbol or another negation. In the case when the sentences in $A \cup \{\neg B\}$ are in $\wedge$-$\vee$-$\neg$ form the natural deduction proof of $\bot$ will be one in which $\vee\mathcal{E}$, $\wedge\mathcal{E}$ and $\neg\mathcal{E}$ are used exclusively. In Exercise 3 you have a chance to find such a proof. This does not mean that the other rules are unnecessary, for, as Exercise 8 shows, they are all used in deriving the $\wedge$-$\vee$-$\neg$ form of a sentence by natural deduction.

Proposition 18.5 If A is a consistent set of sentences then there is some model for it.

Proof : The idea is to construct a larger set of consistent sentences, called A^+, that includes A and for which we can give a model. This model will be a model for A as well.

The construction of A^+ from A uses the rules given below:

1. $A^+ \supseteq A$

2. if $A1 \wedge A2 \in A^+$ then $A1 \in A^+$ and $A2 \in A^+$

3. if $A1 \vee A2 \in A^+$ then $A1 \in A^+$ or $A2 \in A^+$

4. if $\neg\neg A1 \in A^+$ then $A1 \in A^+$

Nothing else belongs to A^+ apart from the sentences forced to do so by (1)—(4). A^+ is constructed by applying the rules above to A until they can be applied no more, choosing in step (3) whichever of $A1$ or $A2$ will maintain consistency.

A^+ is consistent

Rule (2) obviously preserves consistency: if you could prove $\bot$ using $A1$ and $A2$ then you could also prove it without them using $A1 \wedge A2$ and $\wedge\mathcal{E}$. And what about rule (3)? The point is that you have at least one option that preserves consistency. For if you can deduce $\bot$ using $A1$ and you can also deduce it using $A2$ then by $\vee \mathcal{E}$ you could also deduce $\bot$ using $A1 \vee A2$. Rule (4) is left for you to deal with.

An example
$A = \{((\neg P \vee Q) \wedge P) \vee \neg P\}$
$A^+ \supseteq \{((\neg P \vee Q) \wedge P) \vee \neg P\}$ (rule 1)
$A^+ \supseteq \{((\neg P \vee Q) \wedge P) \vee \neg P, (\neg P \vee Q) \wedge P\}$ (rule 3)
$A^+ \supseteq \{((\neg P \vee Q) \wedge P) \vee \neg P, (\neg P \vee Q) \wedge P, P, \neg P \vee Q\}$ (rule 2)
$A^+ \supseteq \{((\neg P \vee Q) \wedge P) \vee \neg P, (\neg P \vee Q) \wedge P, P, \neg P \vee Q, Q\}$ (rule 3)

All the sentences have now been dealt with and to find a model of A^+ just look at the atoms or their negations in A^+, in this case P and Q. The assignment $Q = tt, P = tt$ is a model, as you can check.

This is not the only consistent set that can be constructed by applying the rules. Another one is

$A = \{((\neg P \vee Q) \wedge P) \vee \neg P\}$
$A^+ \supseteq \{((\neg P \vee Q) \wedge P) \vee \neg P\}$ (rule 1)
$A^+ \supseteq \{((\neg P \vee Q) \wedge P) \vee \neg P, \neg P\}$ (rule 3)

This time, $\neg P$ was chosen from $((\neg P \vee Q) \wedge P) \vee \neg P$ to satisfy the third rule. You can check that the assignment $P = f\!f$ and $Q = f\!f$ is also a model of A^+ and A.

(Since A^+ is consistent it cannot contain C and $\neg C$ for any C. Why?)

A^+ has a model
We now show that A^+ has a model I (say). For each proposition symbol X used in sentences in A^+:

If $X \in A^+$ then X is assigned tt in I.
If $\neg X \in A^+$ then $X = f\!f$ in I.
If $X \notin A^+$ and $\neg X \notin A^+$ then X is assigned $f\!f$ in I.

I *is* a model of A^+:
Suppose not, and that Y in A^+ is the smallest sentence in A^+ that is not true in I.

(Use the ordering: a proposition symbol and its negation are the smallest sentences; the constituents of a sentence are smaller than it; so A is smaller than $A \wedge B$, etc.)

Y could be an atom? No, as Y would have been assigned tt.
Y could be $\neg Y'$, Y' an atom? No, as Y' would have been assigned false in I and so $\neg Y'$ is true in I.
Y could be $A1 \wedge B1$ or $A1 \vee B1$? No, as either $A1$ or $B1$ (or both) would be false in I and both are smaller than Y, the supposed smallest false sentence.

278 Models

Y could be $\neg\neg A1$? No, as $A1$ would have been in A^+, too, and also false in I.

Since I is a model for A^+ it is a model for A. □

If A and B are general propositional sentences then Proposition 18.5 can still be used. It does not matter if you replace A by an equivalent set of sentences A': A is consistent iff A' is consistent. Any propositional sentence A is equivalent to one in the ∧-∨-¬ form used in Proposition 18.5 and the ∧-∨-¬ form can be deduced by natural deduction from A and vice versa (see Exercise 8). So every sentence in $A \cup \{\neg B\}$ can be replaced by an equivalent sentence in ∧-∨-¬ form before applying Proposition 18.5.

What has been proved here is often called *weak completeness*. That is, it simply shows that a natural deduction proof exists. But suppose you are trying to derive a sequent and do not follow this 'correct' path (as given by the theorem), whatever it is. You want to know that under reasonable circumstances, the conclusion can still be derived. This is indeed the case, but showing it is belongs to the realm of automated deduction.

Completeness for quantifier sentences

The proof method for propositional sentences can be extended to quantifier sentences as outlined next. Suppose that the problem is to show $A \vdash B$. The construction of A^+ has to be extended so that it includes sentences prefixed by a quantifier. Initially, the context of A^+ is just the context of A, S say. The rule for dealing with $\exists$ will increase this context and so the final context of A^+ will not, in general, be the same as the context of A. We have to take this into consideration when showing that the $\exists$ rule maintains consistency of A^+.

The rules for constructing A^+ now include

5. If $\forall x.\ P[x] \in A^+$ then $P[a] \in A^+$, for all a formed from symbols in the current context S of A^+.
6. If $\exists x.\ P[x] \in A^+$ then $P[e] \in A^+$, for a new constant $e \notin S$. The context is updated to $S \cup \{e\}$.

We can show that rules (5) and (6) maintain consistency:

5. A' is the result of the construction so far, $\forall x.\ B[x] \in A'$ and A' is consistent. $A' \cup \{B[t/x]\}$ is consistent, where t is a term constructed from symbols in the context S' of A'. If not, a proof of $A' \cup \{B[t/x]\} \vdash \bot$ could be converted to a proof of $A' \vdash \bot$ by an additional use of $\forall \mathcal{E}$, giving a contradiction.
6. A' is the result of the construction so far, S' is the context so far and $\exists x.\ B[x] \in A'$ and A' is consistent. $A' \cup \{B[e/x]\}$ is consistent, where

e is a new constant $\notin S'$. If not, a proof of $A' \cup \{B[e/x]\} \vdash \bot$ could be converted to a proof of $A' \vdash \bot$ by using $\exists \mathcal{E}$, which would then be contradictory.

The construction of A^+ will be an infinite process unless there are no function symbols in A (because of step (5)).

Finally, we have to show that the model formed by considering atoms and their negations in A^+ is still a model of A^+. The atoms we consider are all atoms formed from predicates in A and terms using symbols in the final context S^+ of A^+. The domain of the interpretation I is just the set of terms formed from symbols in S^+ and each term is interpreted by itself.

The additional cases cover Y being either of the form $\exists x.\ P[x]$ or $\forall x.\ P[x]$:

Y could be of the form $\forall x.\ P[x]$? No, as then some sentence of the form $P[t/x]$ would also be false and this is smaller than Y.

Y could be of the form $\exists x.\ P[x]$? No, as then every sentence of the form $P[d/x]$ would be false, where $d \in$ domain of I. In particular, $P[e/x]$ would be false, a contradiction as this is smaller than Y.

18.8 Summary

- A *signature* is a collection of extralogical symbols (predicates, functions and constants) with their arities.
- A *structure* (for a signature or for some sentences) gives concrete *interpretations* for those symbols as relations, functions or elements from some particular set, the *domain*.
  Once this is done, any sentence using those symbols is interpreted and it can be determined whether it is true or false.
- A *model* for a sentence is a structure in which the sentence is true.
- The 'failed natural deduction by counter-example' technique can be used to show that $P \nvdash C$.
- Intended interpretations correspond to extralogical deductions.
- Quantifier equivalences can be applied to transform sentences.
- Natural deduction is *sound*:

    If $P \vdash C$ then $P \models C$

- Natural deduction is *complete*:

    If $P \models C$ then $P \vdash C$

18.9 Exercises

1. (a) If $A \vdash B$ then $A \models B$ (soundness of natural deduction). Hence, if $A \not\models B$ then ...?
   (b) If $A \not\models B$ does $A \models \neg B$?
   (c) If $A \models B$ does $A \not\models \neg B$?
   (d) If $A \not\vdash B$ what about $A \vdash \neg B$?
   (e) If $A \not\vdash \neg B$ does $A \vdash B$?
   (f) If $\{S1, S2, \ldots, S_n\} \models T$ is valid does $\{S2, \ldots, S_n\} \not\models T$?
   (g) If S is true in no situations then $\neg S$ is true in every situation. True or false?

2. Complete the missing cases in the proof of soundness of Natural Deduction given in Section 18.5.

3. (a) Apply the method used in the completeness proof to derive a model of the sentences $\{C \wedge N \to T, H \wedge \neg S, (H \wedge \neg (S \vee C)) \to P, N, \neg P\}$. First convert the sentences to the restricted form using equivalences and then apply the method.
   (b) Find a natural deduction proof of $\bot$ from the converted sentences.

4. Show that the following arguments are not valid, that is, the premises $\not\models$ the conclusion. Find two structures in each case in which the premises are true but the conclusion false. Try the 'failed natural deduction by counter-example' technique in order to help you to find the structures:
   (a) $likes(Mary, John), \forall x. [likes(John, x)] \not\models \neg \exists y. \neg (likes(Mary, y))$.
   (b) $\neg \forall x. \forall y. [Diff(x, y) \wedge R(x, y) \to R(y, x)] \not\models \forall u. \forall v. [Diff(u, v) \wedge R(u, v) \to \neg R(v, u)]$.
   (c) $\forall x. [F(x) \vee G(x)] \not\models \forall x. F(x) \vee \forall y. G(y)$.
   (d) $\exists v. F(v) \wedge \exists u. G(u) \not\models \exists x. [F(x) \wedge G(x)]$.
   (e) $\forall x. \exists y. M(x, y) \not\models \exists v. \forall u. M(u, v)$.

5. For each structure and each set of sentences decide the truth/falsity of the sentences in the structure:
   (a) $\{\forall x. R(x, x), \forall x. \forall y. [R(x, y) \to R(y, x)]\}$ Structures:
      i. $D = \{a, b, c\}$, $R(a, b) = R(a, c) = R(b, c) = R(c, b) = t\!t$, $R(a, a) = R(b, b) = R(c, c) = R(b, a) = R(c, a) = f\!f$
      ii. $D = \{1, 2, 3, 4, \ldots\}$, R is the relation $<$
      iii. $D = \{1, 2, 3, \ldots\}$, R is the relation $divides(x, y)$
   (b) $\{\forall x. \exists y. [P(x) \to Q(x, y)], \exists z. P(z), \exists z. [Q(b, z) \to \forall u. P(u)]\}$ Structures:
      i. $D = \{1, 2, 3, \ldots\}$, b is the number 2, $P(x)$ is the relation x is even, $Q(x, y)$ is the relation $divides(x, y)$

ii. $D = \{Fred, Susan, Mary\}$, b is $Mary$, $P(Fred) = Q(Mary, Fred) = Q(Susan Fred) = tt$, $P(Susan) = P(Mary) = ff$, all other pairs for $Q = ff$

(c) $\{\exists z.\ \forall u.\ P(f(u), z)\}$ Structures:

i. $D = \{0,\ 1,\ -1,\ 2,\ -2,\ \ldots\}$, P is the relation $<$, f is the function: $f(u) = |u|$

ii. $D = \{1,\ 2,\ 3,\ \ldots\}$, P is the relation $<$, f is the successor function.

6. Find as many different models as you can for the sentences: $\{\forall x.\ \forall y.\ \forall z.\ [P(x, y, z) \to P(s(x), y, s(z))], \forall x.\ P(a, x, x)\}$

7. Decide on the truth values of the sentences of Example 18.2 in the structure with domain= $\{0, \pm 1, \pm 2, \cdots\}$ and in which A means 0, $P(n)$ means $n \geq 0$, and $Q(m, n)$ means $m^2 = n$.

8. The completeness proof for propositional sentences given in the text can be extended to include all logical operators by using the fact that the following (ND) equivalences can be found:

$\neg(A \land B) \equiv \neg A \lor \neg B \qquad \neg(A \lor B) \equiv \neg A \land \neg B$
$\neg(A \to B) \equiv A \land \neg B \qquad A \to B \equiv \neg A \lor \neg B \qquad \neg\neg A \equiv A$

That is (for example), $A \to B \vdash \neg A \lor B$ and $\neg A \lor B \vdash A \to B$.

(a) Prove each of the above (ND) equivalences.

(b) Once you have proofs of the equivalences they can be used to rewrite any sentence into $\land$-$\lor$-$\neg$ form. The A and B can be any sentences. In particular, prove that if $A \vdash B$, $B \vdash A$, $A' \vdash B'$ and $B' \vdash A'$ then

$\neg A \vdash \neg B$ and $\neg B \vdash \neg A$
$A \land A' \vdash B \land B'$ and $B \land B' \vdash A \land A'$
$A \lor A' \vdash B \lor B'$ and $B \lor B' \vdash A \lor A'$
$A \to A' \vdash B \to B'$ and $B \to B' \vdash A \to A'$

9. Show that quantifiers respect equivalences. That is, if $A(a) \equiv B(a)$ for sentences A and B and some constant a, then $\forall x.\ A(x) \equiv \forall x.\ B(x)$ and $\exists x.\ A(x) \equiv \exists x.\ B(x)$. (HINT: use induction on the structure of A and B.)

10. We say that A occurs *positively* in a sentence F if it is within an even number (or zero) of negations. It occurs *negatively* otherwise. Show that, if A occurs positively in a sentence F and $A \models B$ and replacing A by B in F gives G, then $F \models G$. Also, show that if A occurs negatively in F then $G \models F$.

Appendix A
Well-founded induction

Find a simplest counter-example

One justification for induction arguments is that they say

1. Find a simplest possible counter-example: in other words, all simpler possibilities work correctly.
2. But then from that we manage to deduce that the counter-example, too, works correctly — it is not a counter-example at all.
3. Contradiction: so there are no counter-examples.

(3) is just logic, and (2) depends entirely on the problem to hand (what we are trying to prove). It is the induction step. But (1) depends not so much on what we are trying to prove, as on the things we are proving something about: it says that there is some notion of 'simplicity', and that we can indeed find a simplest. For instance, for numbers, 'simpler' might be 'less than'. Then finding a smallest number is something you can always do with sets of natural numbers but not necessarily with sets of integers or reals.

Well-founded orderings

Suppose we are interested in proving 'by induction', that is, using (1)—(3) above, statements of the form $\forall x : A.\ P(x)$, where A is some set such as nat. We formalize the idea of simplicity with the notion of *well-founded ordering*.

Definition A.1 Let A be a set, and $<$ a binary relation on A. $<$ is a *well-founded ordering* iff every non-empty subset X of A has a minimal element, that is, some $x \in X$ such that if $y < x$ then $y \notin X$.

Note that although $<$ is called an ordering, there is no requirement for it to be transitive or to have any other of the usual properties of orderings.

Theorem A.2 Let A be a set and $<$ a binary relation on A. Then the following are equivalent:

1. $<$ is a well-founded ordering.
2. A contains no infinite descending chains $a_1 > a_2 > a_3 > \ldots$
   (Of course, $a > b$ means $b < a$.)
3. (*Principle of well-founded induction*) Let $P(x)$ be a property of elements of A such that for any $a \in A$, if P holds for every $b < a$ then P also holds for a. Then P holds for every a.

Proof

$1 \implies 3$ (This is really an abstraction of the induction idea presented informally above. The condition on P is the formalization of the step finding that the counter-example is not a counter-example.) Let P be a property as stated, and let X be the set $\{x \in A : \neg P(x)\}$. If $X \neq \varnothing$ then by well-foundedness there is a minimal element a in X ('a simplest counter-example'). For any $b < a$ we have $b \notin X$, so $P(b)$ holds; hence by the conditions on P we have $P(a)$, which contradicts $a \in X$. The only way out is that $X = \varnothing$, that is, $P(a)$ for all a.

$2 \implies 1$ Choose $a_1 \in X$ (possible, because $X \neq \varnothing$). If a_1 is minimal in X, then we are done; otherwise, we can find $a_1 > a_2 \in X$. Again, either a_2 is minimal or we can find $a_2 > a_3 \in X$. We can iterate this, and it must eventually give us an element minimal in X, because otherwise we would obtain an infinite descending chain, contradicting (2).

$3 \implies 2$ Let $P(x)$ be the property 'there is no infinite descending chain starting with x'. Then P satisfies the condition of (3), and so P holds for every a. Hence there are no infinite descending chains at all. □

These three equivalent conditions play different conceptual roles. (1), as in the definition of well-foundedness, is the direct formalization of the ability to 'find simplest counter-examples'. (2) is usually the most useful way of checking that some relation $<$ is well-founded, and (3) is the logical principle.

Box proofs

We can put the induction principles into natural deduction boxes. This is not so much because we want to formalize everything, as to show the proof obligations, the assumptions and goals when we use induction.

The general principle of well-founded induction, given a set A and a well-founded ordering $<$, is shown in Figure A.1.

284 Well-founded induction

$$\begin{array}{|ll}\hline a:A \quad \forall y:A.\ (y<a \to P(y)) & \text{IH} \\ \quad \vdots \\ \quad P(a) \\ \hline \end{array}$$

$\forall x:A.\ P(x)$ induction

Figure A.1

The box, with the piece of proof that you have to supply, is the *induction step*. The formula labelled (IH) is the *induction hypothesis*, and it is a valuable free gift. If it weren't there, then the proof would just be ordinary $\forall \mathcal{I}$ introduction and the goal in the box would be more difficult (or impossible). We shall now look at examples of well-founded orderings, with their corresponding induction principles.

nat

This is the most basic example. You cannot have an infinite descending sequence of natural numbers, so the ordinary numeric ordering $<$ is well-founded. Figure A.2 gives the principle of *course of values induction*:

$$\begin{array}{|ll}\hline n:nat \quad \forall m:nat.\ m<n \to P(m) \\ \quad \vdots \\ \quad P(n) \\ \hline \end{array}$$

$\forall x:nat.P(x)$ induction

Figure A.2

A variant on this is obtained by taking $<$ to be not the ordinary numeric order, but a different relation defined by m '$<$'n if $n = m+1$. Then the induction hypothesis is $\forall m:nat(n = m+1 \to P(m))$, which works out in two different ways according to the value of n. If $n = 0$, it is vacuously true — there are no natural numbers m for which $0 = m+1$. If $n > 1$, the only possible m is $n-1$, and so it tells us $P(n-1)$. Separating these two cases out, and in the second case replacing m by $n-1$, we obtain in Figure A.3 the principle of *simple induction*.

It is no coincidence that these two boxes (the base case and the induction step) correspond to the two alternatives in the datatype definition for natural

$\vdots$ $P(0)$	$n : nat \quad P(n)$ $\vdots$ $P(n+1)$

$\forall n : nat.\ P(n)$ induction

Figure A.3

numbers:

```
num ::= 0 | suc num
```

Note two *non*-examples of well-founded orderings.

1. The integers under numeric $<$: for there are infinite descending chains such as

$$0 > -1 > -2 > -3 > \ldots$$

2. The positive rationals under numeric $<$:

$$1 > 1/2 > 1/3 > 1/4 > 1/5 > \ldots$$

Recursion variants

Let A be any set, and $v : A \to nat$ any function. Then we can define a well-founded ordering $<$ on A by

$\quad x < y$ iff $v(x) < v(y)$ (numerically)

The induction principle is given in Figure A.4.

$a : A \quad \forall y : A.\ (v(y) < v(a) \to P(y))$ $\vdots$ $P(a)$

$\forall x : A.\ P(x)$ induction

Figure A.4

This is course of values induction 'on v'. Plainly *nat* here could be replaced by any other set with a well-founded ordering. The programming examples

Well-founded induction

had P expressing the correct working of some function f, and it could be put into the form
$$P(x) \equiv pre(x) \rightarrow post(x, f(x))$$
where pre and post together give the specification. v is now the recursion variant, and the 'principle of circular reasoning' comes out (after incorporating some $\forall \mathcal{I}$) in Figure A.5.

$$
\begin{array}{|ll|r|}
\hline
a : A & \forall y : A. \ (pre(y) \land v(y) < v(a) \rightarrow post(y, f(y))) & \\
\hline
& pre(a) & \\
& \vdots & \\
& post(a, f(a)) & \\
\hline
& pre(a) \rightarrow post(a, f(a)) & \rightarrow \mathcal{I} \\
\hline
\end{array}
$$
$\forall x : A. \ (pre(x) \rightarrow post(x, f(x)))$ \hfill induction

Figure A.5

Lists

For lists `xs`, `ys`: [*], we can define a well-founded order easily enough by using the length, # (for example, as a recursion variant):

$xs < ys$ iff $\# \ xs < \# \ ys$

However, an interesting alternative is to define

$xs < ys$ iff xs is the tail of ys

This gives the principle of list induction.

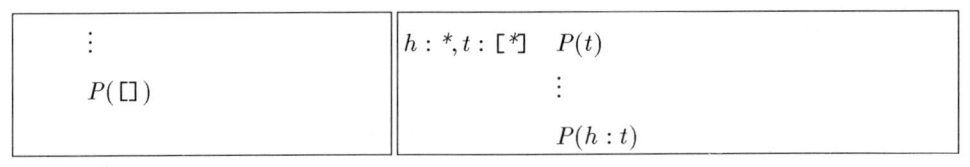

$$
\begin{array}{|c|c|}
\hline
\vdots & h : *, t : [*] \quad P(t) \\
P([]) & \vdots \\
 & P(h : t) \\
\hline
\end{array}
$$
$\forall xs : [*]. \ P(xs)$ \hfill induction

Figure A.6

Figure A.6 contains an example of *structural induction*.

Pairs and tuples

Theorem A.3 Let A and B be two sets with well-founded orderings. We shall (naughtily) write the same symbol '$<$' for both the orderings. Then $A \times B$ can be given a well-founded ordering by

$$(a, b) < (a', b') \text{ iff } a < a' \vee (a = a' \wedge b < b')$$

Proof Suppose there is an infinite descending chain $(a_1, b_1) > (a_2, b_2) > (a_3, b_3) > \ldots$. We have $a_1 > a_2 > a_3 > \ldots$ and it follows from the well-foundedness of a that the a_is take only finitely many values as they go down. Suppose a_n is the last one, then eventually $a_n = a_{n+1} = a_{n+2} = \ldots$ and $b_n > b_{n+1} > b_{n+2} > \ldots$. But this is impossible by well-foundedness on B. □

This can be extended to well-founded orderings on tuples, and it is really the same idea as lexicographic (alphabetical) ordering. BUT note that this depends critically on the fixed length of the tuples. For strings of arbitrary (though finite) length, lexicographic ordering is not well-founded. For example,

$$'taxis' > 'altaxis' > 'aaltaxis' > 'aaaltaxis' > 'aaaaltaxis' > \ldots$$

There is a reasoning principle associated with the well-founded orderings on tuples (see Exercise 2), but perhaps the most common way to exploit the ordering is by choosing a recursion variant whose value is a tuple instead of a natural number.

A.1 Exercises

1. Another variant of the principle of course of values induction, shown in Figure A.2, is obtained by using a well-founded ordering on any subset of the natural numbers (for example, $<$ on the set of even natural numbers). Write down the proof obligations using proof boxes for such a variant.
2. Write down the proof obligations using proof boxes for a reasoning principle based on a well-founded ordering on tuples.

Appendix B

Summary of equivalences

Equivalent propositional forms:

zero law	$P \to f\!f \equiv \neg P$	
complement laws	$P \wedge \neg P \equiv f\!f$	$P \vee \neg P \equiv t\!t$
idempotence	$P \wedge P \equiv P$	$P \vee P \equiv P$
commutativity	$P \wedge Q \equiv Q \wedge P$	$P \vee Q \equiv Q \vee P$
associativity	$P \wedge (Q \wedge R) \equiv (P \wedge Q) \wedge R$	$P \vee (Q \vee R) \equiv (P \vee Q) \vee R$
De Morgan's laws	$\neg(P \wedge Q) \equiv \neg P \vee \neg Q$	$\neg(P \vee Q) \equiv \neg P \wedge \neg Q$
distributivity	$P \wedge (Q \vee R) \equiv (P \wedge Q) \vee (P \wedge R)$	
	$R \to P \wedge Q \equiv (R \to P) \wedge (R \to Q)$	
	$P \to (Q \to R) \equiv (P \wedge Q) \to R$	
	$P \vee (Q \wedge R) \equiv (P \vee Q) \wedge (P \vee R)$	
	$(P \vee Q) \to R \equiv (P \to R) \wedge (Q \to R)$	
others	$\neg(P \to Q) \equiv P \wedge \neg Q$	
	$\neg(P \leftrightarrow Q) \equiv (P \wedge \neg Q) \vee (\neg P \wedge Q)$	
	$P \to Q \equiv \neg P \vee Q \equiv \neg(P \wedge \neg Q) \equiv \neg Q \to \neg P$	
	$P \leftrightarrow Q \equiv (P \wedge Q) \vee (\neg P \wedge \neg Q) \equiv (P \to Q) \wedge (Q \to P)$	

Equivalent predicate forms:

$\forall x. \ \forall y. \ G(x,y) \equiv \forall y. \ \forall x. \ G(x,y)$
$\exists x. \ \exists y. \ F(x,y) \equiv \exists y. \ \exists x. \ F(x,y)$
$\neg \forall x. \ F(x) \equiv \exists x. \ \neg F(x)$
$\neg \exists x. \ F(x) \equiv \forall x. \ \neg F(x)$
$Qx. \ [S \wedge F(x)] \equiv S \wedge Qx. \ F(x) \quad \{Q \text{ can be } \forall \text{ or } \exists\}$
$Qx. \ [S \vee F(x)] \equiv S \vee Qx. \ F(x)$
$\forall x. \ [S \to F(x)] \equiv S \to \forall x. \ F(x)$
$\forall x. \ [F(x) \to S] \equiv \exists x. \ F(x) \to S$
$\forall x. \ [F(x) \wedge G(x)] \equiv \forall x. \ F(x) \wedge \forall x. \ G(x) \{or \equiv \forall u. \ F(u) \wedge \forall v. \ G(v)\}$
$\exists x. \ [F(x) \vee G(x)] \equiv \exists x. \ F(x) \vee \exists x. \ G(x)$

Appendix C
Summary of natural deduction rules

$\wedge\mathcal{E}$, $\wedge\mathcal{I}$, $\vee\mathcal{E}$, and $\vee\mathcal{I}$ rules

- $\wedge\mathcal{E}$

$$\frac{P_1 \wedge \ldots \wedge P_n}{P_i} \quad (\wedge\mathcal{E})$$

for each of P_i, $i = 1, \cdots, n$.

- $\wedge\mathcal{I}$

$$\frac{\boxed{\begin{array}{c} \vdots \\ P_1 \end{array}} \quad \ldots \quad \boxed{\begin{array}{c} \vdots \\ P_n \end{array}}}{P_1 \wedge \ldots \wedge P_n} \quad (\wedge\mathcal{I})$$

- $\vee\mathcal{E}$

$$\frac{P_1 \vee \ldots \vee P_n \quad \boxed{\begin{array}{c} P_1 \\ \vdots \\ C \end{array} \quad \ldots \quad \begin{array}{c} P_n \\ \vdots \\ C \end{array}}}{C} \quad (\vee\mathcal{E})$$

- $\vee\mathcal{I}$

$$\frac{P_i}{P_1 \vee \ldots \vee P_n} \quad (\vee\mathcal{I})$$

for each of P_i, $i = 1, \cdots, n$

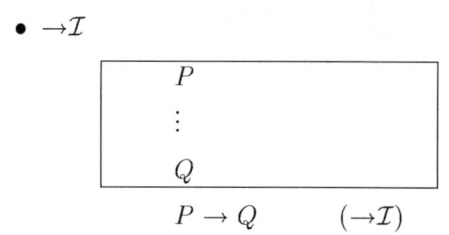

Summary of natural deduction rules

$\to\mathcal{I}, \to\mathcal{E}, \neg\mathcal{I}, \neg\mathcal{E}$ and $\neg\neg$ rules

- $\to\mathcal{I}$

$$\begin{array}{|l|} \hline P \\ \vdots \\ Q \\ \hline \end{array}$$
$$P \to Q \quad (\to\mathcal{I})$$

- $\to\mathcal{E}$

$$\frac{P \quad P \to Q}{Q} \quad (\to\mathcal{E})$$

- $\neg\mathcal{I}$

$$\begin{array}{|l|} \hline P \\ \vdots \\ \bot \\ \hline \end{array}$$
$$\neg P \quad (\neg\mathcal{I})$$

- $\neg\mathcal{E}$

$$\frac{P \quad \neg P}{\bot} \quad (\neg\mathcal{E})$$

- $\neg\neg$

$$\frac{\neg\neg Q}{Q} \quad (\neg\neg)$$

Equality rules

- *eqsub*

$$\frac{a = b \quad S[a]}{S[b]} \quad (eqsub)$$

where $S[a]$ means a sentence S with one or more occurrences of a identified and $S[b]$ means those occurrences replaced by b.

- *reflex*

$$\overline{a = a} \quad (reflex)$$

Universal quantifier rules

- $\forall \mathcal{E}$

$$\frac{\forall x.\ P[x]}{P[t]} \quad (\forall \mathcal{E})$$

    where t occurs in the current context.

- typed $\forall \mathcal{E}$

$$\frac{\textit{is-type}(t) \quad \forall x : \textit{type}.\ P[x]}{P[t]} \quad (\forall \mathcal{E})$$

- $\forall \mathcal{I}$

$$\boxed{\begin{array}{l} c \forall \mathcal{I} \\ \vdots \\ P[c] \end{array}}$$
$$\forall x.\ P[x] \quad (\forall \mathcal{I})$$

    where c must be new to the current context.

- typed $\forall \mathcal{I}$

$$\boxed{\begin{array}{ll} c \forall \mathcal{I} & \textit{is-t}(c) \\ \vdots & \\ P[c] & \end{array}}$$
$$\forall x : t.\ P[x] \quad (\forall \mathcal{I})$$

- $\forall {\to} \mathcal{E}$ and $\forall \neg \mathcal{E}$

$$\frac{\forall x.\ [P[x] \to Q[x]] \quad P[c]}{Q[c]} \quad (\forall {\to} \mathcal{E}) \quad \text{and} \quad \frac{\forall x.\ \neg P[x] \quad P[c]}{\bot} \quad (\forall \neg \mathcal{E})$$

Existential quantifier rules

- $\exists \mathcal{I}$

$$\frac{P[b]}{\exists x.\ P[x]} \quad (\exists \mathcal{I})$$

where b occurs in the current context.

- typed $\exists \mathcal{I}$

$$\frac{is\text{-}type(b) \quad P[b]}{\exists x : type.\ P[x]} \quad (\exists \mathcal{I})$$

- $\exists \mathcal{E}$

$$\exists x.\ P[x]$$
$$\boxed{\begin{array}{ll} c \exists \mathcal{E} & P[c] \\ & \vdots \\ & Q \end{array}}$$
$$Q \quad (\exists \mathcal{E})$$

where c is new to the current context.

- typed $\exists \mathcal{E}$

$$\exists x : t.\ P[x]$$
$$\boxed{\begin{array}{ll} c \exists \mathcal{E} & P[c] \\ & is\text{-}t(c) \\ & \vdots \\ & Q \end{array}}$$
$$Q \quad (\exists \mathcal{E})$$

Further reading

R.C. Backhouse. *Program Construction and Verification.* Prentice Hall, 1986.

R. Bird and P. Wadler. *Introduction to Functional Programming.* Prentice Hall, 1988.

R. Bornat. *Programming from First Principles.* Prentice Hall, 1987.

O. Dahl. *Verifiable Programming.* Prentice Hall, 1992.

E. W. Dijkstra. *A Discipline of Programming.* Addison-Wesley, 1976.

E. W. Dijkstra and W.H.J. Feijen. *A Method of Programming.* Addison-Wesley, 1988.

S. Eisenbach and C. Sadler. *Program Design with Modula-2.* Addison-Wesley, 1989.

D. Gries. *The Science of Programming.* Springer Verlag, 1981.

C. Morgan. *Programming from Specifications.* Prentice Hall, 1990.

S. Reeve and M. Clarke. *Logic for Computer Science.* Addison-Wesley, 1990.

J. C. Reynolds. *The Craft of Programming.* Prentice Hall, 1981.

R. Smullyan. *What is the Name of this Book?* Prentice Hall, 1978.

V. Sperschneider and G. Antoniou. *Logic: A Foundation for Computer Science.* Addison-Wesley, 1991.

N. Wirth. *Programming in Modula-2.* Springer Verlag, 1982.

Index

accumulating parameter, 191
actual parameter, 15
adjacency matrix, 177
aggregate type, 68
and, 9, 198
append, 69, 86
argument, 15, 214
arithmetic, 41
arity, 102, 200, 261
assertion, 143
associative, 69, 209
atom, 199
axiomatic approach, 81

base case, 53, 65, 84
bind, 204
black box, 15
bottom, 222
box proof, 84
built-in functions, 20, 41

characters, 41
Church-Rosser property, 54
circular reasoning, 58
code, 2
comparison operators, 40, 42
completeness, 260, 264, 271
complexity, 181
components, 91
composition, 19

compound types, 96
concatenate, 69
conclusion, 9
conjunction, 198, 206
connectives, 8
cons, 69, 70
consistency, 275
constant, 204
construct, 70
context, 273
contract, 27
contradiction, 209, 222
correct, 7, 214
course of values induction, 60
curried functions, 94
currying, 94

data structures, 68
data types, 40
decidable, 272
declaration, 18
deduction, 197
defensive specification, 29
defining functions, 46
defining values, 45
definition, 18, 21, 38
derived rules, 227
disjunction, 198
domain, 262, 279
double induction, 63

Dutch national flag algorithm, 164

edge, 176
elimination rules, 216
eqsub rule, 249
equality, 247
equation, 17, 47, 247
equivalent, 208
errors, 1
Euclid's algorithm, 56, 63
exclusive or, 11, 202
expression evaluation, 22

falsehood, 209
forall, 9
formal, 9
formal methods, 11
formal parameter, 17
formal parameters, 47, 138
formality, 10
formula, 216
function, 6, 15
function application, 15
functional composition, 18
functional language evaluator, 22
functional term, 200

generic, 99
global, 3
graph, 176
ground term, 238
guard, 48

head, 69, 86
higher-order function, 117

identifier, 44
implication, 9, 198
inconsistency, 275
induction hypothesis, 60, 84
induction step, 84
infinite lists, 73
infix, 50, 200
insertion sort, 76
instantiation, 54

interpretation, 261, 279
introduction rules, 216
invariant, 142
iteration, 186

layout, 47
lazy evaluation, 55, 65
length, 177
lists, 68
local, 3, 52
local definitions, 50
logic, 8
logic operators, 43
logical constants, 134
logical entailment, 260
logical implication, 260
logical notation, 8
loop invariant, 141, 144
loop test, 144
loop variant, 145
looping, 53, 186

map, 18
mapping diagram, 17
mathematical induction, 60
mathematical logic, 197
meaning, 25
mid-condition, 131, 143
model, 260, 264, 279
module, 6
Modus Ponens, 222
mutually exclusive, 48

node, 103, 176
nullary constructor, 102

offside rule, 47, 52
or, 198

partial application, 95
partition, 165
path, 176
pattern, 48, 49, 111
pattern matching, 48
patterns of recursion, 117

296 Index

PC, 227
polymorphic type, 76
polymorphism, 97
post-condition, 28, 29
pre-condition, 28, 29
precedence, 24
predicates, 40, 199
prefix, 50
premiss, 9
preparation, 218
primitive functions, 20
primitive types, 96
Principle of course of values induction, 62
Principle of list induction, 84
Principle of mathematical induction, 60
procedure, 6
procedure call, 133
proof by contradiction, 227
propositional logic, 199

qualifier, 206
quality, 7
quantification, 204
quantifier, 204

reasoned program, 4
recurrence relationship, 53
recursion, 53, 186
recursion variant, 65
recursive, 53, 54
redex, 54
reduction strategy, 55
reflex rule, 249
relation, 176
relational operators, 42
reserved words, 44
result, 15, 139
rule, 17, 47
rule of substitution, 249

scheme, 227
semantics, 11
semi-decidable, 272

sentences, 199
sequent, 216
signature, 261, 279
simple induction, 60
simplification, 54
soundness, 260, 264, 271
specification, 5, 20, 21, 27, 38
string, 71, 87
strong typing, 97
structural induction, 106
structure, 262, 279
substitution, 54
symmetry law of equality, 250
syntax analysis, 97

tail, 69, 86
tail recursion, 186
tautology, 209
terms, 199, 200
theorem, 227
theorem tactics, 230
top-down design, 20
transitive closure, 176, 177
truth table, 201, 211
tuple, 91, 111
type checking, 97
type variables, 98
typed quantifiers, 206
types, 28, 68

union types, 101
unit law, 69
universal quantifier, 204
user-defined constructors, 100
user-defined functions, 44

valid, 9, 214, 260
values, 45
variable, 130, 204
variant, 143

weak completeness, 278
well-founded induction, 64, 282

Prentice Hall International Series in Computer Science (*continued*)

C.A.R. Hoare, Series Editor

POMBERGER, G., *Software Engineering and Modula-2*
POTTER, B., SINCLAIR, J. and TILL, D., *An Introduction to Formal Specification and Z*
REYNOLDS, J.C., *The Craft of Programming*
ROSCOE, A.W. (ed.), *A Classical Mind: Essays in honour of C.A.R. Hoare*
RYDEHEARD, D.E. and BURSTALL, R.M., *Computational Category Theory*
SLOMAN, M. and KRAMER, J., *Distributed Systems and Computer Networks*
SPIVEY, J.M., *The Z Notation: A reference manual (2nd edn)*
TENNENT, R.D., *Principles of Programming Languages*
TENNENT, R.D., *Semantics of Programming Languages*
WATT, D.A., *Programming Language Concepts and Paradigms*
WATT, D.A., *Programming Language Processors*
WATT, D.A., WICHMANN, B.A. and FINDLAY, W., *ADA: Language and methodology*
WELSH, J. and ELDER, J., *Introduction to Modula 2*
WELSH, J. and ELDER, J., *Introduction to Pascal (3rd edn)*
WELSH, J., ELDER, J. and BUSTARD, D., *Sequential Program Structures*
WELSH, J. and HAY, A., *A Model Implementation of Standard Pascal*
WELSH, J. and McKEAG, M., *Structured System Programming*
WIKSTRÖM, Å., *Functional Programming Using Standard ML*